Religion and Popular Culture in America

LINCOLN CHRISTIAN COLLEGE AND SEMINARY

RELIGION AND POPULAR CULTURE IN AMERICA

Edited by Bruce David Forbes and Jeffrey H. Mahan

UNIVERSITY OF CALIFORNIA PRESS
BERKELEY   LOS ANGELES   LONDON

University of California Press
Berkeley and Los Angeles, California

University of California Press, Ltd.
London, England

© 2000 by the Regents of the University of California

Library of Congress Cataloging-in-Publication Data

Religion and popular culture in America / edited by
    Bruce David Forbes and Jeffrey H. Mahan.
        p.   cm.
    Includes bibliographical references and index.
    ISBN 0-520-21324-6 (cloth : alk. paper).
    ISBN 0-520-22028-5 (pbk. : alk. paper)
        1. Popular culture—Religious aspects.
    2. Religion and culture—United States.
    3. United States—Religion—1960– I. Forbes,
    Bruce David.   II. Mahan, Jeffrey H.
    BL2525.R4613   2000
    291.1′7′0973—dc21   99-32106
                                           CIP

Manufactured in the United States of America

08 07 06 05 04 03 02 01 00 99
10 9 8 7 6 5 4 3 2 1

The paper used in this publication meets the
minimum requirements of ANSI/NISO Z39.48-1992
(R 1997) (*Permanence of Paper*). ∞

Contents

Preface

This volume of essays provides an introduction to an area of growing interest among students of religion and culture: the relationships between religion and popular culture. It reflects the wide range of methods that scholars have applied to tease out these relationships: some of the essays take their approach from the social sciences, while others are rooted in the humanities; some bring the tools of religious studies or theological disciplines to bear on popular culture, while others use the tools of film and television studies, anthropology, or other fields of cultural studies. All argue that religion has developed in the midst of, and adapted to the demands of, a consumer-oriented, mass-media culture.

Since such variety of approaches and interests has produced much interesting work, but not yet generated a clear and unified conversation, one goal of this volume is to provide a unifying framework. The division of the book into four parts, as discussed in the introduction, represents the set of key relationships between religion and popular culture which we believe have defined the work to date. We hope this will help students of religion and popular culture to understand and appreciate the work of others trained in different disciplines and methodologies, in order to deepen and enrich the conversation about religion and popular culture.

First and foremost, we owe our thanks to the authors of these essays. Their thoughtful and creative work, and their generous response to the tinkering of the editors, is much appreciated. They have been dialogue partners as well as writers, and their comments have significantly strengthened the volume.

We are also grateful to professors William Dean, Patricia O'Connell Killen, Marty Knepper, John Shelton Lawrence, and Monica Siems for their thoughtful responses to this project. Doug Abrams Arava, Jan Spauschus Johnson, and Reed Malcom at the University of California Press have been supportive, challenging, and encouraging colleagues. Much of Bruce David Forbes's early work on this volume occurred during a sabbatical year generously provided by Morningside College. Morningside and the Iliff School of Theology also provided staff and student assistance: we thank Elizabeth Pexton Connolly, Andy Downing, Lynn Kogelmann, Chris Schulman, Jann Schwab and Katrina Smith for their crucial roles in assembling, organizing, formatting, and proofreading the manuscript.

Earlier versions of the following essays have appeared elsewhere in similar form. Appreciation is expressed for permission to republish them in this volume:

"The Church of Baseball, the Fetish of Coca-Cola, and the Potlatch of Rock 'n' Roll" by David Chidester appeared in the *Journal of the American Academy of Religion,* vol. LXI, Fall 1996, with the subtitle "Theoretical Models for the Study of Religion in American Culture." Reprinted by permission of the editor.

"Like a Sermon: Popular Religion in Madonna Videos" by Mark D. Hulsether is revised from the essay "Jesus and Madonna: North American Liberation Theologies and Secular Popular Music," which appeared in *Black Sacred Music: A Journal of Theomusicology* 8:1, Spring 1994.

"The Disguise of Vengeance in *Pale Rider*" by Robert Jewett is a chapter revision from his book *Saint Paul at the Movies: The Apostle's Dialogue with American Culture,* Westminster John Knox, 1993. It appears by permission of Westminster John Knox Press.

"It's about Faith in Our Future: *Star Trek* Fandom as Cultural Religion" by Michael Jindra appeared under the title "Star Trek Fandom as a Religious Phenomenon" in the journal of the Association for the Sociology of Religion, Inc., *Sociology of Religion* 55:27–51, 1994. © Association for the Sociology of Religion, Inc.

"Rap Music and Its Message: On Interpreting the Contact Between Religion and Popular Culture" by Anthony Pinn is a revision of the chapter titled "Blues, Rap and Nitty-Gritty Theology" in his *Why Lord? Suffering and Evil in Black Theology,* Continuum, 1995. Reprinted by permission of the Continuum Publishing Company.

Jeffrey H. Mahan, Iliff School of Theology
Bruce David Forbes, Morningside College

Bruce David Forbes

INTRODUCTION

Finding Religion in Unexpected Places

Religion appears not only in churches, synagogues, mosques, and temples; it also appears in popular culture.[1] Best-selling popular music has included Joan Osborne's "[What if God Was] One of Us," U2's "I Still Haven't Found What I'm Looking For," and Madonna's "Like A Prayer." The video of "Like a Prayer" features burning crosses, a gospel choir, and a black Christ figure, all mixed together with sensuality. In detective fiction, Harry Kemelman's popular series of mysteries revolves around Rabbi David Small as a sleuth trained in the complexities of Talmudic reasoning. The animated television program *The Simpsons* frequently features the family's interchange with their very religious neighbor Ned Flanders, and even personal appearances by God and the devil. Movies and television shows ranging from *The Exorcist* to *The X-Files* suggest a widespread fascination with demonic possession, vampires, and a variety of occult phenomena. Batman has been portrayed in a crucifix pose on the covers of at least seven comic books in recent years. What does it all mean?

Other examples of intersections between religion and popular culture are quite different in character. When preaching workshops for ministers include advice that sermons should be shortened, to accommodate the television-influenced attention span of seven or eight minutes between commercials, popular culture apparently affects the shape of institutional religion. At other times, aspects of popular culture seem to become a religion: the national hoopla surrounding the Super Bowl has suggested to more than one scholar that this January event has all the trappings of a religious festival. When fans virtually organize their lives around football or basketball, might we say that sport is a religion?

All of these examples both pertain to religion and are drawn from the realm of popular culture, which some people would dismiss as trivial, faddish, or "just entertainment," but which a growing body of scholars finds to be a significant focus for reflection and analysis. This essay, and this book, are about the connections between the two: popular culture and religion. Looking at the various ways these two subject areas interact with one another provides a way to reflect on religion which is quite different from studying religious institutions, their scriptures, and their formal theologians. Approaching the study of religion through popular culture can help us learn more about widespread perceptions of religion, and the role religion plays in the everyday lives of people. The analysis of popular culture also can provide insights about how religions change and are changed by the cultures that surround them. To help frame the discussion of such avenues of inquiry, this introductory essay will attempt to define popular culture, summarize some of the basic terminology and strategies of popular culture analysis, and introduce four different ways that popular culture and religion relate to one another.

DEFINING POPULAR CULTURE

What is popular culture? Most of us already have a rough idea from the very phrase itself, but some clarification might be helpful. Scholars in the field frequently distinguish popular culture from both high (or elite) culture and folk culture. To employ suggestive examples from the realm of food: high culture is a gourmet meal, folk culture is grandma's casserole, and popular culture is a McDonald's hamburger.[2] All three are forms of "culture," which is intended here as a neutral term that includes the whole range of human products and thoughts that surround our lives, providing the context in which we live. Although some advocates of high culture would like to use the word "culture" in a more restricted sense, arguing that the word should be applied only to those human works that are of higher sophistication and quality—so, for instance, a symphony orchestra might be an example of "culture" while a polka band would not—analysts of popular culture use the word "culture" in a wider sense, without making judgments of value, quality, or taste, so that comic books and Faulkner novels, tuxedos and torn jeans, radio talk shows and university lectures, and the three meals mentioned above are all parts of "culture."

The distinctions between the three classifications of culture (high, folk, and popular) have to do especially with the size of their audiences, and perhaps also the means by which they are transmitted. High or elite culture, often transmitted in written form (a literary magazine, the score of an opera, a gourmet cookbook), has a limited audience by its very intention, and is addressed to persons who are perceived to have superior backgrounds or more sophisticated taste. Folk culture, often transmitted orally (family recipes, local legends, regional marriage customs), also has a limited audience, because the oral communication is roughly limited to the more immediate family, community, or other local or regional group. Popular culture might be communicated in many ways, but it most often becomes widespread, and thus popular, through mass media (television, radio, movies, books, magazines, and cyber communication). As its very name implies, popular culture is marked by its larger audience.

At this point a disagreement has arisen among scholars of popular culture about its further definition. How indispensable are the mass media to the concept of popular culture? One circle of scholars is represented by Ray Browne, a key figure in the founding of the Popular Culture Association and the American Culture Association. They consider popular culture to be the broad "way of life of a people" that "has existed since the most primitive times": in other words, even before the advent of the printing press and other developments of mass media.[3] Athenians laughing at the plays of Aristophanes would be an historical example. This approach to the definition makes it possible to discuss the existence of popular culture throughout virtually the entire range of human history. When this definition is used, popular culture and folk culture sometimes merge and are difficult to distinguish in earlier time periods, although they still contrast with high culture.

Another circle of scholars is represented by Russel Nye, also a central figure in the development of popular cultural analysis as an academic field. They contend that truly popular culture requires a mass audience (created by urbanization and democratization) and technologies of mass distribution (the printing press and the various forms of mass media that followed). Thus, writes Nye, popular culture "describes a cultural condition that could not have appeared in Western civilization before the late eighteenth century."[4] In essence, mass mediation is a basic part of the definition for this group of scholars and not for the other. When we move beyond historical questions and consider the present, however, both perspectives agree that popular culture refers to "that which is (or has been) accepted or approved of by large groups of people," and that, today, the mass media are of central importance in its transmission.[5] Thus popular culture includes such expressions as television programs, movies, popular music, supermarket magazines, popular fiction (romance, detective, western), and much more.

The question remains: how widespread must something be in order to be considered popular? For example, if the "top forty" songs are the only expressions of truly popular culture in music, what does one say about country, hip hop, jazz, and other forms of music that are widely accepted among more targeted audiences? Are these not expressions of popular culture as well, within what we might call sub-universes or sub-cultures of the larger national or international cultures? We must acknowledge that we are dealing with spectrums of popularity, and it is difficult to draw clear lines. Yet these very degrees of popularity can be one of the subjects for our analysis, as we ask what it means that certain popular cultural forms flourish in some subgroups and not in others.

These comments, then, do not leave us with an absolutely clear definition. The contrasts between popular culture, folk culture, and high culture are instead simply a suggestive typology, and the pure types do not always precisely fit actual examples. Furthermore, an example of popular culture in one time period or geographical location might be high culture in another setting, such as medieval European morality plays, which may have been popular culture when performed by street players centuries ago but become high culture when presented in an American university theater in the twentieth century. In short, as Ray Browne writes, popular culture "is an indistinct term whose edges blur into imprecision,"[6] but, even with its imprecision, the notion of "popular culture" draws our attention to the widespread, common, frequently commercial, and often entertaining aspects of our cultural context as worthy of attention and reflection.

ANALYZING POPULAR CULTURE

Why should we pay attention to popular culture, even studying it in academic settings? What could we learn? Put most simply, popular culture both reflects us and shapes us, and the implications of that twofold dynamic are profound.

On the one hand, popular culture reflects us. This strikes many as common sense, because it is the general public that makes something popular. For example, creators and producers offer new television series to the public every year, but their manipulation of publicity and time slots cannot automatically guarantee that a show will be a hit; the public decides, sometimes surprising the pundits. "We" make something popular when it touches a chord within us, perhaps expressing our assumptions and values, or portraying our yearnings, or providing moments of escape. There has to be a reason (or reasons) why great numbers of people choose to watch one television series and not another. The trick, of course, is to figure out what the reason is. In the process, we are essentially trying to learn about ourselves.

Jack Nachbar and Kevin Lause, in their introduction to popular culture analysis at the beginning of *Popular Culture: An Introductory Text,* offer a "Popular Culture Formula" that exemplifies this approach. Their formula states simply that "the popularity of a given cultural element (object, person or event) is directly proportional to the degree to which that element is reflective of audience beliefs and values." Thus, we examine elements of popular culture "not as ends in themselves but as means of unlocking their meaning in the culture as a whole." It is a "quest for meaning" to ask "why audiences choose one cultural element over another" and try to discern what this choice says about those audiences.[7]

In a widely used metaphor, popular culture is like a mirror, reflecting who we are. Yet when we look into the mirror, the images are somewhat altered or distorted, because only portions of our realities, interests, values, and desires are reflected back to us, with a selectivity that is influenced by the personal perceptions and intentions of the creative forces behind popular culture. As a result, Nachbar and Lause and others refer to popular culture as a funhouse mirror.[8]

Because popular culture surrounds us, it seems reasonable to assume that its messages and subtle themes influence us as well as reflect us. If popular culture reflects values we already hold, that reflection also serves to reinforce our values and deepen our commitment to them. If selective images emphasize certain groups or experiences and neglect others, our perceptions of reality may be altered. Television programs and commercials of the 1950s, in which African Americans seldom appeared, provide an example. Consistent viewing of such programming helped the dominant white society ignore or forget that African Americans were part of the nation's community, and let African American viewers receive and internalize the message that they were marginal.

Michael Real provides another example of how popular culture shapes us. His book, *Mass-Mediated Culture,* argues that

> Mass-mediated culture primarily serves the interests of the relatively small political-economic power elite that sits atop the social pyramid. It does so by programming mass consciousness. . . . For example, while allegedly "giving people what they want," commercial television maximizes private corporate profit, restricts choices, fragments consciousness, and masks alienation.[9]

Kenneth Myers, an evangelical Christian and a journalist, offers a different critique of the subtle influences of popular culture in "the erosion of character, the spoiling of innocent pleasures, and the cheapening of life itself."[10]

Almost all arguments about popular culture's influence on us, however, include the hope that once we analyze popular culture's subtle dynamics and raise them to a level of consciousness, they will no longer affect us, at least not as powerfully as before. We will be resistant to manipulation; activists then might be able to blunt popular culture's effects, and perhaps even change the production of popular culture in directions the activists find appropriate.

This is an indication of a more general conflict between the creators of popular culture and their critics, which illustrates the twofold claim that popular culture both reflects us and shapes us. When crusaders argue that television programs, advertisements, Nintendo games, and other products of popular culture prompt violence, or demean women, or encourage materialism, popular culture's producers often answer that they are merely reflecting society. On the much debated subject of violence, for instance, critics complain that the frequency of violence on television has helped create a more violent society, while producers argue that their programs simply express the realities of an already violent society. From the perspective of this essay, such a disagreement presents a false choice, because both claims may be true; it remains relevant, however, to argue which direction of influence is more significant than the other.

To examine popular culture as both a reflection and a shaping force, what specific strategies or methodologies might we employ to try to discern the underlying meanings and influences of popular culture? The essays in this book will provide examples of a variety of approaches. However, let me first make two general points.

First of all, some discussions that purport to be popular culture analysis limit themselves to a consideration of the intentions of the creators and the nature of the popular culture text or artifact itself. These discussions are valuable, and are akin to literary analyses, but unless we add a focus on audience reception, on how and why the public receives and responds to the element of popular culture, we will miss the special insights that the study of popular culture can bring. For example, it may be interesting to hear the inside stories told by producers and cast members of the various *Star Trek* television series, including descriptions of their personal backgrounds and motivations, but the central question for popular culture analysis is why and how *Star Trek* became popular. What attracted the audience? What does its popularity say about the audience? How does it influence the audience?

Secondly, we are likely to discern more about the meanings of popular culture when we examine patterns rather than isolated examples. A critic might discuss a unique, groundbreaking novel by a particular mystery writer, but this novel becomes more significant for popular culture analysis when examined in light of detective fiction as a genre, particularly when it represents a continuing or changing pattern rather than a single anomaly. Single examples tend to focus upon creative uniqueness; patterns and genres point to broader themes and popular response.

DEFINING RELIGION

The academic examination of popular culture has flourished in recent years, with the development of the Popular Culture Association and the American Culture Association, presentations about popular culture at other scholarly conventions like the Modern Language Association, the American Academy of Religion, and the American Studies Association, and the advent of popular-culture commentators in the national media. Yet religion is consistently underrepresented in most of these discussions. For example, Nachbar and Lause's *Popular Culture: An Introductory Text*, a reader commonly used in undergraduate courses, contains twenty-nine articles, none of which directly pertain to religion. Such an omission is puzzling, because religion is a pervasive element of the American experience. Ninety-five percent of Americans indicate that they believe in some sort of God or Higher Power; only five percent claim to be atheist or agnostic. Approximately forty percent of the United States population reports attending worship in any given week. The 1993 edition of the *Encyclopedia of American Religions* lists 1,730 religious organizations, large and small, in the United States and

Canada.[11] Certainly, if we are going to examine popular perceptions and behaviors, the topic of religion should be included in the conversation.

If it is to be included, perhaps we should clarify what we mean by "religion." It is tempting to say simply that religion has to do with "belief in God," but such a definition reflects the assumptions of Western religions: Judaism, Christianity, and Islam. The Hindu understanding of Brahman, or Taoist teachings about "the way," or the spirit world of some Native Americans, would not quite fit this reference to "God," and yet all are generally recognized as religions. Even changing the reference to "God or gods," or "a higher power," does not solve the problem. Thus, there is disagreement among scholars about how to describe the focus of attention that makes religion identifiable. We want to be broad enough to include what we generally recognize as religions, without being overly broad.

Another complication arises from the fact that religion can be perceived at several levels. The most readily recognizable manifestation is institutional religion: major world religions such as Christianity, Islam, Judaism, Hinduism, Buddhism, and tribal spiritualities, among others, plus any number of smaller groups. Beyond the institutionalized religions, one often can detect some broad societal movements or tendencies about what is holy or what is valued most highly. Furthermore, many individuals have their own somewhat unique, personal religious beliefs and practices that do not fit with any particular group. It has become commonplace for many to call the institutionalized groups "religions," and to use the label "spirituality" to refer to general movements and private expressions, yet many scholars in religious studies would use "religion" in a broader sense, to include the institutionalized groups, general cultural tendencies, and individual expressions as well.

Thus, some definitions of religion are very broad and inclusive. When the Christian theologian Paul Tillich calls religion "ultimate concern," or when the authors of an undergraduate text define religion as "any person's reliance upon a pivotal value," they see religion as the organizing principle in a person's life, the value or concern to which everything else is subordinate.[12] While such a definition definitely includes major world religions, it also might include some orientations that are less frequently seen as religious: nationalism, or materialism, or athletic competition. It could also include both individual and group expressions. Defined this broadly, the topic of religion certainly ought to arise in the process of analyzing popular culture, because popularity is seen as an indication of what the public values, and that might be called their "religion" in its broadest sense.

Other scholars would use the word religion in a narrower sense, to refer to human expressions that are closer to the traditional religions most people recognize. Julia Mitchell Corbett's working definition of religion in her textbook *Religion in America* is that a "religion is an integrated system of belief, lifestyle, ritual activities, and institutions by which individuals give meaning to (or find meaning in) their lives by orienting themselves to what they take to be holy, sacred, or of the highest value." [13] This definition still is broad enough to include unconventional religions, including the so-called "new age movement" or twelve-step programs, but it is more restrictive than the previous definitions cited. Even when defined more narrowly, religion appears frequently in popular culture.

As with our discussion of the concept of "popular culture," we need not arrive here at one conclusive definition of the term "religion," although we will return to a further discussion of definitions when we ask whether a feature of popular culture like sports might be considered a religion. For now, it is helpful to see the spectrum of subject matter that is associated with the topic of religion. In learning about religion and popular culture, we will find ourselves discussing not only the institutional religions we readily recognize, with rabbis, and cathedrals, and revivals. Religion may be present in discussions of the roles superheroes play as deliverers, or reflections on the struggles of life, or in devotional acts to a celebrity, or in ritual patterns of television viewers.

FOUR RELATIONSHIPS BETWEEN
RELIGION AND POPULAR CULTURE

Religion and Popular Culture is an emerging field of study, with an explosion of interest now underway. Scholars interested in the subject come from very diverse formal educational backgrounds (theology, history, biblical studies, literature, cultural studies, anthropology, and others), and because there exists no graduate program, journal, or scholarly association devoted to the study of Religion and Popular Culture, interested persons often are unaware of each other's work. It is a field in need of definition, articulated methodologies, and fuller awareness of the diverse contributions already made. This book hopes to contribute to the process.

One step is to recognize that religion and popular culture relate to each other in at least four different ways, and each merits examination:

1. Religion in Popular Culture
2. Popular Culture in Religion
3. Popular Culture as Religion
4. Religion and Popular Culture in Dialogue[14]

Religion in Popular Culture

Most of the material already published falls in this category, discussing the appearance, explicitly or implicitly, of religious themes, language, imagery, and subject matter in elements of popular culture, for example the portrayal of Catholic nuns in movies, or the redeemer role played by comic book superheroes, or the many indications of public fascination with angels in the 1990s. How does religion appear in expressions of popular culture? At what points in popular culture is religion strikingly absent? What does it mean?

Movies, which have received more attention from religion scholars than any other feature of popular culture, can provide helpful illustrations of how religion might appear in popular culture, both explicitly and implicitly. First, there are those films that explicitly focus on religion: *The Ten Commandments, The Last Temptation of Christ, The Chosen, Gandhi,* and *Little Buddha* are obvious examples. In addition, many movies include explicit representations of religion or religious figures, although they may not be the focus of the films: priests, monks and nuns, rabbis, evangelists, sun dancers, gothic cathedrals, Muslim prayer rugs, exorcisms, and so on. In all such cases, one might attempt to discern patterns in these portrayals of religion, asking what the patterns reveal about the creative forces behind the images and the audiences who respond.

Religion also makes implicit appearances. For instance, commentators frequently note allegorical Christ figures in movies, such as the extraterrestrial in *E.T.*, a special being with healing powers who came to earth, was loved by many, was misunderstood and feared by authorities, and finally experienced death and resurrection. Charlton Heston, in *Omega Man,* played the role of the only remaining human being with

uncontaminated blood in a doomed world, eventually dying in a cruci-
fixion pose. Providing a non-Christian example of allegory, Eric Greenberg has argued that Superman, a comic book character who also made
it to the screen, is deeply rooted in the Western Jewish experience.
Whether intentionally or not, Jerry Siegel, one of Superman's co-creators
who grew up in a Reform Jewish home, created a character whose Kryp-
tonian name was Kal-el, sounding much like biblical names (Michael,
Gabriel) and incorporating the Hebrew "el," which means "God." Superman was forced to leave a destroyed planet, reminiscent of Jews leaving Jerusalem after its destruction by the Romans. Superman's pursuit of
"truth and justice" and his assistance to the less fortunate parallel major Jewish ethical themes.[15]

Such religious allegories are found not only in characters like E.T. or
Superman, but also in plot structures. Robert Jewett and John Shelton
Lawrence make such an argument in their book *The American Monomyth*. They note that Joseph Campbell wrote about a "classical monomyth," a single archetypal plot in which a hero "ventures forth from the
world of common day into a region of supernatural wonder: fabulous
forces are there encountered and a decisive victory is won: the hero
comes back from this mysterious adventure with the power to bestow
boons on his fellow man." This plot is based on rites of initiation and is
seen in the stories of Ulysses, Aeneas, St. George and the dragon, and
countless others. Yet Jewett and Lawrence are convinced that most of
American popular culture follows a different singular plot, a distinctively American monomyth:

> A community in a harmonious paradise is threatened by evil: normal institu-
> tions fail to contend with this threat: a selfless superhero emerges to renounce
> temptations and carry out the redemptive task: aided by fate, his decisive vic-
> tory restores the community to its paradisal condition: the superhero then re-
> cedes into obscurity.

Western movies in which the hero rides into the sunset at the conclusion,
as well as the stories of comic book superheroes, provide ready illustrations of this plot. Jewett and Lawrence note that the American monomyth is essentially a secularization of Judeo-Christian redemption dramas: "The supersaviors in pop culture function as replacements for the
Christ figure, whose credibility was eroded by scientific rationalism,"
they write. "But their superhuman abilities reflect a hope of divine, redemptive powers that science has never eradicated from the popular
mind."[16]

The American Monomyth is only one example of what might be called a mythological approach, borrowing from the study of comparative religion. Films can be examined for "cross-cultural forms, including myth, ritual, systems of purity, and gods," and studied for "the ways Hollywood reinterprets, appropriates, invents, or rejects" these archetypes.[17]

Finally, in addition to characters and plot structures, there are also implicitly religious themes in products of popular culture. Theologians, often Christian theologians, have for years been eager to discuss what they see as implicit theological themes in film: love, meaning, forgiveness, sin, and death and resurrection. Through the arts and the responses of their audiences, human beings ask questions of identity and purpose and wrestle with possible answers to these questions. Many theologians are interested in viewing movies to see how "the world" poses the questions, are intrigued when the answers seem to parallel their own faith traditions, and offer critiques when they disagree with the implicit answers. A considerable body of theological literature takes this approach. Andrew M. Greeley goes a step further, seeing popular culture in general, and film in particular, as a locale in which one may encounter God. "The film is the sacramental art par excellence; either as a fine or lively art nothing is quite so vivid as film for revealing the presence of God."[18]

Movies have been the focus here, to illustrate how religion might appear on several different levels: through explicit representations, allegorical parallels, and implicit theological themes. Of course, the same variety of manifestations can be found in country music, television comedies, music videos, comic strips, spy stories, science fiction, romance novels, and much more; religion is represented or expressed in many ways in all of these popular cultural forms.

Popular Culture in Religion

This category refers to the appropriation of aspects of popular culture by religious groups and institutions. For instance, when churches or synagogues borrow popular musical styles, or organizational or advertising techniques, or popular-culture slogans and icons, what are the dynamics and influences involved?

These influences can be subtle. The thesis of Neil Postman's *Amusing Ourselves to Death: Public Discourse in the Age of Show Business* provides an interesting example of a cultural influence that is both pervasive and yet largely unrecognized. Postman argues that American culture has moved from a print-dominated age to the Age of Television, and that the shift has literally changed our ways of thinking and the content of our culture. Echoing Marshall McLuhan's aphorism that the medium is the message, Postman maintains that print culture (the Age of Typography, of Exposition), by the very nature of its mode of communication, encouraged coherent, orderly, serious, rational discourse with propositional content. Television, he says, shifts us to an image-based culture that features explosions of images, fragmented rather than coherent, emphasizing sensation and feeling rather than rationality. Postman calls the television era the Age of Show Business, because entertainment is its highest value. He devotes an entire chapter to television's impact on religion, arguing that religion on television is presented simply as entertainment, not because of deficiencies in the televangelists but because of the nature of the medium itself: anything presented on television becomes entertainment. Furthermore, because the pervasiveness of television has shaped the expectations of the entire culture, even when a religious practice (such as a small local church's weekly worship service) is not on television, it is pressured to measure up to entertainment standards. When religion is presented as entertainment, does the basic content and character of religion change? "The danger is not that religion has become the content of television shows," Postman writes, "but that television shows may become the content of religion."[19]

What are other ways that religions consciously or unconsciously borrow examples, images, language, themes, and assumptions from popular culture as tools for religion's purposes? Does such borrowing influence the religion, sometimes in ways it may not recognize? For example, what does it mean when the supposedly distinctive music of an evangelical Christian youth subculture is expressed in hard rock, heavy metal, alternative, or meditative ("new age") musical styles? What is involved in the process, currently so popular in the culture, of casting religion as a wellness program (for instance, Leonard Sweet's *The Jesus Prescription for a Healthy Life*)?[20] When churches adopt "the strategies and techniques of modern marketing" from the business world, and "the audience becomes a market and the gospel is transformed into a product," should religious people view these influences as effective adaptation or a threatening transformation?[21] Of the four relationships between religion and popular culture, this one, the impact of popular culture upon religion, has been the least examined.

Popular Culture as Religion

A third category involves the argument that popular culture serves as religion or functions like religion for many people. Crucial to these discussions, of course, is one's definition of religion, which we already have considered in a preliminary way. Catherine Albanese has provided a helpful, concise summary of three types of definitions: substantive, functional, and formal.

> Substantive definitions of religion focus on the inner core, essence, or nature of religion and define it by this thing-in-itself. They tend to emphasize a relationship with a higher being or beings (God or the Gods) and to be favored by theologians and philosophers. Functional definitions of religion emphasize the effects of religion in actual life. They stress the systems of meaning-making the religion provides and how it helps people deal with the ills, insecurities, and catastrophes of living. Functional definitions are favored by scholars in the social sciences. Lastly, formal definitions of religion look for typically religious forms gleaned from the comparative study of religions and find the presence of religion where such forms can be identified. Religious forms include sacred stories, rituals, moral codes, and communities; and formal definitions of religion tend to be favored by historians of religions.[22]

Most claims about popular culture as religion are based upon functional or formal definitions, but it is possible to find some appeals to substantive definitions as well.

Two general categories of popular culture that many think provide a functional religion for their enthusiasts are sports and television. Do sports or television provide public rituals, private rites, myths and symbol systems through which their followers interpret the world, just as religions do? Other more specific features of American popular culture also invite comparisons with religion: the belief systems, community, and reenactments of *Star Trek* fans; the pilgrimage and religious devotion of those who followed the Grateful Dead; Graceland as a shrine for religiosity surrounding Elvis.

In addition to such comparisons with specific features of popular culture, one might also assert that the sum total of American popular culture expresses an overall cultural religion. John Wiley Nelson, in *Your God Is Alive and Well and Appearing in Popular Culture,* makes just this claim: "Popular culture is to what most Americans believe as worship services are to what the members of institutional religions believe." Nelson, a professor of Christian theology, describes what he sees as American cultural religion, with a belief system regarding the nature and source of problems (evil), the source of deliverance, the nature of a resolved situation, and the proper path to the future. The beliefs of this American cultural religion may or may not be consistent with the formal religions that many Americans claim. He argues that the western movie "is the classic ritual form, the 'High Mass,' of the predominant American belief system." Unlike high art, he says, which "challenges one's self-understanding towards self-criticism and insight," the primary function of popular culture as "worship" is "to affirm already held beliefs and values." The mythic pattern of a western, which may appear in *Casablanca* or television police shows as well as stories set in the pioneer American West, reveals and reaffirms what the dominant culture really believes, such as the general public's conviction that they are relatively innocent and that evil comes from an external source. "Those institutions normally called 'religions' are explicit in announcing precisely what they believe and in scheduling the ritual dramas of reaffirmation, that is, the worship services. American cultural religion is much less recognizably explicit, but no less powerfully persuasive in our lives," Nelson writes.[23]

When Nelson describes what he sees as an "American cultural religion," he focuses upon its beliefs, especially its assumptions about what is unsatisfactory in our present existence and the source of our eventual deliverance. Other scholars give more emphasis to the forms of religion, and the parallel forms that appear in popular culture: rituals, symbols, myths, and icons. Yet another approach is to notice that popular culture and traditional religions function in similar ways, providing meaning and helping people cope with life's problems. Whether the emphasis is upon essential religious beliefs, religious forms, or religious functions, each avenue of discussion makes it possible to claim that aspects of popular culture (sports, television, celebrities, and more) constitute a religion for their most devoted followers.

Religion and Popular Culture in Dialogue

Other interactions between religion and popular culture do not fit well in the three categories considered thus far. The issue of violence in the media, briefly mentioned earlier, is a good example. When church or synagogue leaders become involved in the debate about whether portrayals of violence in movies and on television are harmful to society, it is not a matter of representations of religion in the media (Religion in Popular Culture), nor is it directly a matter of popular culture shaping religion (Popular Culture in Religion). Most of the discussions do not claim that violence has become a sort of religion (Popular Culture as Religion), although it might be possible to make that case. Rather, violence in the media and in society is an ethical issue which concerns both religions and religious people and the general population as well. Religion wants to take part in the broader discussion.

Violence is only one example. Popular culture represents and sometimes advances values and perspectives about gender roles, race, sexuality, economic objectives, definitions of success, the relative importance of youth and the elderly, and so on. These issues are not directly about religion, but they are ethical arenas to which religious values pertain, and thus religion enters into dialogue with popular culture and its creative forces. The meaning of "dialogue" may need to be arbitrarily broadened here, because, from the perspective of religious participants, this dialogue may take several forms:

- listening to the voices of popular culture, being challenged and/or inspired by them;
- philosophically comparing and contrasting values between a religion and the general society represented by popular culture;
- condemning and opposing the influence of popular culture;
- viewing popular culture as an ally in promoting certain causes;
- attempting to transform popular culture when it is not already an ally.

These various responses to popular culture blend into one another, and most critics would identify with more than one.[24]

A wide spectrum of voices is engaged in this dialogue. Within Christian circles alone, they range from Neil Hurley, a Jesuit who sees films as liberating, to Donald Wildmon, the leader of the American Family Association, who sees television as "the most destructive instrument in our society."[25] Others fall somewhere in between, including Michael Eric Dyson and William Fore. Dyson is a minister, university professor, and prominent African American commentator on popular culture, who criticizes gangsta rap for violence, homophobia, and misogyny but who also calls for open lines of communication with gangsta rappers to understand "what conditions cause their anger and hostility"; Fore is a mainline Protestant who has worked in communications for the National Council of Churches, and who seeks to reflect critically on the "central myths" of popular culture, so that religiously committed people "can both clarify their own value system and search for the roots of their faith."[26]

In the United States, Jewish and Christian representatives are predominant in these exchanges. The dialogues can be enriched by the addition of voices from other religious traditions, more direct conversations (even face to face) between creators of popular culture and religious representatives at conferences or workshops, and scholarly assessments of the shape of the dialogue.

CONCLUSION

These four relationships between religion and popular culture are not exclusive categories; in fact, they might better be seen as interactive, helpful in highlighting four directions of scholarly discussion, even though discussions of one aspect can and often do shade into discussions of another. For example, R. Laurence Moore's *Selling God: American Religion in the Marketplace of Culture* describes not only how religion has borrowed commercial practices to promote religion (Popular Culture in Religion), but also how business leaders have employed religion to advance their commercial purposes (Religion in Popular Culture).[27] Christian theologians who highlight the presence of implicit theological themes in novels or television shows (Religion in Popular Culture) often include comparative discussions of religious and cultural assumptions (Religion in Dialogue with Popular Culture).[28] There is fluidity among the relationships between religion and popular culture, but if one's attention tends to gravitate in one direction, the outline of four relationships can be useful in suggesting additional possibilities.

Many of us come to the analysis of popular culture with a particular special interest, related to our own private enthusiasms (comic books, the Beatles, soap operas, or whatever), and we sometimes hesitate to reveal our interest and even fandom to our more "sophisticated" friends. To enter into reflection on the meanings and influences of popular culture out of simple curiosity or because "it's fun" is an effective starting point that requires no apology, and it easily leads to the conviction that we have stumbled upon something that holds promise for significant insight in understanding ourselves, and in understanding religion in the context of our culture.

This volume is intended to survey and widen the discussion, which many of us know only in narrow slices. A broader view allows us to share and borrow methodologies, detect wider patterns, and stimulate our curiosity about new subject areas. The possibilities for research and reflection are endless, because the multifaceted and constantly changing nature of popular culture, and the changing faces of religion as well, assure that there will be no final word.

NOTES

1. This sentence echoes the title of a classic book about religion and popular culture: John Wiley Nelson, *Your God Is Alive and Well and Appearing in Popular Culture* (Philadelphia: Westminster Press, 1976).

2. See Jack Nachbar and Kevin Lause, "An Introduction to the Study of Popular Culture: What is this Stuff that Dreams are Made Of?" in *Popular Culture: An Introductory Text,* ed. Jack Nachbar and Kevin Lause (Bowling Green, Ohio: Bowling Green State University Popular Press, 1992), 1–35, especially 16–7.

3. Ibid., 11.

4. Russel B. Nye, "Notes on a Rationale for Popular Culture," in *The Popular Culture Reader,* ed. Jack Nachbar and John L. Wright (Bowling Green, Ohio: Bowling Green University Popular Press, 1977), 10–6, quotation from 10.

5. Nachbar and Lause, "Introduction," 12.

6. Ray B. Browne, "Popular Culture: Notes Toward a Definition," in Nachbar and Wright, *Popular Culture Reader,* 1–9, quotation from 1.

7. Nachbar and Lause, "Introduction," 5–6.

8. Ibid., 7; see also Michael Medved, *Hollywood vs. America: Popular Culture and the War on Traditional Values* (New York: HarperCollins, 1992), 253.

9. Michael R. Real, *Mass-Mediated Culture* (Englewood Cliffs, N.J.: Prentice-Hall, 1977), xi.

10. Kenneth A. Myers, *All God's Children and Blue Suede Shoes: Christians and Popular Culture* (Wheaton, Ill.: Crossway Books, 1989), xiii.

11. *Gallup Poll Monthly* 352 (January 1995): 14; Robert Bezilla, ed., *Religion in America, 1990* (Princeton: Princeton Religious Research Center, 1991), 45 (some studies based upon field research rather than self-reporting suggest that actual attendance may not be that high); J. Gordon Melton, *The Encyclopedia of American Religions,* 4th ed. (Detroit: Gale Research, 1993). These three statistics are all cited in Julia Mitchell Corbett, *Religion in America,* 3rd ed. (Upper Saddle River, N.J.: Prentice-Hall, 1997), 17, 21–3.

12. Paul Tillich, *Dynamics of Faith* (New York: Harper & Row, 1957), 1–4; Robert C. Monk et al., *Exploring Religious Meaning,* 3rd ed. (Englewood Cliffs, N.J.: Prentice-Hall, 1987), 3.

13. Corbett, *Religion in America,* 7.

14. In addition to the four relationships between religion and popular culture considered here, one might argue for a fifth possibility: "Religion as Popular Culture." If popular culture sometimes functions as religion, can the inverse be true as well? Can religious activity or production not only take on the features of popular culture, but function fully as popular culture? This might apply especially to historical situations where a single religion is central to a culture as a whole, prior to the complications of secularization and religious diversity. Pre-

Lenten carnivals in medieval Europe or camp meetings in nineteenth-century America could be viewed as examples of religious activity and popular culture at the same time; the widespread wearing of crosses or Taoist symbols as jewelry or the activities of New Age believers might be cited as modern examples. Yet all of these could be considered extensions of "Religion in Popular Culture," although they near the limits of the category. We recognize the fluidity of these categories and the possibility that at various points others would find additional categories possible.

15. Eric J. Greenberg, "Did Superman Have Biblical Roots?" *Jewish Week*, 9 February 1996, 41, 56. See also David Peterson, "Superman has Jewish roots, rabbi agrees," *Minneapolis Star Tribune*, 14 September 1996, B10.

16. Robert Jewett and John Shelton Lawrence, *The American Monomyth* (Garden City, N.Y.: Anchor Press/Doubleday, 1977), xix–xx. Their quotation from Joseph Campbell is from his *The Hero with a Thousand Faces* (New York: Meridian, 1956), 30.

17. See the discussion of "mythological criticism" in Joel W. Martin and Conrad E. Oswalt Jr., eds., *Screening the Sacred: Religion, Myth, and Ideology in Popular American Film* (Boulder, Colo.: Westview Press, 1995), 6.

18. Andrew M. Greeley, *God in Popular Culture* (Chicago: Thomas More Press, 1988), 245–6.

19. Neil Postman, *Amusing Ourselves to Death: Public Discourse in the Age of Show Business* (New York: Penguin Books, 1985), 124.

20. Leonard Sweet, *The Jesus Prescription for a Healthy Life* (Nashville: Abingdon Press, 1996).

21. Quentin J. Schultze expresses concerns about such developments in *Televangelism and American Culture: The Business of Popular Religion* (Grand Rapids, Mich.: Baker Book House, 1991), 14–7.

22. Catherine L. Albanese, *America: Religions and Religion* (Belmont, Calif.: Wadsworth Publishing Company, 1981), xxi.

23. John Wiley Nelson, *Your God is Alive and Well and Appearing in Popular Culture* (Philadelphia: Westminster Press, 1976), 16, 30, 196, 19; his general discussion of American cultural religion appears on 20–5.

24. While not identical to H. Richard Niebuhr's five relationships between Christ and culture, his typology is certainly influential in constructing lists like this, and reflection on Niebuhr's discussions in *Christ and Culture* is valuable for general considerations of the relationships between religion and popular culture. See H. Richard Niebuhr, *Christ and Culture* (New York: Harper & Row, 1951).

25. Neil P. Hurley, *The Reel Revolution: A Film Primer on Liberation* (Maryknoll, N.Y.: Orbis Books, 1978); Donald E. Wildmon with Randall Nulton, *Don Wildmon: The Man the Networks Love to Hate* (Wilmore, Ky.: Bristol Books, 1989). The Wildmon quotation is from Tim Stafford, "Taking on TV's Bad Boys," *Christianity Today*, 19 August 1991, 14–8, quotation from 14.

26. Michael Eric Dyson, *Between God and Gangsta Rap: Bearing Witness to Black Culture* (New York: Oxford University Press, 1996), xiii; William F. Fore, *Television and Religion: The Shaping of Faith, Values, and Culture* (Minneapolis: Augsburg Publishing House, 1987) and *Mythmakers: Gospel, Culture and the Media* (New York: Friendship Press, 1990), quotations from 53, 56–7.

27. R. Laurence Moore, *Selling God: American Religion in the Marketplace of Culture* (New York: Oxford University Press, 1994).

28. As two examples among many, see Robert Jewett, *St. Paul at the Movies: The Apostle's Dialogue with American Culture* (Louisville, Ky.: Westminster/John Knox, 1993), and Bernard Brandon Scott, *Hollywood Dreams and Biblical Stories* (Minneapolis: Fortress Press, 1994).

PART ONE

RELIGION IN POPULAR CULTURE

W hen the topic of "religion and popular culture" is introduced, people typically think first of the mention of God in the lyrics of a popular song, the portrayal of Jewish rabbis in network television series, or some similar example of the way popular culture expresses religious values or portrays religious figures. Such examples represent the first of four relationships between religion and popular culture considered in this volume: Religion *in* Popular Culture. This section features essays which discuss the explicit or implicit religious content of popular culture, and offer suggestions about what we might learn from these representations of religion.

Jane Naomi Iwamura considers the portrayal of a figure she calls the Oriental Monk, in American film, television, and advertising. The Monk initiates a westerner, and that westerner serves as a bridge figure who integrates Western and Eastern wisdom. Iwamura argues that rather than being an accurate portrait of oriental religious values and practices, the Monk of American popular culture is a product of Western neocolonial assumptions.

Robert J. Thompson examines the religious content of television Christmas specials. He maintains that in such programs the religious content of the holiday is carried by traditional hymns. However, this theological content is constrained by the surrounding images of hearth and home in ways which subvert religion to serve the interest of American consumerism.

Terry C. Muck considers the way religion undergirds and is expressed in the western literature of Louis L'Amour and Cormac McCarthy. He argues that both authors reflect a postmodern focus on the primacy of individual experience, while still maintaining the notion of universal values. In the process, he finds that traditional distinctions between high and low culture, and high and low religious concerns, cannot be drawn as neatly as some might expect.

Mark D. Hulsether investigates the religious imagery in certain of Madonna's music videos. In response to those who read these images as sacrilegious, he argues that Madonna's combination of eroticism and religious imagery in videos such as "Like a Prayer" delivers messages consistent with liberal and liberationist theologies.

These essays look at religious content in a range of popular media: film, television, literature, and music. They are diverse in ideology and approach. Though Christian symbols and theology predominate, as they do in wider American culture, Iwamura's account of the Oriental Monk demonstrates that other religious traditions are also reflected, if not always very accurately, in American popular culture. What unites the observers and critics is their interest in the way that popular culture draws on, and comments on, traditional religious themes, images, and concepts.

1

Jane Naomi Iwamura

THE ORIENTAL MONK IN
AMERICAN POPULAR CULTURE

Driving down a busy street in Oakland, California, I was met by the larger-than-life presence of the Fourteenth Dalai Lama. He appeared to me in a vision of unparalleled clarity and grace. His direct gaze was gentle, yet intent, and his spiritual repose arresting. For that one moment, the hectic pace of my life was interrupted, and I was transported to another time, another world, another possibility.

Many others who passed that same spot shared a similar vision. To each of us, the Dalai Lama's silent message reverberated: *Think Different*.

The unexpected appearance of such a prominent spiritual figure, in olden days, would undoubtedly be taken as nothing short of a miracle. But in contemporary times, a miracle it is not. The Dalai Lama's "visitation" had been made possible by the Apple Corporation and the spiritual power of advertising. The vision derived its meaning not from a single epiphany, but rather through a series of mass media orientations: glossies in magazines; newspaper photos and references; images in film, television, and the internet. Indeed, at times, His Holiness seemed to be everywhere at once.

The Dalai Lama has become one of the most recognizable spiritual figures of our times. As a non-Christian religious leader, the interest he holds for millions of Americans is unprecedented—save by the Ayatollah Khomeini in the 1980s. And rather than signaling political threat and religious zealotry, as the Middle Eastern patriarch once did, the

Dalai Lama represents an admirable pacifism and spiritual calm ripe for esteem and emulation. Indeed, Americans love the Dalai Lama.

It is this American love and fascination for Eastern spiritual figures such as the Dalai Lama that I am most interested in understanding. Rather than simply recounting the religious and moral qualities these spiritual individuals possess, it is important to discuss the social context from which their attraction emerges. How did the Dalai Lama come to represent all that he does for Americans? Indeed, what exactly does he represent? How have we come to "know" him? Is our ability to embrace someone and something (Tibetan Buddhism) once considered so foreign anything other than a testimony to a newfound openness and progressive understanding?

I'd like to tackle these questions by critically analyzing the history of representation which has contributed to the current image of the Dalai Lama. We "know" the Dalai Lama not simply because of the fact that we may understand his views and admire his actions, but also because we are familiar with the particular role he plays in the popular consciousness of the U.S.—the type of *icon* he has become—the icon of the *Oriental Monk*. To get a sense of what makes the Dalai Lama (and others like him) so popular, we need to get a sense of the history of this icon and how it has been used to express and manage our sense of Asian religions.

The Oriental Monk has enjoyed a long and prominent sojourn in the realm of American popular culture. We have encountered him under different names and guises: as Mahatma Gandhi and as D. T. Suzuki; as the Vietnamese Buddhist monk consumed in flames; as the Beatles' guru, the Maharishi Mahesh; as *Kung Fu*'s Kwai Chang Caine and as Mr. Miyagi in the *Karate Kid*; as Deepak Chopra and, as well, as the Dalai Lama.[1] Although the Oriental Monk appears in these various forms throughout American pop culture, we are always able to recognize him as the representative of an alternative spirituality that draws from the ancient wellsprings of "Eastern" civilization and culture.

Compared with the negative stereotypes of Asians which have historically circulated in the American media (sinister Fu Manchus, inscrutable gangsters, the Yellow Peril, and so on), the icon of the Oriental Monk seems like a noteworthy advance. And indeed, it demonstrates an air of increasing tolerance and respect. But to look at this representation as nothing but admirable progress precludes us from seeing ways in which positive portrayals may reinscribe certain racist notions of the Eastern "other." Indeed, it is important to analyze the icon of the Oriental Monk within the phenomenon of *orientalism*—as part of an orientalist network of representations. According to Edward Said, this network is "framed by a whole set of forces that brought the Orient into Western learning, Western consciousness, and later, Western empire." As a "created body of theory and practice," orientalism divides the world into "two unequal halves, Orient and Occident." Its "detailed logic [is] governed not simply by empirical reality but by a battery of desires, repressions, investments and projections," as well as a "whole series of 'interests.'" Hence, rather than offering a clear and unbiased representation of Asian religions, this system of representation reveals the interests and concerns of the Occidental subjectivity from which it emerges.[2]

The Oriental Monk, drawing from this network of representation, includes within its iconic scope a wide range of religious figures (gurus, sages, swamis, masters, teachers) from a variety of ethnic backgrounds (South Asian, Japanese, Vietnamese, Chinese). Although individual figures point to a diverse field of encounter, they are homogenized within American popular consciousness and culture. Racialization (more correctly, "orientalization") serves to blunt the distinctiveness of particular persons and figures. Indeed, recognition of any Eastern spiritual guide (real or fictional) is predicated on their conformity to general features paradigmatically encapsulated in the icon of the Oriental Monk: his spiritual commitment, his calm demeanor, his Asian face, and oftentimes his manner of dress.

In an analysis of the icon of the Oriental Monk as American, we will see a complex dynamic unfold in which orientalist notions of Eastern spiritual heritages and Western disillusionment and desire converge. These notions are configured in a conventionalized narrative with formulaic aspects that demonstrate the *specific* nature of America's engagement with "Eastern," non-Christian traditions, and its use of the Oriental Monk as a means to symbolically express, manage, and work through its troubled spiritual sense of self. Hence, the Oriental Monk as pop cultural icon and narrative tells us a great deal about the religious ethos of twentieth-century America: he details the fears, hopes, and desires of a society in spiritual turmoil and search. In the following discussion, I will follow the Oriental Monk on his journey through American popular consciousness (or rather, follow this consciousness as it journeys through him), and discuss certain highlights along his spiritual path—his mass media "initiation" through silent film (D. W. Griffith's

Broken Blossoms), his "prominence" in 1980s film and television, and his current "reign" in the form of the Fourteenth Dalai Lama. We will discover that although the monk travels under different guises, primarily dictated by the geopolitical terrain, his basic mission and tale remain strangely the same.

INITIATION

The Oriental Monk makes his on-screen debut in D. W. Griffith's classic, *Broken Blossoms or The Yellow Man and the Girl*.[3] The tale begins in an undesignated Chinese port town where we find the Yellow Man— a devout individual who becomes "convinced that the great nations across the sea need the lessons of the gentle Buddha." He journeys West to "take the glorious message of peace to the barbarous Anglo-Saxons, sons of turmoil and strife." The remainder of the movie chronicles his life in the Limehouse district of London and his encounter with Lucy, a gutter waif (played by Lillian Gish), whom he shelters from her brute of a father, Battlin' Burrows. The Yellow Man is portrayed as the only one who recognizes Lucy's "beauty which all Limehouse missed." But tragedy ensues: Battlin' Burrows discovers his daughter's whereabouts, beats her to death, and then is shot in turn by the Yellow Man. The story ends with the Yellow Man, a knife between his ribs, slumped before Lucy and his Buddhist altar.

Griffith's "masterpiece," produced in 1919, offers a tragic adaptation of Thomas Burke's short story, "The Chink and the Girl." The changes which ensued in the translation of text into film are noteworthy. Most significant is the transformation of Burke's "Chink," a "worthless drifter of an Oriental,"[4] into Griffith's "Yellow Man"—noble and pious in his sense of mission. Indeed, Griffith's main contribution resides in the revised introduction of the story, where he locates the Yellow Man "in the Temple of Buddha, before his contemplated journey to a foreign land." Here, the Yellow Man gains inspiration and guidance not only from the environment of the temple, but also from the Oriental Monks who reside there and provide "[a]dvice for a young man's conduct in the world—word for word such as a fond parent or guardian of our own land would give." Indeed, the motif of the temple which both begins and ends the story offers definite spiritual overtones to the tragic tale.

In his essay, "Modernizing White Patriarchy: Re-Viewing D. W. Griffith's *Broken Blossoms*," John Kuo Wei Tchen cites the "modernized cultural patriarchy" promoted in the film. This new form of dominance and oppression channels the views and prescriptions of the cultural elite into stereotypical representations set in place and reinforced by character and plot development. Tchen exposes the view which undergirds both early silent films such as *Broken Blossoms* and their successors: "Proper society should be managed so Blacks [can] be segregated and kept in their place, and poor whites, immigrants and native alike, [can] be acculturated into bourgeois society."[5] Within a framework of modernized cultural patriarchy, *Broken Blossoms* can be read as the cultural elite's commentary on the marginalized elements of its society in urbanized areas. More specifically, it marks the filmic origin of a device through which this is accomplished—the figure of the "good Asian":[6]

> If anything, [Griffith] eschews the standard stereotype of the "heathen Chinee" already well established in the previous century, and adapts the alternative image of the good-for-the-West "John Chinaman." "John" was the image of the tame, aristocratic, clean, honest, and often Christianized Chinese man promoted by traders, missionaries, and the wealthy who had direct personal interests in promoting good relations with China.[7]

This positive portrayal serves a number of functions: (1) as a "symbolic foil to complain about the abusive, immature authority of lower-class white men" (Battlin' Burrows);[8] (2) to appease China, which the U.S. has "interests" in maintaining good foreign relations with; and (3) to discipline immigrant Chinese who reside in Chinatowns of the West, by providing a representative *measure* and *standard* for the moral behavior of these communities. In these multifarious ways, films such as Griffith's provide a means by which to manage diverse groups via cultural representation rather than through bodily force or direct polemic—a strategy which is the hallmark of the "modernized cultural patriarchy."

For our purposes, it is interesting to note that Tchen emphasizes the "Christian" nature of the Yellow Man's moral and spiritual orientation, since the character is portrayed as definitively Buddhist. I think Tchen is correct in pointing out the "proto-'Christian' values"[9] that the representation masks; at the same time, this easy identification of the Buddhist Yellow Man as Christian in essence misses a significant dimension of Griffith's film.[10] Indeed, Tchen's critical analysis does not account for the brief but crucial encounter between the Yellow Man and two missionizing clergymen in the desolate Limehouse streets:

Christian: "My brother leaves for China tomorrow to convert the heathen."
Yellow Man: "I wish him well."
(The clergymen then offer the Yellow Man a pamphlet entitled "Hell.")

Unbeknownst to the Christian proselytizers, the Yellow Man is a missionary himself, albeit jaded and discouraged by his own experiences in a foreign land. Hence his well-wishing is cast in a sympathetic, yet ironic, tone. The above exchange can be viewed as a brilliant foreshadowing of the Yellow Man's tragic end ("Hell"), but it also serves as a commentary on Christian mission. The viewer is meant to identify with the Yellow Man's disillusioned response. Through this identification, one can read Griffith's (and perhaps the audience's) own relation to institutionalized Christianity as ambivalent at best.

Hence, we must struggle with Griffith's portrayal *as such*. The fact that Griffith associates peace, gentleness, sensitivity, and altruism to the Buddha and his followers in the film constitutes a significant moment in popular consciousness. At the very least, it must assume that a "heathen" religion stands on par with its "non-heathen" counterpart, although I believe much more can be read into this moment: *Broken Blossoms* expresses an already established disillusionment with Christianity and quite possibly a budding fascination with alternative modes of moral and spiritual understanding. Griffith, as "cultural midwife," inadvertently ushers this desire into popular consciousness through the Oriental Monk figures of the Yellow Man and his Buddhist teachers.

Of course, *Blossoms* concludes in tragedy, not hope. This ending reinvigorated the film's elite audience—infused them with "a sense of mission" and justified their "paternalistic efforts" within national borders and without.[11] The film's moral lesson rests on a threat: *If the Christianized West is unable to care for its children, the noble Buddhist East will.* The tone and import of this message is conveyed by the dire consequences of the Yellow Man's intervention (the death of the three main characters); the message is to be taken as a warning for the Christian West to "practice what it preaches." Although this constitutes the intentional aim of Griffith's work, it does not preclude other contrary effects as well: Eastern spirituality has been representationally idealized and operates kindly in its new Western home. In this way, *Broken Blossoms* sets the groundwork for the West's further engagements, and later spiritual identification, with the East. As we will see, the message will be transformed from one of threat and consequence to one of desire and hope: *If the Christianized West is unable to care for its children, the noble Buddhist East will!*

PROMINENCE

Times have obviously changed since Griffith's day, and, along with them, attitudes towards non-Christian religions. This transformation is for the most part due to the events of the 1960s, which embodied a refreshing challenge to the American Christian establishment (in the form of "alternative" lifestyles and spiritual experimentation) and a new tolerance towards "peoples of color" (in the form of the Civil Rights Movement and 1965 Immigration Act). At the same time, this transformation was underwritten by a sense of loss—a loss configured by the wounds of war (the World Wars, the Vietnam War), the impact of technology and global capitalism, domestic racial strife, and growing disillusionment with traditional forms of religious faith and worship. Out of this context emerged the archetype of the American religious subject as a "spiritual seeker" who journeys in search of new religious ground for reconciliation and healing.[12]

The cultures of Asia offered the unparalleled promise of finding such ground. The search for spiritual renewal in the East found popular expression in *Kung Fu* (1972–75), the first popular offering to make explicit the spiritual underpinnings of Eastern martial arts practice. It is thus the progenitor of both the many martial arts movies that were produced from the early 1970s through the late 1980s, and later representations such as *The Karate Kid* (1984) and *The Teenage Mutant Ninja Turtles* (1990), which transformed the adult entertainment of *Kung Fu* and its more violent martial arts successors into family-oriented fare.

Kung Fu, The Karate Kid, and *The Teenage Mutant Ninja Turtles* all share a similar narrative: lone monk figure—oftentimes with no visible family or community, unrecognized by the dominant culture—takes under his wing a fatherless, often parentless, child.[13] This child embodies a tension: for example, *Kung Fu*'s Kwai Chang Caine is half-American, half-Chinese;[14] Daniel in *The Karate Kid* hails from a working class, ethnic background; and, of course, the turtles are mutant. Although these figures half-signify the dominant culture in racial terms, they have an ambivalent relationship with that culture; this allows each to make a break with the Western tradition radical enough to embrace their marginalized half. The Oriental Monk figure seizes this half, develops it, nurtures it. As a result of this relationship, a transmission takes place: oriental wisdom and spiritual insight is passed from the Oriental Monk figure to the occidental West through the *bridge figure*. Ultimately, the Oriental Monk and his apprentice(s) represent future salvation of the dominant culture—they embody a new hope of saving the West from capitalist greed, brute force, totalitarian rule, and spiritless technology.

Hence, the modernized cultural patriarchy set forth decades ago in *Broken Blossoms* becomes firmly established in the '70s and '80s. Like *Blossoms*, these contemporary films enact a commentary on and prescription for ethnic and working-class communities built upon the ideological figure of the spiritual Asian male. But in these later renditions, the Oriental Monk travels down a path not foreseen by Griffith. If *Blossoms* were rewritten in more contemporary terms according to the above narrative, the Yellow Man would arrive as noble and pious as before, but this time as a kung fu master with magical powers. He would rescue Lucy from her depraved, abusive father, care for her, and finally train her in the spiritual ways and practices of the East. Battlin' Burrows, now a frustrated blue-collar worker obsessed with war and guns, would then attempt to reclaim his estranged daughter, and the film would culminate in a final showdown between the two father figures and their respective forms of combat and defense. Lucy would get into the act as well, employing her new talents to disarm her father as gently as possible. The Yellow Man and the girl, through superior human insight and bodily discipline, would triumph over their unruly counterpart. After his definitive defeat, Battlin' would lay aside his weapons, be reunited with his daughter, and the three would join forces to fight evil and corruption in *Blossoms II*. So ends Griffith's classic rewritten for a late-twentieth-century audience—once a cautionary tale and now transfigured into a narrative of spiritual hope and progress.

Indeed, it may appear as if this narrative shift represents a positive trend. Asian religions are no longer portrayed as spiritual systems incompatible with the West, but rather as transformative and life-enhancing influences. But the fact that a particular narrative and representation of Asian spiritual traditions and Asian peoples has become so conventionalized attests to its ideological nature and force. The Oriental Monk figure is portrayed as a desexualized male character who represents the last of his kind.[15] Passing on his spiritual legacy to the West through the bridge figure represents his only hope for survival. Hence, this narrative implicitly argues that Asian religions are impotent within their racial context of origin, and are only made (re)productive if resituated in a Western context and passed on to white practitioners who possess the daring and innovative sensibilities that their Eastern counterparts presumably lack. In this way, the icon of the Oriental Monk and its contemporary narrative—a construction of "racist love"—may be more insidious than negative stereotypes informed by "racist hate," as it allows for the recognition of peoples and cultures of Asian heritage while simultaneously subjecting them to a narrative of their own obsolescence.[16]

Although its characteristic features have remained consistent over the past two decades, the Oriental Monk narrative has become increasingly condensed over time. We have traveled from the more complex narratives of *Kung Fu* and *Karate Kid* to the extremely concentrated signifiers found in *Teenage Mutant Ninja Turtles* and *Alice*. In the original *Kung Fu,* at least half of the movie is given over to explaining Shaolin practices and philosophy. All that remains in *Ninja Turtles* are a few anecdotes thrown in for good measure, and in Woody Allen's *Alice* of the same year (1990), we find the symbol of the Oriental Monk in its crudest form: Allen ironically employs stereotypical "oriental" music and opium den darkness to situate Dr. Yang. Even though Dr. Yang's chain-smoking, caustic persona can be read subversively, he and Chinatown still signal in the viewer's mind Alice's entry into an alternative sense of self. For all the seeming self-reflexivity demonstrated in Allen's ironic invocation of the Oriental Monk figure, Dr. Yang remains merely a symbolic device in the larger plot of Alice's transformation, made productive by a still unchallenged orientalist network of associations.

Along with his condensed form, the Oriental Monk has also acquired more and more fantastic powers in his recent manifestations. Dr. Yang can induce certain states of consciousness and connections with the past through his herbal medications. In *Kung Fu*'s resurrection—*Kung Fu: The Legend Continues* (1993–97)—the extended flashbacks exploring Caine's Chinese philosophical and spiritual training have been replaced by "otherworldly" plots and martial arts scenes filled with implausible stunts. United Paramount Network's *Vanishing Son,* which aired during the same time period (1994–95), did not escape this tendency. Over the course of its short run, the show's protagonist, Jian-Wa Chang, developed supernatural abilities demonstrated by glowing aural meditation scenes and his capacity to connect with the realm of ghosts where his recently deceased brother now resides.[17]

Shifting his disciplined exercise and "grounded" approach into the supernatural arena attests to the full appropriation of the Oriental Monk as America's spiritual "other." Within the categories introduced by early anthropologists to account for the variation in belief systems around the world—magic, science, religion—the Oriental Monk offers an additional alternative: wisdom.[18] This schema, which still resonates in the popular realm, carries with it an implicit racial coding, and in film representations this coding becomes more evident: black magic, white science, oriental wisdom.[19] But as the Oriental Monk narrative becomes more and more conventionalized, the icon condenses and enters the magical realm, to be managed along with other spiritual "alternatives." Indeed, as the Oriental Monk takes on more and more (supernatural) "powers" within the narrative, he seems to enjoy less and less "power" outside the narrative (i.e., as an antihero and counternarrative challenge).

A final dimension of the Oriental Monk narrative should also be taken note of. Many of the above films and television programs entail a return to the East in some fashion or another: Kwai Chang Caine liberates a camp of his fellow Chinese railroad workers; Mr. Miyagi and Daniel return to Japan in *The Karate Kid II* (1986), to prevent Miyagi's home village from being overrun by a greedy capitalist Japanese gangster; the Turtles and Splinter return to seventeenth-century Japan in *Teenage Mutant Ninja Turtles III* (1993); and Alice heads for India to work with Mother Theresa. Here we find that the East also suffers despair and corruption and requires the help of the protagonists. Asia cannot save itself, but looks toward the powers of the newly "enlightened" Westerner: the bridge figure has come to signify salvation not only for Western culture, but for "the Orient" as well. In this way, the modernized cultural patriarchy of the U.S. uses the Oriental Monk and his narrative to transform its disillusionment into a new spiritual imperialism and a renewed sense of mission. The proven success of the Monk now establishes it as one of the reigning icons in American popular cultural consciousness.

REIGN

With much acclaim, the Fourteenth Dalai Lama received the Nobel Peace Prize in 1989. In the tradition of Mahatma Gandhi and Martin Luther King, Jr., he continued a line of world peacemakers whose vision was shaped by a mixture of profound spirituality and political awareness. The Nobel Peace Prize hurled the Dalai Lama and the small Asian country of Tibet into the public eye, and what happened next only solidified the Dalai Lama's status as an American popular cultural figure. Hollywood actor Richard Gere personally adopted the Dalai Lama's spiritual and political mission as his own, promoting the cause at the 1993 Academy Awards and becoming the Founding Chair of the Tibet House in New York.[20] Many of Gere's contemporaries followed suit: "the Power Buddhist/Free Tibet contingent" includes Harrison Ford, Willem Dafoe, Sharon Stone, Steven Seagal, and Adam Yauch of the Beastie Boys.[21] These celebrity endorsements, along with the long history of the Oriental Monk in American popular culture, offered a Buddhist way of life unprecedented Western exposure and initiated the most recent stage in the development of the icon of the Oriental Monk.

With the Dalai Lama, we witness how the disruptions made by actual teachers are continually minimalized by the overpowering representations which have accrued in American popular cultural consciousness. The teacher of Asian origin instantaneously enters the popular culture realm and is transformed into a celebrity; that realm then exploits the reception of his physical and spiritual presence by marketing it for mass contemplation and consumption. This last stage is exemplified by the big movie productions centered around Tibetan Buddhism and/or the life of the Fourteenth Dalai Lama which have emerged in the 1990s: Bernardo Bertolucci's *Little Buddha* (1993), in which a small Euro-American child from Seattle is selected as one of the subsequent reincarnations of the Dalai Lama; Jean Jacques Annaud's *Seven Years in Tibet* (1997); and Martin Scorcese's biopic of the Tibetan spiritual leader, *Kundun* (1997).[22]

In his physical manifestation, the Oriental Monk is now modeled after the Dalai Lama (note the Tibetan, saffron-robed, shaved-head versions in IBM's OS/2 commercials, who are miraculously able to communicate with each other telepathically). Psychically, this new Monk continues the work of its predecessors in the critiquing of American society—its religious and secular preoccupations:

> We don't need these Buddhist temples, we don't need these Christian Churches. What we need, [the Dalai Lama] says, are the values of the human heart. . . . There's a lot of talk about [the baby boomer] generation being materially satisfied, but the next level of need is not satisfied and that's the spiritual level.

> Buddhism is seen as one way that we might re-create a sense of spiritual meaning and purpose within a directionless society. Amid widespread despair, those who have found Buddhism have a sense of joy and inspiration.[23]

But this version also constitutes a shift in geopolitical focus and mission. The long history of the icon of the Oriental Monk has demonstrated a preference for the Japanese or Chinese model. Indeed, Japan and China were viewed as cultures possessing great spiritual richness, but their challenge in the arena of international politics and the world market in relation to the U.S. was perceived as fairly contained; this combination of factors made them suitable representatives of the East in the American popular imagination from 1970 to the mid-1980s.[24]

In the 1990s, however, Japan and China appear too formidable, with contemporary patriarchies of their own in place which greatly resemble those of the West, whereas Tibet poses less of a threat and offers Americans a new mold.[25] The Tibetan version of the Monk paradigmatically signifies, through his dress and religious practices, a mythic spiritual past. This Oriental Monk also provides his charges with a concrete political mission: Free Tibet. As the inaugural issue of *Tricycle* succinctly summarizes:

- 1.2 million Tibetans have died (one sixth of the population)
- 70% of Tibet's virgin forest has been clear cut
- More than 6,000 monasteries, temples and historic sites have been looted and razed
- All religious practices have been outlawed.[26]

This scenario includes a third world people who are fighting against a global power (China) for their very physical, cultural, and spiritual existence—a noble cause to align oneself with. Hence the Japanese and Chinese variations of the Oriental Monk have for the most part been traded in for the less compromised Tibetan model.

But unrecognized desires underlie the American interest in this politico-spiritual mission. It is interesting to note how Tibet's predicament mirrors and emerges from America's own guilt within and outside its own borders—the millions of human lives it has taken, the deforestation it is responsible for, and its judgment on ways of life foreign to a democratic, secular, capitalist model. Indeed, Tibet represents a manageable cosmos where sins—past and present—can be atoned for. Hence, the Tibetan variation of the Oriental Monk enacts an exchange: a model of ethical behavior and spiritual direction for political and economic support. But this exchange serves the West well: America gains not only psychic resolution and healing, but also unchallenged economic and political patriarchal influence over the exiled nation.

The new regime, which the Oriental Monk and his narrative support, operates according to a uniquely twentieth-century system of domination: the "psycho-spiritual plantation system." Sau-ling C. Wong has introduced this concept to speak of "a stratified world of privileged whites and colored servers/caregivers." [27] She elaborates:

> people of color collectively become "*ideological caregivers*" for whites, in addition to being their literal caregivers. . . . "Ideological caregiving" is typically depicted in a benign light in mass culture, with emphasis placed on the benefits accruing to the care-receiver, the volitional participation of the caregiver, and the general mutuality of the exchange. This wish-fulfilling picture expediently flattens the complex social and emotional dynamics generated when mothering is performed by those who are stigmatized and disenfranchised, in virtually every other context, by the care-receivers.[28]

This "ideological caregiver" "functions mainly as a *resource*, subject to appropriation to salve the insecurities of the master/mistress." [29] Wong focuses on American films and novels whose stories take place in the U.S., and astutely details the domestic presence of the "psycho-spiritual plantation system." But the operations of the Oriental Monk as spiritual caregiver and guardian demonstrate that this new form of cultural patriarchy and spiritual imperialism reaches far beyond our borders, into Asia.

I have examined the historical development and complex workings of the icon of the Oriental Monk in a variety of American popular cultural representations. Although the icon transmutes according to the geopolitical situation operating at the time, the narrative he is associated with remains amazingly similar throughout. The icon reflects a disillusionment with Western frameworks, and the hopes and fears attached with alternative spiritualities of the East. American consciousness plagued by the demands of modernity—imperialist strength and will, Christian progress, disembodied instrumental reason, capitalist accumulation and greed—finds peace and resolution through the Oriental Monk. Also present in the narrative is the vision of the "new man," [30] or, more accurately, the "new West," which has learned its lessons well and combines Western initiative with Eastern spiritual know-how. This bridge figure represents salvation, not only for America, but also for Asia. Armed with a new consciousness and mission, the U.S. justifies carrying on its (imperialist) work with renewed vigor and purpose around the globe.

So what am I and others to make of our sighting of His Holiness on that busy street in Oakland? Mass media images surround us in our daily lives—inundate our imagination and reinforce certain associations—without us really taking into account the power of their repetitive force. Religion, race, class, sexuality, and gender make the representations we encounter meaningful. To understand these dimensions of the popular images we encounter, as well as the sociopolitical contexts in which they are lodged, will inevitably determine whether we will be able to heed the vision to *Think Different* or simply drive on by. . . .

NOTES

The first version of this article was originally presented as part of a panel sponsored by the Religion and Popular Culture Group at the 1995 Annual Meeting of the American Academy of Religion in Philadelphia. I would like to thank Bruce Forbes and Jeffrey Mahan for their always encouraging and patient editorial support and guidance. Others whose comments, suggestions, and care have been invaluable throughout include Rudy V. Busto, Judith Butler, Carolyn Chen, Vivian Chin, Elizabeth Goodstein, Russell Jeung, David Kyuman Kim, Luís León, Marie Lo, Michael Mascuch, Sandy Oh, Young Mi Angela Pak, Greg Thomas, Sau-ling Wong, and Desmond Smith.

1. The genealogy I have constructed (which is far from complete) purposely intertwines historical persons with fictional characters. In a mass-mediated age, "real" figures can no longer be clearly distinguished from imaginary ones, creating a "hyperreal" effect (to use Baudrillard's term) in which both types of representations inform and interact with one another to form a common understanding of "Eastern spirituality" in the U.S. context. This understanding congeals in the icon of the Oriental Monk. For a compelling example of how iconic representation functions in the contemporary U.S., see S. Paige Baty, *American Monroe: The Making of a Body Politic* (Berkeley: University of California Press, 1995).

2. See Edward Said, *Orientalism* (New York: Vintage Books, 1979), 203, 6, 12, 8, 12.

3. D. W. Griffith, renowned as a master of early American film, gained notoriety for his visions of America in works such as *The Birth of a Nation* (1915). Although *Broken Blossoms* is set in London, it too enacts a commentary on American life. Scott Simmon, in his exploration of *The Films of D. W. Griffith* (Cambridge: Cambridge University Press, 1993), discusses how Griffith posited "Anglo-Saxon superiority through British medieval ideals" (143). This romantic link between Britain and the U.S., forged in the filmmaker's mind, intimates his use of *Blossoms*'s London and its degeneracy as a reflective metaphor for the woes of urbanized America.

4. John Kuo Wei Tchen, "Modernizing White Patriarchy: Re-Viewing D. W. Griffith's *Broken Blossoms,*" in *Moving the Image: Independent Asian Pacific American Media Arts,* ed. Russell Leong (Los Angeles: UCLA Asian American Studies Center, 1991), 133–43, quotation from 135.

5. Ibid., 143.

6. The character of the "good Asian" prefigures the myth of the "model minority" so prevalent in contemporary American discourse. Similar to Griffith's deployment of the Yellow Man as a figurative device through which to lodge his commentary and critique of "unruly" sectors of society, the popular press and political leaders valorize and uphold Asian Americans as "model" students and citizens which other racial-ethnic groups (including lower- and middle-class whites) are urged to emulate. In a particularly stereotypical example, Ronald Reagan praised Asian American success and attributed it to "[Asian] values, [Asian] hard work." This assumed ethic falls closely in line with Griffith's representation of the Yellow Man as the uncompromised embodiment of the traditional values of his Asian culture. For an accessible introduction into the "model minority myth," see Ronald Takaki, *Strangers from a Different Shore: A History of Asian Americans* (New York: Penguin Books, 1989), 474–84; Reagan's comment above is quoted on 475.

7. Tchen, "Modernizing White Patriarchy," 137.

8. Ibid.

9. Ibid., 135.

10. For a number of Asian American cultural critics, including Tchen, "Christian" is used with a derogatory overtone. These authors work with a particular view of Christianity in which its exclusionary practice and its imperialist tendencies are highlighted. For an especially incisive deployment, see Frank Chin, "Come All Ye Asian American Writers of the Real and the Fake," in *The Big Aiiieeeee! An Anthology of Chinese American and Japanese American Literature,* ed. Jeffery Paul Chan, Frank Chin, Lawson Fusao Inada, and Shawn Wong (New York: Meridian, 1991), 1–92. The hegemonic view of America as a "white Christian nation" certainly deserves to be dismantled. But a too-easy association between these dimensions—"white," "Christian," "nation"—obscures the complex and changing ways in which this vision generally persists (e.g., liberal pluralism, religious tolerance, multiculturalism). In the particular case of *Blossoms,* Tchen's reliance on this association does not allow him to speak about the contradictions in Griffith's sympathetic portrayal of the Buddhist Yellow Man.

11. Tchen, "Modernizing White Patriarchy," 141.

12. Wade Clark Roof uses the term "spiritual seeker" to refer to the "baby boomers" who came of age in the 1960s. Most notable about the religious sensibility and practice of this generation is their "pastiche-style of spirituality" which draws upon an "expanded number of religious options" including Eastern spirituality (*A Generation of Seekers: The Spiritual Journeys of the Baby Boom Generation* [San Francisco: HarperCollins, 1993], 245). See also Steven M. Tipton, *Getting Saved from the Sixties* (Berkeley: University of California Press, 1976).

13. The martial arts films from the intervening decade make passing reference to the spiritual dimension of their fighting practice, but this dimension is almost always merely assumed, and its presence is used to delineate the "good guys" from the "bad guys." Take for instance *Enter the Dragon* (1973) in which martial arts legend Bruce Lee does battle with an evil drug lord. The superior

fighting skills and heroic stance of Lee's character are taken as signs of his spiritual integrity. A brief but memorable quote affirms his moral rectitude: "You have offended my family, and you have offended a Shaolin temple." Since such films simply presuppose Eastern spirituality, they are less useful for my purposes of showing how this representation gets established and codified for American audiences.

14. Bruce Lee competed with David Carradine to play the role of Kwai Chang Caine, and the reason why he did not receive the part still lingers as a site of controversy and contention. According to David Carradine:

> There are two stories about why Bruce Lee didn't get the part. One: that he was turned down because he was too short and too Chinese; which is a way of saying he was, ironically, a victim of the same prejudice we would be dealing with as our theme in the film. Two: that, for some reason I can't fathom, he was advised by his people not to take the part.
> I was told by someone in the production company that they weren't sure he could act well enough to handle the complexities of the character. I don't know. Whatever the reason, it caused him to quit Hollywood, *go home* to Hong Kong and embrace his destiny. (Emphasis added; note that Bruce Lee was a Chinese American born in San Francisco.)

Kareem Abdul-Jabbar, who claims Lee as a good friend, notes that Lee "would have been perfect, a master working his art before the national audience, but whoever it was that decided such things made it clear to [him] that they didn't think a Chinese man could be a hero in America. They passed over Bruce and gave the part, and the stardom, to David Carradine." David Carradine, *The Spirit of Shaolin* (Boston: Charles E. Tuttle, 1991), 18–9; Kareem Abdul-Jabbar and Peter Knobler, *Giant Steps* (New York: Bantam, 1983), 188–9; see also Darrell Y. Hamamoto, *Monitored Peril: Asian Americans and the Politics of Representation* (Minneapolis: University of Minnesota Press, 1993), 59–63.

15. The gender and sexuality of the Oriental Monk icon are ripe for critical exploration. Richard Fung describes the construction of Asian male in popular films as "sometimes dangerous, sometimes friendly, but almost always characterized by a desexualized Zen asceticism . . . the Asian man is defined by a striking absence down there" ("Looking for My Penis: The Eroticized Asian in Gay Porn Video," in *How Do I Look? Queer Film and Video,* ed. Bad Object Choices [Seattle: Bay Press, 1991], 145–68, quotation from 148).

16. For a discussion of "racist love" and "racist hate," the dynamic between them, and how they operate through racial stereotypes, see Frank Chin and Jeffery Paul Chan, "Racist Love," in *Seeing through Shuck,* ed. Richard Kostelanetz (New York: Ballantine, 1972), 65–79.

17. The pilot and early episodes of *Vanishing Son* did not contain these "supernatural" dimensions, but rather seemed to model themselves after the genre of Hong Kong cinema which is becoming increasingly popular in the U.S. One can speculate that the spiritual references were added in order to serve as a more conventionalized cultural marker and boost ratings for the new series.

18. Sir James Frazer and Bronislaw Malinowski—two forefathers of modern anthropology—grappled with these categories in their respective classic works *The Golden Bough* (1890, 1937) and *Magic, Science, and Religion and Other*

Essays (1925). Although they held different understandings of these three domains, their analyses both relied upon the integrity of these categories. Frazer's conception, which plots magic, religion, and science in a linear evolutionary scheme, was particularly insidious, and his view is still popularly embraced to a certain extent. For a critical discussion of these categories and the legacy of Frazer's and Malinowski's thought, see Stanley Jeyaraya Tambiah, *Magic, Science, Religion, and the Scope of Rationality* (Cambridge: Cambridge University Press, 1990).

19. "Religion" also remains racially coded. As Chandra Talpade Monhanty points out, "The 'third world difference' includes a paternalistic attitude toward women in the third world [which includes] third world women as a group or category [who] are automatically and necessarily defined as religious (read 'not progressive')" ("Under Western Eyes: Feminist Scholarship and Colonial Discourses," in *Third World Women and the Politics of Feminism,* ed. Chandra Talpade Mohanty, Ann Russo, and Lourdes Torres [Bloomington: University of Indiana Press, 1991], 51–80, quotation from 72).

20. For a synopsis of Gere's view, see his editorial, "Tibet a litmus test for U.S. moral resolve," *USA Today,* 13 March 1997, 15A.

21. See Edward Silver, "Finding a New Path," *Los Angeles Times,* 11 April 1995, E1, E8. This contingent has formally expanded into the "Committee of 100 for Tibet" (see the Committee's home page at http://www.tibet.org/Tibet100/).

22. Since the release of these pictures, references to the Dalai Lama and Tibet in magazines, newspapers, television, and the internet have been too numerous to count. One of the most insightful to come along is Richard Bernstein, "Hollywood's Love Affair With Tibet," *New York Times,* 19 March 1997, B1, B4. Other pieces include David Plotz, "The Ambassador from Shangri-La: The Dalai Lama sells the romance of Tibet. The West is buying," http://www.slate.com, 18 April 1997, and Richard Corliss, "Zen and the art of moviemaking," *Time,* 13 October 1997, 82–3. For a compelling historical account of the encounter between Tibetan Buddhism and the West, see Donald S. Lopez, Jr., *Prisoners of Shangri-La: Tibetan Buddhism and the West* (Chicago: University of Chicago Press, 1998).

23. Martin Wassell, documentary filmmaker, and Steven Batchelor, English Buddhist monk and scholar, respectively, quoted in Silver, "Finding a New Path," E8.

24. It is significant to note that the production of *Kung Fu* in 1971 coincided with the U.S. rapprochement with China, and Nixon's much heralded visit to the People's Republic of China took place in 1972, the year of the television film's debut. Although China has been viewed as a "communist threat" ever since the establishment of the People's Republic of China in 1949, it was never figured as America's primary adversary in Cold War and post–Cold War political rhetoric, the way the Soviet Union was. See Stephen Whitheld, *The Culture of the Cold War,* 2d ed. (Baltimore: Johns Hopkins Press, 1996).

As for Japan, the U.S. enjoyed a friendly alliance with that country from 1946—the date of the American Occupation in Japan—into the late 1970s.

Even when Japan emerged as an economic power in the 1980s, relations between the two nations remained conciliatory in the first half of the decade. During this period, the Reagan administration sought Japanese support in its determination "to rebuild American defences and to confront the 'challenges' of the Soviet Union" and emphasized the "shared destiny" of the two as "true global partners." This optimistic rhetoric eventually gave way to the popular view of Japan as an economic threat and unfair trading partner. See Roger Buckley, *U.S.–Japan Alliance Diplomacy, 1945–1990* (Cambridge: Cambridge University Press, 1992), 138–151, quotations from 140.

25. The American conception of Japan's position in the world economic market is readily expressed in survey polls and popular press headlines, e.g., "The Pacific Century" (Bill Powell, *Newsweek,* 22 February 1988, 42–9). From the mid-1980s into the early 1990s, American political rhetoric increasingly figured economic relations with Japan as a nasty "battle," a "challenge" in which the small island nation engaged in unfair play (e.g., imbalanced trade practice, investment binges, appropriating U.S. invention, political corruption, ecological exploitation). Japan's style of "judo-economics" no longer appeared the model to emulate. Instead, "to our own selves be true"—America felt the need to "fight back" in its own way against "the seemingly unstoppable giant." See Philip Elmer-DeWitt, "Battle for the Future," *Time,* 16 January 1989, 42–3; Barbara Rudolph, "Eyes on the Prize," *Time,* 21 March 1988, 50–1; Bill Powell, "The Fallacy of Japan Bashing," *Newsweek,* 11 January 1988, 36–9, "To Our Own Selves Be True," *Newsweek,* 3 April 1989, 45, and "Five Ways to Fight Back," *Newsweek,* 9 October 1989, 68–72; Fred Hiatt, "Japan, the Seemingly Unstoppable Giant," *Washington Post,* 21 January 1990, H7; and Robert J. Samuelson, "Fears and Fantasies," *Newsweek,* 2 April 1990, 25.

While Japan was transformed into America's economic adversary, China emerged as its political one. In 1989—a year that included the fall of the Berlin wall, as well as the Tiananmen massacre—a "giant, powerful, merciless China" was inaugurated. Richard Bernstein, in his analysis of "Hollywood's Love Affair with Tibet," remarks: "The answer [to why Tibet has become the cause du jour for celebrities and non-celebrities alike] has several factors. There is the ferocity of China's actions in Tibet, and China's status in the post-cold-war world as the most important large country still holding another land in subjugation" (B1). It is also interesting to note how this "cold war" has turned into one primarily fought on the playground of commercial representation; the conflict is no longer one expressed solely in terms of national interests (U.S. vs. China), but rather involves a multinational corporate ally (Disney vs. China). See Bernard Weintraub, "Disney Will Defy China on Its Dalai Lama Film," *New York Times,* 27 November 1996, C9, and Jeffrey Ressner, "Disney's China Policy," *Time,* 9 December 1996, 60.

26. "The International Year of Tibet," *Tricycle: The Buddhist Review* 1, no. 1 (Fall 1991): 32–3, quotation from 32.

27. Sau-ling C. Wong, "'Sugar Sisterhood': Situating the Amy Tan Phenomenon," in *The Ethnic Canon: Histories, Institutions, and Interventions,* ed. David Palumbo-Liu (Minneapolis: Minnesota University Press, 1995), 174–210, quotation from 200.

28. Sau-ling C. Wong, "Diverted Mothering: Representations of Caregivers of Color in the Age of 'Multiculturalism,'" in *Mothering: Ideology, Experience, and Agency,* ed. Evelyn Nakano Glenn, Grace Chang, and Linda Rennie Forcie (New York: Routledge, 1994), 67–91, quotation from 70.

29. Ibid., 82.

30. See Carol Clover, *Men, Women, and Chainsaws: Gender in the Modern Horror Film* (Princeton: Princeton University Press, 1992), 90.

2

Robert J. Thompson

CONSECRATING CONSUMER CULTURE

Christmas Television Specials

Until about ten years ago, God more or less stayed out of prime-time television. Religion could be found around the fringes of the broadcast schedule, on Sundays and early mornings, where televangelists, masses for shut-ins, and other low-budget devotional programs were mainstays of the syndicated lineup.[1] Television's big time, though, was prime time, and there you would find the most recognizable shows with the largest audiences and the biggest stars, but not much talk about God.

This was no cause for surprise. In an industry based on popularity and advertising revenue, network executives before the cable era were in the unenviable position of trying to please all of the people all of the time, or at least trying never to offend anyone. Even the mildest controversy was shunned in entertainment programming until the late 1960s. Television bosses took seriously the old saw that any talk about religion or politics would get you into trouble, so they avoided both. Gomer Pyle was a prime-time marine from 1964 to 1970 and he never once uttered the word "Vietnam"; Sister Bertrille, in her three-year novitiate at the Convent San Tanco, was never seen taking communion and seldom prayed. Even after shows like *All in the Family* (CBS, 1971–79) brought contemporary political issues into prime time in the early 1970s, the networks largely steered clear of religious material, with its talk of death and duty.

When television did present clergy as principal characters, there was always a dramatic twist or character quirk to divert attention away from the subject of religion itself, as in *The Flying Nun* (ABC, 1967–70).

Father Murphy (NBC, 1981–84) was about a frontiersman who ran an orphanage in the Old West, but he was just posing as a priest so as not to lose the school's funding. Trying to play against the stereotype of clerical piety, *Hell Town* (NBC, 1985) presented Robert Blake as an ex-convict priest, *Amazing Grace* (NBC, 1995) offered Patty Duke as an ex–drug addict minister, and *In the Beginning* (CBS, 1978) and *Amen* (NBC, 1986–91) brought us MacLean Stevenson and Sherman Hemsley as a pompous and unlikable priest and deacon, respectively. In *Lanigan's Rabbi* (NBC, 1977) and *The Father Dowling Mysteries* (NBC/ABC, 1989–91), yarmulkes, collars, and habits did little more than dress up formulaic television mystery series.

Religious devotion was implicit on wholesome and comparatively unusual series like *The Waltons* (CBS, 1972–81) and *Little House on the Prairie* (NBC, 1974–83), and it even served as a foundation of sorts for the "I can walk again" melodramatics of *Highway to Heaven* (NBC, 1984–89), but in none of these shows— nor anywhere else, from when Bishop Fulton Sheen's *Life Is Worth Living* (Dumont/ABC, 1952–57) left network television until very recently—did anything approaching a thoughtful discussion of the nature of God and our responsibilities toward that God appear during prime time.

Except at Christmas.

If, at most other times, talk about God was considered too delicate or solemn for the timid and escapist mandates of network television, the Christmas season was a notable exception. From its earliest years, television, like radio before it, offered an assortment of special programming for the holiday. One of the most beloved broadcasts from the "golden age of television," *Amahl and the Night Visitors,* was aired on Christmas Eve, 1951, launching the still running *Hallmark Hall of Fame* series. By the mid-1950s, the network schedules for the month of December were filled with special Christmas offerings and Christmas-themed episodes of regular series. This essay will concentrate on one of the most enduring types of special Christmas programming, the musical variety show, but most of what characterizes these programs also applies to other Christmas-themed shows.

The variety show was the dominant genre in the early years of network television. In the first seasons of the 1950s, well over half of the top-rated programs were musical variety series, most of which included extravagant Christmas-themed production numbers and comic sketches whenever the holidays rolled around. Even as the variety genre became nearly extinct in the early 1970s, leaving behind only a few remnants like *The Carol Burnett Show* (CBS, 1967–79) and *The Sonny and Cher Comedy Hour* (CBS, 1971–77), the form would enjoy a brief resurrection every December with a flood of Christmas variety specials. Golden Age veterans like Perry Como, Andy Williams, Bob Hope, and Bing Crosby returned to the air again in the weeks after Thanksgiving, establishing a new Christmas tradition.

Regardless of nineteenth- and twentieth-century mass culture's attempts to reinvent Christmas as a secularized, national season of consumption in which everyone in the melting pot can participate,[2] Christmas does remain a religious holiday, and Christmas television specials are built around a nexus of traditions devised to celebrate an important event in the modern Christian calendar. What gives Christmas television its overtly religious essence is the music. Christmas music constitutes a substantial body of work, and one that is crucial to the experience of the holiday. A Christmas show without traditional holiday music would be like a western without horses. One might argue, in fact, that the subject matter of most of the Christmas variety specials of the last three decades is relatively unvarying. An hour's worth of the same old songs are simply repackaged with different stars in different geographical backdrops, from Johnny Cash's *Christmas in Scotland* to John Denver's *Rocky Mountain Christmas* to Dean Martin's *Christmas at Sea World*.

Although the twentieth century has supplied a selection of secular standards about snow, Santa, and sleigh riding, many of the season's favorite songs continue to be hymns, and the simple act of singing them in prime time is an unusually religious statement for the medium. The lyrics of "Silent Night," "Joy to the World," or any of the familiar Christmas hymns that are sung so frequently on television specials are strikingly explicit about religious belief compared to everything else in prime time during the rest of the year.

In weaving together material to present between songs, some Christmas variety specials come close to becoming Sunday school pageants. In 1980, Perry Como's *Christmas in the Holy Land,* a musical-variety special that is still being rerun on the Family Channel, presents a re-creation of the Nativity, which Como introduces by saying, "We like telling this story because of what it says—and because we know it's true." In the same show, Richard Chamberlain dons New Testament garb and delivers the Beatitudes on the mountain where Biblical scholars speculate that Christ might have delivered them. He sits on the ground, children listen entranced, and we cannot help but see that Chamberlain, with his hair, beard, and cheekbones, looks a lot like Christ as we know Him through paintings, sculptures, and devotional images. (The unbridled hubris of this presentation makes the segment appear a little strange, almost as though Christ were one of the guest stars, there to do his number and get off, yielding the stage to the next guest. But having already seen Chamberlain in a plethora of historical roles in miniseries, seeing him as the Son of God is not as disorienting as it might have been.) Como wraps it all up with a rendering of Ave Maria, performed with his unique brand of understated reverence.

Similarly, in the *Christmas in Washington* specials, which have aired annually since 1982, the separation of Church and State seems to be temporarily annulled. In one of the first of these specials in 1981, Ronald Reagan read the greeting-card poem "One Solitary Life," a popular inspirational piece about the life of Christ. After emphasizing the veracity of the story, he intoned: "If we live our lives for Truth and Love, because that's what He told us to do, and for God, we never have to be afraid. God will be with us. He'll be a part of something larger, much stronger, and much more enduring than any force that has ever existed on Earth." Not surprisingly for the early 1980s, the president celebrated only one aspect of Christianity here—the even-better-than-nuclear power of its God. In the 1995 installment of *Christmas in Washington,* President Clinton played a 1990s Democratic variation on the theme by calling Christmas a time when we celebrate "the birth of a homeless child whose only shelter was the straw of a manger."

These sincere and explicit professions of belief, however, are fairly uncommon, even on Christmas specials. While for many years network executives did not seem terribly concerned about the lack of non-Christians on the shows they aired during the year, they did seem to be wary of alienating non-Christians with overtly Christian Christmas specials. Most of these programs are designed in the perhaps overly optimistic hope of appealing to those who grew up in traditional Christian homes as well as to those who did not.

One common way of attempting this is to secularize the presentations, and characters like Santa, Rudolph, and Frosty are enthusiastically employed toward this end. Many of the songs, images, and stories of Christmas are now safely secular, and many Christmas television shows choose to stick with these. The indictments of Scrooge, the Grinch, Rudolph's exclusionary reindeer pals, and the people who tease little Virginia for believing in Santa communicate warm values associated with Christmas without the gravity of obvious religious belief. *How the Grinch Stole*

Christmas, which communicates a holiday "message" using characters that are not specific to any particular faith, is much more typical of network television than *A Charlie Brown Christmas,* which communicates a similar message by reading from the New Testament.

Granting religions equal time is another way Christmas programming tries to avoid estranging non-Christians. The Holy Land location of the Perry Como special mentioned above allowed Como to explore Jewish and Islamic traditions alongside his familiar renderings of Christmas carols and stories. In a similar vein, a 1995 Christmastime advertisement announced that "Whether it's choirs or Kwaanza, you can count on the U.S. Postal Service to handle the holidays."

Finally, producers often soften the religious content of the Christmas special by reading a religious theme into secular material. A striking example of this strategy occurred in the early 1980s in Anne Murray's special, *Christmas in Nova Scotia,* on which she sang her hit song "You Needed Me." Murray gives the viewer a verbal cue before she begins to sing: "This wasn't written about Christmas," she says with knowing solemnity, "but it could have been." Right from the start, the audience is invited to hear a new message in the song. As she sings, she sings not to a lover, as the lyrics might have suggested ("I sold my soul, you bought it back again"), but to a beautifully panoramic Nova Scotia sunset, a sort of archetypically divine image, the kind of place one would go to pray. And casual attention to the lyrics reveals how easy it is to place a spiritual interpretation on the song. Yet those who do not want to take Anne up on her cue, "This wasn't written about Christmas, but it could have been," can just sit back and enjoy the piece as a popular song illustrated by pretty scenery.

Aside from hymn lyrics, practically none of the network Christmas programming is overtly Christian. Instead, the specials contain the vague trappings associated in the popular imagination with religious life: traditional values, moral living, nostalgia. Christmas programming in general is nearly always characterized by a very heavy emphasis on the home and the extended family, and on the virtue of generosity. Together these are expressive of a faith which Americans—whether Christians, believers of other faiths, or secularists—share.

This American cultural Christmas is a perfect match for television. Christianity itself, a religion based on the word, not the image, and one which rejects wealth, acquisitiveness, and conspicuous consumption, is not well suited for a commercial medium like television, but Christianity as it is reconfigured in Christmas specials to match American expectations is a different story. By focusing on home, family, and generosity, Christmas specials create an uncomfortable emotional state that can easily be comforted by shopping, by patronizing the advertisers of the shows that made the viewer uncomfortable in the first place. This, in the end, is the genius of Christmas television.

The Christmas variety specials may be shot on locations all over the world, but, like most Christmas programming, they are obsessed with a nostalgic reverence for the idea of home and the family. Nearly every location in which a Christmas variety special takes place is somehow tied to the concept of home. Anne Murray went to Nova Scotia because it was where she had grown up, and there she was reunited with parents, aunts, and others in her family tree; Johnny Cash's special returned to his ancestral roots in Scotland, where he too was surrounded by relatives; Perry Como's *Christmas in Williamsburg* tried to identify that city with the collective roots of our country; Dolly Parton eschewed famous guest stars and cast her own friends and family in a special shot in her home town of Sevierville, Tennessee. This strategy continues into the 1990s. Kathy Lee Gifford's entire family gathered around the fireplace and the tree for a special set right in her own house in Colorado, in 1995's *Kathy Lee: Home for Christmas,* and Martha Stewart enlisted the help of her sister and mother in her 1995 special, *Martha Stewart: Home for the Holidays,* shot in her tastefully decorated home. The hearth as well, an archaic symbol of home, still appears over and over in Christmas variety specials, usually with a large family (biological, institutional, or otherwise) singing around it.

This validation and affirmation of a mostly outmoded view of the family has significance beyond mere nostalgia, however. What Anne Roiphe wrote in *The New York Times* about *The Waltons,* one of the key precedents for this type of nostalgia, applies as well to most Christmas television:

> [W]e identify with the Walton family . . . not so much from recognition as imagination or mythical cultural memories of the way it ought to be. Since we think of ourselves as outsiders and we wish we were part of the cohesive, good, happy family, we eagerly sink into the story, two sides of ourselves playing against each other, and in the end we feel pleasurably sad—even though, of course, everything has turned out all right. We are sad because we know things aren't that way at all and yet we're not angry or provoked because we've enjoyed playing around with the images of family life as they might be (we determine, not consciously, to bring our own families closer together), and as

with New Year's resolutions the lack of accomplishment is nothing compared to the sincerity of the attempt.[3]

Dinah Shore, who hosted one of the *Christmas in Washington* specials, unwittingly demonstrated some consciousness of the ephemeral nature of the resolutions Roiphe writes about when, at the end of the show, she invited everyone to sing along "while the glow is still upon us." That "glow," of course, is not only the glow of the "Christmas spirit" but a glow of guilt. These television shows suggest that maybe Christmas spirit is guilt—a temporary, annual, emotional affliction awakened and encouraged by the programs themselves. Television Christmas specials provide the means by which this emotional phenomenon can be harnessed and used for enormous profits. Right after the broadcast of Perry Como's *Christmas in Paris,* following the show's touching finale, a commercial for a national flower delivery service suggested that viewers send a gift of flowers to loved ones by phoning in an order now. The company's advertising agency must have recognized the fleeting nature of the spirit a Christmas special can generate, and they wanted to get our Visa or MasterCard numbers "while the glow [was] still upon us."

This brings us to another defining characteristic of the genre: Christmas television shows are tumescent with presents. Many of the traditions and stories of Christmas have been adapted to support one mandate: the expenditure of capital. The Magi brought gifts to Christ, Santa Claus brings gifts to everyone, and the very definition of a "scrooge" comes from the character in the most well known semi-secular Christmas tale of all, whose hellish descent into his own id is caused by his unwillingness to spot Bob Cratchett a few shillings until payday. After his visits from the ghosts of Christmas Past, Christmas Present, and Christmas Future, Scrooge is redeemed only when he wakes up and starts tossing money around like there was no Christmas Tomorrow. Nearly every television series, from *Mr. Magoo* (NBC, 1962–65) to *Family Ties* (NBC, 1982–89) to *Melrose Place* (Fox, 1992–), has done an episode based on the Dickens classic, and nearly all dramatic Christmas specials resonate with the spirit of giving. On the variety specials, stories are told and songs are sung about giving; gifts are ceaselessly distributed to cast and crew; guest stars frequently make their exits, after performing, with excuses that they have shopping to do. Scripts from the old Perry Como specials reveal a sequence called the "Gifts Montage," in which Perry's sack of presents runneth over. The preponderance of children in Christmas variety specials should be understood in this context: they sing, they decorate trees, but most of all they get presents. Most Christmas television demonstrates that kids like toys, and lots of them, and that we should plan our shopping strategies accordingly. Whether representing frankincense or a sausage basket from Hickory Farms, the mythopoetics of Christmas's cultural traditions have systematically conditioned most Americans to give until it hurts.

In an ingenious sleight of hand, then, popular Christmas stories encourage the purchasing of gifts at the same time they preach of how unimportant material things are. From the Protestant work ethic, which kept pious noses to unrelenting grindstones, to church dress codes, which provided milliners with annual windfalls from the sales of expensive Easter bonnets, Christianity has a long history of being an effective lubricant of the American economic machine. The tradition goes so deep that few recognize the contradiction, even in utter non sequiturs like this coffee advertisement from December, 1995: "As long as the best gifts come without ribbons or tags, Maxwell House will be good to the last drop."

Thematically, these programs set the tone for the commercials within them. Nearly all of the advertisements are designed especially for the season, ready to cash in on the special "glow" that Dinah Shore invoked and that the show tries to create, and featuring the same elements that are in the shows themselves: hearths, families, and emotional, guilt-inspiring incentives to buy. A few years ago, for example, a commercial for a greeting-card company opened with the image of a sweet but very lonely looking old woman sitting on a rocking chair, knitting pathetically. A narrator then offered the interrogative, "Remember Aunt Hildy? She made your first party dress. We wonder who you forgot to remember this year." Hallmark's "When You Care Enough to Send the Very Best," when packaged in a special Christmas commercial, implies an aggressive challenge: "*Do* You Care Enough to Send the Very Best?" Even the Public Broadcasting System, a supposedly noncommercial venue, has shamelessly used this strategy. After the PBS station in Chicago aired a musical special, *A Pavorotti Christmas,* an announcer broke in as the end credits played, asking, "Now that you have been inspired by the spirit of giving, why not call and pledge your support to Channel 11?"

The connection between shows and their commercials goes even deeper, however. In 1980, the *Christmas in Washington* special played an audio tape of Winston Churchill from December, 1941, in which Churchill addressed the problem of how people might get in the mood to give gifts with a war on: "Let the children have their night of fun and laughter," Churchill said. "Let the gifts of Father Christmas delight their play. Resolve that by our sacrifice and daring these children shall not be robbed of their inheritance or denied their right to live in a free and decent world." This comment elevated gift giving to a symbolic prerequisite for living in a free land. And if Churchill's listeners could buy gifts less than three weeks after the bombing of Pearl Harbor, surely a mere recession shouldn't stop us.

In short, commercials thrive in the healthy environment that Christmas television provides. The shows are designed to appeal to many people, and the moods they set are those that will open wallets as well as hearts. The old complaint that "Christmas is too commercial" is a tired cliché, and the claim that "television is commercial" is redundant, but the identity between these two statements is significant. In contemporary American society, the style of Christmas and the style of television are both dictated by consumption.

This was not always the case. Some of the programming of television's "golden age" was serious and moving enough to make the commercial interruptions seem trivial and ridiculous. Other shows were so well liked that sponsors worried that the commercials would get lost in the enthusiastic response. Television critic Mark Crispin Miller points out that commercials are most effective when their messages "are not overshadowed, contradicted, or otherwise threatened by programming that is too noticeably different from the ads," and he cites an ABC executive who wrote that television must attract huge audiences, but must do so without emotionally moving viewers so much that the shows "will interfere with their ability to receive, recall, and respond to the commercial message."[4]

At Christmas, such interference is seldom a problem. The message of the program and the message of the commercials are identical, right down to the music and symbols and characters they each employ. Will the lovers on "The Gift of the Magi" sell their hair and watch for combs and a watch chain? Will the indebted son "reach out and touch" his mother over AT&T lines? They're both the same question.

Once a year, the so-called crass commercialism of television is justified. The advertisements continue to interrupt the programs the same as ever, but the messages are sacred ones. Business as usual is absolved—indeed sanctified—when surrounded by the icons of a holiday which identifies the purchasing of gifts with the achievement of spiritual grace. Television can afford to be reverent at a time of the year when reverence and spirituality take on a consumerist mandate. If the program presents the problem (greed, selfishness, lack of "Christmas spirit"), the advertisements provide the solutions (buy presents, send greeting cards).

The consistent popularity of the Christmas television special might be due, at least in part, to the fact that at no other time do the dramatic and thematic features of the commercials line up so nicely with those of the programs.

As sleazy as this all sounds, though, good things are possible in this profitable bonanza of the ecumenical-industrial complex. Santa, Scrooge, and shopping, while effectively harnessed by national advertisers, also carry messages not entirely hostile to the Christian system. While filled with commands to buy, network television is also filled, for an entire month every winter, with stories and songs that ask us to be nice, not naughty. The messages are for the most part terribly unsophisticated, but they are also a lot kinder and gentler than in the rest of the year. The Grinch, Santa Claus, and even Perry Como can suggest a crude first step in a direction seldom encouraged by television. "For all the billions of dollars in sales that the modern Christmas generates," Leigh Eric Schmidt writes, we should acknowledge the bathwater as well as the baby: "the holiday bazaar has remained a realm of contest, not fiat, a place of disaffection and estrangement as well as joy and excitement, a site of not a little ambivalence, paradox, and contradiction."[5]

It is hard to predict the future of Christmas programming. Despite the growing number of cable channels catering to specialized musical tastes, the network musical variety show is still holding its own each December. The first generation of classic Christmas hosts has been replaced by a new group that includes Kathy Lee Gifford, Martha Stewart, and Vanessa Williams, but the format of the shows is usually strikingly similar to what we have been seeing for decades.

Christmas television is no longer the only place to see religion on prime time, however. In March, 1997, *TV Guide* ran an extensive cover story on "Prime Time's Search for God,"[6] but the trend had been in place for several years before that, most notably in CBS's *Touched by an Angel* (1994–) and its spinoff, *Promised Land* (1996–). Both of these shows remain firmly in the *Highway to Heaven* tradition while at the same time presenting more aggressively religious content.

Surprisingly enough, however, the most innovative use of religion in prime time is now found not in family oriented shows but in series "for mature audiences." The same circumstances that introduced "adult" language, explicit sexuality, and controversial subject matter to prime-time television have, paradoxically, brought religion along as well. Around 1980, with the increased competition brought on by cable and wireless remote control, prime-time network television started to scramble for something new, to keep its viewers from defecting to the vast assortment of choices suddenly available to them without getting off the couch. Networks started looking for programs that were different, programs that would arrest the fickle channel surfer. In an attempt to entice an audience that was shrinking rapidly throughout the 1980s, network executives began searching for programming that would break the very rules that they had been enforcing for decades.

As the creators of television searched for new and original ideas, for something that had not been done before, religion loomed as one of the final frontiers. It provided virgin narrative territory, it had the potential to appeal to a wide variety of audiences, and it was easily integrated into standard genres like cop shows and medical dramas, where a character's confrontation with the meaning and purpose of God's will could be seamlessly incorporated into the life-and-death situations that are so frequent in these programs. *St. Elsewhere* (NBC, 1982–88) flirted with some heady religious discussions, as did *thirtysomething* (ABC, 1987–91), and *Northern Exposure* (CBS, 1990–95) employed spirituality as one of its central themes. *Picket Fences* (CBS, 1992–96) went the furthest, however, featuring both a doctor and a cop among its principal characters, but more concerned with God and religion than with solving crime or saving lives. Rather than the vague, "natural" religion of *Northern Exposure, Picket Fences* actually treated issues of doctrine: Catholic, Protestant, Jewish, Mormon, Christian Scientist, and more. The show included clergy—two of them—in the regular cast of characters. Hardly an episode went by without a mention of God, and often religion was at the center of the story: detailed discussions centering around lapses in faith; the nature of prayer; the extent to which the stories in the Bible are literally "true"; the place of miracles in the mind of a modern, thinking Christian; even the sign of the stigmata.

With the possible exception of *The Simpsons* (Fox, 1989–), the subject of religion has not made as much headway into comedy—Norman Lear's *Sunday Dinner* (CBS) lasted only a month in 1991—but in serious dramatic programs it has become almost a defining feature of the genre. *Homicide: Life on the Street* (NBC, 1993–1999) and *Chicago Hope* (CBS, 1994–) rely especially heavily on these stories, and Christ was portrayed as a character on an episode of *NYPD Blue* (ABC, 1993–). *Oz* (HBO, 1997–), the television series that has gone the furthest to date in its portrayal of graphic violence and "adult" language, features a Muslim leader and a prison chaplain as principal characters, and frequently confronts complex religious questions and problems. That television's most serious, we might even go so far as to say reverent, discussions of religion are being held right next to scenes featuring on-screen rape proves once again that American popular culture is full of surprises.

Turf to which Christmas specials used to have an exclusive claim is now being occupied all year long by regular series programming. Unlike the Christmas specials, however, which for the most part stripped religion of all but its most market-friendly elements, some of this new programming is slouching toward a real and mature conversation about the nature of God.

NOTES

1. A quick overview of this programming can be found in the second chapter of Steve Bruce, *Pray TV: Televangelism in America* (London: Routledge, 1990), 24–53.

2. See Penne Restad, *Christmas in America: A History* (New York: Oxford University Press, 1995); Stephen Nissenbaum, *The Battle for Christmas* (New York: Alfred A. Knopf, 1996); and Leigh Eric Schmidt, *Consumer Rites: The Buying and Selling of American Holidays* (Princeton: Princeton University Press, 1995), 106–91.

3. Anne Roiphe, "Ma and Pa and John-Boy in Mythic America: *The Waltons*," reprinted in *Television: The Critical View*, 2d ed., ed. Horace Newcomb (New York: Oxford University Press, 1979), 8–15, quotation from 13.

4. Mark Crispin Miller, "Deride and Conquer," in *Watching Television*, ed. Todd Gitlin (New York: Pantheon, 1986), 182–228, quotation from 190; the ABC executive is quoted on 191.

5. Schmidt, *Consumer Rites*, 191.

6. *TV Guide*, 29 March 1997, 24–45.

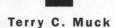

Terry C. Muck

FROM AMERICAN DREAM
TO AMERICAN HORIZON

The Religious Dimension in Louis
L'Amour and Cormac McCarthy

"It was all falling together at last."
—Louis L'Amour, *The Lonesome Gods*

"They rode on."
—Cormac McCarthy, *Blood Meridian*

"What causes fights and quarrels among you? Don't they
come from your desires that battle within you?"
—James 4:1

The western novels of Louis L'Amour and the novels of Cormac
McCarthy set in the West have a religious dimension revealed in the values of their lead characters. Initially, these religious dimensions seem
dead opposites. L'Amour holds up external standards by which to evaluate good and evil as his characters take life journeys toward the American
Dream of prosperity and progress, while McCarthy rejects the American Dream, relocating values in the experience of the journey itself.
Good and evil seem to be left to fend for themselves. As opposite as their
religious visions seem, however, there is a complex complementarity between them: together, L'Amour and McCarthy present complementary
views of good and evil and the way people should live their lives. Together they show a way to navigate life's journey so that both universal
ethical principles and the values of multiculturalism are honored. By

holding these two views in tandem, those who live in the American cultural context[1] can move beyond traditional religions' restrictive understandings of universal values into a postmodern acceptance of the primacy of individual experience in the formation of values, without losing altogether the notion of universal goods. In other words, L'Amour and McCarthy can both be read with profit and without denigrating one or the other.

This thesis does not rest solely on a theoretical argument, but also on L'Amour's and McCarthy's enormous success with different segments of the American audience.[2] L'Amour (1908–1988) wrote well over one hundred westerns and each of them has sold more than one million copies to a popular audience.[3] McCarthy (b. 1933) has written seven novels, and critics of elite literature acknowledge him as one of America's greatest authors, in the same class as Faulkner, Melville, and Hemingway.[4] A key feature of my argument rests on the assumption that L'Amour's and McCarthy's fiction reflect widely held values in a single, complex culture.

This essay has three parts: first, a brief introduction to both authors and their work (which shows the differences between them); second, a comparison of two value complexes (good/evil and the life journey) closely associated with religious worldviews; and finally, a description of the authors' complementarity.

LOUIS L'AMOUR

The facts of Louis L'Amour's life are well known.[5] He obviously lived an interesting life, enjoyed talking about his past, and made a good interview. He was born as Louis Dearborn LaMoore (he only later changed his last name to L'Amour) on 22 March 1908, to a veterinarian / chief-of-police father in Jamestown, North Dakota. Hard times hit this agricultural community in the 1920s, and the fifteen-year-old LaMoore decided to strike out on his own. He headed to the American Southwest, traveling from job to job, eventually journeying by ship to Asia and Tibet. By the time he joined the Navy for World War II, he had worked as a cowboy, hay shocker, fruit picker, circus worker, lumberjack, boxer, longshoreman, sailor, and gold miner. According to his autobiography, *Education of a Wandering Man* (1989), he read voraciously, especially about the history of the American West. After World War II, L'Amour settled in Los Angeles, determined to write. Book reviews, poetry, and short stories followed, but the publication of *Westward the Tide* (1950) settled his destiny.

Westward the Tide was only moderately successful upon its initial publication, but was the first of his many westerns. Literary critics don't spare the rod in evaluating this huge volume of work: style ("Alarming stylistic infelicities . . . commits just about every common error pointed out in basic writing courses"), subject matter ("Old fashioned American virtues: patriotism, loyalty, courage, family, hope . . . corny, but they still ring true to the consuming public"), and success ("Too popular to be defined as a critical challenge . . . embarrassingly readable") all come under heavy scrutiny.[6] According to these critics, L'Amour's literary performance, summarized in report card form, might look like this:

Plots	Great
Scenery	Great
Dialogue	Good
Advice	Plentiful
History	Some
Humor	Little
Violence	Little
Sex	None
Style	Bad

Clearly, "the most popular writer of Westerns ever known"[7] relies heavily on exciting plots and clear, descriptive writing, particularly about the West's geography, to succeed. He uses the seven basic plots all western writers use, but with his great inventiveness and attention to detail he uses them better than anyone else.[8] This skill, combined with a strong work ethic (one critic described him as "an early to rise writing machine" reminiscent of Balzac and Trollope[9]), has produced a great corpus of literature.[10]

CORMAC MCCARTHY

The facts of Cormac McCarthy's life are not as well known as those of Louis L'Amour's; perhaps the best known fact of McCarthy's life is that he refuses to talk about it.[11] To date there is only one published interview with McCarthy, done at the insistence of his agent and publicists after he won the National Book Award for Fiction for *All the Pretty Horses*.[12] McCarthy was born in 1933 in Rhode Island, but his lawyer father moved to Tennessee shortly thereafter to work on Tennessee Valley Authority projects. McCarthy disliked his home life and hated school, although he tried twice to get a college degree at the University of Tennessee. He wanted to write literature and began writing in 1959, at first about Appalachia in *Orchard Keeper* (1965), *Outer Dark* (1968), *Child of God* (1973), and *Suttree* (1979), but then turning West in 1982 when he moved to El Paso, Texas. In both Tennessee and Texas, McCarthy occasionally worked odd jobs to make ends meet, but certainly did not have the traveling adventures of L'Amour. Whereas L'Amour collected odd jobs, McCarthy collected grants, including writing grants from the William Faulkner Foundation, the Rockefeller Foundation, the American Academy of Arts and Letters, and the MacArthur Foundation.

If critics long for a challenge with L'Amour's clear style, they perhaps bite off more than they can chew with McCarthy. One called his prose a "syntactical thorn bush," a hard slog for the general reader.[13] Critics seem to agree that McCarthy is not much interested in the intricacies of plot, but disagree over how debilitating this is.[14] Critics also agree that McCarthy's characters seem flat and lack sophistication.[15] It is McCarthy's use of language—his meditations on creation, looking through appearances, not past them—that is the stunning aspect of his work. But, specifically, he writes about life and death: Saul Bellow describes his writing as full of "life-giving and death-dealing sentences."[16] McCarthy's books are so full of violence, a violence which is so matter-of-factly described, that the reader begins to view the world through violence-tinted glasses. The body count makes Arnold Schwarzenegger movies seem tame. In short, McCarthy's report card might look like this:

Plots	Minimal
Scenery	Great
Dialogue	Different
Advice	Little
History	Some
Humor	Little
Violence	Lots
Sex	Some
Style	Great

DIFFERENT YET COMPLEMENTARY

To say that L'Amour and McCarthy are complementary means that they are different, but that somehow in their difference they contribute to a larger whole. One sharp contrast between the two lies in their respective audiences. The populist L'Amour wanders the earth among the hoi polloi, searching for adventure, and measuring the crisis, climax, and denouement of those adventures against the values of the American Dream: patriotism, loyalty, courage, honesty. On the other hand, the reclusive, elitist McCarthy plumbs the depths of the human condition, reflecting that labyrinth of unarticulated psychic forces by mirroring their complexity with an evocative complexity of language. One author makes the human condition plain, the other manages to "precisely delineate" but only "vaguely define" it.[17]

Yet in the midst of this and other differences lies an essential commonality. On the most obvious level, both write about the American West.[18] The question has been raised whether McCarthy really writes westerns. McCarthy himself perhaps thinks he does, particularly from *Blood Meridian* (1985) on—his second wife has been quoted as saying that McCarthy always wanted to write a great western, and *Blood Meridian* was it[19]—but some critics consider McCarthy a Southern writer in the tradition of William Faulkner and Flannery O'Connor.[20] Still, most critics locate McCarthy as a writer of westerns, even though his first four novels were set in Appalachia and Tennessee, because his books contain many of the elements of westerns: a journey motive, a clear use of landscape as character, a single man undergoing personal transformation, and an emphasis on values such as personal initiative, courage, and skill in facing the vicissitudes of nature.[21]

It is clear that McCarthy is not writing books like L'Amour's—his journeys do not end happily ever after, nature is not always distinct from the conquering traveler, his main characters are not heroes, and the values McCarthy emphasizes, although called by the same names as L'Amour's, seem strangely different. Also, the classic western takes place between 1850 and 1900, while McCarthy's books are set in the early and middle twentieth century. It might be appropriate to recognize both the affinities and differences by calling McCarthy's books "elite westerns."[22]

Yet both contribute to an understanding of the American West and of the religious dimensions implicit in stories that deal with literal and metaphorical journeys and the concepts of good and evil. The western plot always involves a single hero (a man) living his life as a literal journey. He is on the move and the plot, such as it is, comes from the situations created by his journeying. Second, the "adventures" this journeying man faces, and the decisions he makes in the face of such adventures, need some conception of good and evil as the markers by which journeys can be evaluated and decisions validated. In spite of obvious differences in the way L'Amour and McCarthy treat these two topics, in the end they are complementary in that reading both gives a fuller, more complete picture of truth about life journeys and about good and evil than would reading either one alone.

JOURNEY

A journey is a traveling from one locale to another, a trip. Both L'Amour and McCarthy write about journeys; their main characters, homeless men and boys, take trips. Furthermore, these trips involve many of the same elements: they represent freedom from the normal social strictures of family and community; they pit the traveler against the forces of an aggrandized nature; they test the resourcefulness and skill of the traveler who steps up to the task facing him; and in the process the traveler shows great character traits such as courage and the ability to work hard.

In spite of these similarities, the destinies of these trips differ. For L'Amour, the journey moves toward a destination, for McCarthy the journey is life itself. For example, one of L'Amour's classic heroes, Hondo, starts out with a job which is travel exemplified: he is an Indian scout for the United States Cavalry. In the course of his risky duties, Hondo chances upon Angie, a rancher whose husband has deserted her and her young son. Finally, after many adventures—being captured and tortured by Indians, attempting to rescue a doomed cavalry patrol, killing Angie's blackguard husband, warning the fort, protecting Angie—Hondo marries Angie and settles down on the ranch to travel no more. Typical of McCarthy's travelers, on the other hand, is John Grady Cole (*All the Pretty Horses*), who loses his father's ranch (which he considers his inheritance), travels to Mexico, has adventures, and returns across the border to . . . nothing. A lot happens on the trip, but, in the end, nothing. L'Amour's trips are linear, moving from point A to point B to point C, whereas McCarthy's are circular in some cases, totally nondirectional in others.

Both McCarthy and L'Amour are masters of description, but description serves different purposes in their works. L'Amour uses his word power to describe scenes and set tone, both of which move us forward in the plot. If anything his novels are almost too fast paced. He "rushes the action toward the climax . . . with comic strip simplicity."[23] In one of L'Amour's best novels, *Flint,* for example, the action is nonstop. Flint, a gunman from New Mexico, takes in an orphan, Jim Kettleman, teaches him a lot, and is killed; Jim in turn kills some of the killers, goes east, becomes a wealthy man, marries poorly, gets cancer, heads west to escape his vicious wife and die (taking on the alias of his dead benefactor), discovers in the West that his cancer is curable, fights a corrupt railroad magnate and a dishonest cattle rancher to help save a widowed female rancher, learns to enjoy life in the West, marries the rancher, and lives happily ever after—all in 150 pages.

A lot—though not quite that much—also happens in the 335 pages of McCarthy's *Blood Meridian,* the story of a fifteen-year-old boy who in 1849 joins a band of American cutthroats. They embark on a bloody killing spree, searching for Gomez, an Apache leader with a $1,000 bounty on his head. Since there is a bounty on every Apache scalp obtained, the killing seems nonstop, and although the boy escapes the death that finds most of his comrades on this trail of blood, he is eventually killed (while sitting in an outhouse) by another survivor, Judge Holden. Still, although all the elements of an adventure are present, a plot never clearly develops. The plot moves but it does not thicken—one has only a serial progression of adventures. McCarthy's description is not a means to an end, but an end in itself.

Thus L'Amour's novels end in some kind of resolution, usually a "happily ever after" sort of solution to the problem of the plot. "L'Amour's heroes often fight for communities they then live in":[24] the search is for home, ranch, and possibly a family in the future. McCarthy's heroes may be searching for home, but they never find it—as Terri Witek says, both L'Amour and McCarthy find central "the twin desires for permanence of home and freedom of flight," but for L'Amour the former often wins, whereas for McCarthy it rarely does.[25] For McCarthy it would be more accurate to say that the novels stop rather than end. Little if anything is resolved; the real end, the only end in McCarthy, is death. Death for L'Amour is the enemy; for McCarthy it is the one sure event against which the rest of life can be measured. Death is described in unrelentingly evenhanded tones; the effect is to put the most horrific scenes on the same level with a description of a magnificent sunset, the death of a she-wolf, or a lovemaking scene. The horror is there in all its graphic description, but McCarthy does not prescribe the tools that insure the reader will muster the appropriate moral horror—readers are left to their own devices.

Taken together, these elements of the journey—direction, description, and result—add up to different reasons for undergoing such journeys. For L'Amour, the individual journey of the westward-yearning hero is coterminous with America's journey. The chaotic West is slowly but surely brought under the hand of civilization. The destiny of democratic values and the values of individualism—courage, initiative, honesty—are assured by individual heroes like Hondo and Flint, whose efforts, multiplied thousands of times by other, unknown heroes like them, ensure the dominance of the American Dream. Like scores of Homeric heroes winning the world for Greek civilization, the western hero carves out the future of the American people.

For McCarthy, there is no dream to realize. His lead characters are more like Dante's, searching for personal redemption, or more often for the least amount of punishment. Beyond this almost incidental self-discovery, their journeys have no immediate purpose and little direction. They never end in any satisfactory sense. The most that can be said for McCarthy's characters is that by relentlessly moving on toward the horizon they have caught glimpses of truth, but the horizon is always receding, and the journey never ends. The truth the characters see comes in lightning flashes which may illuminate the horizon momentarily, but which have no enduring reality or discernible pattern. If L'Amour's journeys are to achieve progress, McCarthy's enable the protagonists to understand process.

GOOD AND EVIL

How does one evaluate what happens on these epic and existential journeys? What is required is a sense of L'Amour's and McCarthy's conceptions of good and evil. It is tempting to say that L'Amour cares a great deal about good and evil and the difference between the two, and that McCarthy rarely thinks either about good and evil or their distinction. One could marshal a great deal of evidence to support such an argument. One of the most common words in all of L'Amour's novels is the word "evil," as in "evil men" and "evil deeds," while his heroes are good by definition, and even when they are forced by circumstance to do a mildly bad thing, it is clearly for a good cause. McCarthy, for his part, describes in detail some of the most horrific deeds in the annals of American literature, and leaves the reader wondering what he or she should think about them.

But such a view is overly simplistic and masks a much more subtle use of good and evil by both authors. Because L'Amour tends to identify good with good men and bad with bad men, and digresses frequently with advice-giving passages, he is often saddled with the designation of moralist. A careful look at some of his heroes reveals a moral complexity that dispels that notion. In *Hondo,* Angie saves Hondo by a flat lie, and Hondo lies to her when he tells her her cowardly husband died a brave death. The hero of *Crossfire Trail,* Rafe Caradec, participates in a "justifiable" shipboard mutiny in order to get ashore to carry out an important mission of mercy. Marshals and sheriffs frequently take the law into their own hands to pursue some notion of justice outside the letter of the law. If L'Amour is a moralist in any sense, he is a complex moralist.

Because McCarthy, on the other hand, does not tell readers explicitly what to think about the deeds appearing in front of their faces, one is tempted to label him a relativist with little regard for abstract notions of good and evil. Yet his main characters are constantly doing heroic, L'Amouresque deeds. In *The Crossing,* Billy Parham, the teenaged son of a Texas rancher, traps a she-wolf that has been terrorizing his father's cattle. Seeing that she is pregnant and has wandered over the Texas-Mexico border, he determines not to kill her and instead returns her to her home in the Mexican highlands. His brother eventually joins him and as they wander through Mexico looking for the murderers of their parents (killed while Billy is away on his expedition), they eat whenever good people take pity on them and offer them food. Clearly McCarthy's characters are capable of doing very "good" deeds. They are most often unexpected good deeds and they rarely follow any cultural pattern, but they are good deeds nonetheless. If L'Amour is a complex moralist, then McCarthy often seems to be a simple romantic, especially in his later novels. As a result, despite the differences between moralism and romanticism, L'Amour's complexity and McCarthy's simplicity bring the authors closer together on the question of good and evil than a first glance might suggest. Both recognize that the lines between and among the good, the evil, and the ambiguous are often difficult to draw.

Still, it is the differences regarding the two novelists' views of good and evil that are the most revealing. One way to get at those differences is to begin by saying that because L'Amour locates good values and bad values "out there" in an objective sense, he also finds himself better able to identify good men and bad men because they can be measured by the deeds they do, and how those deeds stack up against the objective realities. This is classic western novel stuff—heroes and villains. Of course, creating realistic characters is never quite that easy. Believability demands that L'Amour's heroes not appear perfect. A wart here and there is necessary to make any character real. Yet L'Amour rarely identifies a good man with an evil deed. Instead he relabels the deed: a villain may lie, a hero bluffs. A villain is disloyal to his comrades, a hero displays a lapse of relational judgment. L'Amour occasionally even allows for a bit of cultural relativity. For example, one of his strengths is his portrayal of Native Americans, at least when measured against the faceless way pulp fiction writers (and television cowboy-and-Indian programming) usually portray them.[26] L'Amour recognizes that there are good Native Americans and bad Native Americans (just as there are good whites and bad whites), but he also recognizes differing value systems. The strength of L'Amour's understanding of good and evil is its clarity, its ability to hold up clear models of what contributes to human flourishing and what doesn't, even across different cultures. The weakness of his understanding of good and evil is that reality often proves remarkably resistant to clearly identifying where evil ends and good begins.

McCarthy's approach goes a long way toward addressing this last problem. He begins by clearly recognizing that strictly good or evil men do not exist, that the mixture of good and evil in the world is every bit as much a quagmire within human beings as it is without.[27] He locates the good and evil confrontation as taking place "in here" rather than "out there." This frees McCarthy's characters from having to be heroes. They can clearly do evil things without McCarthy having to relabel them.

Those who have recognized McCarthy's indebtedness to Faulkner also recognize that it is precisely at this point that he diverges from Faulkner. "What's missing [from McCarthy vis-à-vis Faulkner] is all those elaborate socio-moral codifications with which Faulkner gave formal structure and thematic coherence to the complex life of Yoknapatawpha County." This, actually, is what makes McCarthy a western author rather than a Southern author, although as an elite western author he internalizes the good/evil battle so that "no . . . basis for moral judgment or conflict [is] to be found anywhere."[28] The strength of this approach is that it resonates more profoundly with what we sense to be true about ourselves—that, as John Donne notes in "Hymne to God My God, in My Sicknesse," we all have within our breasts the capacity for great glory and great evil.[29] But it too has weaknesses as a theory of good and evil. It relies too strongly on our idiosyncratic intuition to sort out the good/evil question, thus making it extremely difficult to understand the author as developing good or evil characters.

As a result, it is no accident that critics of McCarthy's work have consistently noted the flat nature of his characters.[30] Moral acts are simply a series of moral decisions with little connection to one another or anything else. One of McCarthy's most interesting characters is Cornelius Suttree, the protagonist of *Suttree*. Suttree is an educated dropout from a well-to-do family who has chosen to live in a dilapidated houseboat in Knoxville on the Tennessee River. The novel follows his adventures—eking out a living fishing, relating to other characters on the river and the skid row of Knoxville, loving, being addicted, and nearly dying—yet at the end of *Suttree* one still has little idea of who he is and how all these adventures have affected him. There are no lessons to learn from *Suttree,* other than some vague acknowledgment of perseverance.

Despite all this, one still comes away from McCarthy's novels with a clear sense of good and evil. As one critic said, there is no question that McCarthy is a writer with a "deep imagination of evil," and that he helps the reader see human nature plain, "as an evil nature, but . . . [with] room for redemptive forces." [31] In this leaving room for "redemptive" forces, what another critic calls McCarthy's recognition of "transcendental codifications," [32] McCarthy somehow manages to overcome the weaknesses of L'Amour's objectivism and paint characters truer to actual (as opposed to ideal) moral life, while leaving open the question of a transcendent dimension to existence. He recognizes the "authority of the secular" [33] (the fact that violence and evil do dominate the world) without giving up on the possibility of God. It is in plumbing the depths of this feature of his novels that the reader touches most closely on McCarthy's (and L'Amour's) religious sense.

L'AMOUR, MCCARTHY, AND RELIGION

Many have recognized and attempted to describe the implicit religious dimension in Louis L'Amour and Cormac McCarthy.[34] Usually that dimension has been oversimplified. As mentioned above, L'Amour has usually been characterized as a moralist pure and simple, and in the religious realm that makes him closer to the right wing, Protestant fundamentalist brand of Christianity than any other.[35] Taking his metaphysic and extrapolating a theology from it produces a dualistic theology of people progressing down the pilgrim's road of life, fighting against the devil and trying to conform to God's will in the process. The end of this struggle is death for the bad and eternal life in heaven for the good. This description of the religious task is remarkably similar to the basic plot development of the classic western. L'Amour and orthodox Christianity make congenial bedfellows.

As suggested, however, this view of L'Amour needs to be nuanced. A simple moralist he is not. It does seem clear that L'Amour's worldview lends itself to an understanding of the cosmos with God in heaven championing a set of values such as honesty, courage, hard work, freedom, and patriotism, and that our task is to find a place where we can live out those values in obedience to God and for the good of our fellow human beings. Yet L'Amour is a novelist, a good one, and his craft demands more faithfulness to the reality of the human condition than simple moralism allows. As a result of what I earlier called L'Amour's complex moralism, his heroes turn out to be real men, capable of error (although not evil), and not the priggish pseudosaints one would expect from a moralist.

This view also implies that L'Amour has accepted the lessons of the Enlightenment and is what you might call a religious humanist. God (and country) is the standard against which we measure success, but it is the individual human being who tramps the earth in search of redemption. Using his wits and the gifts God has given him, the western hero acts as a free moral agent, carving out by his decisions a life rewarded and punished by the quality of his actions.

McCarthy presents a more complex problem, and the religious conclusions critics have drawn from his novels are by no means consistent. All seem to agree that whereas L'Amour's "theological" task (were he to undertake it) would be to find consistency between God's standards and human actions, McCarthy internalizes the struggle that results from this basic cosmological construction of heaven and earth. The conflicts "out there" are real enough, but of remarkably little moral importance. Violence does predominate, even a fool can see that, but it is difficult, if not impossible, to accurately assess the moral value of it—to lay blame as it were. The real struggle takes place within the human breast.

But if external standards with which to measure moral worth are absent, what standards are there? Here is where McCarthy's critics disagree. One group says that for McCarthy there are no standards. McCarthy is the first author of postmodern westerns.[36] There are no standards, because there is no truth. What one envisions as truth is simply that which is historically or culturally conditioned—useful perhaps, but temporary. When it comes to morality, what you see is what you get, and it is delusionary to make any more of it than that.[37]

A second response is to deny the basic cosmological dualism of heaven and earth. McCarthy not only moves the moral battle into the human heart, but he changes the conditions of the fight. The task is not to line up on the right side of some battle between good and evil forces, but to understand that all of the material side is evil and unreal and to be overcome. Material existence is unrelieved evil, fallen from an original state of purity, perhaps, but evil all the same; the only good is the spiritual. In other words, when it comes to religious designation, McCarthy is a gnostic.[38]

The third answer is the opposite of the second. Like the gnostic interpretation, it denies the basic cosmological war between heaven and earth, between good and evil. In its place it sees McCarthy suggesting that the religious task is one of affirming the material as real and the spiritual as illusory. By denying the spiritual realm and removing human beings from any kind of privileged position vis-à-vis physical nature and the animal kingdom, McCarthy is saying that moral meaning can only come from persevering in the existential task of living.[39]

The existence of these three different answers could mean that McCarthy's approach to questions that lead one into the religious realm is (a) inconsistent, (b) complex, or (c) unfamiliar. Perhaps it means all three of those things. His approach is inconsistent only because there does seem to be some development in McCarthy's novels from an early nihilism that might make the postmodern interpretation stronger, to a materialism in the middle novels (*Suttree* and *Blood Meridian*), to more evidence of a gnostic search mode in the Border Trilogy (*All the Pretty Horses, The Crossing, Cities of the Plain*). This development does not mean a repudiation of any of the work, but simply an increasingly complex view that adds newer and richer layers of religious meaning. This complexity then breeds unfamiliarity. By contrast, L'Amour's work is so consistent with traditional American civil religion (and the American Dream) that it is easy to understand. McCarthy seems to be reaching to describe what religion in America is becoming as the old civil religion consensus breaks up in the face of multicultural realities and accompanying religious pluralism. This makes his metaphysic seem strange and incomplete.

MCCARTHY'S METAPHYSIC

It is not necessary to choose between the materialist or the gnostic interpretations of McCarthy. Both approaches can be, and have been, argued responsibly, but the fact that both can be argued with good supporting evidence suggests that something more may be going on here. McCarthy's writing supports both, not because either one by itself represents his position but because he is defining a religious location that cannot be described analytically. McCarthy's position must draw on insights of the "border" to define itself, as it resides in the uncharted land between gnosticism and materialism. McCarthy attempts to carve out and enlarge an area between the authoritative reality of the spiritual and the concrete nowness of the material. This is extremely difficult to do. It can only be done with a non-spiritual, non-material medium—McCarthy chooses language. He creates an ambiance with pure language as not only the medium of expression, but also as the via media of plot, and the standard of measure.

How does McCarthy do this? With an exquisite use of language, he writes about the arena of interplay between the objective and the subjective, using the evocative power of words to communicate the nature of the terrain, and in the process he gives us a truer picture of knowledge and affect than we could ever get by a more direct approach. He uses language not in the service of the material, and not in the service of the spiritual, but language in its truest meaning, as a signpost to the inexpressible realm of being and relationship.

So many things can go wrong in this endeavor. One can overemphasize the feelings created by language and write the secular equivalent of the pietist devotional; one can overemphasize the objective content of the plot and become the secular equivalent of the systematic theologian; one can overemphasize the standard of measure and become the secular equivalent of a homiletician or catechetical teacher; one can overemphasize the universal unknowns and become the secular equivalent of a mystical writer. McCarthy avoids all four of these forms, but he does more as well. When he describes the indescribable, the result is not a denial of the border realities of the objective and the subjective, but an enriched affirmation of both. He does not deny the objective, he simply avoids deifying it in a way that denies other dimensions exist—or relegates them to second-class status. He does not deny the subjective, but he refuses to make human beings the measure of themselves. The farthest he will go is to give individuals the responsibility to understand themselves and their place in the world. He does not deny the moral task, but he does question persuasively the dogma of progress, the idea that we can count on moral improvement, let alone perfection. In McCarthy's own words, "The notion that the species can be improved in some way is dangerous. . . . It enslaves you, takes away freedom, makes life vacuous." [40] Redemption? Possible, if decoupled from the idea of progress. In truth, the objective and subjective attain reality only when connected to this middle realm.

WHY L'AMOUR AND MCCARTHY
ARE COMPLEMENTARY

Why are these two writers complementary? Why is their fiction best served when they are not seen as antithetical, but are read together? [41] The answer is that they complement one another in their approach to values, and they need one another in order to be fully understood. Dana Phillips, in his fine article on McCarthy, notes that McCarthy "does not wholly reject the notion of values, but the values [his work] describes are not ones for which we have ready terms." [42] Perhaps it would be as useful to say that McCarthy still uses the terms for common values, but changes something about the values themselves. John Grady Cole, for example, the young wanderer in *All the Pretty Horses,* at times seems "like a younger but equally laconic John Wayne." [43] He comes into contact with the young daughter of a powerful rancher in Mexico. They fall in love. Unlike John Wayne (who found himself in such a situation time and again in his movies), John Grady dares to despoil her and suffers the consequences. The value is clear in both instances: neither moral nor practical good would come from sleeping with the daughter. John Wayne would not sleep with her (and none of Louis L'Amour's heroes would either), because the external moral code is the center of the story—if the hero does in rare cases break the code he does so only in service of a higher external moral value. For McCarthy, breaking the code is a fact (and in this case the hero suffers serious consequences, a jailing that almost costs him his life), but the story misses not a beat because the external moral code does not determine the lead character's internal moral struggle. McCarthy does not abandon the value, but something about the value changes. What?

First, the location of the impact of the value changes from the objective, external sphere to the subjective, internal sphere. Whether John

Grady sleeps with Señorita Alejandra makes a difference all right, but the crucial difference is located within Grady (and correspondingly within Alejandra). Is this the right thing for him (and her) to do?

Second, the function of the value changes. The value—call it chastity—is not an end in itself, but a means to learn a bigger lesson. For L'Amour such a value, along with others already mentioned—honesty, loyalty, hard work, patriotism—is an end in itself, and the cumulative observance of these values adds up to the moral life. For McCarthy values are not ends but means. They function to reveal lessons about life that are much larger than the simple value in question or even an aggregate of such values. Values are, to use Charles Taylor's term, "epiphanies of the eternal." [44] How one chooses to relate to a value one's society deems very important (whether one follows common wisdom about it or not) reveals meaning that goes far beyond simple observance. Values, in this reading, are like windows to the eternal instead of being mirrors that reflect one's essential character.

Third, the way we understand, accept, and act on a value changes. Already L'Amour has moved beyond the premodern way of accepting values as divinely revealed. For L'Amour, one learns by trial and error the value of holding to values, and painstakingly builds a moral character value by value, much like a bricklayer builds a wall. This is the modernist view.

McCarthy moves us beyond modernism. In his three early novels, he moves us a full turn away from the modernist position by questioning whether values exist anywhere at all, at least anywhere except in the internal constitutions of our own historically, culturally, and existentially constructed lives. In the process of doing this, he ironically becomes even more of a western writer than L'Amour, making the individual not only the center of action but the measure of all things.

But in his later work, he turns his readers a half step back—not a full step back to L'Amour's dualism, but back to where he seems to recognize the existence of "transcendental codifications" and yet holds fast to his really significant contribution, his reflection of modern religions' recognitions that human beings are unable to even come close to understanding or acting on the eternal truth.

With such a realization comes the true meaning of values. They are like cosmic seeds able to grow only in the soil of human nature; they surely exist without human beings, but they only become what they really are when combined with the catalyst of human subjectivity. And as the soil of each of our subjectivities changes, so the resultant plant changes—

same species, different variety. Thus values do not exist in any ideal form (although they do not *not* exist either); and values do not really exist in any human codifications of them. McCarthy cannot clearly describe a value, nor can he show it to us pure in any one of his characters. He can only bounce us back and forth between the two realms, the universal and the cultural, with his flat, mystical use of language, and trust that the message comes through.

So why does Cormac McCarthy need Louis L'Amour? Practically, because both of them succeed with the same overall culture, although probably with varying segments of that culture. Both reflect truths about American culture that participants in that culture need to hear. Logically, because even as McCarthy's novels reflect an emerging facet of American religiosity, L'Amour reminds his readers of a facet of that same religiosity that is as true as the one McCarthy implies. Philosophically, because our increasingly multicultural society impresses on us the vision that truth is multifaceted, eluding in some way even the very best codifications of it. In such a situation, the value of truth must be seen as an interplay between complementary visions of it. Readers will never move completely beyond L'Amour's vision of the world nor into Cormac McCarthy's vision of the world. Even though current conditions (and our individual locations on the cultural spectrum) may make it appear that the different cultural segments are moving on a continuum away from one or the other, neither emphasis will ever be lost. They are both necessary, providing insights that prepare readers for a more profound multicultural existence that belies the very violence McCarthy uses to teach us. It is in the interface between the popular and elite segments of any single cultural group that one learns both the wisdom and the specific techniques for living at peace in broader, more complex multicultural societies.

NOTES

1. I am using the word "culture" in a general sense, to refer to what *Webster's Dictionary* calls "the concepts, skills, arts, and institutions of a given people in a given period." This usage corresponds most closely to the way the word is used when people discuss issues of "multiculturalism." I recognize that anthropologists, sociologists, and aestheticians all have specialized definitions of culture, but because of the interdisciplinary nature of this article this general definition serves best.

2. These segments are often called "popular" and "elite." Sometimes those

terms are used normatively, but I am not placing any value on them other than descriptive. I am also assuming that the relationship between culture and religion is dialectical; that is, they influence each other. This makes me more Weberian than Durkheimian, although understanding Durkheim's *The Elementary Forms of the Religious Life* (New York: Free Press, 1965) is a must, particularly his statement that "religious representations are collective representations which express collective realities" (10). See also "The Social Psychology of the World Religions," in *From Max Weber: Essays in Sociology*, ed. H. H. Gerth and C. Wright Mills (New York: Oxford University Press, 1946), 267–301: "No economic ethic has ever been determined solely by religion. . . . [R]eligion is, however, one of the determinants of the economic ethic. . . . Of course, the religiously determined life is itself profoundly influenced by economic and political factors" (268). For an introduction to the ways of describing the relationship between religion and American popular culture, see Catherine L. Albanese, "Religion and American Popular Culture: An Introductory Essay," *Journal of the American Academy of Religion* 64, no. 4 (Winter 1997): 733–42.

3. These are actually underestimates, since all of L'Amour's books are still in print and selling briskly. All are published by Bantam and hereafter will be referred to by title and page number in the text.

4. He won a National Book Award for Fiction for *All the Pretty Horses* (New York: Random House, 1992). All of McCarthy's books are published by Random House (in their Vintage imprint), and will be referred to by title and page number in the text.

5. Robert Gale, *Louis L'Amour* (Boston: Twayne, 1985). This critical summary of L'Amour's life and work, written three years before L'Amour's death, suffers from an acknowledged lack of critical distance, but is reliable as an account of the facts of L'Amour's life.

6. Gale, *L'Amour*, iii, 108, iv, 18, 30.

7. Gale, *L'Amour*, 1.

8. As summarized by Frank Gruber in *Pulp Jungle* (Los Angeles: Sherbourne Press, 1967), the seven plots are the Union Pacific Story, the Ranch Story, the Empire Story, the Revenge Story, the Outlaw Story, the Marshal Story, and the Indian Story (184–6). See also John Cawalti, *The Six Gun Mystique* (Bowling Green, Ohio: Bowling Green State University Popular Press, 1971), who expounds his own list (35–7).

9. Gale, 77–9.

10. It is difficult to get a handle on L'Amour's writing unless one has the time to read all of the more than one hundred novels, the short stories, and the critical commentary. For someone not interested in that kind of reading commitment, I suggest the following short list, which is both calculated and arbitrary—calculated in that it attempts to take pieces from each decade of L'Amour's writing career, and arbitrary in that I have chosen what I judge to be the best works: "Ride, You Tonto Raiders," an early short story in *Law of the Desert Born*; *Westward the Tide* (1950), L'Amour's first novel; *Hondo* (1953), a L'Amour classic made into a movie starring John Wayne; *Crossfire Trail* (1954); *Last Stand at Papago Wells* (1957); *Sitka* (1957); *Flint* (1960), chosen as one of the twenty-five best westerns of all time; *Bendigo Shafter* (1979); *The Lonesome*

Gods (1984); *The Walking Drum* (1984); and *Education of a Wandering Man* (1989), L'Amour's autobiography.

11. Vereen M. Bell, *The Achievement of Cormac McCarthy* (Baton Rouge: Louisiana State University Press, 1988). As John Aldridge puts it, "McCarthy preserved his privacy to such a remarkable degree that it became the most reliable fact known about him" ("Cormac McCarthy's Bizarre Genius: A Reclusive Master of Language and the Picaresque, On a Roll," *Atlantic Monthly,* August 1994, 89–97, quotation from 89).

12. Richard Woodward, "Cormac McCarthy's Venomous Fiction," *New York Times Magazine,* 19 April 1992, 28–31, 36, 40.

13. Gregory Jaynes, "The Knock at the Door," *Time,* 6 June 1994, 62.

14. Sven Birkirts, rev. of *The Crossing, The New Republic,* 11 July 1994, 38–41, especially 38. Aldridge ("Bizarre Genius") seems to see McCarthy's disinterest in plot as a weakness, Dana Phillips as a strength ("History and the Ugly Facts of Cormac McCarthy's *Blood Meridian,*" *American Literature* 68, no. 2 [1996]: 433–60).

15. See, for example, Birkirts, rev. of *The Crossing,* 40.

16. Quoted in Woodward, "Venomous Fiction," 30.

17. Aldridge, "Bizarre Genius," 92.

18. Complex cultures have distinctions other than popular vs. elite, for example geographical differences. For America, one of the most important geographical concepts is the idea of the West, which, according to Henry Nash Smith, has symbolically represented all that is good and distinctive about America. See *Virgin Land: The American West as Symbol and Myth* (Cambridge: Harvard University Press, 1950), vii.

19. Woodward, "Venomous Fiction," 36.

20. See Phillips, "History and Ugly Facts," 434–5. Phillips summarizes both arguments, McCarthy as "Southern" writer and McCarthy as "Western" writer, and opts for the latter.

21. See James Folsom, *The American Western Novel* (New Haven: College and University Press, 1966); Richard Etulain, "Origins of the Western," in *Critical Essays on the Western American Novel,* ed. William T. Pilkington (Boston: G. K. Hall, 1980); Richard Etulain and Michael T. Marsden, eds., *The Popular Western: Essays Toward a Definition* (Bowling Green, Ohio: Bowling Green University Popular Press, 1974); and Jane Tompkins, *West of Everything: The Inner Life of Westerns* (New York: Oxford, 1992). Westerns have traditionally dealt with men. There is, however, a series of popular westerns with women as the heroines, which includes Nora Roberts, *Montana Sky* (1996); Barbara Samuel, *Dancing Moon* (1996); Elaine Coffman, *If You Love Me* (1997); Linda Miller, *My Outlaw* (1997); Krista Janssen, *Sky Legacy* (1997); Susan Ledbetter, *Colorado Reverie* (1997); and others. Among writers of elite westerns, of course, we have Willa Cather, whose *Song of the Lark* is the story of Thea Kronberg, a gifted girl whose artistic talents are stifled by the Colorado frontier town in which she is raised.

22. Other terms occasionally used include "antiwesterns," "modern westerns," and "postmodern westerns," but McCarthy's books are not antiwesterns because their form is not against the old western but simply responsive to new

cultural conditions. They are definitely not modern westerns—if anything, L'Amour is a writer of modern westerns because his heroes display a modern capacity for Enlightenment reason and a baby-boomer sense of life as a journey. The best argument that can be made for McCarthy as a postmodern writer would look at his first three novels (*The Orchard Keeper, Child of God,* and *Outer Dark*), where the postmodern absolutes of relative truth, changing culture, and history as determiner of all we are and know seem to dominate. See Steven Shaviro, "The Very Life of the Darkness: A Reading of *Blood Meridian,*" *Southern Quarterly* 30 (Summer 1992): 111–21. I agree with Phillips ("History and Ugly Facts," 435, 456 n.), however, that McCarthy expresses a definite point of view in his later novels that makes the postmodern label a difficult one to sustain.

23. Gale, *L'Amour,* 102.

24. Tom Sullivan, "Westward to Stasis with Louis L'Amour," *Southwest Review* 69 (Winter 1984): 78–87, quotation from 78.

25. Terri Witek, "Reeds and Hides: Cormac McCarthy's Domestic Spaces," *Southern Review* 30 (Winter 1994): 136–43, quotation from 136.

26. Robert Gale gives a good analysis of L'Amour's strengths and weaknesses as far as Western history, Indians, and women are concerned in *L'Amour,* 111–6.

27. For "darkness" (a metaphor for evil) as something real and permanent inside human beings, see Phillips, "History and Ugly Facts," 438.

28. Aldridge, "Bizarre Genius," 90.

29. "We thinke that Paradise and Calvarie, / Christs Crosse, and Adams tree, stood in one place; / Looke, Lord, and finde both Adams met in me" (*The Complete Poetry and Selected Prose of John Donne* [New York: Modern Library, 1941], 271–2).

30. For example, Aldridge says that McCarthy's characters do not interact on any level of sophistication: they "are completely isolated and unsocialized, do not work, inhabit no community, obey no law unless one is forced upon them from outside, and own no property" ("Bizarre Genius," 91).

31. Birkirts, rev. of *The Crossing,* 38, 40.

32. Aldridge, "Bizarre Genius," 94.

33. Aldridge, "Bizarre Genius," 94.

34. There are many ways to analyze a "nonreligious" novel for implicit religious meaning. One can choose to identify specific references to religion (what Suttree says about God in *Suttree* or Judge Holden in *Blood Meridian*), or relate an author's work to an existing religious system (as Robert Coles did in "The Stranger," his review of McCarthy's *Child of God* in the *New Yorker,* 26 August 1974, 87–90), or identify values that have religious importance and extrapolate from those. I have chosen this latter approach here.

35. This connection has been drawn by Robert Gale ("L'Amour is an ultra-conservative, anathema to modern revisionists" [*L'Amour,* 113]).

36. Shaviro, "Very Life of Darkness."

37. By this account, McCarthy would be closest to Richard Rorty's understanding of these matters. See *Contingency, Irony, and Solidarity* (New York: Cambridge University Press, 1989).

38. This seems to be the view of Vereen Bell, *The Achievement of Cormac McCarthy* (Baton Rouge: Louisiana State University Press, 1988). Birkirts also takes this view of McCarthy as a gnostic (rev. of *The Crossing*).

39. See Phillips, "History and Ugly Facts."

40. Quoted in Woodward, "Venomous Fiction," 36.

41. Other writers have noticed the relationship but on different levels. Birkirts, for example, calls McCarthy, "Louis L'Amour rewritten with a bloody pen" (39).

42. Phillips, "History and Ugly Facts," 45.

43. Aldridge, "Bizarre Genius," 95.

44. Charles Taylor, *Sources of the Self: The Making of the Modern Identity* (Cambridge: Harvard University Press, 1989), 479.

4

Mark D. Hulsether

LIKE A SERMON

Popular Religion in Madonna Videos

STUDYING MADONNA AFTER
THE ACADEMIC MADONNA BOOM

This essay argues that some of the most important and interesting texts in recent U.S. culture which have overlapping concerns with liberation theologies are by Madonna. There . . . I said it. Anyone who wants to turn the page in disgust can do so now. I only ask that before you begin a jeremiad about the nihilism and vacuity of scholars these days, you let me clarify what I am—and am not—attempting to establish.

As I explain below, I am not making global claims about all liberation theologies or speculating about Madonna's conscious intentions; I am simply exploring how a select handful of her videos relate to black and feminist theologies in specific contexts during the years around 1990. My goal is not to single out Madonna as especially exemplary. In fact, she is only one among many high-profile stars—some of whom are better musicians—who articulate strong religious themes in their work. A short list of such musicians, drawn only from consensus superstars whose music overlaps with Christianity, might include the Artist formerly known as Prince, Bob Dylan, Aretha Franklin, Bob Marley, Stevie Wonder, and many country artists. A list drawn from lesser known performers and encompassing both Christian and non-Christian spiritualities could be virtually limitless.

Nor do I claim that the videos I address are "typical." Just as no one can walk into a bookstore and choose a good book at random, one must be selective to find popular music with interesting religious content, especially the sort of oppositional political-religious content that interests me the most.[1] I do maintain that much popular music has a strong religious content which goes underappreciated. Only someone who is not listening or has an extremely narrow definition of faith could say, with Christian Coalition leader Ralph Reed, that "one searches in vain for a positive portrayal of faith in popular culture."[2] Listening to Madonna suggests what can be gained if we pay more attention to religion among a wider range of popular musicians.

It is important to clarify how this article relates to what Simon Frith calls the "boom in the academic Madonna business—the books! the articles! the conferences! the courses!"[3] If you have managed to remain unaffected by this orgy of analysis, I can bring you up to speed in four easy steps. Most of this writing—however emotionally overheated when written for television or bloated with jargon when written for academia—fits somewhere within the following ideal conversation.

At level one, the Madonna-hater (or MH) says "Popular culture is morally bankrupt, flagrantly licentious, and utterly materialistic—and Madonna is the worst of all." (Thus the Parents Music Resource Center says that Madonna teaches girls to act "like . . . porn queen[s] in heat.")[4] The Madonna-lover (ML) retorts "Can't you cultural conservatives see what she is trying to do—to annoy people like you! If you don't like it, don't listen to it. Stop trying to police my morality."

At level two, the MH responds "I don't mind rebellion against conservative teachings on the family, but she does it in a way that reproduces sexist stereotypes. Jeesh, look at her dress up like Marilyn Monroe, name her company 'Boy Toy, Inc.,' and celebrate being spanked. What kind of rebellion is that?" The ML replies "Can't you see that her Boy Toy jokes are ironic, that they use ridicule to tweak conventional gender roles?" (Thus when Madonna was asked whether she really enjoys being spanked, she replied "It's a joke . . . it's play. I say I want to be spanked, but it's like 'Try it and I'll knock your fucking head off.'")[5]

By level three, any honest critic who has not seriously studied Madonna's videos should keep silent, although few of them do. The MH says "All well and good, but can't you see that irony is not enough? It is too thin as a foundation for oppositional politics." (One writer says that "the postmodern entices us to enjoy nothing more than the free play of our own chains.")[6] The ML retorts "Can't you see that irony is a lot?—especially about issues of gender and sexuality. Granted it is not everything, but who can address everything?" The MH and ML argue into the night: "But she's too compromised." "Is not." "Is too." "Is not." . . .

At level four, the academic Madonna boom takes off, feeding on endless debates about which cultural discourses she reinforces and which ones she destabilizes. The key to unlock this debate is simple once you get the hang of it. If you are speaking to anyone who perceives more ironic destabilization of conservative traditionalism than you do, you say "What's the matter with you white middle-class postmodernists, get a life, write about something really important!" (Then, since you are certain that postmodernists are the enemy, feel free to quote them out of context.) If you are speaking to someone who sees less destabilization, you sniff "You old stuck-in-the-mud Marxist—and/or Christian, essentialist, bourgeois feminist—you just don't get it! How can you even think about building the revolution—and/or church, theory, movement—without incorporating a postmodern cultural aesthetic?" (Then, try to explain why you were quoted out of context without digging yourself deeper into a hole.) When in doubt you can flip-flop, carrying on a conversation with yourself about the pros and cons of particular videos.[7]

By the time all four levels were fully engaged in the early 1990s, Madonna's videos were a standard locus for debating philosophy and social theory in the field of cultural studies.[8] They became a takeoff point for asking what the words "postmodern cultural aesthetic" mean anyway, whether stable identities of things like gender actually exist, and so on. Meanwhile, as this process snowballed at the hip cutting edge of academic theory, Madonna moved deeper and deeper into the cultural mainstream. Even Norman Mailer could write that "music videos [bear] the same relation to feature films as poetry does to novels" and that Madonna was "our greatest living female artist."[9] (The closest religious analogy was Madonna's embrace by Andrew Greeley.)[10] This created a backlash from scholars who were originally attracted to her because they saw her as transgressive, and the Madonna boom lost some steam. It remains unclear whether ongoing developments, notably her becoming a mother, will breathe more life into this scholarship. Given her reputation as a whore, the tension between images of whores and images of mothers in our culture, and her continuing skill as an artist, it seems premature to close the books on Madonna Studies.[11]

When the editors of this volume asked me to reprint my article on Madonna—first written in 1991—this request came after a lot of water had passed under the bridge.[12] Although my project has snowballed far beyond my original expectations, it began with the modest goal of persuading liberals in religious circles to pay attention to Madonna's anti-racist theology in her hit video "Like a Prayer." Today, there are two senses in which this essay may seem dated. First, it reappears a decade after the videos it discusses, and during this time I have increasingly noticed my students responding to Madonna much as I responded to Elvis Presley when I first heard him in the 1970s: understanding little about his earlier career, I wrote him off as irrelevant. It takes effort to remember when Madonna videos were not moldy oldies on VH-1 and she was a feminist insurgent by the standards of mainstream popular music. Second, this essay was not designed to intervene in high-level theorizing in cultural studies, although it does presuppose some of this theory. In particular, it was never intended to address what became a major locus of Madonna scholarship in the first half of the 1990s: her representation of lesbianism and erotic tastes such as sex toys and sadomasochism in relation to poststructuralist theories of gender.[13]

In a third sense, my article remains fresher. Recall that its goal is to highlight religious nuances in popular music—nuances that are easy to find, if only the critics have ears to hear. Unfortunately, the antennae of critics are rarely tuned to religious bandwidths. A recent call for papers for a national cultural studies conference suggested twenty-nine topics: disciplines from history through art to media studies; categories like class, sexuality, and geography; and subjects including sports, folklore, science, social movements, the internet, and nineteenth-century studies. Nowhere did this list suggest religion as a general subject, nor specific religions, miracles, church-based activism, astrology, feminist spirituality, or millennialism as subtopics. No doubt some speakers addressed religion under rubrics like history and ethnicity, but the list remains revealing, since they could also speak about music under the rubric of gender, art under nineteenth-century studies, and so on.[14]

To appreciate what is lost through this mindset, consider Sinead O'Connor's haunting antiracist lament, "Black Boys on Mopeds." I first heard it with one of the brightest critics I know in the field of cultural studies. Yet when O'Connor sang "Remember what I told you / If they hated me they will hate you" and "Remember what I told you / If you were of the world they would love you," my friend did not realize that O'Connor was quoting Jesus, placing an antiracist understanding of Christianity at the heart of the song.[15] Oblivious that she was missing anything, she was in no position to understand the song's preferred reading, nor the historical resonances and future possibilities it was (at least potentially) suggesting. Obviously, it would not occur to a critic in this

position to explore the audience reception of these meanings or their impact on a larger religious landscape.

True, critics do comment on religious themes that are impossible to
miss—but this does not guarantee subtlety and nuance. Most people
know that O'Connor tore up a photo of Pope John Paul II on *Saturday
Night Live,* after singing Bob Marley's antiracist anthem "War" with a
new verse about abortion rights. For many commentators, that says it all:
this is an open-and-shut case of secular feminist rock star versus mono-
lithic patriarchal Catholicism. A similar framework is typical for approaching religious references by Madonna. No doubt this mindset
illuminates some issues and matches the experiences of many fans. However, it keeps major nuances of Madonna's music and its possible meanings in the shadows. Madonna, too, quotes the Bible. One mix of "Justify My Love" features an extended reading of passages from Revelation
over the music—both affirmations of grace, such as "To the thirsty I will
give water without price," and anathemas rarely heard in decorous
churches, like "They are a synagogue of Satan." [16] How many critics,
even the types that can polish off two volumes of Lacan before lunch, are
willing to read one scholarly book on the politics of Biblical interpretation to inform their interpretation of this song?

E. Ann Kaplan provides a good example of these dynamics in an article that meticulously explores connections between Madonna videos
and the history of film: "Express Yourself" signifies on *Metropolis,* "Oh
Father" alludes to *Citizen Kane,* and so on. [17] The ambition and nuance
of Kaplan's investigation are typical of the work of many other critics,
who expend great effort investigating Madonna's impact on fans and the
dynamics of her popularization of voguing, in which black and Latino
gay men imitate and parody conventional gender roles in elaborate theatrical balls. [18] Just as knowing the Bible helps one appreciate "Black Boys
on Mopeds," these connections deepen the resonance of her videos.

Kaplan does briefly note that "Oh Father" a video she calls a typical
"adolescent story in Western cultural terms," foregrounds Madonna's
"repressive Catholic upbringing and her conflicted relationship not only
to her literal father but also the symbolic one—the Holy Father, the
Law, Patriarchy." [19]

But beyond this comment, Kaplan pays little attention to religious issues in "Oh Father" that cry out for elaboration and investigation. The
particular way that Madonna tells this story about adolescence is through
an elaborate comparison of a literally abusive father, Catholic priests, and
the first person of the Christian trinity—all of whom haunt her psyche

and undermine her attempts to relate to her lover. The video draws on Madonna's childhood experience and dramatizes her efforts to renegotiate these relationships, both psychically, in daily interactions with her lover and father, and in relation to Catholicism, which she references by singing "Oh Father I have sinned" and sitting in a confessional. At all these levels, she seeks peace not through submitting to repression (she sings, "You can't hurt me now, I got away from you") but by transforming the relationships.[20]

Madonna's vision of reconciliation in both "Oh Father" and "Papa Don't Preach," her most famous video about conflict with her father, are grist for the mill at level three of Madonna Studies. ("Too compromised." "Is not." "Is too.") The references to her childhood spark debate on level four. ("Is autobiographical realism passé given the instability of postmodern identities?") But these videos are not merely about rethinking families in general, nor about the "Holy Father, the Law, Patriarchy," if this implies a quick trip from Madonna's body to Lacanian theory with no stops in between. They also reconceptualize Catholic teachings about families and bodies, making them usable in the life of an Italian Catholic taught by nuns—and perhaps by extension usable for fans in a nation where half of the people attend church and 85 percent accept the Bible as divinely inspired.[21] But most Madonna critics simply do not care enough about religion to carry on a nuanced discussion of such matters.[22] After Kaplan's sustained attention to film and German surrealism, for example, she quickly drops the subject of religion. Her footnote captures the priorities of Madonna scholars at large: "Although Madonna's subjectivity is multiple and involves Catholicism, class, and ethnicity as well as gender, my main focus here will be on the latter."[23]

Of course there is nothing wrong with that focus. But what follows is an attempt to shift the focus through analyzing two of Madonna's most famous videos. I seek not to replace a focus on gender with an unrelated turn toward religion, but to integrate attention to religion with race and gender.

WHAT WOULD JESUS DO (IN A VIDEO ABOUT RACISM AND RAPE)?

Critical attention to religious issues in popular music is essential at a time when many young adults build their cultural identities around popular music and express their view of left-liberal Christianity by voting with their feet.[24] In this context, it would be important to analyze popular music in religious terms, even if all this music were diametrically opposed to left-liberal Christian values. But in fact there is often a strong overlap between the concerns of liberation theologies and popular music.

Of course there are many issues critical for liberation theologies—in black, feminist, Third World, and other forms—that Madonna's music does not address. However, liberation theologies analyze religion in relation to specific sociopolitical contexts; they promote ideas and practices designed to overcome specific injustices. Thus they evaluate any given text, like a sermon or song, not in the abstract, but in relation to the problems of particular people.[25] The famous sermon by Archbishop Oscar Romero, in which he commanded Salvadoran soldiers in the name of God to stop killing, does not have universal meaning. It might not strike U.S. youth as relevant to their concerns about racial and sexual identity. Similarly, battles over music censorship and the representation of women on MTV are low priorities for the popular church in Central America. All this is to be expected. What matters is how Romero's sermons and MTV videos function in their respective contexts. MTV's realm of influence is limited, but far from trivial. Even in the shantytowns of Latin America, U.S. television is pervasive, and it matters a great deal to the U.S. peace movement whether MTV promotes shifts from military spending to education and social services.[26]

Since Madonna works in the context of the music industry, it is instructive to compare her work to another video from the 1980s which addresses gender and race in a way that is perhaps more typical. "The Way You Make Me Feel" features Michael Jackson and a few black male peers accosting a woman on an inner-city street. She looks perky yet vulnerable, with a vaguely anorexic figure and an extremely short and tight black dress. Jackson sings about her appearance and his lust above a driving dance beat. He invades her personal space, pursues her as she tries to escape, and makes pelvic thrusts as he faces her. The camera takes his point of view, encouraging viewers to leer at her. She briefly joins a group of female friends who face the men in a somewhat more balanced power relationship. But Jackson chases her away and the climax ensues. She stands alone in the dark as the men surround her. They snap their fingers, make sounds like switchblades, and hump the street, as a fire hydrant squirts water into the air behind them. This can be interpreted as her imagined nightmare or as a come-on which she is supposed to enjoy. Jackson emerges from the shadows to embrace her. In the nightmare reading he is protecting her from rape; in the come-on reading he has successfully worn down her resistance. Either way he wins her and she likes it.

As cultural studies theory stresses, no one can state definitively what any song means, since it can be interpreted in different contexts by various people. Yet songs, like other texts, do have a range of interpretations which have greater or lesser plausibility, especially when considered within specified contexts.[27] It seems fair to say that one context for Jackson's video is the pervasive reality of male supremacy and sexual violence, and that his video promotes images which help to glamorize and perpetuate these problems. Another context is use of images of violent and lustful black males to distort national policy toward minority and low-income people, such as George Bush's demonizing of Willie Horton in the 1988 election and neoconservative laments about the black "underclass." Jackson's song does little to combat this discourse, and may help perpetuate it. I would not stress these points too much, because Jackson's overall impact on race and gender relations is complicated: he is widely lauded as the first African American artist to break into MTV, and is known for his androgynous sexual persona.[28] Moreover, it is possible for musicians to draw on stereotypical images and transform them in helpful ways. In the hands of the best rap artists, such as KRS-One and Public Enemy, "gangsta" images have been used effectively within an antiracist discourse.[29] It seems clear, however, that the pro-black and feminist meanings of "The Way You Make Me Feel" are limited at best.

Thus it is interesting to compare Jackson's video to Madonna's "Like a Prayer," which also represents the threat of sexual violence on an inner-city street and interacts with the stereotype of the black rapist. Before turning to this video, let us imagine the ideal song that a group of liberation theologians might desire, if by some miracle MTV offered them equal time to address Jackson's video. Like most Christian theologians, they would seek a song that drew on stories like the Good Samaritan to side with victims of injustice, and which differentiated itself sharply from racist forms of Christianity such as the Ku Klux Klan's. Like a more select subset of theologians, their ideal song would be capable of focusing on the specific injustice and the possibilities for transforming it, as opposed to asking whether "it was all her fault" or if "he could help himself" given the tragic and ineluctable realities of original sin.

The ideal song for a group of liberation theologians would not stop there. It would distance itself from theologies which conceptualize Jesus' death on a cross mainly as individual atonement for individual human sin. Without necessarily rejecting this idea completely, their song would emphasize Jesus' human solidarity or identity with victims of oppression; place the cross in the context of sociopolitical persecution; and call Christians to "take up the cross" and turn toward solidarity. It would envision churches as places of collective empowerment in concrete struggles toward greater social justice. In the context of racism, their model church would promote black culture and combat both police violence and the scapegoating of black males. In the context of sexism, it would promote female leadership and practical responses to sexual violence. Like much feminist theology, their church might stress the importance of the erotic, and human passion and mutuality more generally, for conceptualizing faith. Certainly it would not place human bodies in opposition to "real issues of faith," as if sexuality and spirituality were antithetical.[30]

"Like a Prayer" includes every element of this wish list, endorsed by one of the world's most popular artists. The song gained saturation play on MTV, VH-1, and pop radio stations during 1989. For a brief and bizarre moment, it even became the theme song for Pepsi, whose market strategists apparently hoped that Madonna could make them the hip and antiracist cola. (They quickly bowed to voices from the religious right which pronounced Pepsi the blasphemous cola.)[31] Through it all, the video was largely ignored by left liberal church people. Although I cannot prove this, I suspect that the lack of response Madonna received from this sector of her public is one reason she gave less attention to religious themes in subsequent years.

As the video opens, Madonna flees for safety to a church because she has witnessed three white males attack a white woman, then stare menacingly at Madonna. Inside the church she prays in front of a shrine with a statue of a black male, perhaps a saint, who is clearly marked by his dress as a Christ figure.[32] She soon falls into a dream which lasts for most of the video, and within the dream the statue comes to life. It begins to cry, then leaves the safety of the church for the dangers of the street. Madonna sings that she hears a voice which calls her name and makes her "feel like home," but at this point it is unclear whose voice it is—that of Christ or that of a lover.

The music and images intensify, and we see a flashback to the assault. We learn that as the attackers escaped, a young black male aided the victim. The Christ figure who left the church and this "Good Samaritan" are the same person. At this moment, the police arrived, accused him of the assault, and hauled him away—and everyone knows what happens to blacks accused of raping white women. Urgently Madonna sings "I hear you call my name," and it seems clear that "you" is the Christ figure and the "call" is to solidarity. If so, this makes sense of an earlier scene which is initially shocking. As Jesus leaves the church and Madonna debates whether to follow, she cuts her palms; this reference to Christ's stigmata has fueled charges of blasphemy, but is easily read as a call to "take up her cross and follow." In any case, it remains unclear how she will respond.

The camera comments on the assault and unjust arrest by cutting abruptly to burning crosses. Madonna dances defiantly in front of them as the music builds to an extreme tension. Then, in a striking musical shift akin to putting a car in overdrive, a black gospel choir (Andrae Crouch's group) takes over the musical mix and the video church. In scenes of joy and collective empowerment, Madonna dances with the choir. The black female preacher who is presiding lays hands on her head in a commissioning scene. A prone Madonna kisses "Jesus." Like many saints and songwriters before her, her faith includes an erotic dimension.[33] Thus we learn the answer to our earlier question. She is not choosing between Christ or a lover, but singing about Christ as a lover, linked in a relationship which balances his call (which is mediated through the gospel music as Madonna sings "you are a mystery" and "no choice, your voice can take me there") with her active response ("I'll take you there").[34] As a powerful gospel chorus repeats and fades, Madonna awakens from her dream and goes to the police station. The camera cuts from the statue of Christ, now inanimate again behind the steel bars of the shrine, to the arrested Christ in a jail cell. Madonna testifies on his behalf and he is released. A curtain falls on the stage where the passion play has been acted and the actors take their bows.

Clearly, this is a sophisticated, antiracist statement, far removed from Jackson's vision of gender roles. Indeed, it is among the more powerful statements of some major themes of liberation theologies that I have ever seen in the mainstream U.S. media. But, like any text, it has limitations as well as strengths. First, it is so complex that parts may be unclear to its audience, or open to negative interpretations—thus compounding the general problem of indeterminacy in interpretation. However, this objection might also be used against exposing teenagers to the Hebrew scriptures or to *Romeo and Juliet*. In each case, a competent reader can gain a relatively clear understanding, and parts of the message will get through to most readers on some level (even if this is not verbal or self-conscious).

Perhaps more seriously, the video centers too much on Madonna and

her good deed to be a fully satisfying vision of the collective empowerment of oppressed groups, despite its focus on combating sexual violence, its call for solidarity against racism, and its heavy emphasis on the
gospel choir. For bell hooks, who perceives the video "mocking" Christianity, this concern completely undermines any positive message.[35] Although I agree that questions about agency are fundamental, hooks's
critique seems unnecessarily harsh. Madonna can play the role of victim
in relation to sexual violence in a fairly unproblematic way, and within
the video she is represented as risking her life. As hooks notes, the issue
of interracial solidarity is more complicated because of Madonna's privilege as a rich white in relation to most blacks, as well as the ways that
white female sexuality has been used in racist discourses.[36] In this context, for Madonna to play the role of "the oppressed" and attempt to
merge herself with black self-empowerment would make no sense. On
the other hand, using racial difference as an excuse to ignore the problem would make her complicit in it. Madonna's only plausible approach
is owning up to her privilege and trying to use it constructively. The video
represents her trying to do just that, even as it places her under the authority of the black community as represented in the gospel choir. The
choir calls and commissions her; through participating in its music, she
taps into an empowering cultural tradition and helps push it forward.[37]
Within this context, she uses her power (derived in part from institutional racism) in ways which might otherwise be purely self-aggrandiz-
ing: she helps rescue the black victim (in the video narrative) and makes
her own use of gospel music within her video (as a businesswoman).

However much these two limitations of "Like a Prayer" reduce its
overlap with liberation theologies, they are limits largely imposed by
Madonna's race and the genre of music video. Five-minute videos featuring white stars are obviously not the only important genre for artic-
ulating liberation theology! But within those constraints, what could she
have done better?

DOES ANYONE GET BEYOND
WATCHING HER CLEAVAGE?

Well, there is the matter of her dancing in her underwear. . . . Does
her sex-goddess image dominate so strongly that viewers can see nothing else? Clearly it does for some people, including conservative critic
Michael Medved, who manages to see Madonna "reaching for her

crotch and simulating masturbation" early in the video as she kneels in front of the statue and then falls asleep.[38] Because Madonna consistently uses sexual images, she can be interpreted as a bimbo with only one over-riding message: pandering to male lust through stereotypical images of women for the purpose of making a buck.[39]

However, Madonna did not invent the stereotypes of female sexuality or the idea that women succeed through using them to influence men. She was born into a system which largely presupposes this, and, many critics argue, works from within these expectations to subvert and transform them in helpful ways (this has been a major theme in the four-stage Madonna argument outlined above).[40] It is useful to approach "Open Your Heart" with this hypothesis because, whereas "Like a Prayer" represents a best-case scenario for the overlap between Madonna and liberation theology, "Open Your Heart" seems at first glance to be a worst-case scenario. If we can read it as pro-feminist, the argument for other videos follows easily.

Madonna's path of least resistance, like that of her fans, is simply to reproduce dominant images like those in Jackson's video. For female musicians, pressure to accept these roles comes with the territory. Throughout the history of rock music, and especially on MTV during its early years, most stars have played the roles and taken the standpoint of rebellious males. It has been difficult for women to create a place except as the groupies of such males or their objects of desire.[41] The "autonomous boy wins objectified girl" plot is typical in music videos, with or without the gross objectification of women evident in Jackson's video or Robert Palmer's "Simply Irresistible" (which actually did become Pepsi's theme song). An especially offensive example is "Girls, Girls, Girls" by the band Motley Crue. This video takes place in a bar and celebrates the band leering at women in various states of undress. The camera takes their point of view; it looks through the legs of women or up from below, focusing on crotches and midriffs.

Madonna's "Open Your Heart" picks up exactly where "Girls, Girls, Girls" leaves off: with men looking at objectified women. Madonna plays a dancer in a peep show. Thus she risks perpetuating her bimbo image— and gains access to an MTV audience. But, in contrast to Motley Crue's video, this video tells the story from her point of view. The men in her audience are separated in little cubicles. The camera takes her perspective, looking down into the cubicles as she tries to make eye contact with the men, which they are unable to return. (She also looks assertively into the camera, demanding eye contact with the viewer.) In contrast to Jackson's video, Madonna's shows her holding power over the men and pursuing them; she is the star they pay to see, and she repeatedly sings "Don't try to run; I can keep up with you; Open your heart to me."

The music has a mournful sound on the verses and a dance groove with a hopeful emotional tone on the chorus; it conveys Madonna's desire to transcend her role and find a mutually respectful relationship. Rather than a man pursuing a vulnerable woman for violent purposes, she presents an assertive woman searching for a lover who accepts her as a full human being. The men in the cubicles prove unable to do this, and there is an undertone of mockery when Madonna addresses them as "baby," shaking her body in an exaggerated come-on. By the end of the video they are isolated and sad, with doors closing on them. In powerful visual and musical imagery, Madonna puts Jackson and Motley Crue in boxes and dismisses them.

Meanwhile, the overall mood is hopeful, because of the sound of the "Open Your Heart" music, but a profound tension has been building between the peep show setting and the music. This tension peaks as the song breaks into the compelling dance groove of the final chorus, but Madonna remains immobile on the floor in a pin-up posture. Only a young boy outside the theater dances—a boy whose attempts to enter the show have been rebuffed by an old man in a ticket booth throughout the video. The tension dissolves as Madonna, standing outside the theater, gives the boy a quick kiss on the lips and wakes him from sleep. Both are clad in loose-fitting gray suits, which gives Madonna an androgynous look, and they dance away playfully with the old man pursuing them. Thus she escapes, leading the boy away from the Motley Crue syndrome.[42]

Feminist viewers must decide whether "Open Your Heart" deserves the benefit of the doubt. It is unquestionably open to negative interpretations.[43] At worst, Susan Bordo sees the "leering and pathetic" men in cubicles and the escape with the boy as "cynically, mechanically tacked on, in bad faith, [as] a way of claiming trendy status for what is really just cheesecake—or, perhaps, pornography." Bordo finds no meaningful reversals in the perspective of the camera, fails to address the music, and argues that "this video is entirely about Madonna's body, the narrative context virtually irrelevant."[44] Even at best, the video risks perpetuating a negative stereotype—"There's Madonna as porno dancer again"—through its attempt to subvert the stereotype. (Rappers who use gangsta images in antiracist ways run analogous risks.) It also risks pandering to pre-adolescent lust. There is no overt representation of anything besides friendship with the boy, but he is trying to enter the show, and he does run off with Madonna as she sings about finding a lover. On the other hand, by escaping with the boy Madonna avoids sexual over-tones that would have been stronger if she had run off with an adult male. More importantly, the video clearly contrasts the exploitation of the peep show with the mutuality of the final scene, and—contrary to what Bordo says—makes this contrast basic to its narrative and musical structure.[45]

There are analogous debates about many of Madonna's videos. Since she often uses irony and promotes controversy, she intensifies the gen-eral interpretive problem of texts having a range of meanings. Some crit-ics see "Like a Prayer" as a bald attempt to use blasphemy as a market-ing tool—some even believe that it endorses cross burnings. Bordo says that Madonna's "message . . . is getting through" in a rap by Ice-T cele-brating gang rape.[46] To what degree should we hold artists responsible for the least flattering readings of their work? Critics have used similar logic to censor Mark Twain's *Huckleberry Finn*. They argue that when Huck debates whether to do the "Christian" thing and betray Jim or "go to hell" by being loyal, this should be denounced as racist rather than understood as a scathing attack on Christian racism. After all, some people might identify with Huck's reasoning (or with the men in Ma-donna's cubicles).

I believe that these videos, especially "Like a Prayer," are fine ex-amples of the overlapping concerns between some U.S. liberation the-ologies and popular musicians. However, we must bear in mind three major qualifications. First, Madonna's work is obviously not allied with critics who seek alternatives to twentieth-century consumer culture as a whole.[47] There are real concerns, both religious and sociopolitical, about building a culture based on the logic of consumer capitalism. From this point of view, Madonna is part of the problem, not the solution. At an-other level of analysis (the one I have been pursuing here), I am not troubled that Madonna makes millions of dollars selling records. So does Michael Jackson, and it matters a great deal which money-making videos gain cultural power.

Second, my discussion brackets a question which holds great fascina-tion, though only secondary importance. What are Madonna's personal intentions? Behind her shifting images and promotion of controversy, does she understand her work as feminist, antiracist, or theological? Or are her detractors correct? Is she a cynical and shallow performer who simply dances to industry scripts that sell records, like a senile Ronald

Reagan reading scripts by his handlers which sell at the polls? I do not find it fruitful to frame a debate between these alternatives. The question about Madonna's self-consciousness is difficult, perhaps impossible, to answer; she is cagey in interviews and far less articulate in words than when expressing herself through music and images.[48] More importantly, there is limited value in asking who holds ultimate creative control in a company such as Madonna's or Jackson's: for example, who wrote the script to "Like a Prayer" or "The Way You Make Me Feel." There is no reason to doubt Madonna's claims to significant control over her art, and reason to suspect sexist bias if someone implies that a "bimbo" like her obviously cannot make substantive decisions for herself.[49] But even if we assume for the sake of argument that industry leaders strongly influence her decisions and she delegates major tasks, the whole argument about intentionality remains secondary. We can debate whether "Reagan's" speeches were scripted by his handlers, but the central question is the meaning that "Reagan" conveyed through these speeches, irrespective of Ronald Reagan's competence to produce them himself. Similarly, the main question about "Madonna"—even for someone who refuses to grant her any credit for sincerity or talent—is how her music can be understood and used.

Thus the third major qualification to my claim that Madonna's music overlaps with liberation theologies concerns the variant meanings of her songs in different contexts. I cannot stress too strongly that the interest of her music varies greatly from song to song and across different discourses of liberation theology and feminism. Not all of her songs are like "Like a Prayer." They highlight issues of race inconsistently, and issues of economic justice and imperialism hardly at all. In the realm of gender, many songs assert female autonomy (such as "Oh Father" and "Papa Don't Preach") or use irony to call received gender patterns into question, as when her brilliant performance of "Vogue" at the 1990 MTV Music Awards used outrageously parodic costumes and role reversals to underline the artificiality of received gender roles. On the other hand, many of her songs reinforce sexist stereotypes, celebrate forms of sexual expression that are no improvement over sexual repression, and make ironic comments which strike me as boring. For example, I see little besides bubblegum pop and cheesecake in a video like "Cherish," despite its somewhat humorous male mermaids. Other videos combine positive dimensions and overall ambiguities: "Justify My Love," for example, features mediocre music, lots of body parts and heavy breathing, and a representation of lesbianism which is unusually positive and explicit by the standards of television. (Guess why MTV censored it?) Her 1991 documentary film, *Truth or Dare,* combines brilliant stage shows, some interesting commentaries on society and spirituality, and a huge dose of self-indulgence. Her 1992 *Erotica* album pushes the theme of liberation from sexual repression to new heights, but seems unpromising from the perspective of most liberation theologies.

Furthermore, the same Madonna songs may be interpreted differently depending on what background theories a feminist critic assumes when approaching sexuality. Insofar as the problem of sexism is identified as male objectification and control of women's bodies, the corresponding feminist attitude toward most sexual expression is suspicion. For such a critic, the sexual revolution and its associated increase in sexual representation in the media merely represent an easier and more dehumanized access by men to women's bodies. The core images for sexuality are rape, abuse, and objectifying pornography. But insofar as the main problem of sexism is identified as the containment, channeling, and repression of sexuality by the "traditional" (i.e., modern bourgeois) family and its associated codes of sexual propriety, then liberation from sexual repression and rigid sexual mores becomes a key to the feminist agenda. The core image is the erotic as the engine of liberation.[50] Many of Madonna's songs appear disreputable to "anti-porn" feminists, while at the same time potentially helpful for "sex-positive" feminist discourses.[51]

Judged in still other feminist contexts, the value of Madonna's work is mixed. Even the most incisive satires and strongest images of female autonomy do not provide all that is needed for a liberatory movement. And her work does more to destabilize "normal" attitudes toward sex and gender than to address the feminization of poverty, female political empowerment, and issues of special concern to women of color.[52] These are not trivial limitations. Still, no song (or any other work) can address all political fronts at once. There are always priorities to set and strategic trade-offs to consider. Madonna's work is no exception.

Thus I do not argue that "Madonna is a liberation theologian," nor that all of her music overlaps with all liberation theologies. I do maintain that "Like a Prayer" and "Open Your Heart" overlap significantly with the broad agendas of many liberation theologies, advancing these agendas more than they hurt them. I believe that this suggests a need for greater attention to religious dimensions of other popular music, and the possibility of alliances between left-leaning Christians and some popular musicians on issues of mutual concern.

NOTES

1. For more on what I mean by "popular" and "oppositional," see my "Interpreting the 'Popular' in Popular Religion" (*American Studies* 36, no. 2 [Fall 1995]: 127–37) and "Sorting Out the Relationships Among Christian Values, U.S. Popular Religion, and Hollywood Films" (*Religious Studies Review* 25, no. 1 [1999]: 3–12), in which I argue that scholars define "popular" in four sometimes contradictory senses: as demographically prevalent, as "authentic" culture uncorrupted by commercialism (similar to what Bruce David Forbes calls "folk culture" in the introduction to this volume), as mass mediated, and as counterhegemonic (as in "popular movements" versus elite groups). For an essay like this one on popular music and liberation theologies, the greatest interest is in the territory where the third and fourth senses overlap—where, in the terms of Forbes's introduction, religion is *in* popular music, but the oppositional aspects of this religious-popular music are in *dialogue* with hegemonic aspects of the larger culture.

2. Ralph Reed, *After the Revolution: How the Christian Coalition is Impacting America* (Dallas: Word Publishing, 1996), 61.

3. Simon Frith, *Performing Rites: On the Value of Popular Music* (Cambridge: Harvard University Press, 1996), 14. The best initial approach to this literature is Cathy Schwichtenberg, ed., *The Madonna Connection: Representational Politics, Subcultural Identities, and Cultural Theory* (Boulder: Westview Press, 1990). See also Lisa Frank and Paul Smith, eds., *Madonnarama: Essays on Sex and Popular Culture* (Pittsburgh: Cleis Press, 1993).

4. Cited in Susan McClary, *Feminine Endings: Music, Gender, and Sexuality* (University of Minnesota Press, 1990), 204.

5. Carrie Fisher, "True Confessions: The *Rolling Stone* Interview with Madonna," *Rolling Stone*, 27 June 1991, 45–9, 78, quotation from 49.

6. Cited in Roseann Mandzuik, "Feminist Politics and Postmodern Seductions: Madonna and the Struggle for Political Articulation," in Schwichtenberg, *Madonna Connection*, 167–88, quotation from 182.

7. For a brilliant commentary, see John Champagne, "Stabat Madonna," in Frank and Smith, *Madonnarama*, 111–38, especially 123, which offers ten readings of the same photograph: Madonna with rapper Big Daddy Kane and supermodel Naomi Campbell in her famous book *Sex* (New York: Time/Warner, 1992). Three of the readings prove that the photograph is progressive, and seven prove it regressive. See also Mandzuik, "Feminist Politics and Postmodern Seductions," 175, on Madonna's 1990 "Rock the Vote" advertisement, which featured Madonna and two black male dancers wearing little except combat boots and American flags. Mandzuik finds the spot good because it "subverts the solemn patriotic and military symbols," but bad because Madonna says "Dr. King, Malcolm X, freedom of speech is as good as sex." Also, the spot makes jokes about Madonna disciplining the dancers, thus "trad[ing] on the racist stereotype" that "white caretakers must compensate for black immaturity." A shot of a dancer spanking Madonna signifies that sexual pleasure (good) is "justified even at the cost of subjugation of others" (bad). Madonna's joke, "If you don't

vote you're going to get a spanking," undermines (bad) the ad's overt message (good). All this is based on a video in which every single shot is ironic; it is hard to see why a satire of flag waving is subversive while a satire of racist paternalism is not.

8. I offer a brief definition of this field and relate it to religious studies in "Three Challenges for the Field of American Studies: Relating to Cultural Studies, Addressing Wider Publics, and Coming to Terms with Religions," *American Studies* 38, no. 2 (Summer 1997): 117–47.

9. Norman Mailer, "Like a Lady: Norman Mailer on Madonna," *Esquire*, August 1994, 41–56, quotation from 56.

10. Andrew M. Greeley, "Like a Catholic: Madonna's Challenge to Her Church," in *Sacred Music of the Secular City,* ed. Jon Michael Spencer (Durham: Duke University Press, 1992), 244–9, and "Desperately Seeking Madonna," in Greeley's *God in Popular Culture* (Chicago: Thomas More, 1988), 159–69.

11. On Madonna as whore, see Laurie Schulze, et al., "A Sacred Monster in Her Prime: Audience Construction of Madonna as Low-Other," in Schwichtenberg, *Madonna Connection,* 15–38.

12. Parts of my argument appear in a severely edited form as "Madonna and Jesus," *Christianity and Crisis,* 15 July 1991, 234–6. An earlier version of the second part of this chapter appeared as "Jesus and Madonna: North American Liberation Theologies and Secular Popular Music," *Black Sacred Music: a Journal of Theomusicology* 8, no. 1 (Spring 1994): 239–53.

13. For example, see Cindy Patton, "Embodying Subaltern Memory: Kinesthesia and the Problematics of Gender and Race," and Lisa Henderson, "Justify Our Love: Madonna and the Politics of Queer Sex," both in Schwichtenberg, *Madonna Connection,* 81–105 and 106–28, and many of the articles in *Madonnarama.* The leading theoretical text I have in mind is Judith Butler, *Gender Trouble: Feminism and the Subversion of Identity* (New York: Routledge, 1990).

14. Call For Papers, "Against the Grain: Cultural Studies as Oppositional Criticism," National Graduate Student Conference in Cultural Studies, March 1–2, 1996, Bowling Green State University, downloaded from internet, 16 October 1995.

15. Sinead O'Connor, "Black Boys on Mopeds," from *I Do Not Want What I Haven't Got* (Chrysalis Records, 1990), paraphrasing John 15:18–20.

16. "Justify My Love, the Beast Within Mix," from *Justify My Love* (Sire/Warner Brothers, 1990). Thanks to Teresa Hornsby for calling this mix to my attention.

17. E. Ann Kaplan, "Madonna Politics: Perversion, Repression, or Subversion? Or Masks and/as Master/y," in Schwichtenberg, *Madonna Connection,* 149–65, quotation from 163.

18. For example, Jane Brown and Laurie Schulze, "Effects of Race, Gender, and Fandom on Audience Interpretations of Madonna's Music Videos," *Journal of Communication* 10 (1990): 88–102; Patton, "Embodying Subaltern Memory"; Kathleen Talvacchia, "Being 'Real,' Using 'Real,'" *Christianity and Crisis,* 15 September 1991, 234–6; bell hooks, "Is Paris Burning?" in *Reel to Real: Race, Sex, and Class at the Movies* (New York: Routledge, 1996), 214–26; Judith Butler, "Gender is Burning," in *Dangerous Liaisons: Gender, Nation, and*

Postcolonial Perspectives, ed. Anne McClintock et al. (Minneapolis: University of Minnesota Press, 1997), 381–95.

19. Kaplan, "Madonna Politics," 163.

20. Unless otherwise noted, all the Madonna videos I discuss are collected on *Madonna: The Immaculate Collection* (1990).

21. For a discussion of Madonna's life, see Lisa Lewis, *Gender Politics and MTV: Voicing the Difference* (Philadelphia: Temple University Press, 1990), 100–8. The other statistics are from Gallup polls in the 1980s, cited by Paul Boyer, *When Time Shall Be No More* (Cambridge: Harvard University Press, 1992), 2–3, 13–5.

22. On popular religion and gender in Italian Catholic families similar to Madonna's, see Robert Orsi, *The Madonna of 115th Street: Faith and Commitment in Italian Harlem, 1880–1950* (New Haven: Yale University Press, 1985), and Colleen McDannell, *Material Christianity: Religion and Popular Culture in America* (New Haven: Yale University Press, 1996); McDannell 63–4 offers an interpretation of "Like a Prayer" which stresses its commercial hijacking of images, the iconography of saints, and the mythology of females bringing statues to life—a fascinating reading which unfortunately says little about the issues of race at the heart of the video.

23. Kaplan, "Madonna Politics," 163.

24. See Wade Clark Roof and William McKinney, *American Mainline Religion: Its Changing Shape and Future* (New Brunswick, N.J.: Rutgers, 1987), and C. Eric Lincoln and Lawrence Mamiya, *The Black Church in the African American Experience* (Durham: Duke University Press, 1990). Evangelical Christians have fared somewhat better, in part due to their embrace of popular culture; see Carol Flake, *Redemptorama: Culture, Politics, and the New Evangelicalism* (New York: Penguin, 1984).

25. Critiques of universalism, and a stress on writing theology "from below" or "contextually," are common in liberation theologies (although variously expressed). Concise introductions include Dorothee Soelle, *Thinking About God* (Philadelphia: Trinity Press International, 1990), and Rebecca Chopp, *The Praxis of Suffering: An Interpretation of Liberation and Political Theologies* (Maryknoll, N.Y.: Orbis, 1986). Books relating cultural studies methodologies to liberation theologies are Kathryn Tanner, *Theories of Culture: A New Agenda for Theology* (Minneapolis: Fortress Press, 1997), and Sheila Greeve Davaney and Dwight Hopkins, eds., *Changing Conversations: Cultural Analysis and Religious Reflection* (New York: Routledge, 1996).

26. For basic information on the music industry and youth identities, see E. Ann Kaplan, *Rocking Around the Clock: Music, Television, Post-Modernism and Consumer Culture* (New York: Routledge, 1987), and Lawrence Grossberg, "MTV: Swinging on the (Postmodern) Star," in *Cultural Politics in Contemporary America,* ed. Ian Angus and Sut Jhally (New York: Routledge, 1989), 254–69. George Lipsitz, *Dangerous Crossroads: Popular Music, Postmodernism and the Poetics of Place* (London: Verso, 1994), treats the international aspects of popular music.

27. For example, see Simon During, *The Cultural Studies Reader* (New York: Routledge, 1993); John Fiske, *Reading the Popular* (Boston: Unwin Hyman,

1989); George Lipsitz, *Time Passages: Collective Memory and American Popular Culture* (Minneapolis: University of Minnesota, 1990); and John Storey, *Cultural Studies and the Study of Popular Culture: Theories and Methods* (Athens: University of Georgia Press, 1996).

28. Michael Eric Dyson, "A Postmodern Afro-American Secular Spirituality," in Spencer, *Theology of American Popular Music,* 98–124, offers a sympathetic reading of Jackson videos (including "Thriller," which is quite similar to "The Way You Make Me Feel"). Phillip Brian Harper, "Synesthesia, 'Crossover,' and Blacks in Popular Music," *Social Text* 23 (1989), 110–3, is a hostile treatment of Jackson's role as the first black artist on MTV in 1983.

29. See Michael Eric Dyson, *Reflecting Black: African-American Cultural Criticism* (Minneapolis: University of Minnesota Press, 1993); Robin D. G. Kelley, "Kickin' Reality, Kickin' Ballistics: 'Gangsta Rap' and Post-industrial Los Angeles," in *Race Rebels* (New York: Free Press, 1994), 183–227; and Tricia Rose, *Black Noise: Rap Music and Black Culture in Contemporary America* (Middletown: Wesleyan University Press, 1994).

30. On the issue of passion, Judith Plaskow and Carol Christ, eds., *Weaving the Visions: New Patterns in Feminist Spirituality* (San Francisco: Harper and Row, 1989) includes several influential articles, including Audre Lorde, "Uses of the Erotic" (208–14), Alice Walker, "God is Inside You and Everybody Else" (101–4), and Beverly Harrison, "The Power of Anger in the Work of Love" (214–25). See also Carter Heyward, *Our Passion for Justice* (New York: Pilgrim, 1984); Dorothee Soelle with Shirley A. Cloyes, *To Work and to Love: a Theology of Creation* (Philadelphia: Fortress, 1984); and Rita Nakashima Brock, "The Feminist Redemption of Christ," in *Christian Feminism,* ed. Judith Weidman (San Francisco: Harper and Row, 1984), 55–74.

31. Among others who complained, Donald Wildmon's American Family Association threatened to boycott Pepsi. Madonna was paid five million dollars for the ads anyway. See Brown and Schulze, "Effects of Race, Gender, and Fandom," 91.

32. Mary Lambert, the filmmaker who directed the video, says the statue is meant to represent St. Martin de Porres (see McClary, *Feminine Endings,* 209).

33. There is sexual imagery in many standard Protestant hymns, such as "Jesus, Lover of My Soul." McClary (*Feminine Endings,* 163–4) also points to classical music such as "Bach's pietistic bride and groom duets," and discusses how Madonna is "tapping into" the tradition of Saint Teresa and other female Roman Catholic mystics. She leaves open the question of Madonna's self-consciousness about this tradition.

34. Mark C. Taylor, *Nots* (Chicago: University of Chicago Press, 1993), 199–207, sees Madonna seducing Christ and reads this not as mutuality, but as Madonna usurping power. However, Taylor also says that Madonna "lies seductively on a nearby pew . . . and provocatively rubs her genitals" (200)—in a scene where I see her go to sleep and rest her hand on her abdomen for half a second after kneeling in prayer. He says "the stroke of her hand brings the statue to life" (where I see him responding to the victim's cries). He says that a shot of Christ crying tears of blood is a symbol of Madonna castrating him, and that the

statue's return behind bars represents "displacement of the savior" in which "this latter-day anti-Christ [i.e., Madonna] repeats the proclamation of Nietzsche's madman: 'God is dead . . . and we have killed him'" (202). Thus Taylor abstracts from the major issues structuring the video: the black church and the "mystery" of faith versus racism and sexual violence. He implies that when Madonna "castrates" Christ—in a shot linked to an image of burning crosses— she aligns herself with the KKK and the history of white women manipulating black men. Taylor is more persuasive when he grants that "the most obvious reading of [the bleeding eye] is that one of the bullets or arrows hurled at the suffering servant hits its mark" (202). Taylor usefully accents how Madonna helps Jesus escape his usual role in churches (which makes sense of her words "you are not what you seem"). However, if there is a castration, the obvious preferred reading is that the police and cross-burners are responsible, with Madonna opposing them.

35. bell hooks, "Madonna: Plantation Mistress or Soul Sister?," in *Black Looks: Race and Representation* (Boston: South End, 1992), 157–64, especially 161–2, says that Madonna exchanges white maternalism for white paternalism and that her black characters are as stereotypical as "singing black slaves in the great plantation movies." She objects to the video's focus on a white woman and black male, claiming that black women have no role except "to catch (i.e., rescue) the 'angelic' Madonna when she is 'falling,'" which is "a contemporary casting of the black female as Mammy." (This refers to a shot of the presiding female minister welcoming Madonna at the beginning of her dream.) For a reading closer to my own—despite its dubious contention that the kiss between Madonna and Jesus has no necessary erotic dimension—see Ronald Scott, "Images of Race and Religion in Madonna's Video 'Like a Prayer,'" in Schwichtenberg, *Madonna Connection,* 57–79. See also Stephen Young, "Like a Critique: A Postmodern Essay on Madonna's Postmodern Video 'Like a Prayer,'" *Popular Music and Society* 15, no. 1 (Spring 1991): 59–68.

36. See Barbara Andolsen, *Daughters of Jefferson, Daughters of Bootblacks: Racism and American Feminism* (Macon, Ga.: Mercer University Press, 1986), and Susan Thistlethwaite, *Sex, Race, and God: Christian Feminism in Black and White* (San Francisco: Harper and Row, 1989), as well as hooks's own *Ain't I a Woman: Black Women and Feminism* (Boston: South End, 1981).

37. On gospel music, its relation to other musical forms, and its role in oppositional struggles, see John Chernoff, *African Rhythm and African Sensibility* (Chicago: University of Chicago Press, 1979); James Cone, *Spirituals and the Blues: An Interpretation* (New York: Seabury, 1972); Lawrence Levine, *Black Culture and Black Consciousness* (New York: Oxford, 1977); and John Michael Spencer, *Protest and Praise: Sacred Music of Black Religion* (Minneapolis: Fortress, 1990). Three special issues of *Black Sacred Music: A Journal of Theomusicology* explore connections between African American popular music and theology: *Theology of American Popular Music* (1989), *Sacred Music of the Secular City* (1992), and *Theomusicology* (1994).

38. Michael Medved, *Hollywood vs. America: Popular Culture and the War on Traditional Values* (San Francisco: HarperCollins, 1992), 77. Appar-

ently this refers to the same extremely brief shot in which Taylor sees Madonna "rub her genitals"—when after praying by the statue for a long time, she goes to sleep with a hand resting lightly on her abdomen. If one insists on pursuing a sexually reductive reading of this video, it would be much more promising to claim that "the true meaning" of Madonna's dance in front of the burning crosses is to show off her cleavage. At least most viewers notice this. Either way, such readings say as much about the viewers as they do about Madonna.

39. Such critiques from the left include Daniel Harris, "Make My Rainy Day," *Nation,* 8 June 92, 790–3, and Susan Bordo, "'Material Girl': The Effacements of Postmodern Culture," *Michigan Quarterly Review* 29, no. 4 (1990): 653–77, reprinted in Schwichtenberg, *Madonna Connection,* 265–90. For critiques from the right, see Allan Bloom, *The Closing of the American Mind* (New York: Simon and Schuster, 1987), 68–81. McClary provides many examples of hostile attacks, as when she quotes the *Village Voice* saying: "The trick behind the crucifixes, opera gloves, tulle, chains, and the recent rosary-bead girdle is that they lead only back to themselves, signifying nothing" (*Feminine Endings,* 209).

40. Major statements include Fiske, *Reading the Popular,* 95–132; McClary, *Feminine Endings;* and several essays in Schwichtenberg, *Madonna Connection.* Lewis, *Gender Politics and MTV,* argues that Madonna and stars such as Tina Turner pioneered a "female-address video" which expanded female spaces in rock, laying a foundation for later stars.

41. See Leerom Medovoi, "Mapping the Rebel Image: Postmodernism and the Masculinist Politics of Rock in the U.S.A.," *Cultural Critique* 20 (Winter 1991–92): 153–88; Sut Jhally, *Dream Worlds: Desire/Sex/Power in Rock Videos,* independent documentary film, 1990.

42. Similar readings include McClary, *Feminine Endings,* and Lewis, *Gender Politics and MTV,* 141–3. Thanks to Carolyn Krasnow for discussing this video with me at an early stage of this project.

43. Brown and Schulze, "Effects of Race, Gender, and Fandom," documents a range of student responses: men who enjoyed it as a pornographic spectacle, women who disliked it for the same reason, men who saw it attacking pornography and/or felt uncomfortable watching it, and women who identified with Madonna being trapped in her job and trying to escape.

44. Bordo, "'Material Girl,'" 674. This article is framed as an attack on McClary's *Feminine Endings.* It persuasively attacks the tendency for some postmodern theory to dissolve into a celebration of abstract "difference" unrooted in particular contexts of struggle—in which case "difference" reduces to liberal individualism—and Bordo argues this important thesis more fully in "Feminism, Postmodernism, and Gender-Skepticism," in *Feminism/Postmodernism,* ed. Linda Nicholson (New York: Routledge, 1990), 133–56. (Mandzuik, "Feminist Politics and Postmodern Seductions," attacks Madonna along similar lines.) Unfortunately, Bordo analyzes "Open Your Heart" in an unnecessarily narrow context, saying that "*the* context in which it is historically embedded" is the "containment, sexualization and objectification of the female body" (674, emphasis added).

45. Lewis, *Gender Politics and MTV,* goes so far as to discover feminist

virtues in shots of Madonna's body at the peep show. For Bordo, this is pornography and cultural support for anorexia, because Madonna flaunts a thinner and more muscular body than in her earlier videos, but for Lewis, Madonna's new look "gave a physical embodiment to the strength she had already acquired" as an artist. It "attenuat[ed] any impression of abject victimization" and "represent[ed] power" as much as sex (142).

46. Bordo, "'Material Girl,'" 675–6.

47. Such critics highlight the power of consumerism to dissolve collective traditions and moral visions—whether they stress conservative traditions (as in Bloom, *Closing of the American Mind*), liberal ones (as in Robert Bellah, et al., *Habits of the Heart: Individualism and Commitment in American Life* [Berkeley: University of California, 1985]), or radical ones (as in Soelle, *To Work and to Love*). Commonly they reduce popular music to a commodity, as when Harper states that "music videos are really nothing more than advertisements for the audio recordings they feature" ("Synesthesia," 120). Scholars like Lipsitz and McClary are more optimistic about the possibility that radical visions can be mediated through popular culture, although they stress that this is circumscribed. Without denying limits caused by commodification, they stress other dimensions of meaning. For an eloquent statement, see McClary, "Terminal Prestige: The Case of Avant-Garde Music Composition," *Cultural Critique* 12 (1989): 77–82.

48. Madonna refuses to be pinned down about her views on feminism or religion, but often throws out suggestive quotes. In Adrian Deevoy, "Madonna Talks," *US*, 13 June 1991, 18–24, she says "I've always known that Catholicism is a completely sexist, repressed, sin- and punishment-based religion" but "I go to church. . . . I love the rituals . . . and the mysteriousness of it all" (20). In Mikal Gilmore, "The Madonna Mystique," *Rolling Stone*, 10 September 1989, she states "Men have always been the aggressors sexually. . . . So I think sex is equated with power . . . I think it's scary for women to have that power—or to have that power and be sexy at the same time" (57). Such evidence does not satisfy those who interpret her whole career as a set of poses, since her interviews also contain much that is disturbing from feminist and religious points of view.

49. Sexist bias is often built into criticisms of mass culture; see Andreas Huyssen, "Mass Culture as Woman: Modernism's Other," in *Studies in Entertainment: Critical Approaches to Mass Culture,* ed. Tania Modleski (Bloomington: Indiana University Press, 1986), 188–207. McDannell, *Material Christianity,* 163–97, demonstrates how religious leaders often share the same attitude; I believe that she should draw out the implications of this argument for her discussion of Madonna.

50. For an incisive interpretation of this debate, see Alice Echols, *Daring to Be Bad: Radical Feminism in America, 1967–1975* (Minneapolis: University of Minnesota, 1989), 288–91. At one extreme, Mary Daly, *Beyond God the Father* (Boston: Beacon, 1973), 123, compares the sexual revolution to a gang rape by an invading army. At another extreme, *Re-Making Love: the Feminization of Sex* (New York: Anchor, 1986), by Barbara Ehrenreich, et al., finds a "women's sexual revolution" in cultural phenomena like Beatlemania and *The Total Woman*.

51. Bordo's visceral hatred of "Open Your Heart" can be understood in light of the former approach—recall her statement that "the context" for Madonna was the "sexualization and objectification of the female body."

52. On the diversity of feminist discourses see Nicholson, *Feminism/Postmodernism;* Plaskow and Christ, *Weaving the Visions;* Alison Jaggar and Paula Rothenberg, *Feminist Frameworks,* 2d ed. (New York: McGraw-Hill, 1984); Cherríe Moraga and Gloria Anzaldúa, eds., *This Bridge Called My Back: Writings By Radical Women of Color* (Watertown, Mass.: Persephone Press, 1981).

POPULAR CULTURE IN RELIGION

T he preceding section of this volume explored the first of our four relationships between religion and popular culture, the way religion influences and is expressed in popular culture. But in the relationship between religion and popular culture, influence does not run only in one direction: it is also possible to think about *Popular Culture in Religion*. Here, the focus is on how traditional religions utilize elements of popular culture, and on how such borrowings have affected the form and content of religion. The three essays in this section give special attention to evangelical Christianity, which has been especially interested in using the tools and motifs of the wider popular culture for evangelical purposes. The essays look at the religious expression and practice produced by these evangelical borrowings, and at the same time consider how evangelical Christianity is changed by its interactions with popular culture.

William D. Romanowski reviews the world of contemporary Christian music, asking how it was changed by efforts to cross over into the world of popular music. His work leads him to examine the claims that evangelism is the primary justification for such music, noting that in fact its principal audience is evangelical Christian youth. Rather than converting the world, contemporary Christian music serves to confirm the faith and identity of its already Christian audience. Yet, in efforts to expand its popular acceptance, contemporary Christian music has been influenced by marketing practices, cultural trends of leisure and consumption, and celebrity adulation.

Gregor Goethals looks at the world of religious broadcasting in light of the historic rejections of icon and ritual during the Protestant Reformation. She examines the way television preachers conform to the expectations of the medium. Ironically, television's dependence on the image requires television evangelists to re-embrace ritual, and transforms the descendants of the radical reformation into mass-mediated icons. These reflections lead her to consider the way in which a similar process of ritual and image invests secular spectaculars, like political conventions or the Super Bowl, with a religious quality.

For Stewart M. Hoover, the use, and absence, of the cross at Willow Creek, a prominent megachurch, provides an opportunity to think about how the megachurch movement has adapted to a world created by television and corporate culture, and about how we might study and discuss contemporary religious practice. He suggests that religious prejudice and inadequate critical tools lead us to discount the real religious depth of the megachurch's popular-culture-influenced services.

These authors help us to see, in the context of a mass-media culture, the cultural face of Christianity. It should be noted, however, that this influence of popular culture is not found only among evangelicals. Churches in the traditional mainline denominations are also bringing popular music and video projection screens into the sanctuary. Other traditions are also reshaped by their interactions with popular culture: on the cover of a book about the impact of media on traditional cultures (*O What a Blow that Phantom Gave Me* [New York: Holt, Rinehart and Winston, 1972]), Edmund Carpenter features a picture of a Kachina doll from the 1950s with a Mickey Mouse head, which is just one example of how widespread these influences are. What unites those who study Popular Culture *in* Religion is their interest in how existing religions are changed by their interactions with popular culture.

5

William D. Romanowski

EVANGELICALS AND POPULAR MUSIC

The Contemporary Christian
Music Industry

The contemporary Christian music industry was established by American evangelicals in the early 1970s as a religious alternative to the mainstream, "secular" entertainment business. It began as a fledgling venture, with members of the youthful Jesus Movement using existing rock and folk music to communicate the gospel message to alienated youth of the Vietnam era. Shaped by evangelistic designs, these evangelical hippies created "Jesus Music," the precursor to contemporary Christian music, by co-opting existing musical styles and adding "Christian" lyrics in the current vernacular. As a contemporary form of "gospel" music, contemporary Christian music was perceived by the secular media as a curious oddity in American religious life—a strange synthesis of rock (the "devil's") music and Bible-based song lyrics. Although the use of contemporary entertainment formats to reach the spiritually lost has historical precedents in earlier American evangelical revival movements, contemporary Christian music is the most extensive attempt to merge religious music with the commercial and industrial apparatus of the entertainment industry.

Throughout the 1970s, the evangelical music industry tried to counteract several common difficulties: a lack of audience acceptance for contemporary musical styles, technically inferior record production, severely limited radio exposure for artists, and a small and inefficient network for distribution, limited mainly to Christian bookstores.[1] The industry scaffolding began to go up as concert halls replaced coffeehouses and church fellowship halls, record labels replaced custom recordings, and contemporary music radio formats replaced prerecorded tapes of local preachers. Increased commercialization and industrialization, justified by expanding opportunities for evangelization, pioneered the growth of a major evangelical commercial enterprise ($300 million to $500 million or more by some estimates).[2] Today, the evangelical music industry has its own roster of "stars" who sell millions of records, appear on national talk shows, tour major arenas across the country, perform at major sporting events and at the White House, and are featured in mainstream magazines, including in *People*'s annual list of the 100 Most Beautiful People.

This essay investigates the limits and possibilities of the Christian music industry in the marketplace. I examine the coalescing of evangelical interests in spirituality, evangelism, and business, a development that created "religious" popular art out of the forces of leisure and consumption, marketing and profiteering, and the celebrity cult of power. The Christian music industry both influenced and was influenced by trends, practices, and strategies in the mainstream entertainment industry. This does not mean that these evangelical Christians simply "sold out" their evangelical heritage; nor, however, does it mean that the industrialization of contemporary Christian music did not influence evangelicalism. The contemporary Christian music industry evolved with conflicts and contradictions. It can be understood as a process of incorporation: a general process of change that involves not only industrial and business organization, but also communicative and social relations, including the remaking of cultural perceptions.[3] This evangelical venture in popular music making undeniably created discord and confusion both inside and outside the Christian music industry. Arguably, this is because of tensions in their common assumptions about the Christian life and cultural activity, which in turn, ironically, limited the possibilities of success for contemporary Christian music.

In brief, the Christian music industry existed initially as a separate religious alternative to mainstream business. In contrast to the secular industry, the business of contemporary Christian music, at least in the rhetoric of industry leaders and artists, was ministry and the evangelization of youth. "When you ask somebody what our songs are about there's no ambiguity," one of the early Jesus musicians explained. "It's right there in plain simple language with no deep intellectual vibes. What we're saying is Jesus, one way. If you want the answer follow it."[4] This conception shaped the way evangelicals thought about, produced, and consumed culture, emphasizing evangelistic value as the primary evaluative standard. This, in turn, fostered a naive acceptance of assumptions about the entertainment industry and its audience, especially regarding the supposed neutrality of musical styles and the potential effectiveness of popular music for evangelism. In addition, the Christian music industry fostered a movement in churches to consider the weekly gathering for worship as a vehicle for evangelism. To make services more appealing to non-Christians, local congregations debated the inclusion of popular music and entertainment formats, a challenge to cultural tradition for many; some have even used demographic studies to target a potential "audience."

As the Christian music industry was increasingly incorporated by mainstream industrial practices, however, evangelistic ideals were eclipsed by business imperatives. Intense competition ensued between gospel record companies and independent religious distributors battling for slim profit margins in the small evangelical market. Evangelical record labels and distributors sued each other over contract disputes. Songwriters and publishers battled radio programmers over appropriate licensing fees. In order for Christian artists to be successful outside the evangelical market, gospel companies had to cooperate with secular ones, blurring boundaries between religious and secular both in cultural perception and in industrial reality. Codistribution deals let evangelical artists "cross over" onto the mainstream charts, but with songs "about life experience *without any hidden spiritual agenda* [emphasis mine]," as Amy Grant said about her *Heart in Motion* album.[5] The crossover music confused evangelical consumers; there was seemingly nothing to distinguish Christian music from its secular counterpart. In other words, industrial advances necessitated new cultural understandings of the purpose of the music. Gospel executives continue to debate the measure of the industry's success based on commercial and spiritual standards. "We've got the best distribution we've ever had, we've got the best capitalized companies we've ever had, we've got more sophistication than we've ever had and we're selling less records," one executive complained. Another thought that the industry had made a mistake "trying to blend the mainstream culture and the church culture into one. It's like metric and standard."[6]

This study also illuminates ways that religious subcultures are co-opted, perhaps even converted, by the dominant American consumer culture. The rise of mass culture in twentieth-century American society both fueled the rise of "democratic" culture and homogenized it, suppressing the personal, ethnic, and religious identities associated with traditional subcultures. Media saturation eventually reshaped society, lessening familial and religious authority and eroding Americans' sense of time and place. The unprecedented size of the baby boom generation and post–World War II affluence created a national consumer-oriented youth culture that for the first time cut across social and economic lines. Commercial products — everything from blemish cream to movies—targeted the baby-boom demographic, and rock music was a staple in the postwar youth culture's consumer diet.

By adopting both rock music and the ethos of the popular culture industries, contemporary Christian music thrust evangelical youth into the new consumer-oriented youth culture, or at least into an evangelical version of it. Clinging to particular religious convictions and cultural assumptions meant isolation in an evangelical ghetto, limited resources and rewards, and an inferior status in the dominant culture. A very successful Christian record, for example, only sells 100,000 copies or more; very few go gold (500,000 units sold), platinum (1 million), or multiplatinum, standard markers in the mainstream business. Religious radio reaches only 2.1 percent of the national audience, compared with the top music formats (Adult Contemporary, Country, Top 40) that account for over 10 percent each. On the other hand, venturing into the commercial mainstream, while it could result in an expanded market or "ministry," greater financial success, and even "star" status, threatened the loss of specific religious identity to the homogenizing effects of mass culture.

Ecclesiastical purposes originally supplied the "sacred" justification evangelicals needed to record and perform "secular" music and to establish the Christian music industry, but these rules limited acceptable lyrical content to "confessional" themes for worship and evangelism. Such a utilitarian view of music making proved inadequate for gospel artists to thrive in the mainstream business, where evangelical songs with redundant lyrics about "Jesus" were not only unappealing to secular listeners, but perceived by producers and programmers as potentially offensive to large audience segments. Nevertheless, from the very beginning, the effort to create a demand for evangelical rock music committed the Christian music industry to the goals and strategies of the commercial marketplace—industrial growth, increased market share and greater profits. This, in turn, encouraged the popularization and dilution of the evangelical message necessary to build a large mass market. The evangelical artists who have been most successful on the mainstream charts, like Amy Grant and Michael W. Smith, scored with wholesome love songs and not the "confessional" lyrics that originally qualified as contemporary Christian music.

Consequently, the Christian music industry promoted an evangelical popular culture based on the rules of commercialism and not those of churches, elevating consumer values and taste at the expense of doctrine and tradition. In that sense, contemporary Christian music made a place in which the confluence of religion and the marketplace could shape both personal and communal identity for baby-boom evangelicals and their children. The merchandising of contemporary Christian music shifted "ministry" from collective spiritual matters to personal consumer habits, concentrating the practice of faith on the individual instead of the larger religious community. Contemporary Christian music thereby subordinated a church affiliation and denominational creeds to a highly individualistic and personal faith centered in the popular "born again" experience that was perhaps the hallmark of the popular evangelicalism that grew out of the Jesus Movement.[7]

The Christian music industry, then, was forged with a dual purpose that had a decisive impact not only on the creation of evangelical popular music, but also on the establishment and evolution of the industry, its relation to the larger church community, and its fortunes in the world of American entertainment. In religious terms, the music was supposed to be a means of evangelistic outreach, with artists stepping in for ministers and singing "minisermons" to spiritually lost youth. In business terms, gospel artists and record companies competed for a share of the marketplace. The intent may have been to save souls and minister to young Christians, but the Christian music industry brought evangelical religion even further into the free-for-all competition of the consumer marketplace. Ironically, the synthesis of evangelism and marketing led to the gospel industry's own co-optation by the mainstream recording business.

THE ART WORLD OF
CONTEMPORARY CHRISTIAN MUSIC

The contemporary Christian music industry is best understood as an art world, an institutionalized social network with established conventions, rationales, and philosophical justifications that serve to identify roles for art and standards for production and evaluation.[8] Perhaps the key feature of this evangelical art world is that it has a stronger religious orientation than it does a particular aesthetic.[9] At first, adding confessional lyrics to imitations of commercially successful styles was the basis of evangelical music making: "Contemporary Christian Music has nothing to do with the musical style. It has only to do with the lyrics," Sparrow Records founder Billy Ray Hearn said. And, as another Christian artist explained, "My music is not gospel music by the strict definition. It's contemporary music with a Christian message. If you took the lyrics away and changed them to a secular message, I don't think you would be able to tell the music apart from pop, contemporary, rock-oriented music." [10] Contemporary Christian music became a musical chameleon, adapting existing styles from other commercial music producers. Musical style, seen as neutral, was left to secular innovation and mere Christian imitation; evangelical popular music was literally "not of this world," but a parasite on secular industrial and artistic achievements, sanitized versions of various secular styles. Contemporary Christian music emerged primarily as religious propaganda—designed to persuade—and became a diluted expression of so many disparate musical styles that it lacked a religious, or even a cultural, home. In addition, the Christian music art world places spirituality and morality over aesthetic and cultural considerations, a feature with little correlation in the mainstream entertainment business. When prominent Christian artists admit to extramarital affairs, for example, many religious radio stations remove their music from playlists and retailers pull their records from the shelves.

No other form of popular music is distinguished solely by its "spiritual" dimension, as displayed in the lyrics (and sometimes an artist's personal lifestyle), without regard for musical style. Even traditional gospel music—that is, southern gospel and country gospel—have musical uniqueness, as well as followers outside the evangelical church community. This is especially true of black gospel, which has a strong cultural compatibility with other forms of popular music. Differences between sacred and secular music are perhaps more cultural than artistic: music serves different functions in the life of a community and is identified by thematic content, purpose, and physical location—the church as opposed to the dance club, for instance.

Contemporary Christian music also differs from traditional gospel in that it was marketed almost exclusively to a religious subculture, namely the burgeoning evangelical youth culture and not the traditional gospel audience. Contemporary Christian music became the musical mainstream of the reformulated gospel market, 12- to 35-year-old white evangelicals, not the "unsaved youth" for whom the music was allegedly written. The extent to which the industry mirrored the shifting tastes of its consuming public became painfully clear at the Gospel Music Association (GMA) Convention in 1991. In the GMA's effort to appease its growing constituency of white evangelicals, and to secure and maintain a television sponsor for its Dove Awards ceremony, the black gospel community was overlooked. Black gospel artists and executives complained about a lack of programming and seminars addressing the unique and specific needs of the black gospel industry. The black gospel "Spectacular" artist showcase was absent from the week-long schedule of concerts, and black gospel categories were excluded from the telecast portion of the Dove Awards. The GMA was charged with tokenism and insensitivity to the black gospel community. "According to scripture, they're about as non-Christian as you can get," one black gospel artist said. "What most upsets me is that they consider their music as Christian, and ours as black Christian, but God is a Spirit." [11] The powerful impersonal forces of marketing and demographics, rather than musical tradition or religious perspective, had come to largely define the Christian music industry.

The assumption that evangelicals have to compete for people's attention in the world of popular culture and entertainment fueled the industry's ambition to take religious music out of the church and into the marketplace. The effect and ensuing controversy matched that of earlier revival movements. Just as eighteenth-century mass revivalist George Whitefield's fusion of drama and preaching blurred distinctions between the theater and the church, so also the evangelical use of popular music and associated social practices for the purpose of ministry confused the sacred and the profane, soul-saving and entertainment.[12] By fusing religious themes and purposes with secular music, practices, and settings, traditional roles for church music—worship, praise, confession, and evangelism—were mixed with non-ecclesiastical functions for popular music, like dancing, diversion, exercising, enjoyment, or other aesthetic purposes. This may have helped forge an evangelical popular culture, but it also ripped religious popular music from the tradition and cultural life of the church. The lines between sacred and secular became increasingly blurry as the Christian music industry promoted a consumer-oriented culture that copied, even in some sense usurped, many functions of institutional religion. Concerts became worship services or evangelistic meetings. Consumer commodities (CDs, T-shirts, and other paraphernalia) became symbols representing religious faith. For some evangelical fans, social rituals, like going to a Christian concert or listening to a gospel recording on headphones, could qualify as a religious experience as much as attending a church service with a local congregation.

All this was not without effect. Turning mass recordings and rock tours into a form of "ministry" took church pastoring from the world of local, personal relationships, premised on trust and familiarity, into the impersonal world of entertainment, characterized by the market-driven terms of production and consumer choice. Furthermore, the Christian music industry had an impact on traditional worship styles and church ministries, as part of a broad range of changes instituted by the baby boomers who were once evangelical "hippies": the rise of megachurches, the use of popular music and charismatic styles in worship, and the decline of denominationalism. Ironically, while conservative evangelicals today advocate "traditional" values, they have also incorporated contemporary music and entertainment formats in church services, clearly distinguishing their manner of worship from historic and more traditional styles.

Nevertheless, establishing an evangelical recording network seemed perfectly reasonable to evangelicals in the Christian music industry. To them, the marketing strategy of the mainstream entertainment business matched the evangelistic goals of the gospel industry. The success of evangelism was calculated by the number of souls that were saved; "souls" were consumers, as measured by record sales, airplay, and concert tickets. "What we are are packagers of ministries," explained one gospel record executive. "We package an artist's ministries in such a way that it can be multiplied to the greatest number of people." [13] People in the gospel industry believed that this fusion of marketing and ministry would simultaneously save souls and generate profits. Soon, however, evangelism became industry rhetoric—justifying the propaganda value of the industry's work — not spiritual reality.

The need for such a spiritual justification for evangelicals' participation in the production and consumption of contemporary music was paramount, considering the church's long history of antagonism with the "worldly" amusements, from the theater and women's novels in the nineteenth century to popular music, dance, and movies in the twentieth, to name only the most recent examples. [14] Religious groups often perceived entertainment as a threat to familial and religious identity and authority, and were more inclined to ban entertainment as being "on the side of Satan" than to seek to transform it for the service of God and neighbor. The more conservative religious groups denigrated popular culture; fundamentalists even demonized it.

Because of their passion for proclaiming the gospel, however, it was not unusual for American evangelicals to employ contemporary entertainment formats and new communication technologies for the purpose of mass evangelization. The antebellum revivals and camp meetings were probably the first large-scale popular entertainments in the United States.[15] From radio evangelist Charles D. Fuller's national radio broadcasts in the 1940s, to televangelist Pat Robertson's Christian Broadcasting Network, evangelical groups have used contemporary idioms in radio, recording, television, film, and advertising. Music, in particular, has been central to the emotional style of evangelical revivals, from post–Civil War preacher Dwight L. Moody, and song leader and composer Ira B. Sankey, to Billy Sunday revivals in the early twentieth century, to Billy Graham crusades beginning in the 1950s. Similarly, the Christian music industry justified its existence and activities on the assumption that contemporary popular music was an effective vehicle for bringing the evangelical message of personal salvation through Christ to the modern youth culture and promoting "traditional" beliefs and values.

Some evangelicals, however, were not sure. One writer in an evangelical magazine observed that, as a communication process, evangelical rock sent conflicting messages. Christian groups, he explained, were "on stage wearing eye make-up and with shirts split open to their navels and with pelvises grinding to a 'heavy metal' sound; and they tell teenaged boys who may be struggling with gender confusion how God can fulfill their masculinity, or try to convince teenaged girls that they must cap their sexual urges until they are married." [16] A *Time* critic referred to contemporary Christian artists as "indistinguishable—except for their lyrics—from their secular counterparts." [17] Given such mixed signals, many evangelicals concluded that there was little difference between contemporary Christian and secular rock. Pentecostals and fundamentalists who thought rock music was inherently evil and irredeemable for evangelical ministry labeled evangelical versions of rock music "spiritual fornication" and "of Satanic origin." [18] Christian music apologists continued to argue for the neutrality of musical style as a defense against assertions that the beat of rock was inherently evil. At the same time, gospel artists and executives welcomed criticism that portrayed the evils of secular rock music. The gospel industry had much to gain by encouraging evangelical record buyers to forsake secular recordings and purchase their Christianized versions instead.

Despite harsh criticism from Pentecostals and fundamentalists, a significant slice of the evangelical market accepted contemporary Christian music's evangelistic purposes, along with the ideas that musical style does not matter and that lyrics alone make the music "Christian." The result, however, was not exactly what gospel industry people anticipated. Without access to the mainstream's national and international systems for exposure (radio, television, video channels) and distribution (retail stores, record clubs), the gospel industry had little choice but to use religious broadcasting stations and bookstores to create an alternative evangelical network modeled after its secular counterpart. As a result, contemporary gospel music reached few non-evangelicals. The use of popular music as a means of evangelizing youth entrenched the religious audience in its own impotent subculture.

This was problematic for Christian music entrepreneurs. To be successful, in either business or ministry terms, contemporary Christian music had to sell. But disparate motives and strategies within the growing industry resulted in an extreme lack of cooperation among bookstores, media, and producers—the different facets of the industry responsible for production, distribution, and exposure. Because of this, contemporary Christian music reached a plateau in the 1980s in terms of musical development, product sales, and market exposure.

First, cooperation among different sectors of this subcultural industry declined during the 1970s, when evangelical artists began using diverse musical styles—from folk and soft rock to heavy metal—which subdivided the evangelical market along the lines of taste groups. This reduced the size of the potential audience for any single recording, thus limiting record sales. Also, this wide variety of musical styles further stymied evangelical radio stations, which were already alienating potential listeners with formats that included, for example, a diverse mix of pretaped sermons and music.

Second, "mom-and-pop" religious bookstores, which were the main retailers for these recordings, initially showed little interest in promoting Christian music merchandise. But as sales of Christian music grew, music became a staple item in religious outlets, renamed "book and record stores." Despite the industry's dream for contemporary gospel to reach nonbelievers, however, Christian retailers protested when gospel labels established deals with mainstream distributors. Fear of competition from conventional retail chains also drove retailers' resistance to the Christian Bookseller's Association's adoption of the SoundScan monitoring system, which put contemporary gospel artists on the mainstream sales charts in the 1990s.

Finally, disagreements over the commercial character of the music stymied cooperative efforts among retailers, producers, artists, and even local concert promoters. When Christian artists and record companies began to see increased revenues from concert fees and record sales in the late 1970s, some artists rebelled against the direction the industry was taking, arguing that ministry should be free. They refused to charge set fees for concerts or records and relied instead on freewill offerings and donations. Eventually, a group of musicians protested that the growth of the evangelical music industry actually hampered their ministries: "We who feel called as ministers of the gospel of Jesus Christ feel that [the industry] is reflecting an unfortunate trend in Christian music brought on in part by the proliferation of airplay and sales charts and album reviews." [19] All of these differences and disputes within the industry highlighted growing tensions over the purpose and direction of contemporary Christian music.

Many Christian artists continue to feel that the industry's altruistic dreams about evangelism and Christian discipleship have become lingering but distant ideals, largely eclipsed by the drive for business success. In 1997, musician Steve Camp went so far as to liken himself to sixteenth-century reformer Martin Luther and issue "A Call for Reformation in the Contemporary Christian Music Industry." In broad generalizations, Camp denounced contemporary Christian music as "a Christless, watered-down . . . God-as-my-girlfriend kind of thing," and boldly demanded that gospel record labels "return all the money they have received to their respective secular counterparts that purchased them and divorce alliances with them." This polemic, supported with 107 theses, demonstrates the kind of muddled cultural and aesthetic theorizing that can go on in the industry (as well as poor Biblical exegesis). Nevertheless, it garnered an audience and media attention by tapping into unresolved issues that still haunt the evangelical music industry.[20]

MAKING MUSIC FOR THE MAINSTREAM MARKET

Christian entrepreneurs were building an evangelical entertainment industry that paralleled its secular counterpart not just in musical styles and trends, but in marketing techniques, management, concert production, publicity, and glamorization. Controversy aside, the result was a steady increase in record sales. In 1977, a Warner Communications study put gospel music in the "All Others" category, which accounted for only 3 percent of all record sales. By 1983, gospel had its own category and accounted for almost 6 percent of total industry sales. Gospel was suddenly outselling both classical and jazz recordings.[21]

The GMA identified gospel's market as born-again Christians under 35 with an annual income over $20,000. A Gallup poll found that from 50 to 60 million Americans were in that category. The only significant issue was marketing: how to reach the popular evangelical audience. Although two-thirds of WORD Records' sales came through Christian bookstores, research revealed that fewer than 10 percent of all evangelicals frequented these outlets. Also, a 1983 survey by the National Religious Broadcasters found that the number of U.S. radio stations with religious formats had increased 13 percent in the previous year, but religious stations had a meager 1.6 percent share of the listening audience in the United States. That put religious programming ahead of Spanish-language, "solid gold," and jazz and classical stations, but hardly in the big leagues of popular music. A controversial survey report from WORD Records that year "painted a vivid picture of an infant industry still struggling for a significant share of the marketplace—often using antiquated (if any) marketing research."[22] These were harsh reminders of the shabby state of affairs in the gospel music network. Gospel industry people were all the more dissatisfied with the situation and determined to change it.

During the 1970s and early 1980s, several mainstream record companies established joint production, marketing, and distribution deals with gospel labels, hoping to turn evangelical songs into pop records that would capture mainstream airplay and break into national sales charts. "I'll not pretend that we're here because of some new burst of religious faith," a CBS record executive said. "We're here because of the potential to sell records in the gospel market. We want to put gospel records in stores that don't currently carry them. We want to transform gospel from a specialty market to a mass-appeal market."[23] Dismal sales and the quick dissolution of these pacts, however, convinced gospel record executives that contemporary Christian music had to be made by and for young evangelicals. The key to crossover success was to reach the larger evangelical audience through mainstream exposure and distribution without estranging apprehensive Christian music followers.

Mainstream record companies renewed their interest in the gospel business when Amy Grant's *Age to Age* album (1982) sold over one million copies in the evangelical market. Grant's platinum certification was a milestone in gospel music and all the more incredible because it happened without the benefit of national radio or video exposure. How much more business could Christian music's top artist generate if she were to have access to these exposure media? Executives at A&M Records, who identified contemporary Christian music with the growing population of evangelicals and the conservative social and political agenda of the Reagan era, signed a coproduction and distribution deal with WORD, Grant's record company. WORD continued to service Christian radio and retailers; A&M worked mainstream radio and marketed to conventional stores hoping to reach the large number of evangelicals who did not shop at religious bookstores or listen to evangelical radio.

This "crossover" affair brought tensions in the Christian music paradigm to the surface, exposing the limitations of both the Christian music aesthetic and the evangelical industry. Grant had achieved unprecedented stardom in the gospel field with religious-oriented songs like "My Father's Eyes," "El Shaddai," and "Praise to the Lord." Building on her success with the evangelical audience, Grant began producing music that would appeal to the mainstream Adult Contemporary market. With each successive A&M/WORD project, Grant and her producers heightened her imitation of Top Forty sounds and selected lyrics more compatible with the Hot 100 and Adult Contemporary listings. The "celestial singer," as *Time* noted, was "shooting for secular success." [24]

Fueled by the A&M/WORD initiative, Grant's extraordinary career (by gospel standards) was marked with unprecedented achievements that completely transformed contemporary Christian music in terms of record sales and audience potential. Even prior to her 1991 release, *Heart in Motion* (which alone sold over 5 million copies and generated several Top Ten hits on the Billboard charts), Grant had earned five Grammy Awards and numerous Dove Awards, and sold over 10 million records. A contemporary Christian artist had finally achieved full commercial status and broad popular appeal. But popularity required religiously shallow lyrics, which elicited harsh criticism from Christian separatists. Grant was blasted by fundamentalists. "*Unguarded* isn't Christian music; it's moral and ethical humanism with a very slight religious perspective," one *CCM Magazine* reader wrote of her first A&M/WORD album (1985). "From Amy's ungodly album cover to her mediocre message, I see no attempt at true evangelism." A note attached to a bouquet of flowers presented to her at a concert read: "Turn back. You can still be saved if you renounce what you've done." [25] Even people within the gospel industry had to wonder about the effect of contemporary Christian music's move into the mainstream. When other WORD artists grumbled at not being selected for crossover projects, an A&M promotion director explained, "it could be because they're *too evangelistic* for secular listeners." [26] The evangelistic ideals of Christian music were easily clouded by the business imperatives in the major leagues of popular music.

When Grant became the first gospel solo artist to reach the top of the Billboard Hot 100 in April 1991, *CCM Magazine* (the monthly magazine for evangelical music fans) declared the moment perhaps "the most significant single event in the history of contemporary Christian music." [27] But Grant "entered the realm of pop-culture history," as the editor asserted, by topping the Billboard Hot 100 with a jejune love song entitled "Baby Baby." Ardent Christian music fans were confused about the message their most popular artist was spreading via the mainstream channels. Most religious stations excluded "Baby Baby" from their playlists. One general manager even removed Grant's records from the station's library and started a campaign urging other stations and religious bookstores to follow suit. Much of the controversy was centered on the "Baby Baby" video about a young couple in love, the "baby" being "a flirty, touchy guy," as *USA Today* put it.[28] An A&M press release rightly called the video clip "teasingly ambiguous."

Grant's gradual crossover into the mainstream was interpreted by some evangelical fans and critics as a violation of the spiritual standard for "Christian" music. If Grant was not producing and performing music for the purpose of ministry, they reasoned, then the crossover venture was little more than secular profit making. Even the mainstream press noted the difference. "Has Amy Grant traded in hallelujah for hubba hubba?" a writer in the *Los Angeles Times* asked. "It wasn't that many years ago that the singer enjoyed an exceptionally demure image and sang almost strictly devotional songs." [29] Grant was, according to the gospel industry's own definition, a Christian performing sanitized versions of secular love songs. There was little to distinguish this evangelical project from secular Top 40 fare. To secure mainstream success, contemporary Christian music's biggest star abandoned explicitly religious lyrics, the sole distinguishing feature of gospel music and the symbolic rock of the entire evangelical music effort in the early days. *Heart in Motion* seemed to signal the assimilation of Christian music's top artist—

and, symbolically at least, the entire evangelical music industry—into the ethos of the mainstream recording industry.

In one sense, Grant's career can be understood as that of an artist recognizing and overcoming the limitations of one socially constructed definition of popular music. Clearly, she challenged the narrowly defined concept of "Christian music" as it evolved from the Jesus Movement. But the concerted marketing and promotional strategizing, and the enormous revenues generated by the crossover projects, make it impossible to reduce her musical campaign to simple artistic expression. For, in the gospel music industry, ministry was increasingly subjugated to popularity and financial profits as gospel record executives gradually acquiesced to equating missionary goals and marketing requirements. Grant was one artist in a growing industry of companies and corporations. Whatever she did she could not change the incorporation of contemporary Christian music: she could work only in the world of business and industry if she truly sought to reach millions of people with her music. As one artist manager argued at the GMA Convention in 1989, the goals of ministry and business are "exactly the same—market share." [30] To be successful in the mass market, popular music must capture broader myths than those of a particular religious group. In effect, then, as the Christian music crossover trend illustrates, the dominant consumer culture may have a greater impact on religious subcultures in the United States than the other way around.

The success of the Christian music crossover demanded a new, or at least revised, justification for evangelical support. Grant proposed replacing evangelism with a new apologetic for contemporary music made by Christians. "Some feel that if music doesn't have some kind of evangelical content, it doesn't have any value," Grant said. "I feel differently. I want to be able to turn on the radio and hear fun songs where I'm not being pressured materially, sexually or violence-wise." [31] But it was difficult to remake the cultural perceptions of many evangelicals who, after more than two decades of contemporary Christian music, now believed that confessional lyrics alone distinguished evangelical popular music and that only explicit "ministry" legitimized the industry. To them, such a change in value seemed in retrospect more like rationalizing than reestablishing guiding principles. Consequently, the Christian music crossover caused disarray within the gospel industry; there was little consensus on what constituted "Christian" music, or on the means, motives, and expected outcome of evangelical popular music. The industry was split into two camps: those determined to cross over with "sanctified entertainment," and purists content to make music for the evangelical market.[32] Try as they might, Christian music apologists seemed unable to escape the very limiting view of culture they had propagated in order to justify evangelical use of contemporary popular music. Moreover, the traditional Christian music industry, from religious radio and television to Christian bookstores, generally sided with the purist, anti-crossover believers.

The debate reached a critical moment in 1997 with the release of Amy Grant's *Behind the Eyes,* an album that contained no explicit references to God or Jesus. Reviewers, radio programmers, and retailers debated the "Christian" merits of the record, while at the same time an album by country singer LeAnn Rimes, *You Light Up My Life: Inspirational Songs,* settled in for a long run at the top spot on the Christian album chart. The GMA had to launch a re-evaluation of its guidelines for the Dove Awards, and solicited reports from consultants to try to determine just what constitutes "Christian" music. The whole affair showed just how much industry growth had widened the cracks in the contemporary Christian music art world, which had become a confusing mixture of ministry as consumerism, evangelism, and entertainment.[33]

CONCLUSION

The commercial success of Amy Grant, Michael W. Smith, BeBe and CeCe Winans, dc Talk, and other popular evangelical artists suggested that contemporary gospel could transcend the limitations of the evangelical market and perhaps even thrive in an age of "family values." In the early 1990s, amidst predictions that gospel would follow country music as the next breakthrough genre, secular media conglomerates began purchasing the most salient gospel recording and distribution companies: EMI-Capitol purchased Sparrow Communications and, within days, WORD, the largest gospel company, was purchased by Thomas Nelson (sold to Gaylord Entertainment in 1997). Gospel companies fell like dominos in the next few years; entertainment conglomerates were to exploit the evangelical market niche while giving gospel releases access to conventional retail outlets and overseas markets.

In a short time, however, corporate reshuffling began, along with speculations that secular parent companies were becoming disenchanted with evangelical business prospects. For years, industry executives com-

plained that minuscule production budgets, inferior distribution and retail systems, and inadequate means of product exposure hampered the
advance of Christian music, not only in the evangelical market, but also
in efforts to penetrate the mainstream. Still, even as it largely overcame
these problems, contemporary Christian music never reached the anticipated popularity and music sales. One gospel executive concluded: "Even
if the music product measures up on so many levels—creatively, artisti-
cally, commercially—there's still the spiritual dimension, and sometimes
at least, our Christian agenda continues to be an obstacle." [34]

The intermingling of sacred and secular cultures that characterized
the contemporary Christian music enterprise became a very complex affair. To the degree that people in the gospel industry drew a line between
religious and non-religious subjects or aspects of life, we can talk about
a trend toward secularization. The Christian faith might have mattered
for church, personal morality, and family life, for example, but people
in the Christian music industry relied on secular perspectives in the affairs of business, management, and the production and distribution of
popular art. Secular motivations and goals—increased profits and larger
market shares— equated with expanding ministries but revealed the divided allegiance of the Christian music industry as it tried to serve both
God and mammon.

The results are mixed. The Christian music industry played a major
role in popularizing basic evangelical beliefs and values through the
commercial apparatus of the entertainment industry. There are plenty of
Christian music fans who would testify that they have been edified by
contemporary Christian music. Evangelical rock also fulfilled separatist
desires, as a safe religious alternative to the vulgarity and rebelliousness
of much rock music. Grant's manager, Dan Harrell, said that "[w]hat
Heart in Motion did was give Christian kids something to be proud of.
They could say 'Hey, we're normal.' " [35] As an imitation of contemporary
secular music and fashion, contemporary Christian music bolstered the
identity of young evangelicals who feared being alienated from their peers
because of their religious faith. At the same time, however, by its inces-
sant promotion of media consumption, the contemporary gospel industry subtly affirmed American materialism as a guide to personal happi-
ness. Evangelical records and videos often were advertised as solutions
to family problems, parent-child conflicts, and adolescent struggles.

Despite enlarged commercial success, evangelical artists did not have
the impact, spiritual or artistic, that the Christian music community envisioned they would have on the world of secular music. Also, the unique-

ness and force of contemporary Christian music was confounded by successful Christian artists like Bruce Cockburn and U2, whose music explored new styles on secular labels. Instead of writing and performing songs that imitated current musical fashions with redundant Christian motifs, they forged distinctive sounds and themes that won both commercial success and critical acclaim. Finally, the Christian music industry was rocked by its share of personal scandals and broken lives, breached contracts and multimillion-dollar lawsuits, competitive battles for larger profits, and ambitious jockeying for increased market shares. The fusion of business and religious values and purposes still plagues the Christian music industry. It remains something that people in the industry apparently have yet to understand, or at least publicly acknowledge, let alone use as a point to begin to critique and transform evangelical popular music.

NOTES

1. See William D. Romanowski, "Contemporary Christian Music: The Business of Music Ministry," and Quentin J. Schultze, "The Invisible Medium: Evangelical Radio," both in *American Evangelicals and the Mass Media,* ed. Quentin J. Schultze (Grand Rapids, Mich.: Zondervan, Academie Press, 1990), 143–69 and 171–95.

2. A recent report put revenues from record sales and concert tickets at $1.3 billion. Some people in the gospel music industry, however, question the validity of this figure, since it includes artists like LeAnn Rimes and Barbra Streisand, who released inspirational albums but are not considered contemporary Christian artists. See Adam Sandler, "Christian Music: The Word Is Out," *Variety,* 4–10 May 1998, 32, 101.

3. Alan Trachtenberg, *The Incorporation of America: Culture and Society in the Gilded Age* (New York: Hill and Wang, 1982), 3–4.

4. Chuck Girard, quoted in Patrick Corman, "Freaking Out On Jesus," *Rolling Stone,* 24 June 1971, 24–5, quotation from 25.

5. Amy Grant, quoted in Thom Granger, "Amy Grant: Relatively Speaking," *CCM Magazine,* March 1991, 20–3, quotation from 23.

6. Dan Harrell, from Blanton-Harrell Entertainment, and Terry Hemmings, former president of Reunion Records, quoted in John W. Styll, "Facing the Music: Christian Music In Period of Realignment," *CCM Update,* 21 October 1996, 1–2, 4, quotation from 4.

7. The effect is basically the same as what religious historian Harry S. Stout observed of eighteenth-century Protestant revivalism: "The process of commercialization necessarily transformed concepts of religion and religious experience generally: they came to be viewed in more individualistic and subjective terms.

'Experience,' 'taste,' and 'attraction' became sufficient criteria for purchase" (*The Divine Dramatist: George Whitefield and the Rise of Modern Evangelicalism* [Grand Rapids, Mich.: Eerdmans, 1991], 36).

8. See Howard S. Becker, *Art Worlds* (Berkeley: University of California Press, 1982).

9. See Romanowski, "Roll Over Beethoven, Tell Martin Luther the News: American Evangelicals and Rock Music," *Journal of American Culture* 15, no. 3 (Fall 1992): 79–88.

10. Billy Ray Hearn, quoted in John Medearis, "Sparrow Finds Markets Beyond Gospel," *Los Angeles Times,* 14 November 1989, D9A; Chuck Girard, quoted in "God, Me & My Guitar: Insights From Five Christian Musicians," *HIS,* January 1979, 16–20, quotation from 18.

11. Marv Winans, quoted in "GMA Under Fire From Black Gospel Industry," *CCM Update,* 6 May 1991, 1–2, quotation from 1. Ironically, while white CCM artists have had difficulty maintaining the gospel message in their Adult Contemporary offerings, the distinction of the black gospel tradition is recognized in the general market. This acceptance gives credence to religious themes in the work of African American artists like BeBe and CeCe Winans and Kirk Franklin & The Family, and, conversely, allows a pop star like Whitney Houston to keep gospel numbers in her repertoire.

12. Stout even labels Whitefield "Anglo-America's first modern celebrity" (*Divine Dramatist,* xiii).

13. Stan Moser, quoted in "Word Records: A MusicLine Salute," *MusicLine,* March 1985, 17–48, quotation from 25.

14. See Romanowski, *Pop Culture Wars: Religion and the Role of Entertainment in American Life* (Downers Grove, Ill.: InterVarsity Press, 1996).

15. R. Laurence Moore, *Selling God: American Religion in the Marketplace of Culture* (New York: Oxford University Press, 1994), 45.

16. David Hazard, "Holy Hype: Marketing the Gospel in the '80s," *Eternity,* December 1985, 32–4, 39–41, quotation from 40.

17. Gerald Clarke, "New Lyrics for the Devil's Music," *Time,* 11 March 1985, 60.

18. David Noebel and Jimmy Swaggart, quoted in "Can Religion Rock?" *CCM Magazine,* October 1981, 21; John W. Styll, "Swaggert: One Man's Opinion," *CCM Magazine,* September 1980, 5.

19. "An Open Letter," editorial in *Contemporary Christian Magazine,* February 1986, 5–6, quotation from 5.

20. Camp's declaration was issued as a four-foot poster and website. See Lindy Warren, "Reformation Rumble," *CCM Magazine,* January 1998, 14–5; John W. Styll, "Camp's 'Call' Misses the Mark, But Hits Everyone," *CCM Update,* 17 November 1997, 1–2, 8.

21. Steve Rabey, "Fast-growing Gospel Music Now Outsells Jazz and Classical," *Christianity Today,* 16 March 1984, 42–3.

22. Bob Millard, "Gospel Music Meet Buoyed By Rising Sales: Execs See Bright Future In New, Upscale Market," *Variety,* 20 April 1983, 179; Bob Darden, "Word's 30 Years Net 70% of Christian Record Sales," *CCM Magazine,* Jan-

uary 1981, W-17–8; "Religious B[road]casting Study Finds Growth in 1983," *Billboard,* 21 January 1984, 46; Bob Darden, "Christian Radio: Reach and Impact Grow As Struggle Continues for Greater Share," *Billboard,* 27 August 1983, G-12.

23. Dick Asher, quoted in Carol Flake, *Redemptorama: Culture, Politics, and the New Evangelicalism* (New York: Anchor Press, 1984), 177.

24. "Pop Angel," *Time,* 6 May 1991, 43. For a full treatment of Grant's crossover career see Romanowski, "Move Over Madonna: The Crossover Career of Gospel Artist Amy Grant," *Popular Music and Society* 17, no. 2 (Summer 1993): 47–68.

25. "Feedback," *Contemporary Christian Magazine,* January 1986, 5–6, quotation from 6; note to Grant quoted in Bob Millard, *Amy Grant: A Biography* (New York: Doubleday–Dolphin Books, 1986), 162.

26. Don Bozzi, quoted in Moira McCormick, "The A&M/Word Impact: Next Six Months are 'Critical' For Gospel's Mainstream Voyage," *Billboard,* 19 October 1985, G-3, 20, 32–3, quotation from G-32.

27. John W. Styll, "Intro," *CCM Magazine,* June 1991, 4. Grant did have an earlier Number One hit on the *Billboard* Hot 100: a 1987 duet with Peter Cetera, "The Next Time I Fall."

28. David Zimmerman, "'Baby' puts Amy Grant on top of the pop chart," *USA Today,* 22 April 1991, D2.

29. Chris Willman, "Faithful in Her Fashion," *Los Angeles Times,* 16 April 1991, F3.

30. Dan Harrell, quoted in Quentin J. Schultze and William D. Romanowski, "Praising God in Opryland," *Reformed Journal,* November 1989, 10–4, quotation from 13.

31. Amy Grant, quoted in Walter Scott, "Personality Parade," *Parade,* 24 November 1991, 2.

32. John W. Styll, "Amy Grant's Sanctified Entertainment," editorial in *Contemporary Christian Magazine,* July/August 1986, 4.

33. See Romanowski, "Where's the Gospel?" *Christianity Today,* 8 December 1997, 44–5.

34. Terry Hemmings, quoted in James Long, "Terry Hemmings: Dropped in the Desert," *CCM Magazine,* March 1997, 18–20, quotation from 20.

35. Dan Harrell, quoted in Paul O'Donnell with Amy Eskind, "God and the Music Biz," *Newsweek,* 30 May 1994, 62–3, quotation from 62.

6

Gregor Goethals

THE ELECTRONIC GOLDEN CALF

Transforming Ritual and Icon

Distinctions typically made today between so-called "popular art" and "fine art" simply did not exist in earlier cultures; nor, in fact, did the modern concept of "art." We stroll through museums today enjoying classical reliefs from the Parthenon, for example, or look at fragments of sculpture from the tympanum of a medieval church, relating to them as "art" in this artificial setting, but we are really viewing fragments of a public, popular art taken out of context. As cultural historian Johan Huizinga has pointed out, medieval forms are examples of applied art, of images that worked in particular environments. "Art," Huizinga writes, "was not yet a means, as it is now, to step out of the routine of everyday life to pass some moments in contemplation; it had to be enjoyed as an element of life itself." The purpose and meaning of images took precedence over any purely aesthetic value.[1] Given the widespread illiteracy at the time, for example, pictorial representations adorning religious buildings were essential instruments for communicating ideology and reinforcing belief.

Although people's experiences, education, and piety in these earlier cultures were very different, the carved and painted pictures they viewed were constant, shared symbols which communicated vital myths and stories of the community. For individuals, images in liturgical spaces helped to define who one was and what the society, even the universe, was like. For religious institutions, rituals and icons functioned as forms of social integration, building and maintaining a belief structure. Thus the paintings, stained glass, and sculpture of churches were a form of popular culture insofar as they were accepted and appreciated by a diverse laity.

In this essay I will consider the mutual interaction of traditional forms of religious communication and contemporary technologies. How have religious and secular institutions been able to extract the dynamics of rituals, appropriating them for secular or civic functions? To explore the later electronic transformations, I will first look at the basic elements of traditional forms of religious communication. Selected examples from commercial television will then indicate how spectacular television "rituals" differ from those in traditional religion.

Particular attention is given to how religious denominations responded to the revolutionary communication technologies of modern popular culture. As we shall discover, the traditions that historically rejected images have, ironically, made the greatest use of television. Spiritual descendants of John Calvin and Ulrich Zwingli are welcoming the new electronically vivified icons. Has the tradition that once shunned visual images formed a new covenant with them?

RESISTANCE TO IMAGES

Even in medieval Christianity, there were churchmen who objected to the artistic extravagances of some churches. In the twelfth century, the most outspoken critic of images was Bernard of Clairvaux; although he recognized that pictures could be helpful for devotions of the laity, he lashed out against their presence in monasteries. Monks need no images in their worship, Bernard reminded them, "but we, who have now come forth from the people; we who have left all the precious and beautiful things of the world for Christ's sake . . . whose devotion, pray, do we monks intend to excite by these things?" [2]

Later, leaders of the Reformation in the sixteenth century were divided in their attitudes about the use of images in worship. For Martin Luther, the visual arts were important for instruction and for enhancing liturgy. Spirit and flesh were never disjoined; the sacraments were an integral part of religious life. In his devotions, Luther was "aided by the sight of the crucifix, the sound of the anthems, and the partaking of the body of Christ upon the altar." [3] The reformers inspired by Luther in Germany neither defaced nor destroyed the art work in churches.

Radical aesthetic transformations, however, were initiated by John

Calvin and Ulrich Zwingli. Their reforms came with such force that the very nature and function of ritual and icon were shattered along with church images. These Swiss reformers stripped worship spaces of all visual representations. Calvin rejected images, even the crucifix, as aids to devotion; he permitted only a simple cross. Although Calvin allowed the congregation to sing psalms, Scripture alone was the primary resource and guide for devotion and worship. Zwingli, for his part, eliminated both music and images. Unlike Martin Luther, he also dismissed the homage that a medieval culture brought to the eucharistic mystery, and so desacralized all material elements of worship. The churches in Zurich became highly rationalized, functional spaces in which liturgy consisted essentially of preaching and hearing the word of God. "Faith," writes Zwingli, "is from the invisible God, and is something completely apart from all that is sensible. Anything that is body, anything that is of the sense cannot be an object of faith." When all images were removed and the churches whitewashed, Zwingli found the walls to be "beautifully white," positively luminous.[4] Thus all the visual arts that had borne witness to Christian faith for centuries were unequivocally rejected.

Without doubt, there is a particular beauty in unadorned architectural spaces. The flow and interconnectedness of spaces, the play of light and shadow on surfaces, and the ordering of abstract geometric shapes combine to form an aniconic or imageless aesthetic. The visual syntax is one of pure form, shorn of any representation. This aniconic aesthetic had a telling impact on the architecture and worship practices of some religious groups in the United States. Calvin and Zwingli would have been pleased, for example, with the architecture of the seventeenth-century New England meeting house. The simplicity of its interior space, oriented toward a pulpit which is centered and elevated above the pews, dramatizes the ascendance of the Word. While other forms of architecture have supplanted the meeting house, some American churches exhibit an enduring suspicion of rituals and icons. Preserving the aniconic spirituality that spearheaded the reforms of radical Protestants, many congregations keep the sanctuary free of visual images. The reading of Scripture and the sermon remain paramount in the worship service.

Yet the aesthetic which nurtured representational arts and sacramental rites did not simply vanish. When some religious groups cast out rituals and icons, such forms found new and fertile soil in political and social environments, reappearing and flourishing in the secular realm. In contemporary culture, visual images and ritual arts function most powerfully not in the service of liturgy, but in the service of a consumer society. Commercial establishments in the United States have been quick to recognize the persuasive power of images, and elaborate icons and rites have become powerful secular instruments of social integration.

Contemporary icons, however, are radically different from the earlier ones fashioned with pigments, stone, and glass. Most frequently, the images which saturate our contemporary consciousness are independent of any architectural context, and are instead promoted through the advertising media. With television, we have witnessed an unexpected and rapid renaissance of both ritual and icon. The accelerated transformation of symbolism from a religious to a secular milieu remains tied to revolutions in communication technologies.

THE TRANSFORMATION OF RITUAL

For more than a decade, scholars have used ritual as an analogue for various forms of popular culture. Among the first to explore these interconnections was the anthropologist Victor Turner, who spoke of the "spreading rings" of his work and thought over a range of data drawn from pluralistic cultures. Turner points out that

> with religious pluralism, there is sometimes a veritable supermarket of religious wares. . . . [S]ymbols[,] once central to the mobilization of ritual action, have tended to migrate, directly or in disguise, through the cultural division of labor, into other domains, esthetics, politics, law, popular culture, and the like.[5]

To better understand the nature of this "migration," it helps to review some of the basic concepts of ritual that have been used in previous discussions of religion and popular culture.[6]

From the rhythms of a Hopi rain dance to the liturgical motions and gestures of priest and communicants, ritual is a deeply rooted human activity. At its most fundamental level, ritual is the enactment of myth. Traditionally, religious myths gave members of a community a sense of their personal and corporate origin and destiny. Religious ritual, different for each tradition, depends upon formative myths and history. For some groups, ritual enacts events in the life of historical figures such as Jesus of Nazareth or the Buddha. In the eucharist, for example, the Christian believer "takes part" in the passion and resurrection of Jesus, entering into an extraordinary liturgical time. For those who partake of the eucharistic bread and wine, there is indeed a suspension of the ordinary world; they participate in a transcendent order of being that is "outside" the time and space of our everyday life. This experience of a sacred, timeless order enables the believer to return to the mundane world individually renewed in spirit and confirmed as a member of a larger community of faith. In traditional religious rituals, such as the Catholic mass, it is the sacred dimension that underpins both the existential and the social functions of the rite.

While the mythic substance and aesthetic form of ritual differs from one community to another, two operative functions remain the same: providing an immediate, direct sense of involvement with the sacred, and confirming a shared world view. The innermost spiritual life of the individual is nurtured through its encounter with the sacred, and, at the same time, the believer becomes integrated into a larger, cohesive whole. Today, religious rituals in churches, synagogues, and mosques continue to offer opportunities for spiritual renewal and communal identification.

For many theorists, ritual is defined by its substantive mystical core— the salvation and redemption of the individual and community. From the perspective of these theorists, ritual is inherently sacred, and thus in the absence of a specifically transcendent and redemptive dimension there is, by definition, no ritual. It is, however, the focus of this essay to indicate how the analogy of "ritual" can be a revealing lens through which to observe and analyze some secular events. Some theorists may insist that secular events can only be "ritual-like"; nevertheless, the analogy of ritual is critical to understanding the power of the media. If we bracket the transcendent element of ritual, underscoring instead its function of social integration, then we find striking secular parallels to religious ritual activity. In particular, we can better grasp the efficacy of the media in expressing, shaping, and maintaining community beliefs and values.

Boundaries in Ritual: Religious and Secular

Focusing on the integrative power of ritual to identify and promote community loyalties, we can legitimately compare secular rites and ceremonies to traditional religious rituals. Rituals become secularized when the events enacted or celebrated are clearly separated from sacred dramas. Whenever I refer, therefore, to secularized rituals, it should be understood that I am foregrounding a functional definition of ritual, concentrating not on the rite's theological mystery, its drawing us into the supernatural realm, but on its power to reinforce beliefs and to foster a sense of community. As I shall argue, there are similar structural elements present both in sacred rituals and in secular ceremonies: specific boundaries of time and of space, and the active participation of "believers."

One basic component of sacred ritual is the space in which the action occurs. This space is extraordinary, set apart from the ordinary places of daily life and specifically designated for supernatural events. Its sacredness, however, does not depend upon architectural complexity. Rites may take place within a unique natural rock formation or at a special ground that is consecrated, as in the ceremonies of the Australian aborigines, for example. Religious rituals may also occur within a very intricately designed space, like that of Chartres Cathedral. Although these spaces are dramatically different, they both define an area which is holy—clearly set apart from the traffic of daily life and routine. These sacred zones mediate the presence of the divine.

We are also accustomed to spatial boundaries that designate extraordinary spaces for the "hallowed" events of our secular life. Contemporary professional sports have created spaces which for some enthusiasts have become almost "holy." For devoted fans, certain baseball diamonds are so sacred that the fans passionately resist any modernization or change in the physical space. Such was the case with Wrigley Field in Chicago. On the other hand, even disinterested observers immediately recognize the shape of a baseball diamond, acknowledging its unique spatial function. Moreover, it has become increasingly profitable for cities to develop a particular "bowl" space for leading college football teams. But this secular zoning is not particular to sports. In politics as well, we have very elaborate visual planning for the spaces of the Democratic and Republican conventions. The boundaries of space are indeed critical to the fashioning of secular rites.

A second fundamental component of ritual is that of time. Like ritual space, ritual time is extraordinary in quality, not at all the ho-hum clock time of our workdays. The time of ritual is a carefully structured, cohesive unit, with a distinct beginning, middle, and end. In time as we ordinarily know it, we can point to a beginning, our birth, and we anticipate, ultimately, an ending in death. While we may mark certain "beginnings" and "endings" in our life cycle, we can only experience the flow of the process. Traditional religious rituals deal with origin and destiny, the beginning and the beyond, casting us into measures outside ordinary time. In ritual, the flow of everyday existence—open-ended and unresolved— is suspended; the believer leaps timelessly into creation and into eternity.

The temporal component of secular rituals has no link to the supernatural world. Rather, the rhythms of these rituals depend very much on the rules of the game or on the fixed structure of the events being celebrated. The conventions of political parties, for example, usually have two nights which feature major politicians and the philosophy of the party. These events lead up to the third evening, when a candidate will be officially nominated. Finally, the climax of the convention comes with an address by the nominee on the last evening. In sports, the periodicity is determined by the regulations of a particular sport: "clocks" are set according to quarters, halftime, numbered time-outs, innings, and so on. While the ritualized events of our secular society reveal diverse temporal patterns, they all depend upon an intentional and ordered structure of time.

The third element, perhaps the most important for understanding both sacred and secular rituals, involves the active participation of individuals. If one is to experience ritual power as a form of social integration, one cannot be a detached observer: one must enter into the truth of a myth. Participants in ritual are actors, and their bodily gestures, speech, and motions affect others in the drama as well. It is this ritual participation that enables one to transcend human separateness and experience a sense of social unity.

In *Take Time for Paradise,* A. Bartlett Giamatti (former President of Yale University and Commissioner of Baseball) writes eloquently of the power of sports to nurture a sense of community. Giamatti discusses particular experiences of transcendence and transformation for the players themselves—a kind of self-forgetfulness through intensive participation. Yet a kind of transcendence and vital bonding is possible for devoted spectators as well. Giamatti's emphasis upon the communal experience of sports is central to a discussion of secular ritual. He reminds us that we experience sports in cities and that fans develop a special loyalty to, and identity with, local teams. Baseball, he insightfully notes, like all sports, lives in the world—not "on the mountaintop but in the valley." In these "valleys," sports shape enthusiastic fans into a cohesive, embodied whole—an experience of community which some might not otherwise enjoy.[7]

Thus we see that ritual action is significantly rooted in a propensity for order rhythmic patterns of time and demarcations of hallowed space. Further, our participation in certain ritual activities organizes and renews our loyalties and values, thus shaping a sense of community. Underscoring these basic elements of time, space, and attentive participation, we can expand the ritual analogy to civic events, to sports, and to public entertainment. More importantly for my purposes here, the analogy helps us examine television's adroit coverage of these secular events. The electronic medium, perhaps more than any other, has amplified and reshaped the ritualistic dimensions of our worldly experiences.

Electronic Ritual Presence

With a power analogous to that of traditional ritual, television technology extends the boundaries of time and space. Media coverage of public "rituals" can transport countless viewers to "sacred" zones once accessible only to a chosen few. There is now an unprecedented opportunity for public participation, including participation by people not physically present at the televised event. In fact, television's capacity to extend these boundaries has engendered ritualistic forms in many aspects of our common life, particularly in politics and sports.

Even so, political, economic, and racial tensions among various segments of the American population make it difficult to point out rituals which organize and unify the entire national community. Although the Republican and Democratic conventions have become increasingly lavish, they tend to attract mostly the partisans of each group. To grasp the ritual power of television to extend boundaries of time and space and to unify a country, one would perhaps have to go back to November 1963, when people around the nation collectively mourned the death of John F. Kennedy. For several days following his death, television networks provided continuous coverage of the events in Dallas and the nation's capital. The American people gathered in electronic space to witness and to be "present" in rites of mourning. Television "transported" those who grieved through space and time. Viewers "joined" ordinary people lining the streets, and were able to enter the Capitol and view the flag-draped coffin, the president's widow and children, the international leaders walking in the funeral procession, the riderless horse. And, finally, they "stood" among those at Arlington National Cemetery and heard the poignant sound of taps. It was through television monitors that a community of millions mourned their president.

In the 1990s, the ritualistic dimensions of popular culture are most apparent in sports. One has only to think of the highly elaborate telecasts during the World Series, or the playoffs leading up to that quintessential television ritual, the Super Bowl. Fans watching in living rooms or in local bars are "present" and "take part" in the extraordinary time and space of telecast games. Unlike those in the stadium, television viewers can even "hang" from a blimp high above the field and in the next instant be shoulder to shoulder with the cheering crowd.

The Super Bowl of 1991 is worth noting for its unusual coalescence of fervent patriotism and team loyalty. While some debated propriety of having the game during a national crisis (the Persian Gulf War), those in charge decided that it would be good for the morale of the country to go ahead with the contest. Those in the stands and viewers around the nation were caught up in the drama of the game, but there was also a deep, anxious sense of involvement in a larger cause: the war in the Middle East. The telecast of this event transformed a celebrated sports ritual into a civic one which reinforced a sense of belonging to a great national cause. Support and confirmation of the war effort became a major motif throughout the telecast: viewers looked down from the blimp upon a sea of waving American flags, as those in the stands held aloft banners that celebrated and honored the troops sent abroad; representatives from the armed services who participated in the opening ceremonies were portrayed in dazzling montage techniques; there were tight shots of stalwart faces, exquisite patterns of company insignia, and a formation of F-16 fighters zooming over the stadium. Crowning these opening rites was Whitney Houston's singing of "The Star-Spangled Banner," which she sang with the passion and exuberance of a great liturgical hymn. Layers of images floated across the screen as she performed: countless waving flags; patriotic banners supporting the war; the football players standing at attention; the faces of singing fans. Once the game began, the heroic action on the field was interrupted not only by commercials, but by reports from the war front as well.

Years later, it is possible to look back on this event from a jaded perspective, especially as more information about the actual conditions of the conflict is disclosed. At the time, however, Super Bowl XXV functioned as a momentous civic ritual that confirmed many Americans' loyalties to sports, consumerism, and to the Gulf War. The action of the game, punctuated with commercials, symbolically fused with the action of the troops into a single mythological embodiment of the American Way.

The electronic rituals of secular television resonate with and reinforce the deepest values of a national consumer society. But how do religious broadcasters use mass media and popular culture? I would like to turn now to the appropriation of electronic communication by religious groups. How have new media technologies interacted with their patterns of worship?

THE ELECTRONIC TRANSFORMATION OF THE WORD

Religious institutions have responded to the forms of popular culture and their symbolic environment in various ways. On any given Sunday morning, one may surf the local channels to see and hear how churches are using this medium. Typically, a television presentation is related to the liturgical tradition of the congregation—Catholics, for example, especially those who can no longer get to church, may find spiritual comfort in a televised presentation of the mass, while other congregations may choose to highlight an eloquent pastor or a music program. But how many religious groups really understand the extensive presence and power of televised rituals and icons? How many have considered how adopting the forms of popular culture will change the shape of their worship life and subtly alter their message? Or comprehend the ways in which ideologies are communicated through commercial television? Unlike America's corporate and advertising institutions, few religious groups seem to grasp the encompassing symbolic function of the medium, either as a means of social integration or as a way to perpetuate a value system.

However, some of the Protestant television evangelists—heirs of those who stripped bare their churches—have, perhaps inadvertently, rediscovered the persuasive role of images. Moreover, in their reintegration of images into religious communication, they have conferred a new status upon these images. Historically, their denominations have been part of the American Protestantism described above, strictly committed to the teachings of Calvin and Zwingli and standing firmly against the use of images in worship spaces. Their churches have continued to emphasize the reading and hearing of the Word, with no visual representations to compete with the written and spoken text. During the later twentieth century, however, the communication revolution has had a remarkable impact upon some adherents of this aniconic worship aesthetic. While maintaining a suspicion of visual representations in the sanctuary, followers of the radical reformers have become the most sophisticated practitioners of electronic technology, beginning with radio and later moving into television. Electronic preachers have, paradoxically, granted to religious images a power greater than that of medieval liturgical icons.

Rituals without Space

While ritual and icon—liturgical forms of a sacramental tradition—migrated to a secular society, a countermotion has occurred among some conservative, evangelical churches: electronic revolutions of radio and television have decisively shaped forms of evangelism and worship. During the early history of American radio, evangelical and conservative religious groups outside mainstream denominations were denied access to free public service time. To get their messages on air they began to buy time; eventually, they became owners and operators of religious stations. An evangelist of the 1940s, Charles E. Fuller, used radio to broadcast his sermons and Bible-study lessons to thousands of unseen listeners. Real liturgical space became unnecessary. His congregation consisted of "friends in radio land," a church with no walls. Fuller admonished his listeners to get out their Bibles and follow his messages and interpretations. Participation depended on the turn of the radio dial and correspondence by mail with the radio pastor.

Later evangelists quickly saw how television enhanced religious messages for a mass audience. Jerry Falwell was among those who used technology to shape religious communication, and his regular telecast services from the Thomas Road Baptist Church in Lynchburg, Virginia, typify the new alliance between electronic technology and some forms of Protestant worship. In his *Old-Time Gospel Hour,* Falwell uses television techniques to visually enhance and modify the formal elements of a free church evangelical service. Television cameras provide a variety of angles and close-up shots, giving the viewer the sense of being present in a sacred space. Falwell standing behind the central lectern, flanked by flowers, reads and preaches; he is the visual focal point for congregation and television viewers alike. While still focusing worship upon the Word, Falwell also uses television technology to provide a dynamic visual dimension to the reading of the Bible: as he reads from the Bible, a camera films the page; printed passages become highlighted and fill the viewer's screen. Other modifications serve to completely change the formal style and timing of his preaching. For example, an illustration or extension of Falwell's message, previously recorded on tape, may be inserted into his sermon. Electronic magic thus reconfigures the traditional rhetoric of preaching.

In the evangelical tradition, the sermon is typically followed by an invitation to come forward and profess one's faith, signifying an experience of being "born again." Underscoring this dynamic, Falwell and others have expanded this moment in the worship service to introduce a particular cause or issue. This flexibility of emphasis reveals a shift in the purpose of these televised worship services. Nationally broadcast interpretations of social issues perform an educational and political, rather than a strictly liturgical, function. While instruction may not be clearly separated from the preacher's call for repentance, Falwell's advocacy for particular causes plays an equally important role at this point in the service. In this sense as well, telecasts have modified the flow and rhythm of a traditional evangelical service.

Unlike Falwell and other electronic preachers, some earlier developers of mass media evangelism made no attempt to use traditional sanctuaries. Experimenting with a variety of contexts in which to preach and heal, Oral Roberts was among the first to transform a broadcast studio into "liturgical" space. A pioneer of this "studio church," Roberts converted a variety show into a sacramental occasion for Christian witnessing. Roberts brought in guests who were nationally recognized cultural heroes, such as movie stars and popular entertainers. They shared with him and the viewing audience their own conversion and healing experiences. In addition, Roberts's program sometimes had an orchestra and chorus dressed not in choir robes, but in stylish gowns and formal attire. In this respect, Oral Roberts was following the lead of secular variety programs such as Lawrence Welk's, and perhaps even Johnny Carson's and Ed Sullivan's.

While Roberts used a sermon as the climax to his show, faith healing became a major part of his message. He constantly stressed the power of the sacred in his messages to viewers, and he used the technology of television to enhance his ministry to those who were ill. Attentive viewers tuned in to see and hear the evangelist testify to God's healing power. Indeed, through the technology of television, the power of the Holy Spirit would be channeled to those in need. Proclaiming God's presence and power, Roberts accepted the television monitor as a bearer of grace and healing; at one point in his career, Roberts invited viewers to put their hands on the video image. Television technology was here offering more than simply image and sound: it provided the faithful with electronic icons that, like the older ones, could put them in touch with a transcendent power.

Pat Robertson enlarged and elaborated the studio-based religious program when he created *The 700 Club*. Among the video evangelists, he developed the most complex type of programming, with features styled after those of commercial television. Employing the latest electronic technology, Robertson and his colleagues refined stage properties, lighting, and performance. Robertson invited to his program celebrities from all walks of life—sports, politics, entertainment—and ordinary people as well. In imitating talk show hosts like Merv Griffin and Phil Donahue, Robertson seems to have appropriated and baptized a popular secular format of television entertainment.

As his religious broadcasts grew in popularity, Robertson altered and expanded his programming. The studio space was refurbished from time to time, changing from a traditional sitting room to a more contemporary setting while maintaining a comfortable, middle-class style. The program eventually included talk-show routines, financial advising, and cooking adventures modeled after those of Julia Child. Robertson also introduced news summaries, documentaries, commercials for becoming a Christian, and at one time even tried a soap opera. Robertson's guests came to bear witness to their extraordinary religious experiences. The common theme of such diverse segments was the testimony to God's power in the lives of individuals and in society. This was consistently amplified in Robertson's prayers and teaching. In addition, he regularly presented editorials and commentaries on social issues and political events, pointing to God's revelation in the present and future. As talk-show host, television newscaster, teacher, preacher, prophet, and producer, Robertson orchestrated complex genres of programming into a cohesive whole, largely through his television persona.

The Imagery of Persuasion

While video evangelists differ in style and content, we can observe some basic similarities among them. These core elements, drawn from a Protestantism that emphasizes the reading and preaching of the Word, are charismatic leadership and the conversion experience.

The central dynamic among the electronic evangelists is a charismatic leadership which downplays the ritual office of priest and the role of the sacraments. Instead, spiritual authority rests with the Bible, individually interpreted. The power of the charismatic religious leader does not reside in the priestly office but in the calling to preach, teach, and heal through the inspiration of the Holy Spirit—all in accordance with Biblical text. Radio, and later television, brought with them unprecedented opportunities to focus on the personality and forcefulness of religious leaders. Indeed, charismatic religious leaders of all church affiliations have benefited from television technology. As they enter the world of television, electronic images of their preaching, prophecy, instruction, and healing take on dimensions of "real life" for millions of viewers.

Much of the success of these charismatic preachers depends upon special qualities of body, mind, and spirit, qualities that are highlighted by the television monitor. Television techniques can intensify the zeal of the evangelist and bring viewers into intimate visual contact with a speaker. We are all familiar with the eyeball-to-eyeball images provided by a zoom lens: fiery or tear-filled eyes, the passion of prayer and supplication. Engineered by the television camera, such close engagements are shared by thousands at the same moment—something that could not have happened before the electronic revolution.

Such persuasive visual and aural rhetoric is, of course, not limited to preachers. It is equally well understood by politicians, talk-show hosts, and rock stars. William McLoughlin, scholar of American religion, has shown how the series of great awakenings in this country, with their large mass tent meetings, may be seen as prototypes of what we now call media events.[8] The difference is that our contemporary "tent" revivalists—comprised now of a wide range of public and popular figures— are seen and heard in the context of one's living room.

A second element in television evangelism is the emphasis upon a change of heart, the conversion principle. While the electronic preachers and broadcasters work in different styles and environments, the fervent appeal to individuals to make a decision, a profession of faith, is shared by all. Thus the preaching of charismatic religious leaders is generally *persuasive* in tone and style. Sermons build up to a climax, and those in the pews or viewers on their sofas are urged to look inside their hearts and make a change. What the televangelist seeks in others is a conversion, a "turning around," or, in religious language, an experience of being "born again."

Television has thus become an ideal medium for charismatic religious leaders. Through their spirited exhortation they work a magic over the airwaves, transforming living rooms into generic sacred spaces where altar calls can be seen and heard by millions. Yet, the lone viewer at home before the television screen may respond to these images and sounds in a deeply personal, private way.

Mediated Holy Objects

Just as ritual space and time have been appropriated and changed by electronic communication, icons also have undergone transformations of form, function, symbolism, and context. In their liturgical settings, paintings and sculptures are placed on church walls or screens as aids to devotion and as a means of divine encounter. Like ritual, traditional icons give people a basic orientation to human experience by presenting the faithful beholder with a concrete, meaningful world. They also serve as models for human behavior. Pictures of extraordinary or exemplary personalities bring inspiration or comfort to bored or disillusioned individuals. Traditional icons—whether they portray sacred personages mediating grace or present visual narratives of religious heroes—depict luminous human beings who hold out special hope for ordinary persons. These representations of saints and heroic mythic figures offer the less privileged at least a vicarious experience of adventure, risk, and endurance. In addition to presenting world views and role models, icons frame important questions and answers. In visually depicting moral and religious situations, icons thus focus attention on questions that institutions consider essential both to individuals and to the group as a whole.

The evangelical ministries, perhaps unwittingly, have developed their own special icons and have promoted what might be called a technological sacramentalism. Nationally known evangelists discovered that, as in ancient and medieval times, people want some concrete, material expression which nurtures a sense of belonging and which bestows tangible contact with a remote authority and power. Parishioners of the churches without walls, the folks who regularly tune in to religious programming, are offered an assortment of palpable symbols to cement their identification with a larger whole. Modern technology has provided the video evangelists with techniques for distributing devotional materials to their constituencies and for maintaining regular communication with them. Along with innumerable books, pamphlets, charts, and pins, viewers can also obtain various kinds of audio and visual tapes. Traditional holy images have been technologically updated by decorative, colored plastics and by moving, talking shapes. VCRs and headphones can now attune the devout to the spiritual world of video ministry.

Furthermore, television's star system promotes celebrity and confers an almost superhuman status upon the heroes and heroines of popular culture; the pervasive images of the electronic preachers have similarly been elevated into a new kind of religious iconography. Viewers repeatedly attend to the dramatic faces on the monitor as they teach, pray, and heal. For some devoted followers, the representations on the television screen have become icons in action, imbued with a power which surpasses that of the older ones. Traditions which once condemned images in religious communication have given new life to visual devotional forms, but instead of static portraits of saints, we now have moving, persuasive images that talk to us "directly." Demystified and rationalized, the new holy images are the evangelists themselves.

Implications for Televised Religion

Ritual and icon may be useful analogues for understanding certain dimensions of both secular and religious popular culture, but we should also be mindful of their limits. The analogies falter when there is no mystical dimension to the events celebrated; they are more applicable when we emphasize their role in forming and maintaining a sense of community. In addition, we need to acknowledge that theological and liturgical differences among religious traditions affect the ways in which television can be appropriated.

Television technology has limited use, for example, in churches where the eucharist is central to worship. Watching the movements of the participants in liturgical spaces, including the shots of those taking communion, may have little personal significance to a television observer. To some viewers, it may even cause discomfort—as if they were intruding upon the privacy of the communicant. For others, watching television only accentuates the sense of being "outside" the worshiping community. Thus churches embedded in the sacramental tradition do not readily adapt to telecasting. Real presence—moving to the altar, receiving communion—cannot occur via the television monitor.

Even so, consider the extensive use of television by Pope John Paul II. Beginning with his Inaugural Mass, the pope pronounced blessings on all who were "present" through radio and television. In the many travels which have marked his papacy, he has continued to use mass media technology to address those who could not be physically present. I would argue, however, that the pope's use of radio and television is most effective not for sacramental participation, but for the worldwide dissemination of his homilies and non-liturgical addresses. As a climax to his Cuba visit, for example, John Paul II celebrated mass in Revolution Square, a hallowed place for Cuban political leaders. On this historic occasion, the pope spoke critically about the embargo on Cuba tenaciously maintained by the United States. At the same time, he was equally critical of a Cuban political environment that denied certain basic human rights. Those who watched this address on television or listened to it on the radio would have felt, to some degree, part of an extraordinary event.

Even though these "participants" did not receive communion, television did give them limited access to this ritual. It allowed this pope to speak as pastor and prophet to the world—to those present and to those who saw or heard his words through the electronic media. In many ways, television is responsible for making a visual icon of this important religious figure of the twentieth century.

In any case, the religious denominations that de-emphasize the sacraments and focus rather on the reading of Scripture and the sermon are the ones which have developed an eminently pragmatic partnership with mass-media technologies. When Oral Roberts, for example, in his heyday as evangelist and healer, used the television so effectively that some of his devoted followers experienced a healing power, Roberts's picture seen on the monitor and his accompanying words marked the presence of the Holy Spirit. For the televangelist and his viewers, electronically enhanced word and image suffice as channels of divine mercy and healing. Thus faithfulness to the Word now includes, paradoxically, a dependence upon electronic images, and as long as the Word and conversion are valued above all else, mass media can play a major role in worship and religious communication.

More significantly, the television medium has given new power to the evangelical tradition. There is an astonishing intimacy between the electronic preachers and their "congregations." For many viewers, the close up portraits of the evangelists—the details of their eyes, the furrowed brow, the head uplifted in prayer—reinforce their appeals for conversion; an object (the television set with its electronic images) fosters a kind of "sacramental" experience, a mediated "presence." Since the charisma of the preacher is critical to effecting a change of heart, his "presence" and words seem as "real"—perhaps more real—to the viewer at home than to the person in the pew or studio. In their adaptations of programming and technology, then, the television evangelists have successfully transformed electronic space into ritual space. Each week, attentive viewers can enter a "shared" worship space through the television monitor and privately repeat or relive experiences of renewal. Thus television introduces a ritualistic dimension into a religious tradition that historically rejected ritual.

If we pursue the principles of Calvin and Zwingli, the Word is the source of grace. Thus, for many contemporary believers, it does not matter whether we encounter it via radio, via television, or in the space of a church. Yet what has happened to the community that nurtures and supports individual believers when that community consists of viewers in isolated spaces, focused on their television monitors? In times of deep human distress, what do the images of the televangelists or their electronic mailings—the video tapes and pamphlets—provide? Is it help enough to viewers in need to offer a telephone number or an internet address?

Implications for the Larger Society

Of course, those who tune in to religious programs comprise a relatively small group, especially when compared to the large network audiences of mainstream programming. In contrast to the limited numbers of believers who watch religious programs on television, millions participate via television in the extravagant secular rituals of professional sports and politics. Even though television preachers are adept at appropriating television imagery, the most pervasive rituals and icons of American culture belong to the commercial world.

Still, the analogy of ritual continues to be helpful as long as we emphasize the integrative function of commercial television. The medium uniquely enhances the secularization of ritual by enlivening its components of time and space in unprecedented ways. One measure of the vitality of these secular rituals is the cost of the commercials that pay for the television coverage. During the 1998 Super Bowl, every second of commercial time was worth approximately $43,000. The sponsors, however, got their money's worth. Viewers were intensely "there"—right down to the last few seconds of the game. They were "present" among the Denver Bronco players who triumphantly lifted John Elway and carried him aloft through the crowd. The excitement of the game flowed into the ceremony that followed. At one point the Bronco hero held the trophy high for all the crowd to see. In moments like this, the "participant" in the television ritual was "there"—experiencing a sense of belonging as keenly as the fan in the stadium at San Diego.

Strangely enough, in spite of their different aims and audiences, the creators of television commercials, as well as televangelists, recognize the psychological power of conversion. Disdained though it may be, the television commercial may be the most significant example of a fortuitous interaction of media and "religion" in contemporary American society. Television advertisement draws upon the "born-again" philosophy of evangelical denominations, since the dynamics of a religious heritage— namely, an emphasis on salvation and choice—are embedded in the structure of many advertisements. Echoing the passionate pleas of the preacher, advertising images evoke in us both fear and desire; products now offer salvation, and the consumer's decision, whether about a new car or a can of beer, marks a turning point that makes life excitingly fresh and different. Thus the conversionist religious motif itself is refurbished in a consumer society.

Furthermore, commercials do more than advertise individual products; taken collectively, they promote an encompassing faith in the American Way. In buying products and services, we become members incorporated in the mystical body of those who have been redeemed through consuming. Informing both commercials and televangelists' messages is a highly individualist psychology, focussing on the inner core of the self. If one is not mindful of a condition of discomfort or pain, then the words of the commercial or preacher admonish us to turn inward and look critically at the self, its graying hair or sense of unworthiness. Equally powerful is the assumption that, once a person is aware of a condition, he or she can make a significant choice about his or her fate. Finally, the language of commercials and persuasive preachers assert that our decisions will be efficacious: the self will be different, marked by significant changes in body or spirit.

In appropriating television, the electronic evangelists develop a unique relationship to contemporary popular culture. The medium enables them to use images very effectively, even as using these images in places of worship is disavowed. Electronic imagery allowed them to have it both ways, so to speak: to proclaim the iconoclastic principles of the radical reformers and their emphasis upon the Word, yet at the same time to build extravagant churches without walls, resplendent with icons—particularly, the images of the evangelists themselves. While voicing a suspicion of ritual, the evangelists have also benefited from television's tendency to ritualize all kinds of programming. Worshippers across the country are gathered together as the television monitor frames the places and times into which they enter for worship. Tuned in, the faithful viewer awaits the "real presence" of the preacher.

NOTES

1. Johan Huizinga, *The Waning of the Middle Ages* (Garden City, N.Y.: Doubleday, 1956), 244.

2. Elizabeth Gilmore Holt, ed., *The Middle Ages and the Renaissance,* vol. 1 of *A Documentary History of Art* (Garden City, N.Y.: Doubleday, 1957), 19.

3. Roland H. Bainton, *Christendom: A Short History of Christianity and Its Impact on Western Civilization* (New York: Harper & Row, 1966), 2:25.

4. Charles Garside, Jr., *Zwingli and the Arts* (New Haven: Yale University Press, 1966), 160.

5. Victor Turner, "Variations on a Theme of Liminality," in *Secular Ritual,* ed. Sally F. Moore and Barbara G. Meyerhoff (Assen and Amsterdam: Van Gorum, 1977), 36–52, quotation from 36.

6. For a fuller discussion, see Gregor Goethals, *The TV Ritual: Worship at the Video Altar* (Boston: Beacon Press, 1981) and *The Electronic Golden Calf: Images, Religion and the Making of Meaning* (Cambridge, Mass.: Cowley Publications, 1990).

7. A. Bartlett Giamatti, *Take Time for Paradise: Americans and Their Games* (New York: Summit Books, 1989), 14, 48.

8. William McLoughlin, *Revivals, Awakenings and Reform: An Essay on Religion and Social Change in America. 1607–1977* (Chicago: University of Chicago Press, 1978), 208.

Stewart M. Hoover

THE CROSS AT WILLOW CREEK

Seeker Religion and the
Contemporary Marketplace

My only visit to a true megachurch took place a few years ago when I sat in with a delegation of mainline church communication officers at Willow Creek Community Church near Chicago. Willow Creek is in many ways the prototype of the megachurch, also known as the seeker's church or "next" church. One incident during my time there stands out. As this group sat in the church's huge auditorium, the tour guide asked them to name anything they thought was missing from the space. "There's no cross," said several, almost in unison. "That's right," replied the guide, who went on to say:

> In fact, you will see no Christian symbolism here at all. The metaphor or image we are trying to project here is corporate or business, not traditional church. Now, we do have a cross. We bring it out for special occasions, like baptism. When I was baptized here, all of us were asked to write our sins on pieces of paper and stick them on the cross as we came forward. I'll never forget looking up from the baptistery at that cross, covered in paper. I had not really understood atonement until that moment. So we think of the cross as a prop.

The reaction of these visitors from more conventional churches and denominations was predictable. Most felt that it was disingenuous, if not downright irreligious, for Willow Creek to so consciously eliminate the long-standing trappings of the faith from its walls. But most of the discussion centered around the notion of the cross as a "prop." This was obviously meant as the theatrical term for stage paraphernalia, not the idea of the cross as a spiritual crutch of some sort to "prop" one up. But the idea struck most of my fellow attendees as a trivialization of the central symbol of the Christian faith. That the cross would only have the status of "prop" substantially devalued it in their eyes.

I will return to this story because I think it enables us to understand some things not only about the megachurch as a phenomenon, but also about the state of contemporary religious practice and the role that the commodities of the media and popular culture have played and will continue to play in it. We are well beyond the time when we can see the intersection between religion and culture purely in cause and effect terms. That is, it is both unsatisfying and misleading to ask either how religion affects the media or how the media affect religion. The deeper, more profound, and more helpful question is how media and religion as social and cultural spaces and practices are interacting in contemporary life, and how we can better understand the prospects of religion in a media age.

THE MEGACHURCH

It is obvious that I see the phenomenon of the megachurch as a source of helpful insight. The implications of the anecdote above, and of the whole phenomenon of "seeker" religiosity which megachurches benefit from, are best understood when they are historically and theoretically grounded. Megachurches such as Willow Creek are much more than the sum of their various parts.

The characteristics of megachurches are well known. They are large, typically with several thousand members. They are Protestant, and generally associated with the evangelical side of the Protestant ledger. They emphasize service of members' needs and interests, and see religion as a consumer "demand" rather than as a "supply" issue. Willow Creek, for instance, is well known for regularly conducting market surveys of its geographic area, and adjusting and shaping its ministries to fit the results.

These elements of Willow Creek—its conscious "market" orientation and the programs that have resulted—make it emblematic of a new kind of religious practice that Wade Clark Roof, a sociologist of religion, has described in *A Generation of Seekers*.[1] According to Roof, baby-boom religiosity is coming to be dominated by an emphasis on seeking more than on belief or belonging. The focus is on developing a religious faith that is unique to the individual person and oriented toward their own needs and interests. The market research of Willow Creek has placed it in a unique position to be able to respond to this "seeker religiosity."

The most common criticism of megachurches relates to their religious authenticity. The market-driven approach so typical of the media and popular culture seems to some observers necessarily to devalue the core activities of these institutions. Using market logic to create programs, services, and even products to respond to religious "seeking" turns religion into a commodity. Worse still, religion becomes just one commodity in a culture of commodities, and therefore necessarily less "authentic," "meaningful," and "truly religious." Seen in this light, the cross being used and manipulated in the way described above suggests that the overall effect of the megachurch is to undermine important and authentic symbols and practices of the faith.

While Willow Creek itself is not a media church of any kind, I wish to argue that its religious practice places it very much in the commodity culture of the media sphere. Such a view can provide important insights into the evolving religion of the media age, and raise the possibility that this religion is, contrary to critics, authentic in important ways. The status of the cross at Willow Creek tells us something about how religious seekers, as children of the television era, understand symbols and their meanings, and suggests that Willow Creek actually understands contemporary religious seeking more deeply than critics realize.

MEDIA AND RELIGION

Accounting for religion and media is a large and complex task. As has been argued, the whole literature of media and religion has been typified by a sort of dualist instrumentalism which sees the question solely in terms of cause and effect, as though "media" (or commodity culture, or popular culture) and "religion" are more or less equivalent and autonomous historical categories and it is possible to understand them only as competing with and contesting one another.[2]

This view, however, is too limited. First, it has not gotten us very far in understanding the contemporary scene. The impressionistic and anecdotal evidence suggests that the media and religion occupy some of the same turf in modern life. People seem to be seeking religious meaning in mediated cultural commodities, at the same time that media and popular culture regularly address and use religious themes. Second, the traditional view turns out to lead to a blind alley whether one begins with the proposition that the media affect religion, or the other way around. We simply find, in both cases, that the same ground is being trod by these two areas of cultural practice (religion and commodity culture), but there is no conceptual scope to finally account for their relationship to one another. Third, the traditional view tends to ignore powerful theoretical and conceptual tools which have become available in recent years in anthropology, cultural studies, religious studies, ritual studies, linguistics, and so on. These disciplines have started concentrating on questions of meaning in contemporary consciousness, and are gradually coming to provide insights into how we might look at the intersection between religion and contemporary culture. Finally, and most importantly, the traditional view has systematically overlooked phenomena in both religion and culture which point toward the emergence of entirely new ways of doing and understanding religion. Before I return to the megachurch and to my experience at Willow Creek, I would like to describe in a bit more detail what I mean by this.

I have argued elsewhere that the contemporary religious scene can be best understood when we step outside received categories of analysis (dictated to us largely by nineteenth-century and early-twentieth-century social theory: secularization, functionalism, social movements, positivism, institutional studies, social structure, and the like) and instead follow the lead suggested by anthropological scholarship. We should see cultural practice as the central category, and understand the practices of contemporary lived lives as efforts to embody an evolving religious understanding.[3] From this perspective, it is possible to look at important social categories such as structure, class, institutions, social movements, and so on, but in a way that grounds them in lived lives and lived experience, and which takes account of their cultural, symbolic, and discursive dimensions.

Such an approach immediately illuminates some tantalizing trends in both media culture and religious practice. Today's media scene is one of tremendous diversification (I am speaking here of diversification of channels and outlets, not necessarily of ownership—another critical matter). Whole new channels and services have emerged in the last ten years, and new cross-media marketing and programming alliances mean that the current atomization, combination, and recombination will continue for the foreseeable future.

There are good reasons to expect an eventual limit to this diversification (audiences, for example, cannot be broken into smaller, more specialized segments ad infinitum), but in any case the diversification to date

important implications for my considerations here. Media market-
are coming to recognize that in today's marketplace, traditional
h" marketing must give way to a new "pull" marketing. That is, the
y to interact with audiences and consumers is not to think that you
can push goods or ideas or services on them; they now have a greater capacity to choose, not only what they buy but even what they have access
to, and marketers need to encourage them to "pull" goods or ideas or
services towards themselves. The days are long gone when one program
or one advertiser could be assured of a majority of the audience just by
virtue of location or position on the television dial. The situation is now
far more fractured and competitive.

At the same time, the media have also learned in recent years that the
traditional bifurcation of audience members' interests into public and
private or "rational" and "emotional" categories no longer makes much
sense. In the golden age of broadcasting, marketers tended to operate
with an easy confidence that social theories of secularization (at their
most simplistic) were right: with industrialization and increased education, audiences were becoming more rational and less spiritual, more
systematic and less symbolic, more secularized and less interested in religion.[4] With the new diversity of channels has come a whole panoply of
material that transcends these oppositions. This material includes much
more than mere "televangelism": from films and television programs to
whole "emotional" channels (such as the "Recovery Network" and "Pax
Network"), self-help books, magazines, websites, and pop music songs
and videos, the list could go on almost indefinitely.

A good deal of this material admittedly fits into what Roof has called
the "therapeutic" turn in establishment American religion,[5] and this is
significant in itself. Roof's more recent work, as well as that of Robert
Bellah and his associates (among others), has demonstrated the power
and volubility of a new faith and spiritual practice oriented toward perfection of the self.[6] In popular parlance, this has been called "new age
spirituality," but it in fact extends far beyond the boundaries of the
"new age" movement.[7]

In a way which connects with (but is not necessarily caused by) these
trends in the media, religion is becoming more diverse, fractured, and
personal. This has been called the rise of personal autonomy by some[8]
and "Sheilah-ism" by others, a term named after Sheilah Larson, one of
the respondents in Bellah's study. Larson has come to embody a kind of
religious practice oriented toward the self and conceiving of religion as
a conscious search for a variety of inputs, which can then be coalesced

into an identity for which the individual considers him- or herself responsible.[9] This practice, of course, has little room for institutions or for classic religious dimensions such as structure, authority, or legitimacy. Instead, it is self-legitimating and self-orienting.

It can be said, of course, that this "seeker" religiosity is, at its root, narcissistic, limited, and superficial. Against such a view, as argued by Bellah himself, R. Stephen Warner has suggested that it is a mistake to think of seekers as anything other than "morally serious" in what they are doing.[10] That is, while this practice may not fit traditional religious behavior, it should not be dismissed out of hand. At the same time, the seeker model has allowed whole new categories of consciousness and spirituality—women's, indigenous, experiential, invented, and others—to emerge in theory and scholarship.

THE EMERGING MARKETPLACE

The essential question is thus how to understand the common ground forming under these parallel trends. As the authority and legitimacy of traditional religious and institutional practice declines, and as the individual becomes more and more responsible for his or her own faith, a sort of horizontal "symbolic marketplace" is emerging, where an inventory of symbols, networks, movements, groups, sources, relationships, and practices is made available to religious seekers. This marketplace is, increasingly, a commodified, media-based marketplace.

To a great extent, this marketplace's "commodities" are the symbolic and practical resources which have long been repressed in the American (particularly the Protestant) context: the visual, the body, objects, experience, and rituals.[11] As the "pull" marketing described above comes to the center of this "seeker" religiosity, the most valuable commodities of exchange have become those which address hungers and needs not met by conventional religious practice. Modern media culture is profoundly tactile, visual, embodied, and "effervescent" (to use a term from Durkheim), which lets its programs, services, and symbols contest, by their very nature, the tried-and-true communicational paradigms of traditional religion.

What, specifically, are the underlying needs which contemporary commodity culture aims to fulfill? While it is misleading to limit our sights to one generation or one cultural milieu, there are nevertheless sound reasons for locating the core of these trends in the "baby boom" generation, the group Roof has called the "Generation of Seekers." The central spiritual motivation of this group is lodged in a host of historical, social, and cultural factors, but as Roof succinctly summarizes:

> The concern is to experience life directly, to have an encounter with God or the divine, or simply with nature and other people, without the intervention of inherited beliefs, ideas, and concepts. Such striving is understandable, not simply because secondhand religion can be empty of meaning, but because only personal experience is in some sense authentic and empowering. Individuals are inclined to regard their own experiences as superior to the accounts of others, and the truths found through self-discovery as having greater relevance to them than those handed down by way of creed or custom. Direct experience is always more trustworthy.[12]

This need for direct, even tactile experience in religion is powerfully expressed by Barbara Wheeler, discussing ethnographic research she conducted in an evangelical seminary:

> Evangelicals turn out stuff: thousands of Christian recordings; even more books—a new Christian gothic novel, I was told by an avid reader of them, is published every week—along with almost every other kind of fiction, poetry, Bible translations and paraphrases, advice, celebrity biography, and countless devotional volumes; magazines, pamphlets, newspapers, broadsides, leaflets; plaques, posters, greeting and note cards, bumper stickers, ceramics, jewelry. As various as they are, and as much as they have in common with the rest of American mass material culture, most evangelical artifacts are self-evidently evangelical. . . .
> [In contrast,] mainline Protestantism does not have enough of a culture. By comparison with the prolix popular culture of the evangelicals, the mainline Protestant inventory of symbols, manners, iconic leaders, images of leadership, distinctive language, decorations, and sounds is very low indeed.
> In fact, mainline Protestants do not handle much of anything. I never would have realized this if I had not done research in such a different milieu. What I further gained from the evangelicals and now have to offer my own religious community is the realization that our lack of paraphernalia is a dangerous situation. We do not need the evangelicals' particular dry goods or pious practices, but we, like the evangelicals, are bodied beings, and a religious tradition that has little or nothing to look at, listen to, and touch cannot sustain us very long.[13]

So it is at this very direct and concrete level of practice, of actually touching and feeling objects, that a kind of piety can increasingly be invoked by, and satisfied by, commodity culture.

While evangelicalism may have the most obvious and, in a way, superficial range of objects, the religious marketplace, and a marketplace approach to religion, is far from a recent phenomenon. R. Laurence Moore, for example, finds evidence of its emergence around the time of American independence:

> I am persuaded that the transformations of market societies in the nineteenth century as they affected the United States did transform the issues, changing the whole texture and meaning of activities labeled "spiritual." Clearly the First Amendment was a major factor in accelerating the process of religious commodification. Even before it was enacted, as Harry Stout has demonstrated in his work on the eighteenth century, religious leaders, "in order to make religion popular," understood that they had "to compete in a morally neutral and voluntaristic marketplace environment alongside all the goods and services of this world."[14]

Still, there has clearly been an acceleration and deepening of these marketplace approaches recently: they have become institutional, systematic, and even industrial in ways that transcend our traditional categories of analysis. Furthermore, this development has received a great part of its momentum from the parallel evolution of the media sphere and its interrelated practices of cultural commodification. Finally, the resulting inventory of symbols has also deepened and broadened over time, moving beyond evangelical and orthodox categories to include such offerings as Deepak Chopra, Robert Bly, and various forms of "the Goddess." These illustrate the extent to which the sort of totemic *objects* Wheeler discusses are only one element of the story. As ritual theorists have argued,[15] and as is obvious in the quotation above from Roof, there is also an *experiential* dimension to religious seeking, and experience can also be a marketplace commodity.

THE MEGACHURCH AND THE MARKETPLACE

It is a fairly short step from the argument I have been developing here to the phenomenon of the megachurch, which caters to "seeker" religion in its most refined and focused form. Megachurches make certain that their parking lots are large and convenient. They provide childcare and other things which make attendance more accessible. Many have shops and coffee bars. Some provide recreational facilities, aerobics, and the like. Willow Creek is known for self-consciously organizing its weekly program around the process of seeking: in fact, its Sunday services, designed so as to not conjure up conventional church to an audience of Roof's generation of seekers, are called "seeker services," while the "real services" take place at another time, on a weeknight.

Two elements of the typical megachurch match the emerging picture of religion in the marketplace particularly well. First, most of the megachurches place great store in conventional market research as a way of understanding their members and potential members. Writing in *Atlantic Monthly,* Charles Truehart recalls meeting the pastor of one of these churches and seeing "a handsome framed woodcut on the wall of his study . . . [which] read, 'What is our business? Who is our customer? What does the customer consider value?'" [16] Second, the core of the megachurch's "service" of these customer needs is a panoply of "ministries"—typically support groups, fellowship opportunities, or combinations of these—pegged to the particular stresses and strains of contemporary life. Truehart provides a typical list for a typical church: parenting workshops; twelve-step recovery groups "by category" (i.e., alcohol, drugs, gambling, etc.); premarital couples classes; classes for "homebuilders"; a "women in the workplace" brunch; and so on. The megachurches typically make the effort to schedule these groups in times and locations that are as accessible as possible. [17]

Of course, megachurches have their share of critics.

> The Next Church movement makes many traditional church leaders, and many active Christians, nervous, because it implies a rejection of the tried and once-true and the somehow holy; it also suggests to many people an unseemly market-driven approach to building the Kingdom of Heaven. But its obvious success in building congregations and communities alike is making many believers out of skeptics. [18]

Most of the credit for the success of the megachurch is given to its facility in making itself intellectually as well as physically accessible, and this intellectual accessibility is criticized as well. The gospel is watered down in the megachurch, the argument goes. It is brought nearer to the grasp of the seeker or believer. It is made easy—too easy—and thus is "cheap grace."

These criticisms go to the heart of the transitional moment we have been considering here. As the seeker mode of religiosity comes to the fore, making the faith and its symbols accessible is absolutely central. The megachurch phenomenon is simply taking advantage of this transition in religious practice; in it, we can see the modes of practice typical of our times and of the largely commodified and media-saturated context in which we live. To say this, however, is not to say that the media have "made" religion what it is today. They have, however, participated in the creation of—and are now themselves typical of—the conditions and contexts which make the emergence of the megachurch a logical outcome.

SYMBOL AND MEANING AT WILLOW CREEK

Most of what I have said about the megachurch and about the seeker religiosity it relates to has been grounded in the rational and practical spheres. Megachurches use modern research and marketing. They find that people want and need certain kinds of services, and make those services as available as possible. But religion is more than rational and practical: it is, of course, also about symbolically binding the adherent to larger narratives of the ordering of reality. Thus I want to turn now to how the megachurch also represents a transition in contemporary religion on the symbolic level. The argument I have made about the current period of "transitional religion" [19] lets us see that the essential question in this realm as well concerns the authenticity of these practices.

I argued above that seeker religiosity is, in fact, "morally serious," which implies that it is "authentic" to a certain degree. But what we must meet head on is the question of whether commodified symbolic practice can be authentic in terms of its relationship to religious consciousness. That is, are commodified symbols in some way less powerful because of their place in the logic of the contemporary cultural marketplace?

There is a theological dimension of this discussion, which I will leave to the theologians to resolve. I wish to provide some additional insight into the discussion, however, by probing the issue of symbolism in a bit more detail. As with everything I have been considering here, the topic is deeper, more nuanced, and more complex than is often appreciated.

Let me begin by pointing out that the science of signs is a well developed and rich discipline, and one with strong and vibrant debates about the nature of symbolic (or metalinguistic) communication. In the simplest of terms, semiotics and semiology (the two subdisciplines in symbolic scholarship) concern themselves with relationship between signs and referents. All signs refer to something, although in actual practice there is a good deal of flexibility and negotiation in these relations. Many signs are relatively fixed referentially, but others vary widely, and it is the capacity to manipulate such signs that in part defines us as human beings. Certain of these readings become conventionalized over time, and under certain institutional regimes, and the ability to establish and maintain such definitions is an important source of the cultural currency of social institutions. The ability of a government, a corporation, or a church to control and define its own symbols is an important source of power, perhaps more so in today's sign-suffused cultural environment than at any point in history.[20]

I would further add that the whole question of the status of signs within religious practice is one of the least understood and least theorized fields of contemporary scholarship. Semiotics and semiology have tended to be infected by the same disease that has been epidemic in all of academe during the middle of this century—a wholesale rejection of the serious study of religious phenomena. At the same time, theologians and religious thinkers have tended to undertheorize and underproblematize the structure and practice of public communication in general, and visual symbolism in particular.[21]

There are a number of reasons for this. At the most superficial level, it appears as though Western Christianity, and American Protestantism in particular, have a very particular understanding of symbols, an approach that Douglas Kellner has called (in an entirely different context) "representational realism."[22] This means that Protestantism has looked at signs only in terms of their capacity to directly represent unequivocal referents in creedal doctrine. The place of the cross, for example, has been described with rich metaphor over the centuries, but within a relatively narrow range of possible referents. Its status is defined by its place within those historic categories. Other images, particularly popular or vernacular ones such as Warner Sallman's Head of Christ,[23] are derogated because of their relationship to popular piety and their potential for undermining the historic claims of Protestantism to be a faith of "the head as well as the heart."

This is a complex argument, too complex to fully develop here. But I want to argue that one of the things that defines the religion of this transitional moment is a particular relationship to signs. If, as I have said, the religious practice of today is rooted in the cultural practice of the marketplace, then the *symbolic* practices of the marketplace should be apparent in the world of lived religion.

THE CROSS AT WILLOW CREEK

And, in fact, the particular approach to symbolism at Willow Creek (their description of the cross as a "prop" and their particular understanding of its status) is directly and powerfully rooted in an approach to symbolism that is more consonant with broader cultural practice than the conventional, representational approach taken by mainstream Protestantism, and places the sign in a more central position.

Tillich's classic formulation of the symbol as something that points beyond itself to a transcendent reality,[24] and the assumption made by many that the symbol is thereby negated (i.e., the sign is no longer present, only the necessarily implied transcendent reality is), is an example of the more mainstream approach, but contemporary practice is better described by a poststructuralist semiotics. The school of Charles Sanders Peirce, in particular, holds that the sign and the referent continue to exist in a material sense, and that the relationship between a continuing sign and a continuing referent constitutes the actual object of the whole enterprise of symbolization: meaning.[25] Thinking again about the cross at Willow Creek, we can see that the experience of the cross in the mind of that speaker was a profound, referential, and spiritual one. But the physical object, the cross, continued to participate in an act which constructed meaning. The cross did not disappear by referring to some external idea of atonement; the cross materially represented atonement as a physical object in space and time.

By saying that the cross is a "prop," the speaker was therefore saying that the physical manipulation of the cross, its availability for use in a very concrete sense and moment, makes manifest a transcendent meaning. This is one of the particular and unique symbolic practices of transitional religion. Consonant with broader trends in commodity culture, religious practice here takes objects (in this case the cross) and appropriates them in new ways, in a postmodern (or late-modern) practice of meaning construction. I take the cross at Willow Creek, then, to represent the broader trends I spoke of earlier— a new, voluble, embodied, and effervescent kind of religiosity articulated to cultural-symbolic practices which it can never fully escape.

The suppression of this kind of effervescence—of the body, the totem, the experience, ritual, and in particular the image—has generally been considered one of the legacies of John Calvin. Indeed, the term "Calvinism" has come to mean precisely the denial of the physical and expressive in American cultural discourse. However, in an important work on early American Puritanism, Ann Kibbey has demonstrated that this is entirely too narrow a view of Calvin's ideas. In fact, he did not oppose visual imagery in general, only in the case of religious imagery that might veer toward the idolatrous.[26]

It is, of course, the area of religious symbolism that Calvin was most

concerned with, but Kibbey argues that his approach to symbols and images was more complex than he is often given credit for. First, he held
that the problem with the idols he condemned in Catholicism was that
they were merely representational.

> Calvin's theory of visual art is that of a materialist who fears that he can think
> no further than he physically sees. . . . Quoting Augustine, he explains the
> vulnerability of the onlooker: "For the shape of the idol's bodily members
> makes and in a sense compels the mind dwelling in a body to suppose that
> the idol's body too has feeling."[27]

Thus Calvin condemned a certain kind of approach to symbols—that is,
direct representation—which encompassed the traditional ways symbols such as the cross have been used.

The second significant thing about Calvin's theory of symbolism is
that he calls for a use and manipulation of material symbols very much
like that in my example from Willow Creek. The problem with representation, he felt, was fetishization:

> [Calvin] candidly summarizes, "Men's folly cannot restrain itself from falling
> headlong into superstitious rites." Images have such power over people that
> the mere presence of the image compels fetishistic adoration. Calvin assumes
> that this response to an image is a universal quality, and thus, whatever
> Catholics may say about the value of representational art, he insists that they
> believe in their images as a fetishist believes in icons.[28]

Calvin then tries to transcend the fetishistic, representational notion of
symbols by contending that symbolic properties are only valid when
they are embodied and used. To simplify Kibbey's argument: she sees
Calvin deriving a theory of symbolization from his understanding of the
sacrament of communion, and of the bread in particular. He rejects the
notion of transubstantiation, holding instead that the power of the bread
is not in its transcendent qualities as consecrated bread, but instead in
its commonness as ordinary bread. Its connection with the "spiritual
essence" only works, in his view, if it is seen to be common bread that is
thus engaged in the transaction.

Kibbey then goes on to a stunning claim. Calvin's view of symbols is
remarkably similar to Karl Marx's theory of commodities in the capitalist market: Both of them hold that the real power, the real transcendence in objects, and hence their real symbolic role, is neither in the things
themselves, nor in their merely pointing unequivocally to something
else, but in their use and their exchange. Both of them, Kibbey points out,
warn against the dangers of fetishizing the object itself.[29] This would im-

ply that using the cross as a "prop," far from being a trivialization, is a more profound and more meaningful use than simply hanging it on a wall, week after week, so that it is never manipulated, appropriated, or used. As currency in a cultural exchange, the cross at Willow Creek becomes an object in an ongoing discourse of contemporary, transitional religion. Its use in this way is both embedded in, and emblematic of, the broader prospects of religion in an age of commodity culture.

NOTES

1. Wade Clark Roof, *A Generation of Seekers: The Religion of the Baby Boom Generation* (San Francisco: HarperCollins, 1993).
2. See Lynn S. Clark and Stewart M. Hoover, "At the Intersection of Media, Culture and Religion: A Bibliographic Essay," in *Rethinking Media, Religion and Culture,* ed. Stewart M. Hoover and Knut Lundby (London: Sage, 1997), 15–36.
3. See Hoover, "Media and the Construction of the Religious Public Sphere," in Hoover and Lundby, *Rethinking Media, Religion and Culture,* 283–97.
4. See Stewart M. Hoover and Douglas K. Wagner, "History and Policy in Broadcast Treatment of Religion," *Media, Culture and Society* 19, no. 1 (January 1997): 7–27.
5. See Wade Clark Roof, "America's Voluntary Establishment: Mainline Religion in Transition," in *Religion and America: Spirituality in a Secular Age,* ed. Mary Douglas and Stephen M. Tipton (Boston: Beacon Press, 1982), 130–49.
6. See Roof, *Generation of Seekers,* and Robert Bellah et al., *Habits of the Heart: Individualism and Commitment in American Life* (Berkeley: University of California Press, 1985).
7. See Catherine Albanese, "Fisher Kings and Public Spaces: The Old New Age in the 1990s," and Martin Marty, "Where the Energies Go," both in *Annals of the American Academy* 527 (May 1993): 131–43 and 11–26.
8. Phillip Hammond, *Religion and Personal Autonomy: The Third Disestablishment in America* (Greenville: University of South Carolina Press, 1993).
9. Bellah et al., *Habits of the Heart,* 221.
10. R. Stephen Warner, "Work in Progress Toward a New Paradigm in the Sociological Study of Religion in the United States," *American Journal of Sociology* 98 (March 1993): 1044–93.
11. For more complete discussions, see Albanese, "Fisher Kings and Public Spaces," and Hoover, "Media and the Religious Public Sphere."
12. Roof, *Generation of Seekers,* 67.
13. Barbara Wheeler, "We Who Were Far Off" (paper presented to the Religious Research Association, St. Louis, November 1994).
14. R. Laurence Moore, *Selling God: American Religion in the Marketplace of Culture* (New York: Oxford University Press, 1994), 7, quoting Harry S.

Stout, *The Divine Dramatist: George Whitefield and the Rise of Modern Evangelicalism* (Grand Rapids, Mich.: William B. Eerdmans, 1991), xvii. See also the intriguing parallels in Colleen McDannell's *Material Christianity* (New Haven: Yale University Press, 1995), and further support for the general argument of a seeker or market metaphor for religious involvement in Peter Berger's classic *The Sacred Canopy: Elements of a Sociological Theory of Religion* (New York: Anchor Doubleday, 1967): "The pluralistic situation [that is, the religious situation of modernity] is, above all, a market situation. In it . . . religious traditions become consumer commodities. . . . [A] good deal of religious activity in this situation comes to be dominated by the logic of market economics" (138).

15. See, for example, Catherine Albanese, *America: Religions and Religion* (Belmont, Calif.: Wadsworth, 1981); Catherine Bell, *Ritual Theory, Ritual Practice* (New York: Oxford University Press, 1992); Ronald Grimes, *Symbol and Conquest: Public Ritual and Drama in Santa Fe* (Albuquerque: University of New Mexico Press, 1976); and Robert Wuthnow, *Meaning and Moral Order: Explorations in Cultural Analysis* (Berkeley: University of California Press, 1987).

16. Charles Truehart, "Welcome to the Next Church," *Atlantic Monthly*, August 1996, 37–58, quotation from 40.

17. Ibid., 39

18. Ibid., 38.

19. This term is taken from Roof, *A Generation of Seekers.*

20. Alf Linderman, "The Reception of Religious Television: Social Semiology Applied to an Empirical Case Study," *Acta Universitatis Uppsaliensis, Psychologia et Sociologia Religionum 12* (Stockholm: Almquist and Wiksell, International, 1996).

21. See Hoover, "Media and Moral Order in Post-Positivist Media Studies," *Journal of Communication* 45, no. 1 (1995): 136–145; Hoover and Shalini Venturelli, "Religion: The Blindspot of Contemporary Media Theory?" *Critical Studies in Mass Communication* 13 (September 1996): 251–65; David Morgan, *Visual Piety* (New Haven: Yale University Press, 1998).

22. Douglas Kellner, "Popular Culture and the Construction of Postmodern Identities," in *Modernity and Identity*, ed. Scott Lash and Jonathon Friedman (Oxford: Blackwell, 1992), 141–77, especially 145.

23. See David Morgan, "Imaging Popular Piety: The Icons of Warner Sallman," *Religion and American Culture* 3, no. 1 (Winter 1993): 29–47.

24. Paul Tillich, *Theology of Culture* (New York: Oxford University Press, 1959).

25. Linderman, "Reception of Religious Television"; for a thorough discussion of Peirce in this regard, see 17–62.

26. Ann Kibbey, *The Interpretation of Material Shapes in Puritanism: A Study of Rhetoric, Prejudice, and Violence* (New Haven: Yale University Press, 1986), 44.

27. Ibid., 46–7.

28. Ibid., 47.

29. Ibid., 52.

PART THREE

POPULAR CULTURE AS RELIGION

Some commentators suggest that it is possible to think of particular forms of Popular Culture *as* Religion. This approach constitutes our third relationship between religion and popular culture. For these cultural critics, the emphasis is not on traditional forms of religion, but on the way that significant cultural activity takes on the social form and purpose of religion. They ask us to consider whether this cultural activity should be regarded as religious, or at least as analogous to religion.

Most often, these scholars draw on understandings of ritual, myth, and symbol derived from anthropology and religious studies, to suggest that when secular activities take on the forms of religion they also take on the function of religion and become bearers and shapers of cultural values and beliefs. Earlier in this volume, Gregor Goethals made use of the concept of ritual in her discussion of how television ritual transforms evangelical Christian worship. In this section, four writers consider the way that specific popular cultural activities seem to take on religious function when they take on the forms of religion.

Michael Jindra's work on *Star Trek* fandom emphasizes the rituals and beliefs of the participants and the way these expressions of popular culture provide interpretive frameworks analogous to religion for thinking about life and values. In doing so, he helps us understand the role of belief and ritual in bonding a distinctive subculture.

Michelle M. Lelwica examines the world of dieting and eating disorders among young women, attending to religious language as well as ritual practices. She finds in the literature and practices designed to re-shape the female body a striving for an "ideal" which is expressed in religious terms and pursued with religious zeal.

Joseph L. Price takes a similar approach to a different cultural activity. His consideration of sports and sports fans suggests that the rituals, symbols, and their transformative experiences constitute at least "a form of religion."

David Chidester focuses more generally on the question of what constitutes a religion. He illustrates how different definitions of the religious lead us to reflect on different features of popular culture, examining in detail the "church" of baseball, the "fetish" of Coca-Cola, and the "potlatch" of rock 'n' roll.

8

Michael Jindra

IT'S ABOUT FAITH IN OUR FUTURE

Star Trek *Fandom as Cultural Religion*

From *The Wizard of Oz* to the *Davy Crockett* series of the 1950s, to movies such as *E.T.* and *Star Wars,* Americans in the twentieth century have been entertained and inspired by vivid and captivating narratives utilizing the new visual media. Through television and film, popular culture has become an influential, even dominating, force in many areas of our society. As the essays in this volume make clear, popular culture often draws upon religious themes, but in this essay I will argue that the entertainment industry also creates meanings that begin to function in religious ways for consumers of popular culture.

This should not be too surprising, for there has always been a relationship between religion and popular culture. Popular culture originally split from "learned," formal religious culture after the Protestant and Catholic Reformations,[1] but it continued to complement religious culture. The pre-Lenten Carnival was a direct product of church culture, as were the patron saint festivals and the cults of images of early modern Europe. Because of this close connection, popular culture was not a completely distinct alternative to religious culture.

Today, however, popular culture has lost its direct connection with the religious heart of society and has taken on a life of its own, creating its own stories and myths through which people find meaning and identity. Popular culture has become an independent producer of mythical narratives, a reflection of cultural themes and a producer of new ones. Though often using traditional religious themes and imagery (as in *E.T.*

or *Star Wars*), the narratives and messages have been formally cut off from the religious traditions that have dominated Western culture over the centuries. In other words, parts of popular culture have taken their place alongside the mainstream religious traditions and political ideologies which have guided people's lives down through the centuries.

There is no better example of this than the *Star Trek* fan phenomenon. As a television and movie production, *Star Trek* has gone through several installments, but the fan phenomenon it sparked has been going strong since the original *Star Trek* was first broadcast in 1966. The fan phenomenon first became apparent when the original *Star Trek* television series was threatened with cancellation after its second year. Fans immediately organized a letter-writing campaign to keep *Star Trek* on the air.[2] When it was canceled after its third year, the show went into syndication, which is when the "fandom"[3] phenomenon really started to take off. The first *Star Trek* convention was in New York in 1972, and by then noncommercial *Star Trek* fan magazines ("fanzines") and commercial *Star Trek* books, manuals, and novels were being published for fans hungry for more knowledge about the *Star Trek* universe.

Efforts to revive *Star Trek* broadcasts, in some form, continued for years. An animated series was produced from 1973 to 1974, and in 1979 the first of nine (to date) *Star Trek* movies was released. In 1987, *Star Trek: The Next Generation* was first aired, and during its seven-year run this series was often the highest rated hour-long show among males 18 to 49 years of age, and a top-rated show among other viewer categories, including females. This success has led to still more spinoffs, including *Deep Space Nine* and *Voyager*.

No other popular culture phenomenon has shown the depth and breadth of fan activity that *Star Trek* has. The numbers are staggering: over 2 billion dollars in merchandise sold over the last 30 years; over 4 million novels sold every year (often bestsellers); several dictionaries of *Star Trek* alien languages, along with institutes that study them; "fanzines" numbering in the thousands; hundreds of fan clubs, conventions, online computer discussion groups, *Star Trek* role-playing and computer games, and now even entertainment centers and tourist sites; plus of course the endless reruns, broadcast in over 100 countries. Captain Kirk and Mr. Spock, the two main characters on the original series, became household names not only in the U.S. but in other English-speaking countries, along with the name of the spaceship they travel on, the *Enterprise*. Other popular culture productions, such as *Star Wars,* have fascinated fans, but none have produced the level of fan involvement and activity that *Star Trek* has sustained for over 30 years.

STAR TREK AS A RELIGIOUS PHENOMENON?

When I undertook research on the fan phenomenon, my earliest intention was to focus on how *Star Trek* draws a picture of the future that is attractive to many Americans. Early on, however, I realized I was dealing with something much bigger and more complex than I had anticipated. As I will show in this essay, *Star Trek* is not limited to science fiction fans, nor is it just a pop culture phenomenon created for corporate profit.

Instead, *Star Trek* fandom seemed akin to a religious movement. It has features that parallel a religious movement: an origin myth, a set of beliefs, organizations, and some of the most active and creative members found anywhere. Fans fill out a mythological universe and keep it consistent through the formation of a "canon" of acceptable and unacceptable *Star Trek* events. Within fandom, there are also the schisms and oppositions that such movements typically engender. Finally, there is a stigma associated with *Star Trek* fans that is similar to that directed against serious devotees of other religions. To address *Star Trek* as a religious phenomenon, however, we first need to understand the place of religion in our society, how it is changing, and what it is changing into.

RELIGION IN CONTEMPORARY AMERICAN SOCIETY

Most Americans think of "religion" as a system of private, conscious, and articulated beliefs, usually expressed in churches and formal creeds, and set off from the other "spheres" of life such as work, politics, or leisure. This view of religion, however, stems from the specifically Western process of societal "differentiation,"[4] in which institutional religion was given a specific function. After the medieval era, when religious practice was intimately connected to everyday life, the practice of Christianity became "abstracted," or disconnected from everyday life.[5] As a result, we now tend to regard "religion" as something connected to institutions such as churches and denominations. Alternatively, we view it as something personal and private, a psychological aid that is only peripherally connected to a person's public life.

This view of religion severely limits our understanding of it. A less ethnocentric definition regards religion as the daily, lived expression of an individual's or a society's most important values.[6] In many cultures, religion is not articulated as "belief," but is more often an ongoing experience, lived out and taken for granted.[7] But we often fail to recognize religion in our own society when it lacks an institutional and creedal form, and is instead "disguised" under various political or cultural forms. The fact that nearly every group has a religious dimension is regarded as obvious in many parts of the world, but is foreign to us, and makes us blind to religious aspects in many areas of our lives.[8]

Since at least the nineteenth century, scholars such as August Comte have been predicting the imminent downfall of religion in society. Religion may now be more "segregated" into its own private sphere, but Christianity has remained a potent force. New forms of religion have also developed, many of which are individualistic and express belief in the power of humanity and our mastery over the environment, whether through science or quasi-scientific or mystical philosophies. These modern-day religions are expressed in many areas of our culture, including popular culture, as Bruce David Forbes makes clear in the introduction to this volume. "New age" groups, for example, favor smaller networks and reject large-scale organization, but have a commonality fostered by commercialization and expressed in popular culture. In this essay, I argue that *Star Trek* is also a primary location for the expression of contemporary religious impulses.

SOMETHING TO "BELIEVE" IN:
THE WORLDVIEW OF STAR TREK

Star Trek is one of the most visible locations to witness religion in popular culture. Not only does it have an identifiable belief system and vision of the future, but the activities of its adherents are oriented toward participating in that vision and bringing it to fruition. *Star Trek* is a subset of the larger category of science fiction, which itself has been called a religion with a "central myth" of progress that "helps people live in or into the future." Science and technology are the vehicles by which this future will be brought into existence, "and should be understood in religious terms" as that which "breathes new life into humankind." [9]

The "positive view of the future" portrayed in *Star Trek* is one of the most common reasons fans give for their attraction to the show.[10] On

Star Trek, problems such as poverty, war, and disease have been eliminated on earth, and threats are normally from alien forces. Faith is placed
in the ability of humanity to solve its social and technical problems
through application of reason, science, and technology.

Star Trek mixes the scientific and technical ideals of America with its
egalitarian ideology, to produce a progressive world where people from
all races work together in a vast endeavor to expand knowledge. One fan,
recounting his first impressions of *Star Trek,* said: "We noticed people
of various races, genders and planetary origins working together. Here
was a future it did not hurt to imagine. Here was a constructive tomorrow for mankind, emphasizing exploration and expansion." [11]

As a result, *Star Trek* has taken its place in American mythology
alongside the "frontier" myth of westward expansion exemplified by
television westerns. Essentially, *Star Trek* is a projection of America's ex-
pansionist past into the future, a continual quest for more knowledge,
space, and resources. Anthropologist Conrad Kottak argues that *Star
Trek* is "a summation of dominant American cultural themes . . . a transformation of a fundamental American origin myth," akin to a "secular
myth" that emphasizes humanity's power to change the planet through
science and technology. [12]

This utopianism can be traced back to notions of Christian eschatology that foresee, in the context of a linear history, a future perfection.
Also tied in with utopian impulses is the Western notion of "order" out
of which came the "project" of the West, that of universal assimilation. [13]
On the heels of these beliefs have come many utopian religious movements, and such political religions as orthodox Marxism. It is this cul-
turewide ideological inclination towards future utopias that *Star Trek*
fandom draws upon. [14]

The belief in progress and a "positive view of the future" was explicitly articulated by the late creator of *Star Trek,* Gene Roddenberry. In
1991, just months before he died, a 30-page interview with Roddenberry was published in *The Humanist,* the official magazine of the American Humanist Association, to which Roddenberry had belonged since
1986. There he reveals that he had a very conscious humanist philosophy that saw humans taking control of their own destiny, and thus able
to control the future. Roddenberry's intention was to express his philosophy in *Star Trek,* but he had to keep this intention secret lest the network cancel his show. [15]

Others besides Roddenberry have used *Star Trek* to express their philosophy publicly. Jeffrey Mills has taught courses at various colleges on

"The Cultural Relevance of *Star Trek.*" He points to the Prime Directive (forbidding interference in another culture), the pluralistic Vulcan philosophy of IDIC (Infinite Diversity in Infinite Combination), and the cooperative governing structure of the United Federation of Planets as the kinds of ideas that we need to act on if we are to survive into the twenty-fourth century. By watching *Star Trek,* studying it, and applying its lessons, we can make the world a better place, Mills has written. "[I]n this light *Star Trek* almost becomes a sort of scripture, doesn't it? What the Bible does in 66 books, *Star Trek* does in 79 episodes. . . . I can't think of a series that really spoke to the future of humankind with as much clarity and vision as *Star Trek.*" [16]

In sum, *Star Trek* has strong affinities with a religious outlook, namely an underlying ideology and mythology that ties together messages about human nature and normative statements about social life with a construction and presentation of future society. Fans see *Star Trek* as a sign of hope for the future: not for personal salvation, but for the future of the collective "we," our society, our species. It is a myth about where we have come and where we are going. "I" will not live until the twenty-fourth century, but "we" certainly will, according to the *Star Trek* future. Fans, through their participation in fan activities, have shown they want to be a part of forming that destiny.

THE FANDOM COMMUNITY

Star Trek as a religious phenomenon can be understood as a set of beliefs, but the activities of its fans give us a much fuller picture of its religious potential. *Star Trek* fandom is in part the culmination of a phenomenon that began in the post–World War I era, when science fiction pulp magazines had a small but loyal readership. From the beginning, science fiction fans formed a group set apart from the rest of society. These fans formed a community, at first exclusively male, but with females entering later: "fans married fans and raised their children to be fans; there are third- and even fourth-generation fans beginning to show up these days at the 'cons'" [conventions]." [17]

It was out of science fiction fandom that the first *Star Trek* fans came. The story of the origin and growth of *Star Trek* fandom has itself taken on mythological proportions. A preview of the pilot episode of *Star Trek,* shown at a science fiction convention in 1966, is recounted almost in terms of a conversion experience:

"After the film was over we were unable to leave our seats. We just nodded at each other and smiled, and began to whisper." "We came close to lifting the man [Roddenberry] upon our shoulders and carrying him out of the room. . . . [H]e smiled, and we returned the smile before we converged on him." [18]

From then on, according to the author, the convention was divided into two factions: the "enlightened" who had seen the preview, and the "unenlightened" who had not.

Soon after *Star Trek* was first broadcast, fans formed organizations. *Star Trek* fan clubs have since grown into a diverse worldwide circuit of clubs, with over 500 clubs and chapters in nearly 20 countries. Many of these clubs are modeled after *Star Trek* ships, in a fan attempt at participation in the *Star Trek* universe. Hierarchy is established within each club by the titles given to leaders (Admiral, Captain, etc.). Members move up the hierarchy by being active in group events, much like in the Boy Scouts. Many fan clubs stress community service projects, which distinguishes them from a mere fan group and underlies the seriousness with which they take their beliefs about building a better world.

Star Trek fans often describe their fellow fans and clubs as a "family." They celebrate personal milestones such as birthdays and anniversaries, and console each other over misfortunes. Many remark that they are closer to fellow fans than they are to their own family members. Fans often meet at the nearly 100 annual *Star Trek* conventions. One fan described a convention in the following way:

> If you've never been to a convention, it's an experience that is difficult to explain. It's like being ushered into another world, where every facet of the day has something to do with STAR TREK. It might be seeing the incredible variety of merchandise in the dealers' room or seeing a star of the series in person and having the opportunity to ask questions. To describe it as a time warp would not be far from wrong. You're very much cut off from the real world in a convention. You can easily forget your own troubles as well as those of the world until the con ends and you have to come down to earth again.[19]

In other words, conventions are an opportunity to immerse oneself further in the *Star Trek* "experience," much as one is immersed in ritual. Using the religious language of "immersion" is not just a rhetorical move on my part. Witness the following quote, a response to a questionnaire I sent out over the internet:

> At a convention I went to a while back they had this thing about the "Temple of Trek." I stayed and watched—even participated in the chanting. They had some woman who was there with her baby—fairly newborn. And they "baptized" the kid into this pseudo-church. Pretty bizarre—even though it

was all just a joke. But I must admit—I was kind of wondering at the time if everyone there was really taking it all as a joke.

This ambiguity over the seriousness of Trek practice reveals, I believe, its underlying religious potential.

Fan activities that seek to promote a family atmosphere are in a sense "symbolic communities" that resist the secularization and rationalization of modern life.[20] Yet there is a paradox here if we seek to apply this to *Star Trek* fandom, because the ideology expressed in *Star Trek* and adhered to by many of the fans is an expression of rationalistic modernism itself, the progressive belief that we can construct a better tomorrow. In other words, the modernism that is exemplified by *Star Trek* is, in the final analysis, itself a faith that is practiced in the various types of communities that make up *Star Trek* fandom.

STAR TREK TOURISM, PILGRIMAGE, AND PARTICIPATION

For fans, *Star Trek* exhibitions and tourist sites have become popular places where fans can see and experience the *Star Trek* universe up close. The Universal Studios theme park in California has a *Star Trek* set in which selected tourists are filmed, in full uniform, taking on characters' roles and acting out a *Star Trek* plot. I visited one fan who proudly showed me the video of her visit there. The scenes of role-playing tourists were spliced with actual footage from one of the movies, giving the appearance that they were actually part of a *Star Trek* film. This fan described the experience "as a dream come true," which made the 2,000-mile trip "worthwhile." "We pilgrimage out there; it's our Mecca," she told me. Another fan showed me numerous pictures of herself posing in uniform on a mock-up of the *Enterprise* bridge that was built for a convention. It is the fan's dream to actually be on the show, and the closest thing to it are bridge mock-ups and studio tours. The ritual act of sitting on the bridge in uniform and being photographed or filmed brings one into direct participation in the *Star Trek* universe.

Participation in the *Star Trek* universe is even more direct through "simming" (playing *Star Trek* simulations over the internet with other fans). These games allow fans to take a position as a crew member on a "ship" and role-play adventures with other fans. Fans move up through the ranks as they gain experience. As one player described it, simming "allows anyone who embraces the precept of *Star Trek* and its premises of a bright future to be a part of that future," by providing "their own unique interpretations of how the future might look or how far 'we' might evolve in our quest for knowledge and our thirst for exploration." [21]

Finally, fans participate in the *Star Trek* universe by buying vast amounts of *Star Trek* merchandise and amassing videotaped collections of episodes and movies, a "capturing" of the *Star Trek* universe that enables fans to enter it at any time. Religion often points us to another world; *Star Trek* does the same.

LINKING THE STAR TREK UNIVERSE WITH THE PRESENT

The *Star Trek* universe is not a totally separate, fantastical universe unconnected to the present. In various ways, the *Star Trek* universe is "linked" with the contemporary world. The lead-in to every *Next Generation* episode ("Space: the final frontier. These are the voyages of the Starship *Enterprise* . . .") begins with a close-up of the earth, and then a gradual "tour" through the other planets of the solar system, until the camera finally focuses on the *Enterprise*. This sequence orients the viewer to envision the events as taking place in his own universe.

Other "linkage" is accomplished by the *Star Trek* manuals and novels. *Star Trek Chronology: A History of the Future* compiles a history of the universe, incorporating both actual historical events and *Star Trek* history through the twenty-fourth century.[22] This world is a direct projection from the present into the future. Furthermore, through time travel, many of the show's plots actually take place in twentieth-century time. One fan I talked to focused on how space and time is manipulated in time travel plots, which allows one "a second chance . . . to set things right again." Time travel allows us this ritualistic recourse, in much the same way healing rituals or rituals based on origin myths do. Origin myths often take place "in the beginning," but are really a message for all time, a model to be attained, enacted through ritual.[23]

Star Trek, like a religion, has profound effects on fans' lives. Actors often relate how fans have been inspired by the show to do well in school and eventually become engineers, doctors, or scientists.[24] *Star Trek* has given people hope for the future, inspiring them to take control of their lives in the same way many self-help movements and quasi religions do.[25] Fans also want to make "real" life more like *Star Trek*. *Star Trek* fans have been enthusiastic supporters of increased funding for the space program, and science fiction becomes science fact when "fans actively engineer events to make it true,"[26] such as by naming the first space shuttle prototype the USS *Enterprise*. Fans also point to devices such as the communicator, which foreshadowed today's portable phones.

FILLING OUT STAR TREK AND MAKING IT "REAL"

Star Trek, like many other shows, actively encourages a "suspension of disbelief" and sets itself up as a "reality" in which fans can exist. The reality of this universe is important to many people. As Richard Weiss, technical advisor to the Air Force, former head of a jet propulsion lab, and an "avowed trekkie," says, "I believe in *Star Trek*. It's all within the realm of possibility."[27] Dale Adams, who quit his job as an aerospace engineer to sell *Star Trek* merchandise, proclaims that "*Star Trek* isn't about a television series, it's about faith in our future."[28]

There has been an entire industry built up around "filling out" the *Star Trek* universe. Reference books such as the *Star Trek Encyclopedia* and *Star Trek: The Next Generation Technical Manual* (which details the specifications of Starfleet ships) have been among the most popular.[29] Dictionaries have been compiled for the languages of three *Star Trek* alien species: Klingon, Vulcan, and Romulan. The entire history, geography, philosophy, and even the purported location of the planet Vulcan has been described, sometimes with the full cooperation of people at academic institutions and even NASA.[30] There is a journal for the study of the Klingon language (*HolQed*), and a Klingon language camp one can attend. The *Star Trek* universe has been filled out with just about everything to make it a full, consistent reality, to enable one to live within this universe. This universe is much larger and more complex than any other fictional universe, such as that of the J. R. R. Tolkien novels and the game somewhat based on it, Dungeons and Dragons. *Star Wars* has also become an extremely popular universe, but without the realism and science found in *Star Trek*.

The coherence of this alternate universe must be maintained in order for fans to continue their "suspension of disbelief." As a result, there is a *Star Trek* "canon": as a regularly posted guide to one internet Usenet newsgroup defines it,

> "Canon" means that Gene Roddenberry (or his duly appointed representative) has declared something to be officially part of the "Star Trek" universe.

This includes the television episodes and the movies. "Non-canon" is every-thing else (the books, the animated series, comic books, the story you made up when you were playing "Star Trek" with your friends during recess . . .).[31]

The fans of *Star Trek* have taken this given universe of *Star Trek*—the canon—and filled it out in order to make a consistent, utopian world in which science has given us control over the problems of life we experi-ence and read about in the papers. Ironically, in order to complete the *Star Trek* universe, both the creators of the show and the fans have to rely on both science and magic. The technology used is given a veneer of scientific reality, but most fans recognize that most of the technology is made up, and is thus closer to magic. Science thus turns into magic, a state of affairs anticipated in new religions where magic/science is relied upon to provide control in areas outside our ability to master.[32]

I would argue that all of this fan creativity—the invention and filling out of an entire universe—is a creation of mythology similar to pro-cesses of mythological creation in other cultures through the ages. The anthropologist Claude Lévi-Strauss uses the term *bricoleur* (French for "handyman") to illustrate the process of creating mythology: *bricoleurs* use the available "tools" and "materials" of the culture to create a myth-ological structure over a period of time.[33] *Star Trek* fan *bricoleurs* act not on their own culture, but on the alternative (but related) one they have constructed. Creating new plots and stories and ironing out existing ones—discussing the canon and writing new fan literature to fill in gaps in character biographies, planet details, or technology—is essentially a way to resolve the contradictions which are an affront to the consistent universe that fans so desperately want to create.

In calling the activities of *Star Trek* fandom "mythological," I do not intend to eliminate the "playful" or entertainment aspect of *Star Trek* and claim that it is only serious. There is certainly a mix of entertain-ment and seriousness about *Star Trek* among fans, but this coexistence is also present in the creation of "primitive" mythology. Do the tradi-tional consumers of mythology take it to be only literally true? Here too, there is an ambiguous mixture of reality and unreality, of entertainment and mythology. One can see this in rituals that involve masking, where the masked figure personifies the ambiguity between the person under-neath the mask and the spirit which is the mask. Participation in a masked performance, as in the *Star Trek* universe, often involves pretending, but utterly serious pretending.[34]

Play is serious business, as Victor Turner makes clear in his discus-sion of the ludic aspects of ritual.[35] In industrial societies, however, play and seriousness have become separated. *Star Trek* fandom, I believe, is an example of play and ritual coming back together, back to their "natural" condition of coexistence and ambiguity. *Star Trek* fandom does not have the thoroughgoing seriousness of more established religions, but it is not mere entertainment. This interplay of seriousness and entertainment, I argue, is a sign of its vitality.

Religious movements are often persecuted or looked down upon because of their zealousness. And indeed, there is a stigma associated with *Star Trek* fandom. Non-fans react against the "seriousness" of *Star Trek* because they believe it should remain totally in the realm of entertainment, and the fact that people take it seriously offends them. *Star Trek* fans, in turn, want to be respected and understood, and want their devotion to be recognized as legitimate, even as many of them try to distance themselves from a segment of fans whom they believe to have gone "too far" in their fan activities. *Star Trek* elicits this type of controversy because it exists in the liminal area between entertainment and seriousness. It is in this interplay between "seriousness and diversion," a common feature of religion,[36] that we see the roots of the tension over *Star Trek* between its fandom and the general public.

CONCLUSION

In a society that has become more diverse (or, as some say, "disunited"), mass popular culture has become the new unifying element. By providing a certain commonality and unity of purpose for a wide variety of people, *Star Trek* takes on many elements of "civil religion": a generalizing of religious belief necessary for an integrated society, as a counter to pluralizing trends that divide society. In the U.S., it is expressed in a sense of national purpose and destiny, and includes notions of both moral and material progress.[37] These humanistic ideals become a model for others. This is exactly what seems to have happened by the time of *Star Trek*'s United Federation of Planets, the guardian of universal peace, prosperity, and self-determination, and a direct outgrowth of twentieth-century American faith in science, humanity, and a positive future. Fans latch on to the *Star Trek* vision that these ideals will eventually triumph, and they enthusiastically continue to fill out and participate in the *Star Trek* universe.

Americans are traditionally forward looking, and it is events like the space race that animate them. For many fans of popular culture, orga-

nized religion seems less relevant, partly because they perceive it as back-
ward looking rather than forward looking. Exceptions are to be found
among some conservative religious denominations that speak in specific
terms about the future, but enthusiasm for mainline denominations is
lacking among baby boomers, who regard them primarily as community organizations which can teach their children good values.[38]

Meanwhile, popular culture, especially television and film, attempts
to fill the religious void. In the ways described above, *Star Trek* has become a "cultural religion" (as discussed in the introduction to this volume) that reflects many Americans' most widely held beliefs. *Star Trek*
fandom expresses Americans' idealism, and offers fans reasons for hope
in the future. In this sense, it is a phenomenon born in popular culture
that has taken on serious, religious functions.

NOTES

1. See Peter Burke, *Popular Culture in Early Modern Europe* (New York:
Harper & Row, 1978).

2. See Bjo Trimble, *On the Good Ship Enterprise* (Norfolk, Va.: Donning,
1983), 22 ff.

3. "Fandom" is a term that is commonly used to describe people who actively follow specific TV, film, or other popular culture productions.

4. See Olivier Tschannen, "The Secularization Paradigm: A Systematiza-
tion," *Journal for the Scientific Study of Religion* 30 (1991): 395–415.

5. Talal Asad, "Anthropological Conceptions on Religion: Reflections on
Geertz," *Man* 18 (1983): 237–59, 245.

6. This corresponds with the "functional" definition of religion described by
Bruce David Forbes in the introduction to this volume.

7. Jean Pouillon, "Remarks on the Verb, 'to believe'," in *Between Belief and
Transgression*, ed. Michel Izard and Pierre Smith (Chicago: University of Chicago, 1982), 1–8.

8. Two writers who stress the changing and disguised forms of religion are
Thomas Luckmann ("Religion Old and New," in *Social Theory in a Changing Society*, ed. Pierre Bourdieu and James Coleman [Boulder, Colo.: Westview, 1991],
167–82, especially 169) and William H. Swatos, Jr. ("Enchantment and Disenchantment in Modernity: The Significance of 'Religion' as a Sociological Category," *Sociological Analysis* 44 [1983]: 321–338).

9. Frederick Kreuziger, *The Religion of Science Fiction* (Bowling Green,
Ohio: Bowling Green State University, 1986), 84, 15.

10. Numerous fans have stated this in personal interviews with me. See also
Jacqueline Lichtenberg et al., *Star Trek Lives!* (New York: Bantam, 1975), and
David Gerrold, *The World of Star Trek* (New York: Bluejay Books, 1984), first
published in 1973.

11. Alan Asherman, *The Star Trek Compendium* (New York: Pocket, 1989), 2.

12. Conrad Kottak, *Prime Time Society* (Belmont, Calif.: Wadsworth, 1990), 101–2; the phrase "secular myth" is from Pierre Hegy, *Myth as Foundation for Society and Values* (Lewiston, Maine: Edwin Mellen, 1991), 21.

13. See Michel-Rolph Trouillot, "Anthropology and the Savage Slot," in *Recapturing Anthropology*, ed. Richard Fox (Santa Fe: School of American Research, 1991), 17–44.

14. The popularity of the optimistic, progressive view of the world has normally been much stronger than the apocalyptic, pessimistic view (which also goes back to biblical apocalyptic themes). There have been popular science fiction movies in the apocalyptic vein (e.g., *Blade Runner*), but the initial draw of these movies did not coalesce into the popular universe created by the vast cultural acceptance of *Star Trek,* which demonstrates the resonance of a future universewide utopia.

15. See David Alexander, "Gene Roddenberry: writer, producer, philosopher, humanist," *The Humanist* 51 (March/April 1991): 5–38.

16. Steve Paulson, "Free Enterprise," *Isthmus,* 27 September 1991, 27–9, quotation from 29.

17. Frederik Pohl, "Astounding Story," *American Heritage* 40 (Sept/Oct 1989): 42–54, quotation from 47.

18. Alan Asherman, *The Star Trek Compendium* (New York: Pocket, 1989), 2.

19. James Van Hise, *The Trek Fan's Handbook* (Las Vegas: Pioneer Books, 1990), 90.

20. See Ken Thompson, "Secularization and Sacralization," in *Rethinking Progress,* ed. Jeffrey Alexander and Piotr Sztompka (Boston: Unwin Hyman, 1990), 161–81.

21. Jim Rubino, "Signing On for the New Voyages," *Dateline Starfleet* 21, March 1992.

22. Michael Okuda and Denise Okuda, *Star Trek Chronology: a history of the future* (New York: Pocket, 1993).

23. See Mircea Eliade, *Patterns in Comparative Religion* (New York: Meridian, 1958), especially 410 ff.

24. See, for example, James Doohan (with Peter David), *Beam Me Up, Scotty* (New York: Pocket, 1996), 209.

25. See Arthur Greil and David Rudy, "On the Margins of the Sacred," in *In Gods We Trust,* ed. Thomas Robbins and Dick Anthony (New Brunswick, N.J.: Transaction, 1990), 219–32, especially 226.

26. James Van Hise, *The Trek Fan's Handbook* (Las Vegas: Pioneer Books, 1990), 14.

27. "Defense Cuts Worry Departing Scientist," *Los Angeles Times,* 21 June 1993, B-14.

28. "Trekking Off to Harvey," *Chicago Tribune,* 27 June 1993, "Tempo SW"-2.

29. Michael Okuda et al., *The Star Trek Encyclopedia: A Reference Guide*

to the Future (New York: Pocket, 1997); Rick Sternbach and Michael Okuda, Star Trek: The Next Generation Technical Manual (New York: Pocket, 1991).

30. See, for example, the letters page of Sky & Telescope 82, no. 1 (July 1991): 5.

31. Otto Heuer, rec.arts.startrek "FAQ" (usenet post, 1992).

32. Swatos, "Enchantment and Disenchantment," 330. The 1997 Heaven's Gate suicide cult members are an example of those who mix science with pseudoscience, and they were also avid watchers of Star Trek.

33. Claude Lévi-Strauss, The Savage Mind (Chicago: University of Chicago Press, 1966), 16 ff.

34. Lessa and Vogt, Reader in Comparative Religion, 414.

35. Victor Turner, From Ritual to Theatre: The Human Seriousness of Play (New York: PAJ Publications, 1982), 32.

36. Lessa and Vogt, Reader in Comparative Religion, 414.

37. Robert Bellah, "Civil Religion in America" in American Civil Religion, ed. Russell E. Richey and Donald G. Jones (New York: Harper and Row, 1974), 21–44, especially 38–41.

38. Dean Hoge, Benton Johnson, and Donald Luidens, Vanishing Boundaries: The Religion of Mainline Protestant Baby Boomers (Louisville, Ky.: Westminster/John Knox Press, 1994), especially 75–7, 147–50, 159.

9

Michelle M. Lelwica

LOSING THEIR WAY TO SALVATION

Women, Weight Loss, and the
Salvation Myth of Culture Lite

On any given day, the majority of girls and women in the U.S. worry about their weight and its appearance on their bodies. Nearly two-thirds of adult women surveyed report that one of their greatest fears is becoming fat. Roughly the same percentage of high school girls monitor what and how much they eat, and in some urban areas up to 80 percent of fourth-grade girls have dieted. While the average woman in the U.S. is 5'4" and weighs 144 pounds, the average female model is 5'10" and weighs 111 pounds. Not surprisingly, diet books outsell any other books on the market, except the Bible. Meanwhile, nearly 5 percent of adolescent girls and young women suffer from anorexia, and up to 20 percent of college women suffer from bulimia.[1] Still, it is not unusual to see television ads like the one for "Nutri Systems," in which a slender, young, white woman announces that "Changing your body is as easy as changing your mind."

What are so many girls and women trying to change through their pursuit of a thinner body? What social conditions and popular-cultural images and rituals make this transformation seem not only possible, but necessary? The current craze of eating disorders has been the subject of numerous studies in the fields of psychology, sociology, and medicine, and a growing number of these studies underline the continuities between eating patterns that are deemed "pathological" (i.e., the self-starving and/or binge-and-purge tactics of anorexics and bulimics) and those that are widely recommended to girls and women as "healthy." However, few of these studies consider the religious resonances of these problems. In this essay, I explore the popular pursuit of female slenderness from a cultural and religious studies perspective. More precisely, I analyze and assess the language and ethos of a quasi-religious system that invites women to "save" their souls by shrinking their bodies.

SACRED AND SECULAR RITUALS: COMPLICATING THE DISTINCTION

This analysis presumes that the distinction between "secular" and "religious" meanings is less obvious than has traditionally been assumed. In his classic essay, "Religion As a Cultural System," Clifford Geertz cites the difference between ascetic fasting and dieting to illustrate the distinction between "religious" and "secular" behavior. This distinction, Geertz argues, is based in these practices' diverging ends, and thus the varying frames of meaning and dispositions they foster. Whereas weight reduction aims to achieve a "conditioned" goal, religious fasting is "directed toward an unconditioned end"; whereas dieting is tied to worldly values (presumably health and beauty), religious fasting takes its meaning and motivation in reference to "a conception of all-pervading vitality," a picture of "a general order of existence."[2]

At first glance, Geertz's distinction makes a lot of sense. One need only watch TV for an evening, page through a popular women's magazine, listen to a schoolgirl insist she is "too fat," or hear a doctor telling you to "watch what you eat" to witness the this-worldly quality of America's pursuit of thinness. And yet, a closer reading of these weight-reduction discourses suggests that something more, something of vast importance, is being summoned, weighed, and reckoned in this pursuit, especially among its female participants. The more one probes this "something," the more the distinction between "secular" and "religious" behavior fades, and the more one begins to see that for many girls and women, creating a slender body has become a matter of all-pervading significance, an end whose achievement feels tantamount to ultimate salvation.

Over thirty years ago, anthropologist Mary Douglas, in her book *Purity and Danger,* recognized the fluidity of the distinction between sacred and secular practices.[3] More recently, Catherine Bell's work highlights how power operates in the creation of this distinction. In *Ritual Theory, Ritual Practice,* Bell uses the concept of "ritualization" to draw attention to the culturally embedded and power-laden character of meaning production in ritual activity.[4] For Bell, the significance of ritual practices rests not in their inherent distinction from other ways of acting, but in their capacity to constitute themselves as different from, and holier than, more mundane ways of acting. Rooted in the "ritualized body," ritual meaning is strategically generated both in relation to prevailing social values and norms, and in reference to "realities thought to transcend the powers of human actors."[5]

FEMALE DIETING AS A POPULAR-CULTURAL RITUAL AND A "NEW RELIGION"

In short, Bell's work offers a way of thinking about female dieting as a popular-cultural rite of womanhood: a ritualizing practice through which a woman's body is distinguished and sacralized, her anxieties and dreams generated and regulated, and the prevailing social order negotiated and reproduced. As part of a broader system of cultural beliefs and practices, weight-loss rituals do not simply create an ideal female body; they generate a worldview, an embodied sense of self-definition, and a precarious method for coping with the conflicting possibilities of life in the late twentieth century. "After a time," a woman who dieted compulsively writes,

> the number on the scale became my totem, more important than my experience—it was layered, metaphorical, metaphysical, and it had bewitching power. I thought if I could change that number I could change my life. . . . I would weigh myself with foreboding, and my weight would determine how went the rest of my day, my week, my life.[6]

In the U.S., land of maldistributed abundance, most girls know the language of dieting, often from firsthand experience, by the time they are ten years old. Rituals of avoiding some foods while measuring others are not only common among females in this culture: they are habitual. So too are the ritual encounters with the number on the scale, and so are the losses of control that often follow restricted eating. To be sure, the range of dieting varies considerably. Some diets involve specific food plans; others focus on technique. Some are formally prescribed by doctors; others are commercially bought and sold. Still others are informally devised and implemented, broken and resumed.[7] Despite these variations, however, dieting involves the routinization, calculation, and regulation of eating. For many women, this disciplined mode of nourishment is not only habitual: it is, true to its name, "a way of life."[8]

The desire to minimize the female body's appetites and size is, of course, neither natural nor universal. In most cultures, especially those where food supplies are unstable, large female bodies are not only tolerated, but desired.[9] Even in this culture, prior to the twentieth century, female plumpness was generally seen as a sign of health, beauty, and prosperity, and calculating one's food intake entailed an interruption of ordinary ways of eating.[10]

A network of historical shifts and cultural conditions have made slenderness the prevailing ideal, and weight loss a seemingly viable strategy for making meaning among women today. In particular, the axiomatic belief that women can and should monitor what they eat stems from a confluence of modern developments, including the belief that "the self" is an autonomous individual, the reconception of the body as a machine, and the rise of new scientific, technological, and economic systems of power, in conjunction with a long-standing and still-powerful symbolic association between women and bodily concerns.

The various threads of this confluence are evident in the history of dieting in the West, a story that begins not with the notorious fasting practices of medieval holy women but with the new mode of restricted eating that emerged with the rise of modern scientific authority.[11] Beginning in the sixteenth century, this new way of eating combined the quest for spiritual truth with the pursuit of improved health; it focused on measuring and regulating one's food intake; and its rules and guidelines were encoded in the texts of religiously motivated men.[12] By the seventeenth and eighteenth centuries, the practice of restricting one's eating to augment one's health was bolstered by a mechanistic worldview, which reconceptualized the body (seen as an extension of the natural world and similarly gendered feminine) as passive, manipulable, subject to and in need of rational mastery and control.[13]

According to Bryan S. Turner, the rise of a mechanistic worldview in the modern period involved a "secularization of the body," whereby the body as the site of sin and salvation became the object of scientific scrutiny.[14] But this transfer of meaning was neither stable nor complete. For even as the growing authority of science was eroding religious reasons for appetite surveillance by the turn of this century, a new set of moral meanings ("bad" and "good") were attached to bodies ("fat" and "thin"), thus suggesting a lingering relevance of religious models and meanings. In the rational codes of modern science, variation came to mean deviation, for which there was scant excuse given the presumed autonomy of the self and mechanics of the body: if 3,500 calories equals one pound, then losing weight is a matter of simple arithmetic.[15]

For all its scientific underpinnings, the expanding pursuit of the narrow body hinged on a symbolic system whose patterns resembled some of the moral codes and ritualizing techniques of traditional Christianity. In her historical account of this society's obsession with weight control, Roberta Seid suggests that the fervor with which contemporary Americans pursue thinness borders on the religious:

> If sloth and gluttony have always been condemned as sins, we have taken those sins as the cornerstone of a new faith. We believe in physical perfectibility and see its pursuit as a moral obligation. The wayward are punished with ugliness, illness, and early death. The good get their just rewards: beauty and a blessedly long, happy, and fulfilling life. The virtue that presumably will put us on this road is our ability to control one of our most fundamental instincts— eating.

In Seid's view, this "new religion" has become so pervasive, and so persuasive, in the latter half of this century because it meshes so well with some of America's most cherished beliefs, including a faith in the objectivity of science and a belief in the ideal of individual self-control.[16]

"CULTURE LITE" AND THE FITNESS ETHIC

During the past few decades, these beliefs have been incorporated into and promulgated by the systems of consumer capitalism. In particular, they support a network of industries, products, and programs designed to reduce our appetites and bodies. Organized around the pursuit of thinness, especially the flab-free female form, this soteriology (salvation myth) draws on and sustains a language and ethos through which female dieting makes sense. Its objectifying vision and reductive measures underwrite this culture's prevailing iconography of womanhood (exemplified, e.g., in magazine images of "model" women). It is the other side of the prevailing cultural war on fat. I refer to it as "Culture Lite."

Mainstream manifestations of Culture Lite are evident in the explosion of various slenderizing industries and products during the second half of this century. In the 1950s, sales of weight-loss aids (from bathroom scales to diet books, low calorie foods to amphetamines) began to soar.[17] By 1984, nearly a fifth of the $290 billion spent on retail foods in the U.S. went for "lite" and "lo-calorie" foods. At this time, diet food and soft drink sales were increasing three times as fast as those of regular foods and beverages. Meanwhile, revenues of commercial diet centers grew exponentially, despite statistics indicating that over 90 percent of those enrolled in these programs regain their weight within two to seven years. Over-the-counter drugs for weight control have also become increasingly popular, not to mention profitable, with sales climbing at a rate of 20 percent each year. In 1995, the book about the diet that made Oprah Winfrey thin was hailed as "the fastest-selling book in history." Dieting today is estimated to be a $50 billion business, and by this century's turn, Americans are predicted to spend $77 billion trying to shed their "excess" flesh.[18]

The mechanisms of Culture Lite have not simply accelerated during the past few decades; they have also changed, making the pursuit of the fat-free body more dispersed, more mandatory, and more deeply entrenched in profit-seeking ventures. This trend is illustrated in the rise of the "fitness ethic," a prominent but distinct current within Culture Lite that emerged in the late 1960s.[19] What distinguishes this ethic's practices from its mainstream counterparts is that both its marketers and consumers claim that its primary goal is not slenderness per se, but overall "health," signified by a body that is light and lean.

Like the ascetic Christian disciplines that it implicitly takes as its models, the fitness ethic began as a countercultural critique. In particular, it challenged mainstream eating and dieting practices, promoting nutritious food and moderate exercise as means for mental and spiritual renewal. Before long, however, this alternative was absorbed by the very powers it meant to criticize: the giant food and weight-loss industries. While this co-optation produced the current markets for "natural" foods, it also reinterpreted the fitness ethic beyond recognition. Concerns about healthy eating and "living lightly," by which the counterculture meant watching the earth's resources, came to mean counting calories and fat grams, whereby mostly middle-class white women were encouraged to watch their waistlines.[20]

As it turns out, the difference between "mainstream" weight-loss practices and those comprising the "fitness ethic" is far from clear. In the wider context of Culture Lite, the call to "overall health and fitness" is not easily distinguishable from the imperative to lose weight. Given this culture's axiomatic preference for female slenderness, fitness-oriented rhetoric usually implies the need for women to reduce. Surveys indicate that most women who exercise do so primarily in order to lose weight.[21] Commercial enticements and exhortations to "Get Healthy! Feel Fit! Lose Weight!" (to quote an ad for Joan Lunden's *Workout America* home video) end up conflating health, aesthetic, and moral concerns. This conflation contributes to the apparent "naturalness" of the thin ideal, an aura that makes the call to slenderness all the more difficult to contest.

THE QUASI-RELIGIOUS POWERS OF CONSUMER
CAPITALISM AND THE CULT OF THINNESS

The adoption of the "fitness ethic" by commercial weight-loss industries illustrates the mechanics of modern domination: prevailing cultural hegemonies (systems of power) operate by accommodating and profiting from new developments within the social order, even when these developments are critical of its systems. In many ways, the profit-seeking ethos of consumer capitalism seems both omnipresent and omniscient, supplanting an omnipotent creator as the invisible ground of transcendent power. Given its quasi-religious function, it is not surprising that some of this system's rhetorical maneuvers employ the terms of traditional religion, particularly the language of this country's dominant tradition: Christianity.

The degree to which this rhetoric alludes to or conjures up recognizably religious motifs varies considerably among advertising texts and their viewers. Still, such techniques are relatively common amid the symbolic galaxy of consumer/media culture. Choir music and personal confession are regular features of television commercials; words like "ultimate," "pure," "total," and "perfection" are used to sell a wide assortment of consumer items, from breakfast cereals to new cars. Given that the average American is exposed to 1,500 ads each day and is likely to spend one-and-a-half years of her or his life watching television commercials, it is reasonable to suggest that advertisements are a crucial conduit for communicating traditional religious values, both in spite of and because of their "secular" content.[22]

The commercial use of traditional religious idioms and terms has come to play a particularly prominent role in the soteriology of Culture Lite. Within this system, producing a body that is fit and trim has become a middle-class mode of spiritual "enlitenment." That such enlitenment depends on consumption is not a problem within the logic of late capitalism. A magazine ad for a fat-burning candy bar, featuring a lean, athletic-looking woman, tells us that by eating this product we can "Burn it off." The ethic of control that underwrites this trope of forgiveness is seen in another ad for a fat-burning product, which summons its readers to "Show those pesky fat cells no mercy." More subtle tactics of domination / enlitenment are sold in products like "The Cellulite Solution," the "Chews to Lose" weight-loss gum, the "Totally Fit" workout video (available in Spanish), or the "Think Like A Thin Person" tape series (at Sharper Image for just $69.95).

TRADITIONAL RELIGIOUS DISCOURSE IN THE CONTEMPORARY CULT OF THINNESS

Precisely because weight-reducing rituals engage their users' hungers for a sense of meaning, many of their terms and promises resemble those of traditional religion. The penitential aspects of losing weight are implicit in the New Year's cover stories of *People* magazine: "Diet Wars: Who's Winning, Who's Sinning" (1992) and "Diet Winners and Sinners of the Year" (1994).[23] Indeed, the continuities between the salvation myth of Culture Lite and the discourses of biblical religion are sometimes quite explicit. A weight-loss program called "Happy Losers" motivates its members with the saying:

> The diet is within me I shall not cheat
> It leadeth me to choose the legal food
>   whenever I have the urge to eat
> Yea though I may wish to eat sweets or cake
> I shall eat them never
> For the diet is with me
> And I shall reach my goal
> And remain slim forever. Amen.[24]

In other cases, the weight-loss "gospel" is constructed and preached through conversion idioms of before-and-after. Several diet franchises were founded by women who confessed and capitalized on their "personal" weight-loss sagas.[25] The evangelical tone of these enterprises echoes in the words of "fitness diva" Susan Powter: "Four years ago . . . I was an unfit person—a very, very, very unfit person," referring to the days when she allegedly weighed 260 pounds. Now weighing 115 pounds, with shaved and bleached white hair, she quips: "I'm just a housewife who figured it out."[26]

Confessed and converted, Powter presents a female rendition of the "American Dream." Unlike the famous fitness gurus of previous decades (e.g., Jack Lalane and Richard Simmons), Powter displays a female body that many women can envision themselves becoming. Moreover, in contrast to her female counterpart, Jane Fonda, Powter appeals to women without unusual social privilege: women like herself, she claims, reminding disciples of her unhappy fat days in the Dallas suburbs, where her husband abandoned her and her two children for a woman who was thin. In the spirit of the fitness ethic, Powter criticizes "mainstream" weight-loss programs such as Jenny Craig. Her "alternative" includes a "wellness kit" (which has five motivational audio cassettes, an exercise video, a booklet with recipes and fat guides, and a caliper to measure body fat), in addition to her best-selling book *Stop the Insanity,* a quarterly audio newsletter, and a paid infomercial which reached nearly 50 million viewers every three days when it first aired. Needless to say, Powter is a millionaire. But that, she says, is not the point. Her goal, she insists, is to empower women like herself, which can only happen when they slim down and shape up so the world will take them seriously.[27]

Powter's mixture of evangelical tone and democratic rhetoric is a recurrent theme in Culture Lite, where distinctions of worth are made by transforming the ordinary practices of daily life into opportunities for self-improvement:

> Park a few blocks away from work and walk; or better yet, ride your bike. And take the stairs instead of the elevator. Stand rather than sit. Walk rather than stand. Walk briskly rather than slowly. This way you can nudge up the caloric expenditure.[28]

On an obvious level, such advice suggests that burning calories is the underlying goal of fitness-oriented activities. More subtly, however, the mundane focus of this rhetoric masks the ritualizing function that weight-loss strategies implicitly serve. Walking briskly rather than slowly, taking the stairs rather than the elevator . . . such practices create more than a taut and trim physique. They also produce a sense of purpose, an embodied sense that links an individual's experience to a wider social order, and ultimately (if implicitly) to a cosmic scheme, a conception of "the general order of existence" (Geertz) within which life is meaningful.

The ritualizing function of Culture Lite, its capacity to transform life's banal materials into ultimate meaning, is further illustrated in popular food products whose labels bear the saving words: "lo-cal" or "fat-free."[29] An ad for Diet Coke, featuring the standard figure of a slender young white woman, entices consumers by reference to ecstatic religious experience. "To the Novice," the copy reads:

Many of our loyal drinkers equate the indescribable taste of a Diet Coke with that of something in the spiritual realm. However, if this is your first time, we do advise that after drinking one, you resist the urge to run out into the street, toss your beret in the air and exclaim to a slightly bewildered crowd "I'm gonna make it after all!!" While we are not disputing these emotions of exuberance, a display of this kind could be confusing to the non-Diet Coke drinker, thus resulting in ostracism from the community, perhaps to a strange land that does not serve Diet Coke.[30]

Such is the longed-for rapture that the monotonous fare of Culture Lite can engender. Though the details of its products, rhetoric, and programs vary, the "truths" around which the pursuit of thinness spins its often vicious circles seem as indisputable as the numerical values (both scientific and monetary) through which they are measured. In the words of a smiling woman, who in an ad for Weight Watchers testifies that she lost over 8 pounds in 14 days: "The scales don't lie."

THE SOCIAL POLITICS OF DIVERSION:
FUELING AND EN-GENDERING THE MYTH

The salvation myth of Culture Lite is fueled by a broader culture of self-deception, however. More specifically, the search for a sense of meaning that America's battle with the bulge both masks and reveals represents a large-scale attempt not merely to manage this society's apparent abundance, but more importantly to divert attention away from the damaging effects of its grossly uneven distribution. According to the ethos and logic of Culture Lite, it is good to have excess in your billfold but not on your body, and it is right to want to change your thighs but dangerous, indeed crazy, to want to change the world.

Organized around the pursuit of female slenderness, Culture Lite is a central nerve in this society's politics of distraction: the wide-scale diversion of attention away from the prevailing values and actual conditions that undermine individual and social well-being. On one level, the prominence of diet culture stems from its ability to synthesize a number of authoritative discourses and beliefs, thus offering diverse Americans what traditional religion no longer does: a common, public frame of meaning which appeals and applies across competing party lines. On another level, this prominence stems from its resonance with certain paradigms and values of traditional Christianity, especially those which sanctify oppressive relations of power by defining salvation as a state of perfection one achieves (or receives) in another space and time.

The salvation myth of Culture Lite is not simply otherworldly: it is also both patriarchal and feminized. For the modern beliefs that fuel the quest for the lean and well-managed body, particularly the notion that individuals can and should control their own destiny, have special meaning for those whose destinies have historically been tied to their anatomies. More specifically, the long-standing view of women as spiritually uncomplicated servants of men and as objects of devotion or temptation, together with women's historical exclusion from formal realms of power, and their modern duties as household servants, ornaments of beauty, domestic scientists, and consumers, has cast them in a leading role in the quest for the fat-free body. In this drama, modern beliefs in the autonomy of the self, the manipulability of the flesh, the authority of science, and the promises of consumer capitalism merge with traditional visions of womanhood, revising without upsetting women's age-old identification with and through their bodies by demanding their increasingly strict mastery over them. In a society whose prevailing symbols, rituals, and social arrangements continue to conflate female anatomy and destiny, it is not altogether surprising that women learn to seek salvation both from and with their bodies. In a culture where female anatomy is evaluated largely according to its size and contours, it makes sense that rituals aimed to regulate the body's weight and appetites figure prominently in this soteriological quest.

THE REWARDS OF PUNISHMENT: HUNGRY BODIES, SOCIAL APPROVAL, AND SELF-DEFINITION

Despite this grim description, my analysis of the operations and conventions of Culture Lite suggest that this quasi-religious system of meaning is best seen as a context, rather than as a conspiracy. No one forces girls and women to diet. At the same time, losing weight has become an extremely compelling, if often debilitating, practice for so many of them. To understand this conundrum is to recognize that what makes this plan of salvation so compelling among so many different girls and women are the rewards it promises and, at least partially, delivers.

Practices aiming to slenderize the female body create their own rewards, including a sense of social approval and a feeling of self-determination. Women's own accounts of their weight-loss quests illustrate the extent to which the applause of others is an enticing factor in their struggles to be thin: "The more the clothes hung, the more the compliments grew. 'What kind of diet are you on; you haven't looked this good in ages; why, you look like you've lost ten years. . . .'"[31] For girls and women of color, losing weight may represent not so much an acceptance of prevailing (i.e., Euro-American) ideals of feminine health and beauty, but rather a rejection of widespread cultural stereotypes. A young Black woman who temporarily lost forty pounds following "The Model's Ten Day Diet" recalls: "Afterwards, no one dared to call me Fat Alberta, and my relatives extolled me for my weight loss and referred to me as a 'real teenager,' as though prior to the weight loss I was insignificant."[32] Undeniably, the social applause that accompanies weight loss may temporarily ease the pain of long-standing cultural stereotypes and prejudices. It does so, however, by reinstating the narrowly defined standards and values that keep an unjust social order intact.[33]

In addition to the social approval it generates, losing weight is a compelling practice because of the autonomy it requires and fosters. By deciding what, how much, or whether to eat, a woman exercises a kind of self-determination that has historically been the prerogative of men. In her daily rituals of self-surveillance (counting calories, doing leg-lifts, checking in mirrors, refusing dessert, etc.), a woman gains the feeling of control that she does not experience in other areas of her life. In one woman's words: "Food was power and control. Food was making my own decisions about what I would eat, when I would eat, how much I would eat. Food was taking control over what I looked like."[34]

The fact that some of the primary rituals this culture proffers girls and women for cultivating a sense of agency and worth require obedience to prevailing ideals of womanhood suggests the limits of the power that dieting produces. Frigga Haug's work on female socialization suggests that these everyday rites are precisely the means whereby "society as a whole re-creates itself."[35] As Susan Bordo points out, weight-loss practices reward women with a sense of autonomy by rendering them more subservient, more pliable and more "useful" to an oppressive social order.[36] Although such rituals can foster a sense of agency and purpose, they do so by reproducing the classic scenario of patriarchal religion, in which a woman's salvation depends on her sacrifice, self-denial, and submission.

EMBODYING PURPOSE, PRIVILEGE,
AND SELF-CONTROL

By ritualizing some of the most banal of all human activities—eating and moving—women's weight-loss practices harness the power of those two elements that history seems to have granted them: food and body. Through the privileged contrasts they create, these rites generate opportunities for experiencing something more, something better, something beyond the vicissitudes of life on earth, something sacred in a disenchanted world. In these rites, necessities become possibilities. And possibilities become profits. In the U.S. today, reducing the female form is highly profitable business, not simply because of its almost perfectly predictable lack of permanent success, but also because of the sense of purpose it fosters among those who are overwhelmed by the inequities and pluralities of life today.

On some level, weight-loss rituals "work" by creating simple and accessible solutions to the questions "What do I want?" and "What should I do?"—questions that have grown ever more complicated amid this culture's movements and backlashes. The industries of Culture Lite capitalize on the eclipse of Truth and the dispersion of meanings that these shifts entail by providing an array of "Answers," even before any questions are raised. The attraction of these "Answers" rests in the agency they presume, and in the tangible and immediate results they imply. Promotions for diet programs often begin with the promise "In Just One Week. . . ." A television ad for Bally's fitness centers assures potential converts / consumers that "Twenty-four dollars is all it takes to turn your life around."

In particular, diet industries cash in on the changing expectations of womanhood that have emerged during the past three decades, by appropriating and reinterpreting the feminist assertion that "biology is not destiny." An article in *Vogue* entitled "Redefining the Body" encourages women to use "body sculpting" to produce a "look" that is "both strong and feminine." This technique involves "chiseling one's body fat to expose the muscle." Such a standard applies to every woman, the author warns, "no matter what shape you're born with." [37] A similar article on body sculpting features a close-up of a woman's firmly shaped butt, grabbed by her hand which bears an expensive-looking ring. The copy at the corner of the page explains: "A firm fundament announces to the world that the owner controls her own destiny—and can wear an ass-grabbing thong with aplomb." [38]

The growing popularity of body sculpting among economically elite women suggests the multiple ironies through which popular codes of womanhood are ritually defined and consumed. Women, who are generally born with a higher ratio of fat on their bodies, are seen to perfect themselves in proportion to the amount of fat they eradicate from their bodies, especially those parts of their bodies seen to mark them as "female" (hips, buttocks, stomach, thighs). That breasts are supposed to stay inflated and plump while the rest of the body is flattened and trimmed underlines the unattainability, aside from surgical alteration, of this bodily ideal. Moreover, muscles, which have traditionally been associated with masculinity and working-class life, are transcribed onto female bodies to signify social privilege: these are bodies whose "owners" have time and money to spend at the health club.[39] Finally, women of color, who have been virtually excluded from the public sphere except when their labor was needed for jobs that nobody else cared to do, now have role models like Black fitness guru Victoria Johnson instructing them to "shape up for summer without ever leaving home."[40]

Despite its egalitarian coating, the salvation myth of Culture Lite reproduces an association between the fat-free body, material privilege, and individual self-control. A magazine ad for Nestle's dark chocolate fudge diet product called "Sweet Success" illustrates this nexus. The ad features a slender female torso wearing an elegant black dress. The figure is outlined in a way that conveys an image of a paper doll: depthless, playful, and ultimately headless. Given prevailing definitions of female "success" in the U.S. today, losing weight is not only a gendered practice, it is also racially, generationally, heterosexually, and economically inflected. Market research profiles of the typical dieter—a woman who is white, urban, married, employed, well educated, financially sound, and between the ages of 25 and 44—underline this point.[41]

The belief that undergirds the call to slenderness, that every body can and should get fit "no matter what shape you're born with," ignores women's uneven access to the cultural "goods" that the fat-free body requires. Neither the time nor the accoutrements through which middle- and upper-class female bodies are trimmed and distinguished (health clubs, home exercise equipment and videos, and so on) are affordable to women from lower income brackets. Even exercise that seems to be free, such as walking or jogging, is a limited option for those who live in neighborhoods where simply being outside is unsafe.[42] Commercial diet foods are expensive, and so-called "healthy" or "lo-fat" foods usually cost more (even though they are often cheaper to produce).[43] As it turns out, creating a flab-free female body is far from free, and despite occasional moments of color, Culture Lite is very white.

By highlighting the social hierarchies that underwrite the soteriology of Culture Lite, I mean to underline the varying meanings and effects of this pursuit among girls and women in different social locations. By showing how this plan of salvation is constructed through various forms of gender, racial, economic, sexual, and generational privilege, I want to question the quality of the "freedom" and "purpose" that slenderizing rituals produce. As more and more girls and women turn to weight loss as a strategy for making meaning out of the inequities and contradictions that fill their lives, as consumer markets encourage them to shape up and burn fat "without ever leaving home," as elite women worship and imitate an ideal defined through economic and racial exploitation, as minority girls and women join the majority in hating their bodies, as industries' profits get fatter by making female bodies and imaginations smaller, those with critical consciousness and religious faith must take a serious look at what is really being gained and lost in the saving promises of Culture Lite.

REINVENTING WOMANHOOD:
"IS THIS A NEW RELIGION?"

A few years ago, I came across a magazine ad for Avia running shoes, whose text inspired my present inquiry. "Is This a New Religion?" the boldfaced copy asked its readers. The central image of the two-page ad features a young, taut, and sweating female body, dressed in a leotard, arms extended in a gesture that recalls a crucifix. This image is flanked by two others: on one side, the same sweating woman bent over and lifting weights, muscles and bosom accentuated by a bluish haze; on the other, a close-up of the shoes cast in the same mystifying light. Together these images form a triptych, but the religious motifs do not stop there. In the upper corners of each page, the ad addresses its own query:

> This is not about guilt. It's about joy. Strength. The revival of the spirit. I come here seeking redemption in sweat. And it is here I am forgiven my sinful calories. Others may never understand my dedication. But for me, fitness training is something much more powerful than exercise. It is what keeps my body healthy. It is what keeps my mind clear. And it is where I learn the one true lesson. To believe in myself. AVIA.

On an obvious level, this text illustrates the affinities between, on the one hand, contemporary diet and fitness rituals, and, on the other hand, the terms and beliefs of traditional Christianity. More subtly, however, it suggests that women's subordination within traditional religion makes them prime candidates for this "secular" substitute. Defined through an ostensibly progressive rejection of biblical religion's most notoriously harmful features, its degradation of women and the body, this commercial alternative proffers a new ultimate point of reference, Womanhood Herself: revived and redeemed, made powerful and clear through a diligently trained and slender body. Juxtaposing a stereotypical view of Christianity (characterized by guilt, damnation, and belief in female weakness) with a liberal vision of "a New Religion" (defined by joy, redemption, and affirmation of female strength), this ad speaks to those whose need for meaning remains unfulfilled by the promises of traditional religion, and whose dreams have been further delayed or lost in the shuffle of a rapidly changing and unevenly conflicted world.

In the end, perhaps, the question that the Avia ad raises is not simply whether women's pursuit of physical perfection constitutes a new religion, but also what kind of religion this pursuit turns out to be.

NOTES

1. A number of surveys indicate that the majority of women in this country already see themselves as "too fat." A 1984 survey conducted by Drs. Susan and Orland Wooley in conjunction with *Glamour* magazine found that 76 percent of its readers wanted to lose weight ("Feeling Fat in a Thin Society," *Glamour,* February 1984, 198–201). A 1994 survey conducted in connection with *Essence* magazine found 71.5 percent of the respondents to be preoccupied with the desire to be thinner, and over two-thirds engaging in potentially dangerous weight-loss practices (Linda Villarosa, "Dangerous Eating," *Essence,* January 1994, 19–21, 87). Kelly Brownell cites a 1987 Harris poll which showed that of the 96 percent of persons who wanted to change something about their bodies, 78 percent of the women desired to change their weight; see "Dieting and the Search for the Perfect Body: Where Physiology and Culture Collide," *Behavior Therapy* 22 (1991): 1–12, especially 6; see also Rita Freedman, *Bodylove: Learning to Like Our Looks—and Ourselves* (New York: Harper and Row, 1988), 82. My statistics for fourth-grade girls reflect studies done in the Chicago and San Francisco areas; among the many places this study is cited is Joan Jacobs Brumberg, *Fasting Girls: The History of Anorexia Nervosa* (New York: Penguin, 1988), 32. Figures comparing average models with average women are cited in Katherine

Gilday's documentary film *The Famine Within* (1992). On the sale of diet books, see Roberta Pollack Seid, *Never Too Thin: Why Women are at War with Their Bodies* (New York: Prentice Hall, 1989), 4, 21. For diet industry figures, see J. Silberner, "War of the Diets," *U.S. News and World Report,* 3 February 1992, 55–60. For statistics on bulimia and anorexia, see W. Cromie, "One in Five Female Undergraduates Has Eating Problem," *Harvard University Gazette,* 7 May 1993, 3, 10; K. A. Halmi et al., "Binge Eating and Vomiting: A Survey of a College Population," *Psychological Medicine* 11 (1981): 483–91; S. Nevo, "Bulimic Symptoms: Prevalence and Ethnic Differences Among College Women," *International Journal of Eating Disorders* 4 (1985): 151–168.

2. Clifford Geertz, "Religion as a Cultural System," in *The Interpretation of Cultures* (New York: Basic Books, 1973), 87–125, quotations from 98, 89.

3. Mary Douglas, *Purity and Danger: An Analysis of the Concepts of Pollution and Taboo,* 1966 (New York: Routledge, 1991). In this work, Douglas argues that "rituals of purity and impurity" such as dietary restrictions and avoidances are central to religious behavior. At the same time, she notes, "very little of our ritual behaviour is enacted in the context of religion" (2–3, 68–9, 72).

4. Catherine Bell, *Ritual Theory, Ritual Practice* (New York: Oxford University Press, 1992), 8, 67, 74. In sum, Bell's theory highlights how rituals make meanings, rather than have or reflect meanings. Ritual practices do not dramatize the symbols they reference; instead, they generate their meanings for practical (rather than logical or universal) purposes. In this understanding, "ritual" has more the quality of a verb than a noun, and its power is productive.

5. Bell, *Ritual Theory, Ritual Practice,* 48–9, 83–5, 90. Bell is drawing on the insights of Antonio Gramsci, Pierre Bourdieu, and Michel Foucault. From Gramsci, she uses the concept of "hegemony" to highlight "the dominance and subordination that exist within people's practical and un-self-conscious awareness of the world. . . . This awareness is a lived system of meanings, a more or less unified moral order, which is confirmed and nuanced in experience to construct a person's sense of reality and identity" (82–3). Bell's notion of the "ritualized body" is close to Bourdieu's concept of the "socially informed body," the body that has been taught to think, feel, act and appear a certain way in a given social milieu (80). From Foucault, Bell picks up the idea that the body is basic to all sociopolitical relations of power (202).

6. Sallie Tisdale, "A Weight that Women Carry: The Compulsion to Diet in a Starved Culture," in *Minding the Body: Women Writers on Body and Soul,* ed. Patricia Foster (New York: Doubleday, 1994), 15–31, quotation from 17.

7. Seid, *Never Too Thin,* 5, 102. Seid lists a number of popular diets in the first chapter of her book.

8. The word "diet" stems from the Greek word *diaita,* meaning "way of life." See Bryan S. Turner, *The Body and Society: Explorations in Social Theory* (New York: Basil Blackwell, 1984), for a discussion of the different meanings of the term, particularly as "a regulation of the individual or a regulation of the body politic" (165).

9. Seid, *Never Too Thin,* 54; see also Susan Sprecher and Elaine Hatfield,

Mirror, Mirror . . . The Importance of Looks in Everyday Life (Albany: State University of New York Press, 1986), 9.

10. A number of historians concur that fatness had primarily positive connotations throughout the nineteenth century. Seid writes: "Fat in the blood, fat on the body, and a new physicality had become the hallmarks of the American female ideal. . . . Throughout this period [1830–1900] body fat had profoundly positive associations . . . abundant flesh symbolized all that was best in middle-class life, especially its comfortable prosperity" (*Never Too Thin*, 76). According to Harvey Levenstein, "Plumpness was widely regarded, by health experts and connoisseurs of female aesthetics alike, as a sign of good health" (*Revolution at the Table: The Transformation of the American Diet* [New York: Oxford University Press, 1988], 13).

11. By situating the beginnings of contemporary dieting in the writings and practices of early modern men rather than the practices of medieval holy women, I am following the work of cultural historians such as Seid and Levenstein, and especially that of Hillel Schwartz (*Never Satisfied: A Cultural History of Diets, Fantasies and Fat* [New York: Free Press, 1986])—all of whose studies suggest greater threads of continuity between the practices of early modern dieters and those of present-day girls and women.

12. Schwartz, *Never Satisfied*, 16–7.

13. Carolyn Merchant charts the emergence of a mechanistic worldview and its gendered implications in her book *The Death of Nature: Women, Ecology, and the Scientific Revolution* (San Francisco: HarperCollins, 1980). For a discussion of the construction of gender implicit in the scientific view of knowledge as the subjugation of nature, emotion, and the body, see Genevieve Lloyd, *The Man of Reason: "Male" and "Female" in Western Philosophy* (Minneapolis: University of Minnesota, 1984).

14. Turner, *Body and Society*, 36–7. Also see Turner's more recent book, *Regulating Bodies: Essays in Medical Sociology* (New York: Routledge, 1992).

15. Alongside new medical theories about the detriments of obesity, psychoanalytic models not only blamed obesity on overeating, but also assumed that people who overate did so because of unsatisfied emotional needs. In psychoanalytic theories, "[t]he overfed body was, strangely, an empty body" (Seid, *Never Too Thin*, 126). According to Schwartz, during the forty-year period following World War I, psychoanalysis shifted the cause of obesity from biological to psychological disturbances (*Never Satisfied*, 192–4, 153–5).

16. Seid, *Never Too Thin*, 18–9.

17. Seid, *Never Too Thin*, 105–6, 108.

18. For figures of diet food and soft drink sales, see Schwartz, *Never Satisfied*, 245, 255; Levenstein, *Revolution at the Table*, 205. According to the President's Council on Physical Fitness and Sports, Americans spent $31 billion on diet and fitness in 1984; see A. Thresher, "Girth of a Nation (Diet Entrepreneurs)," *Nation's Business* 74 (December 1986): 50–1. In "War of the Diets," Joanne Silberner cites figures indicating that about 53 million adult Americans—mostly women—were expected to go on diets in 1992, spending $36 billion in the process (*U.S. News & World Report*, 3 February 1992, 55–60). On com-

mercial weight-loss centers, see A. Miller, "Diets Incorporated," *Newsweek,* 11 September 1989, 56–60. On the failure of commercial weight-loss programs to keep weight off, see "Losing Weight: What Works. What Doesn't," *Consumer Reports,* June 1993, 347–57. On the revenues for programs like Weight Watchers, see B. O'Reilly, "Diet Centers are Really in Fat City," *Fortune,* 5 June 1989, 137. On scandals and debates that have hurt this industry, see M. Schroeder, "The Diet Business Is Getting a Lot Skinnier," *Business Week,* 24 June 1991, 132–4. On pharmaceutical dieting, see Schwartz, *Never Satisfied,* 245, and Seid, *Never Too Thin,* 106, 138–9. The $77 billion figure, which does not include money spent on "aesthetic" surgery, is cited by Andrew Kimbrell, "Body Wars," *Utne Reader,* May/June 1992, 52–64, especially 53. O. W. Wooley notes that the total number of articles listed in the *Reader's Guide to Periodical Literature* under "diet" decreased by half between 1955 and 1965, and skyrocketed after 1965, especially in women's magazines, where over 79 percent of diet articles appeared (". . . And Man Created 'Woman': Representations of Women's Bodies in Western Culture," in *Feminist Perspectives on Eating Disorders,* ed. Patricia Fallon, Melanie Katzman, and Susan Wooley [New York: Guilford, 1994], 17–52, especially 37). Statistics for contemporary and future expenditures in the diet industry are detailed in Laura Fraser's new book, *Losing It: America's Obsession with Weight and the Industry that Feeds It* (New York: Dutton, 1997), 8.

19. See Seid, *Never Too Thin,* 164–6.

20. See Warren Belasco, *Appetite for Change: How the Counterculture Took on the Food Industry,* 1989 (Ithaca: Cornell University Press, 1993), for an account of the countercultural critique of mainstream eating and dieting practices in the 1960s and 1970s, the social challenge underlying this critique, and its eventual absorption by mainstream culture and capitalist markets.

21. For example, in a survey conducted by *Essence* on issues related to troubled eating and body-hatred, 74.5 percent of respondents said that they exercise to burn calories (Villarosa, "Dangerous Eating," 19).

22. Statistics for advertising exposure are cited in Jean Kilbourne's "Still Killing Us Softly: Advertising and the Obsession with Thinness," in Fallon, Katzman, and Wooley, *Feminist Perspectives on Eating Disorders,* 395–418, especially 395.

23. Marjorie Rosen et al., "Diet Wars: Who's Winning, Who's Sinning," *People,* 13 January 1992, 72–82; Karen Jackovich and Allison Lynn, "Diet Winners and Sinners of the Year," *People,* 10 January 1994, 36–53.

24. Quoted by Lois Fine, "Happy Loser," in *Eating Our Hearts Out: Personal Accounts of Women's Relationship to Food,* ed. Lesléa Newman (Freedom, Calif.: Crossing Press, 1993), 134–6, quotation from 136. In addition, Seid cites several diet books and programs whose titles make explicit reference to the rhetoric of traditional religion, including Rev. C. W. Shedd's *Pray Your Weight Away,* which equates fat with sin, arguing that "God really made us all thin, except for the glandular cases, and if our bodies really are to be temples of the Holy Spirit, we had best get them down to the size God intended." According to Seid, the 1970s saw a number of evangelically inspired weight-loss groups: "The Prayer-Diet Clubs of the fifties gave way to Overeaters Victorious, the Workshop in Lenten Living, 3D (for Diet, Discipline, and Discipleship), and the Jesus

System for Weight Control." Other examples of Christian diet books include Frances Hunter's *God's Answer to Fat—Lose It!* (1976) and Joan Cavanaugh's *More of Jesus, Less of Me* (1976). See Seid, *Never Too Thin,* 107.

25. Alison Thresher charts this trend in "Girth of a Nation," 50–1.

26. Quoted in Rebecca Sherman's "Stop the Lies," *Boston Phoenix,* 14 January 1994, 3, 5–8, quotations from 3, 8.

27. Sherman, "Stop the Lies," 3, 8. See also James Servin, "Lean and Mean," *Allure,* October 1993, 114; Elizabeth Kaye, "Powter Keg," *Lears* 6 (1994): 56–8, 91, especially 58, 91.

28. Melanie Menagh, "Starting Late: How to Get Fit When Your Life Gets in the Way," *Lears* 6 (1994): 60–3, quotation from 63.

29. For more examples of the use of religious discourse in advertisements for weight-loss products, see Kilbourne, "Still Killing Us Softly," especially 409–11.

30. The ad appears in *Self,* April 1995, 117.

31. Pamela Gross, "A Separation of Self," in Newman, *Eating Our Hearts Out,* 63–7, quotation from 65.

32. Retha Powers, "Fat Is a Black Women's Issue," *Essence,* October 1989, 75, 78, 134, 136, quotation from 78. For a more detailed discussion of such stereotypes, see Patricia Hill Collins's chapter "Mammies, Matriarchs, and Other Controlling Images" in her book *Black Feminist Thought: Knowledge, Consciousness and the Politics of Empowerment* (New York: Routledge, 1991), 67–90.

33. For a Womanist critique of the damaging effects of Euro-American standards of beauty for African-American women, see Cheryl Townsend Gilkes, "The 'Loves' and 'Troubles' of African-American Women's Bodies: The Womanist Challenge to Cultural Humiliation and Community Ambivalence," in *A Troubling in My Soul: Womanist Perspectives on Evil and Suffering,* ed. Emilie Townes (Maryknoll, New York: Orbis, 1993): 232–49.

34. Barbara Katz, "Weighing the Cost," in Newman, *Eating Our Hearts Out,* 189–93, quotation from 189.

35. Frigga Haug, *Beyond Female Masochism: Memory Work and Politics* (New York: Verso, 1992), 9, 26. See also Haug, ed., *Female Sexualization: A Collective Work of Memory* (London: Verso, 1987).

36. Susan Bordo, *Unbearable Weight: Feminism, Western Culture and the Body* (Berkeley: University of California Press, 1993), 27.

37. Deborah Pike, "Redefining the Body," *Vogue,* January 1994, 105, 166, quotations from 105.

38. Martha Barnette, "Perfect Endings," *Allure,* November 1993, 160–3, quotation from 161.

39. Bordo makes this point about the transvaluation of muscles in *Unbearable Weight,* 193–5.

40. See Victoria Johnson, "Body Sculpting," *Essence,* April 1994, 65–9.

41. Schwartz, *Never Satisfied,* 254. According to Schwartz, profiles of male dieters are similar in all respects except for age (which is assumed to be between 35 and 54). In a chapter entitled "Work(ing) Out," Susan Willis suggests that a similar demographic makeup (i.e., white and middle- or upper-class) character-

izes the women who "work out" on a regular basis (*A Primer for Daily Life* [New York: Routledge, 1991], 65).

42. Rosemary Bray makes these points in "Heavy Burden," *Essence*, October 1989, 53–4, 90, quotation from 54.

43. On the economic demography of "healthy eating," see Belasco, *Appetite for Change*, 194, 201, 228.

10

Joseph L. Price

AN AMERICAN APOTHEOSIS

Sports as Popular Religion

THE RELIGIOUS DIMENSION OF SPORTS

Each year, on a Sunday toward the end of January, more than half the American population, and perhaps as much as one-tenth of the entire world's, rivets its attention on a single, remote event. By then, the Super Bowl has dominated public attention for weeks, and viewers tune in to face their televisions like an electronic *qiblah*. In 1985, the Super Bowl commanded such power that the public celebration of Ronald Reagan's inauguration was shifted from the constitutionally required day of January 20, a Sunday, to the following day, a frigid Monday in Washington, D.C. Meanwhile, on Sunday the 20th in Palo Alto, California, Joe Montana and his crew of San Francisco 49ers commanded full national attention as they beat the Miami Dolphins, winning their first Super Bowl trophy. The football championship has not only come to take precedence over national political rituals: economic exchanges and entertainment performances have also become dominated by the event. Fans, in fact, spend more money on the Super Bowl—making a pilgrimage to the game; attending parties bedecked with official Super Bowl paraphernalia; placing bets in office pools and elsewhere—than Americans spend on traditional religious practices and institutions throughout the entire month.[1]

The religious impact of sports, however, extends beyond the popular fascination with this most prominent national sporting event. Every week during intercollegiate sports seasons, fans orient their schedules toward their team's game, devote their attention to plays and players, and put on masks (painting their faces and bodies, dyeing their hair, and wearing color-coordinated jerseys, jackets, and sweatshirts) to increase their identification with their team. The religious significance of their activity is described succinctly by American philosopher George Santayana, who thought of religion as "another world to live in." Yet Santayana "could not have anticipated how, for many millions of [Americans] . . . , what he meant by 'religion' would one day be displaced in the most immediate, existential and emotional sense by organized spectator sports."[2] For tens of millions of devoted fans throughout the country, sports constitute a popular form of religion by shaping their world and sustaining their ways of engaging it. Indeed, for many, sports are elevated to a kind of divine status, in what I would call an American apotheosis.

Sports Illustrated journalist Frank Deford was among the first to identify the kind of religious power that sports exert over modern Americans. Deford suggests that if Marx had lived at the end of the twentieth century in the United States rather than in Victorian England, he would have declared that sports is the opiate of the people, anesthetizing them to the class struggle and focusing their hopes on events that project fulfillment through a vicarious form of participation and through an often delayed form of gratification.[3] This poignant critique of sports and culture also indicts the decline of traditional religion's influence at the end of the twentieth century. Other critics have drawn this conclusion more explicitly: "The decline of religion as a source of significant meaning in modern industrialized societies," Joyce Carol Oates avers, "has been extravagantly compensated by the rise of popular culture in general, of which the billion-dollar sports mania is the most visible manifestation."[4]

The fusion of sports and religion is neither eccentric nor particular to modern America. Throughout history, and across multiple cultures in today's world, mythic and ritual significance has often been recognized in a number of sports events and play activities. In ancient Greece, the Olympic games were only one set of games performed in honor of the gods—for their entertainment, since the gods were thought to be too serious to engage in the recreational play and physical exercise which they nonetheless enjoyed. In Central America, Mayans played ball games officiated by priests, on courts attached to temples, and with victory perhaps demanding the sacrifice of the team captain. Among other tribes and nations of pre-Columbian Native Americans in North America, the game of lacrosse bore religious weight in its ritual enactment of conflict and combat between contestant tribes, and perhaps in the use of its rackets to forecast or foresee future events. For the Oglala Sioux, the seventh sacred rite of Tapa Wanka Yap, or "the throwing of the ball," combined spiritual and sporting dimensions. In Japan, sumo wrestling tournaments still utilize the Shinto purification rituals of throwing salt, and the space for the matches and the hierarchy of wrestlers reflect certain Shinto values. The physical and mental control demanded by karate and other Asian martial arts can be understood as a spiritual discipline. Eugen Herrigel also discusses Asian traditions and discipline in his well-received *Zen in the Art of Archery,* in which archery is called a sport but is also recognized as a disciplined form of spiritual exercise: the archer seeks to become unified with the bow and the target, precisely by not focusing on the athletic aspects of shooting an arrow. Finally, especially in South America and Europe, soccer promotes a sense of national identity that is rightly considered religious.[5]

In America, sports have been identified as a form of civil religion by Michael Novak, as a form of folk religion by sociologist James Mathisen, and as a form of cultural religion by Catherine Albanese.[6] However, several other scholars—trained in literary critical procedures or historical methods, rather than in religious studies or theology—have challenged whether sports could constitute a religion, which, they insist, is characterized by transcendental, sacramental, and uplifting social elements. Sociologist Harry Edwards holds back from calling sports a popular form of religion, suggesting instead that it is "essentially a secular, quasi-religious institution. It does not, however, constitute an alternative to or substitute for formal sacred religious involvement."[7] Other scholars who have focused on the similarities between particular sports and religious life concur with Edwards. In his analysis of collegiate football, Edwin Cady examines the ways in which college games provide a cultural spectacle for intensifying and celebrating rivalries. Yet Cady contends that "The Big Game" is not in itself fundamentally religious, since it is not, as he perceives it, essentially sacramental. Nevertheless, he allows that "The Big Game" might feel sacramental in approximately the same way that good art does, and he identifies "The Big Game" as being "the most vitally folklorist event in our culture."[8] On different grounds, Joan Chandler refuses to classify sport as religion since both priests and believers, on the one hand, and fans and players, on the other hand, would probably not identify the objects of their devotion as addressing or meeting the same needs.[9] Voicing yet another set of concerns, Robert J. Higgs contends that "sports are like religion in many ways just as they are like war in some ways, but they are not equatable with either."[10]

Despite these reservations and protests against classifying sports as a religion, it seems reasonable to do so. Even though sports does not have all characteristics of a religion, neither does any particular religious tradition, because such comprehensive definitions of "religion" are simply ideal norms against which actual religions are measured. And although Charles H. Lippy, in his recent study of popular religiosity in America, hesitates to call sports a religion, he does identify a crucial factor for considering sports as a form of popular religion: the media. The incredible growth of spectator sports, he observes, has corresponded to, if not emerged out of, the expansion of media coverage of sports events.[11] Less than three decades ago, the only sports events that would be televised during weekdays or prime time were the World Series and the Olympics. Triple-header coverage of football games was restricted to the college bowl game day on New Year's. Nowadays, most fall Sundays let couch coaches and quarterbacks view three full NFL games, while channel flipping to at least two others. With cable systems providing increased coverage of college sports, it is possible to view five football games on most Saturdays in season, and to see scores of basketball games throughout the weeks of winter and spring.

As sports coverage of Sunday events began to increase in the mid-1970s, Frank Deford observed that "the churches have ceded Sunday to sports. . . . Sport owns Sunday now, and religion is content to leave a few minutes before the big games." [12] Not only do the overwhelming majority of Americans identify themselves as sports fans, as mentioned above, but "sport, in its spectatorial and participatory forms, permeates our technological society to the extent that few are left untouched by it." [13] And the public's attraction to broadcast sports events represents more than merely the pursuit of entertainment, for "sports affect people, and their lives, far more deeply and for a longer time than mere diversion would." [14]

Among the first scholars to consider the popular religious dimensions of sports in America are sociologist Harry Edwards and theologian Michael Novak, both of whom identify several characteristics common to sports and religion. According to Edwards, these characteristics concern deity, authority, tradition, beliefs, faithful followers, ritual sites, and material elements: superstar athletes correspond to religions' gods and deceased players serve as saints; the coaches and executives who sit on boards and commissions and make and interpret the rules are like religious patriarchs and high councils; the reporters and broadcasters who chronicle sports events and tabulate their statistics are like the scribes of religious traditions; sports trophies and memorabilia are like religious icons; the formally stated beliefs that are commonly accepted about a sport are like religious dogmas; sports stadiums and arenas are like houses of worship; and halls of fame, both the different facilities for different sports (e.g., the Baseball Hall of Fame at Cooperstown, New York, and Pro Football's Hall of Fame at Canton, Ohio) as well as the most local of sports "shrines"—trophy cases—are like religious shrines. Finally, he identifies the faithful or devoted fans of sports with the true believers of a religious tradition.[15] With these perceptive points, Edwards prompts further reflections on how aspects of sports indeed correspond to elements of religions.

Most of Edwards's connections are drawn from a comparison of sports with theistic, scriptural religious traditions. In particular, his association of superstar athletes with gods calls the accuracy of his comparison into question, because sports heroes are living, physical, visible actors, while the gods, for all their presence and potency, remain invisible and nonmaterial.[16] Yet historian of religion Charles S. Prebish supports Edwards in his assessment that sports heroes function as gods: "The child's worship of [baseball great] Ted Williams," Prebish offers, "is no less real than his or her reverential adoration of Christ, and to some, Williams's accomplishments and capabilities in baseball were unquestionably godly."[17]

The reverence and respect accorded to sports heroes and events is not restricted to children or to fans unfamiliar with characteristics of religion. One Saturday afternoon in late November, 1993, more than 7,000 professors of religious studies convened at a hotel in Washington, D.C., for the annual meetings of the two largest professional societies in religious studies. Midway through the afternoon's sessions, a televised event claimed the attention—yea, devotion—of many of the professors. Initially, observers might have thought that the Notre Dame–Boston College football game was quite unlike the religious rituals that the professors studied. But as time wound down in the game, more than a hundred scholars spontaneously gathered around a lobby television set to watch the final kick, and, during the timeout called before the snap and placement, several of them fell to their knees in front of the television set or at the edges of their sofas, while others sat with hands clasped as though in prayer. When the winning kick went through the goal posts, the players on the field and fans in stands leapt into each other's open embraces and cried with tears of ecstasy, and the scholarly supporters of Boston College turned their faces upward, thrust their arms upright, and shouted and whooped with joy in front of the hotel television. Their posture, volume, and spirit resembled a display of spirit-filled believers shouting "Hallelujah!" As theologian Michael Novak notes, the joy of victory in an athletic contest often prompts such a religious response, for winning games generates a feeling that "the gods are on one's side, as though one is Fate's darling, as if the powers of being course through one's veins and radiate from one's action—powers stronger than non-being, powers over ill fortune, powers over death." Victory, Novak asserts, "is abundant life." [18]

In contrast to the jubilation of the Boston College followers, dejected fans of the Fighting Irish reacted with rituals of mourning, first expressing shock that such a "tragedy" (as some of them put it) could occur, then denying that the upset could be real, by proposing scenarios and plays that could have altered the outcome, and finally acknowledging the loss and its pain. "To lose," Novak also notes, "symbolizes death, and it certainly feels like dying; but it is not death." Such a symbolic rehearsal of death, Novak relates, is characteristic of the Christian sacraments of baptism and eucharist, wherein the communicants symbolically experience death and rebirth. [19]

The religious sensibility of sports involves more than the supplanting of divine roles by sports superheroes, or the substitution of religious rites and doctrines with corresponding sports rituals and rules. For the religious sensibility of sports derives from their basic spiritual dimensions and from the public's potential engagement with them. Addressing fundamental questions about the nature of religion and its exemplification in sports, Novak, like Edwards, draws up a list of correspondences between sports and religion. But unlike Edwards, Novak does not restrict the foundation for his comparison to a theistic perspective. In contrast to the somewhat tentative identification of sport with religion that Edwards finally affirms, Novak is forthright, even if ambiguous: "Sports is, somehow, a religion." Throughout *The Joy of Sports,* Novak celebrates the spiritual dimensions and impact of sports, revels in various acts of sporting competition and in the admiration of sports heroes, and, particularly in his chapter "The Natural Religion," specifies the fundamental correspondence between sports and religion—that they are "organized and structured." Like religions, which "place us in the presence of powers greater than ourselves, and seek to reconcile us to them," sports help participants confront the uncertainties of "Fate" by playing out contingencies in games, and by recognizing the role that chance plays in the outcome of contests. Religions regularly help persons confront their anxieties and dreads about failure, aging, betrayal, and guilt, while competitive sports consistently engage participants in situations that "embody these in every combat." Furthermore, because both athletes and believers espouse a self-imposed subordination of their physical bodies to their wills, they develop "character through patterns of self-denial, repetition, and experiment." [20]

Novak also identifies sports with religion by remarking that both establish high standards of expectation, demand discipline, and strive toward perfection. Such pursuit of excellence creates and cultivates a climate of reverence—in religious traditions, manifest in the devotion to saints; in sports activities, evident in the celebration of heroes. In addition, Novak notes, religions normally create a sense of belonging by focusing initially on the bonding of local communities. This sense of affiliation then becomes a paradigm for the germination and nurture of larger commitments—from local to national, from earthly to universal. Sports similarly generate a sense of identity with "the home team" and the loyalty that such a self-understanding entails. One of the means for generating this group identity is through rituals that are common to both religions and sports: even as religions use chants, songs, and certain gestures, so too do sports bond teammates and fans together by using cheers ("Two bits, four bits, six bits, a dollar: All for our team, stand up and holler"), songs ("Take Me Out to the Ballgame," which features the call to "root, root, root for the home team" during the seventh inning stretch, or the singing of the school "fight song" at football games), and bodily movement (clapping, giving "high fives," slapping each other on the back, and so on). With each of these forms of acting and interacting, fans and players unite as a single body.

THE SPIRITUALITY OF SPORTS

Underlying these common facets of religion and sports is the experience of "flow," which Mihaly Csikszentmihalyi defines as "the state in which people are so involved in an activity that nothing else seems to matter; the experience itself is so enjoyable that people will do it even at great cost, for the sheer sake of doing it." Applying his insights on the psychology of optimal experience to persons' participation and performance in sports and games, Csikszentmihalyi recognizes that such opportunities go beyond the boundaries and expectations of ordinary experience. Temporarily set apart from ordinary folks during sports contests and performances, players and spectators cease to act in terms of common sense, and concentrate instead on the peculiar reality of the game.

Such *flow activities* have as their primary function the provision of enjoyable experiences. . . . Because of the way [that sports] are constructed, *they help participants and spectators achieve an ordered state of mind* that is highly enjoyable.[21]

"The peculiar reality of the game," as Csikszentmihalyi refers to it, constitutes the core of the spiritual power and religious significance of sports, and develops out of their ritual aspects—the game's time, space, rules, and purposes. In ritual and in play, Johan Huizinga notes, performance space is set aside, demarcated as the "field of play" wherein a certain set of rules apply. During play or ritual, performance takes shape in a time of its own, certainly surrounded or engulfed by the chronometric measure of ordinary time but set off in such a way that the duration of the game conforms to a different standard of temporal computation, as in the play of baseball with its "innings" or in tennis with its sets and matches. Even the games that utilize a clock, such as football and basketball, run the clock and stop it at appointed times, measuring game time according to a different set of rules than those that govern the calculation of ordinary time. Finally, special rules within the designated space and time for play, such as rules regulating tackling (allowed in football but impermissible in ordinary relations) and taunting (forbidden in basketball, but not in ordinary affairs), create a microcosm, an area and time within whose confines an order is established.[22]

Like Huizinga, historian of religions Mircea Eliade recognizes the worldmaking functions of ritual, although he takes a somewhat different perspective regarding their purpose. Eliade applies the concepts of ritual space and time to his analysis of humans as homo religiosus: for him, the categories of time and space provide the orientation for cosmicization, or the development of a worldview, construing and maintaining one's way of being in the world. All such acts of cosmicization are fundamentally religious because the establishment of order in a new world— even one such as that of a game—replicates the cosmogonic act of the gods in the creation of the world. And sacred time, like play time, is discontinuous with ordinary time. It is reversible and replicable, a different realm of time in which one might forget ordinary time.[23] Like priests performing and laypersons attending religious rites, athletes and spectators lose track of ordinary time when the game is good—when the intensity of play fully engages the participants. It is a realm of time which is satisfying in itself, because the actions that take place are meaningful within the time frame, although they may, in addition, express meaning beyond the block of sacred time or provide release from the strictures of ordinary time.

Obviously, sports are not religions in the same way that Christianity and Islam, Buddhism and Taoism are religions. But sports are "a form of religion," as Novak puts it, because they provide "organized institutions, disciplines, and liturgies" and because they "teach religious qualities of heart and soul. In particular, they recreate symbols of cosmic struggle, in which human survival and moral courage are not assured." [24] Through their symbols and rituals, sports provide occasions for experiencing a sense of ultimacy and for prompting personal transformation.

The kinds of personal and social transformations that sports proffer do not depend upon winning a game or achieving a personal best performance in a contest, although both may certainly generate religious experiences. Instead, the transformative potential of sports themselves extends to all participants, whether or not competition is undertaken. The transformative potential of sports involves, as Prebish puts it, "redemption as well as rebirth into a new type of reality, separated from ordinary reality by its sense of being permeated with ultimacy and holiness, with beauty and freedom." [25] The ultimacy or holiness of the religious experience derives from its location, not in a remote realm of transcendence, but in a sense of alterity generated by the freedom and beauty of the sports activity itself.

When considering the significance of sports as religion, one can distinguish between the sport's spiritual presence and power for athletes, and fans' allegiance to teams and heroes. In established religious traditions, it is not uncommon for priests and laypersons to enjoy various levels of engagement and enrichment in their religious exercise; so too with sports, wherein athletes experience dimensions of selfhood and the quest for perfect performance in ways strikingly different from the experiences of fans.

In her examination of the spiritual experiences of athletes in competition, even where that competition is simply a struggle with oneself to achieve a "personal best" performance, Carolyn Thomas draws inspiration from Jean-Paul Sartre's assertion in *Being and Nothingness* that a person's goal is "to attain himself [or herself] as a certain being, precisely the being, which is in question to his [or her] being." For athletes, Thomas claims, "sport is a lived experience that, despite teammates or fans, is ultimately a solitary quest that reflects highly individual, personal, and subjective intents." Serious athletes, she asserts, "often unknowingly . . .

enter the world of sports in search of self, in search of the reality of a given moment, in search of truth."[26] To engage the most profound level of truth requires that one become introspective and meditative, opening oneself to the Other that resides at the innermost dimension of self. In this sense, then, sports constitute an essential, spiritual pursuit—seeking truth and self-awareness.

> When performers voluntarily enter sport and commit their whole beings to the sport experience, they transcend, or go beyond, outside distractions to a fusion of subject and object that allows them to know both the sport and self in an authentic, profound, special, and very individual way. It is this kind of "knowing" that has the potential to provide a source of meaning, a sense of purpose, and a basis for self-understanding.[27]

Although an athlete might articulate this self-understanding following a performance, he or she might not be conscious of this "knowing" dimension during the performance itself. In fact, the opposite is probably the case, according to Phil Jackson, coach of the Chicago Bulls, son of Pentecostal ministers, and student of Zen Buddhism. The secret for playing basketball well, he says, is "not thinking": a Buddhist sense of being aware of what everyone on the court is doing and responding to, interacting with, and directing the flow of the game, precisely by not thinking.[28] The self-awareness that, upon reflection, leads to an articulation of self-understanding and disclosure of truth is the experience of flow.

A casual observer, of course, would be unlikely to perceive the pursuit of self-awareness and truth in a Division I intercollegiate contest, because of corruption, attempts by some players and coaches to win at all costs, booster clubs that provide illegitimate support for certain players and teams, and the like. "Often portrayed in terms of greed, egocentricity, and immorality, these [Division I] forms of sport . . . that focus on competitive ends . . . seem a far cry from a historic dependence on religion." But even in such contexts, Thomas concludes, sport "provides a place where people can dominate fear and passion; a place where adventure and purpose and commitment can remove a sense of dread that may otherwise prevail."[29]

The spiritual experience of athletes in their performance of sport is not only the introspective pursuit of personal, foundational truths, but also includes their appreciation of simplicity and harmony in team play, and their quest for a perfectly synchronized performance. This quest for perfection arises out of the fundamental dissatisfaction and uneasiness that constitute the human condition, but "sports nourish this drive [toward perfection] as well as any other institution in our society." [30] Even when the pursuit of a perfect performance in sports becomes corrupted or distorted—when it moves toward selfish goals rather than the joy and disclosive possibilities of play itself—it still manifests a fundamental human desire for fulfillment. The willingness to subject personal preferences to the good of the team constitutes a basic religious aspect of team sports. "Even for those who don't consider themselves 'spiritual' in a conventional sense, [the process of] creating a successful team—whether it's an NBA champion or a record-setting sales force—is essentially a spiritual act," asserts Phil Jackson. "It requires the individuals involved to surrender their self-interest for the greater good so that the whole adds up to more than the sum of its parts." [31]

DEVOTION TO SPORTS

In contrast to an athlete's experience of spiritual harmony in team play, fans manifest the religious power of sports in their expressions of allegiance and respect. The most explicit recent example of this was the "religious overtone," as Phil Jackson put it, of the press coverage when Michael Jordan contemplated returning to the Bulls following his eighteen-month retirement. "Perhaps it was just a reflection of the spiritual malaise in the culture and the deep yearning for a mythic hero who would set us free," Jackson mused. "Whatever the reason, during his hiatus from the team, Michael had somehow been transformed in the public mind from a great athlete to a sports deity." And yearning for the possibility of his return—expecting almost an eschatological second coming of sorts—some of the most fervent fans made their way to the United Center, where the Bulls play their home games, and knelt and prayed at the foot of Jordan's statue—a shrine to his transcending the court, his being "Air Jordan." [32]

Certainly, sports fans exhibit a kind of devotion that often is described in terms of religious dedication or intensity. They express their fervor not only in the religious rituals of supplication for success, but also in the negative expressions of prayer for others' destruction or failure. In the Puerto Rican town of San Germán, Jackson recalls, "the fans hated the Gallitos [Jackson's team] so much that they lit candles the night before we arrived and prayed for our death." [33] The most extreme form of this attitude is surely that of the Colombian soccer fans who assassinated Andres Escobar for having accidentally scored a goal against his own team in the

1994 World Cup competition. Most fans, of course, do not resort to death threats and murder, but they express their dedication and devotion by the size of their wagers on favorite teams, the extent to which they will go—the sacrifices that they will make—in order to make a pilgrimage to an important game, and the ludic masking that they often assume in order to establish full identity with their favorite team or its mascot.

One of the most vivid displays of a fan's devotion to a sport occurs in *Bull Durham,* the popular, romantic baseball movie. The opening sequence behind the credits features sepia tones of photographs from the collection of Annie Savoy, whose wall gallery serves as a sort of shrine to bygone baseball superheroes and their seemingly cosmic feats. The soundtrack features a blues singer wailing "Yes, yes, yes" (a secular rendition of "Amen") to a mournful gospel melody. Then we hear Annie deliver her confession:

> I believe in the Church of Baseball. I've tried all of the major religions and most of the minor ones. I've worshipped Buddha, Allah, Brahma, Vishnu, Síva, trees, mushrooms, and Isadora Duncan.
>
> I know things. For instance, there are 108 beads in a Catholic rosary and there are 108 stitches in a baseball. When I learned that I gave Jesus a chance. But it just didn't work between us. The Lord laid too much guilt on me.
>
> I prefer metaphysics to theology. You see, there's no guilt in baseball, and it's never boring. . . .
>
> I've tried 'em all, I really have. And the only church that truly feeds the soul day in and day out is the Church of Baseball.

Annie's experience of awe and sustenance in baseball is not merely aligned with her annual romantic liaison with one of the Durham Bulls. Her enduring love is for baseball, the game itself, and the way it makes sense out of life.

What Annie senses in her devotion to baseball is that somehow the game of baseball dramatizes a myth, a set of contingent relations or a display of possible outcomes that make life meaningful. Scholars have also proposed that baseball enacts elements of a myth whose meaning often corresponds to its athletes' and fans' hopes. For example, A. Bartlett Giamatti, former Commissioner of Major League Baseball, suggests that baseball's space and rules correspond in many respects to the ancient omphalos myth, which reflects upon the creation and ordering of the world from the center of the earth, often a cosmic mountain.[34]

In addition to personal acts of fan devotion such as Annie Savoy's, the group behavior of fans also has religious import. According to a *Sports Illustrated* survey in the 1970s, three-fourths of Americans identified themselves as sports fans.[35] In 1990, the Indiana State High School championship game hosted 41,046 fans, a national record, in the Hoosier Dome at Indianapolis. "Hoosier Hysteria"—Indiana's obsessive love of basketball, especially at the high school level—has been called the state's religion; "indeed it is the church and the team," Barry Temkin observes, "that stand as the two most important institutions in many a town—and not necessarily in that order." [36]

The expressions of devotion by fans are not restricted to fervent individuals; they also extend to communities that often establish their identity by supporting their local team and celebrating its heroes. One of the memorable scenes in the popular basketball film "Hoosiers" reflects such devotion by an entire community, as the headlights on a caravan of cars light the town's pilgrimage to an "away game" on a Friday night. In Kentucky, too, the reverence, hope, and community bonding associated with high school basketball can be seen in the fact that the Metcalf County High School gymnasium seats more fans than the population of Edmonton, the town where it is located. A similar phenomenon has been chronicled by H. G. Bissinger in *Friday Night Lights*, an analysis of a season in the life of the Permian Panthers (Odessa, Texas), and of the community's dreams for justification and validation through the success of this high school football team. In Kentucky, part of a community's dream is that the local high school stars might become immortal by playing for the vaunted University of Kentucky Wildcats. When, at the start of his junior year of high school, Metcalf County point guard J. P. Blevins signed a letter of intent to attend Kentucky, the gymnasium was filled as the entire community celebrated his accomplishment, not merely as a rite of passage for a budding star's achievement but as an enduring validation of their own way of life and their love of Kentucky Wildcats basketball.[37]

CHALLENGES FOR SPORTS AND FAITH

There are at least three points of continuing concern for those who wrestle with comparing the religious creed with the code of the sports cult. The first issue is a theological one. Although religions do not necessarily involve the worship of "God" or "gods," they do orient their followers toward an ultimate force or pantheon of powers, whether personalized as "gods" or identified in abstract ways, for example Buddhism's path of enlightenment or Shinto's abiding sense of family and tradition. One of the primary challenges for religious studies scholars who undertake theological analysis of sports is to identify within sports a source of ultimate powers for evoking and inspiring radical transformation among participants and faithful spectators.

The second issue emerges out of ethical concerns about the inculcation and transmission of values. Not all of the values are negative, as some might be tempted to claim in light of ongoing exposés about the athletes' corruption, the appreciation and practice of violence, the cultivation of bodily deformation as a way to achieve success (as with the use of anabolic steroids), and the use of cheating in order to win at any cost. James Mathisen, among others, challenges the naive notion that sports, in and of themselves, promote the building of admirable character.[38] It should be noted, however, that not all religions adopt and encourage humanistic, pacifist, and compassionate values, so the critique of sports on the grounds that they promote violence, bodily abuse, and an aggressive competitive spirit does not, of itself, separate sports from established religious traditions.

In any case, many celebrate the beneficent aspects of sports, in contrast to these more negative portrayals of the potential evils in store for sports devotees. Michael Novak, for instance, writes: "Sports are our chief civilizing agent. Sports are our most universal art form. Sports tutor us in the basic lived experiences of the humanist tradition."[39] Thus, a challenge for scholars who pursue a religious studies critique of sports is to identify and classify the values in sports that motivate action of players and interaction with and among faithful fans.

Finally, some theological critics have been reluctant to consider sports as religion since they recognize that many traditionally pious persons are also avid sports participants and fans. "Is it possible to maintain multilateral religious affiliations? Can the proponent of sport religion also retain standing within his or her traditional religious affiliation?" Prebish asks. "Ostensibly no!" he responds, reasoning that anyone who identifies sports as his or her religion would be "referring to a consistent pursuit that is also the most important pursuit and a religious pursuit. If this individual were to then state that he or she is also a Jew or a Protestant or a Catholic or whatever," Prebish concludes, "he or she would be referring to cultural heritage only, to the complex series of factors that are essentially ethnic and locational rather than religious."[40] This conflict arises most frequently out of monotheistic concerns, since in monotheistic traditions true believers can adhere to only one form of faith. However, if we recognize, with historians of religion like Mircea Eliade, that it is possible for persons to be simultaneously religious in apparently competing ways, then a new respect for pluralism might arise, and we could consider ways to appreciate the rhythmic or antagonistic forces for allegiance among devoted fans who are also faithful followers of an established religious tradition.

In short, although difficulties exist in trying to specify the exact nature and extent of sports as religion, sports do exhibit many of the characteristics of established religious traditions. Most importantly, they exercise a power for shaping and engaging the world for millions of devoted fans throughout America; they enable participants to explore levels of selfhood that otherwise remain inaccessible; they establish means for bonding in communal relations with other devotees; they model ways to deal with contingencies and fate while playing by the rules; and they provide the prospect for experiencing victory and thus sampling, at least in an anticipatory way, "abundant life." In America, quite simply, sports constitute a form of popular religion.

NOTES

1. See Joseph L. Price, "The Super Bowl as Religious Festival," *Christian Century,* 22 February 1984, 190–91. Statistics about the extent of gambling on the Super Bowl appear in Bill Christine, "The Big Gamble," *Los Angeles Times,* 3 February 1999, D1, D6.

2. Joyce Carol Oates, "Lives of the latter day saints," *Times Literary Supplement,* 12 July 1996, 9.

3. Frank Deford, "Religion in Sport," *Sports Illustrated,* 19 April 1976, 88–102, quotation from 91.

4. Oates, "Lives of the latter-day saints," 9.

5. For an excellent introduction to the religious functions of the Greek Olympiad, see Judith Swaddling, *The Ancient Olympics* (Austin: University of Texas, 1984). For an explanation of the Mesoamerican ballgames, see S. Jeffrey K. Wilkerson, "And Then They Were Sacrificed: The Ritual Ballgame of Northeastern Mesoamerica through Time and Space," in *The Mesoamerican Ballgame,* ed. Vernon L. Scarborough and David R. Wilcox (Tucson: University of Arizona Press, 1991), 45–71. For information about the religious significance of lacrosse, see Stewart Culin, *Games of the North American Indians* (1902–3; reprint, New York: Dover, 1975), 563 ff. For an exploration of the religious origins of the rite of throwing the ball, see *The Sacred Pipe: Black Elk's Account of the Seven Rites of the Oglala Sioux,* recorded and ed. Joseph Epes Brown (New York: Penguin Books, 1971), 127–38. For a discussion of the spiritual dimensions of the martial arts, see, for example, Peter Payne, *Martial Arts: The Spiritual Dimension* (New York: Crossroad, 1981). For an imaginative, literary exploration of the connections between discipline, spirituality, and one of the martial arts, see Harry Crews, *Karate Is a Thing of the Spirit* (New York: William Morrow, and

Company, 1971). Eugen Herrigel's examination of the spiritual challenge of archery is *Zen in the Art of Archery*, trans. R. F. C. Hull, intro. D. T. Suzuki (New York: Vintage Books, 1971). For an analysis of Brazilian soccer as a civil religion, see "Sports in Society: Futebol as National Drama," in *Concilium: Religion in the Eighties, Sport*, ed. Gregory Baum and John Coleman (Edinburgh: T & T Clark, 1989), 57–68.

6. Michael Novak, *The Joy of Sports: End Zones, Bases, Baskets, Balls, and the Consecration of the American Spirit* (New York: Basic Books, 1976), 18–34; James A. Mathisen, "From Civil Religion to Folk Religion: The Case of American Sport," in *Sport and Religion*, ed. Shirl J. Hoffman [Champaign, Ill: Human Kinetics Books, 1992]), 17–33, especially 21–4; Catherine Albanese, *America: Religions and Religion* (Belmont, Calif.: Wadsworth Publishing Company, 1981), 322.

7. Harry Edwards, *Sociology of Sport* (Homewood, Ill.: Dorsey Press, 1973), 90.

8. Edwin Cady, *The Big Game: College Sports and American Life* (Knoxville: University of Tennessee Press, 1978), 78.

9. Joan Chandler, "Sport is Not a Religion," in Hoffman, *Sport and Religion*, 55–61, especially 55.

10. Robert J. Higgs, "Muscular Christianity, Holy Play, and Spiritual Exercises: Confusion about Christ in Sports and Religion," *Arete* 1, no. 1 [1983], 59–85, quotation from 63. Since publishing his essay in the initial issue of *Arete*, the journal sponsored by the Sports Literature Association, Higgs has published a more expansive study of the convergence of sports, religion, the military, and education: *God in the Stadium: Sports and Religion in America* [Lexington: University Press of Kentucky, 1995). Rather than focusing on issues pertaining to the exercise or perception of sports as religion, however, the work studies the development of "muscular Christianity" or "Sportianity" in America.

11. Charles H. Lippy, *Being Religious, American Style: A History of Popular Religiosity in the United States* (Westport, Conn.: Praeger Publishers, 1994), 228.

12. Deford, "Religion in Sport," 92, 102.

13. Thomas, "Sport," 506.

14. Novak, *Joy of Sports*, 26.

15. Edwards, *Sociology of Sport*, 261–262. See also Mathisen, quoting M. C. Kearl: "Like religion, professional sports use past generations as referents for the present and confer conditional immortality for their elect through statistics and halls of fame." Then Mathisen comments: "In our desire to fix in time the achievements of those we look back upon as our representatives for time immemorial, we attribute a sense of sanctity to them and their accomplishments. . . . When a record is broken in sport, we are both happy and sad. Not only has immortality been achieved, but previous immortality proves to have been conditional and so has been stolen from our midst. Maybe we should place an asterisk next to the new record, just to ensure that we do not lose sight of the former one and of the hero who established it" ("Civil Religion to Folk Religion," 24).

For a specific connection of superstar Michael Jordan with a kind of deific projection, see Jim Naughton, *Taking to the Air: The Rise of Michael Jordan*

(New York: Warner Books, 1992), 134. Naughton reminds us of former sportswriter Red Smith's warning against the "godding up of ballplayers," and suggests that, with Jordan's air quality, he embodies the nearest thing to transcendence that we are likely to see.

16. Cf. Oates: "For the 'sports fan' the team or idolized athlete provides a kind of externalized soul: there to be celebrated or reviled but, as the God of the ages apparently was not, there in full public view" ("Lives of the latter-day saints," 9).

17. Charles S. Prebish, *Religion and Sport: The Meeting of Sacred and Profane* (Westport, Conn.: Greenwood Press, 1993), 64.

18. Novak, *Joy of Sports,* 47–8.

19. Ibid., 21.

20. Ibid., xi, 29–30.

21. Mihaly Csikszentmihalyi, *Flow: The Psychology of Optimal Experience* (New York: Harper & Row, 1990), 4, 72.

22. Johan Huizinga, *Homo Ludens: A Study of the Play-Element in Culture* (Boston: Beacon Press, 1955), 1–27. In an effort to connect modern sports to its origins in play and ritual, Allen Guttmann has written three volumes that implicitly, and occasionally explicitly, suggest the religious significance of American sporting events, especially for the fans. Guttmann's earliest work, *From Ritual to Record: The Nature of Modern Sports* (New York: Columbia University Press, 1978), includes the trenchant observation that "one of the strangest turns in the long, devious route that leads from primitive ritual to the World Series and the Fussballweltmeisterschaft is the proclivity of modern sports to become a secular kind of faith" (25). See also *Sports Spectators* (New York: Columbia University Press, 1986) and *A Whole New Ballgame: An Interpretation of American Sports* (Chapel Hill: University of North Carolina Press, 1988), especially chapters 2, 5, and 6, in which Guttmann treats "The Sacred and the Secular" in Native American games, "The National Game" (implying a national identity—and perhaps civil religion—associated with baseball), and "Muscular Christianity."

23. Mircea Eliade, *The Sacred and the Profane,* trans. William R. Trask (New York: Harcourt, Brace, and Co., 1959), chapters 1–2, especially 30–4.

24. Novak, *Joy of Sports,* 31, 21.

25. Prebish, *Religion and Sport,* 70.

26. Carolyn Thomas, "Sports," in *Spirituality and the Secular Quest,* ed. Peter H. Van Ness (New York: Crossroad Press, 1996), 498–519, quotations from 498–9.

27. Ibid., 509–10.

28. Phil Jackson and Hugh Delehanty, *Sacred Hoops: Spiritual Lessons of a Hardwood Warrior* (New York: Hyperion, 1995), 115.

29. Thomas, "Sports," 502, 508.

30. Novak, *Joy of Sports,* 27.

31. Jackson, *Sacred Hoops,* 5, 11–2.

32. Ibid., 16–7.

33. Ibid., 70–1.

34. A. Bartlett Giamatti, *Take Time for Paradise: Americans and Their Games* (New York: Summit Books, 1989), 86 ff. Earlier, I had offered a more extensive

and distinct application of the omphalos myth to baseball in " 'The Momentary Grace of Order': Religious Aspects of a Sport," *Journal and Times of the California Association of Health, Physical Education, Recreation and Dance* 49, no. 6 (March 1987): 16–9. An interpretation of football as reflecting distinct American myths can be found in my brief essay "The Super Bowl as Religious Festival," *Christian Century,* 22 February 1984, 190–1. And myths, more ambiguously suggested, underlie basketball, according to Phil Jackson, *Sacred Hoops,* 7.

35. Cited in Prebish, *Religion and Sport,* xiii.

36. Barry Temkin, "Indiana's 'impossible dream' may soon be no more," *Denver Post,* 11 February 1996.

37. Mark Woods, "Basketball prodigy a Kentucky blueblood," *Denver Post,* 2 February 1997, 11C. See also H. C. Bissinger, *Friday Night Lights: A Town, a Team, and a Dream* (Reading, Mass.: Addison-Wesley Publishing Company, 1990), especially 1–20, 38–52, 173–93.

38. Mathisen, "Civil Religion to Folk Religion," 22.

39. Novak, *Joy of Sports,* 27. Elsewhere in his collection, Novak promotes the potential good in sports even more hopefully: "What I have learned from sports is respect for authenticity and individuality (each player learning his own true instincts, capacities, style); for courage and perseverance and stamina; for the ability to enter into defeat in order to suck dry its power to destroy; for harmony of body and spirit. . . . In sports, law was born and also liberty, and the nexus of their interrelation. In sports, honesty and excellence are caught, captured, nourished, held in trust for the generations" (43).

40. Prebish, *Religion and Sport,* 72.

11

David Chidester

THE CHURCH OF BASEBALL, THE FETISH
OF COCA-COLA, AND THE POTLATCH
OF ROCK 'N' ROLL

What do we mean by "religion" in the study of religion in American popular culture? Consider this: "What has a lifetime of baseball taught you?" Buck O'Neil is asked in an interview for Ken Burns's television series on the history of the American national pastime. "It is a religion," O'Neil responds. "For me," he adds. "You understand?"

Not exactly, of course, because we have no idea what Buck O'Neil, the great first baseman of the Kansas City Monarchs in the 1930s, who served baseball for over six decades as player, coach, manager, and scout, means by the term "religion." What *does* he mean? As Ken Burns would have it, baseball is a religion because it operates in American culture like a church, "The Church of Baseball." Is that how we should understand "religion" in American popular culture, as an organized human activity that functions like the more familiar religious institution of the Christian church?

To complicate the matter, however, consider this: A religion is not a specific institution, but rather "a system of symbols." So says anthropologist Clifford Geertz; so too says Mark Pendergrast in his account of a new religion that was founded in America but eventually achieved truly global scope, the religion of Coca-Cola.

In his popular history *For God, Country, and Coca-Cola*, Pendergrast concludes that the fizzy, caramel-colored sugar water stands as a "sacred symbol" that induces "worshipful" moods which animate an "all-inclusive world view espousing perennial values such as love, peace, and universal brotherhood." [1] According to this reading, therefore, religion is about sacred symbols and systems of sacred symbols that endow the world with meaning and value. As Pendergrast argues, Coca-Cola—the sacred name, the sacred formula, the sacred image, the sacred object—has been the fetish at the center of a popular American system of religious symbolism.

But we can complicate things even further by considering this: "Let's Give It to 'Em, Right Now!" singer Joe Ely screams before the instrumental break in the Kingsmen's 1963 rock 'n' roll classic, "Louie, Louie." In the midst of the clashing, crashing cacophony, with lyrics that are unintelligible at any speed, we are struck by the strained screech of Ely's exhortation, "Let's Give It to 'Em, Right Now!" What kind of a "gift" is this?

In his book-length history of the song, which explores "the secret" of "Louie, Louie," rock critic Dave Marsh proposes that one useful model for understanding this kind of gift-giving appears in the ritualized display, presentation, and destruction of property associated with the potlatch ritual performed by indigenous American societies in the Pacific Northwest. This analogy with a Native American ritual, Marsh argues, can illuminate what he calls the "socioreligious" character of "Louie, Louie" in American culture. In this sense, however, religion is not an institution; it is not a system of symbols; it is the gift.

Church, fetish, potlatch—these three terms represent different theoretical models for analyzing religion in American popular culture. By examining their recent deployment in popular accounts of baseball, Coca-Cola, and rock 'n' roll, I hope to explore some of the consequences of these theoretical models for the study of religion. Among those consequences, I will highlight the force of metaphoric transference in theory building; the implications of these three metaphors—representing the institutional formation of the church, the powerful but artificial making of the fetish, and the nonproductive expenditure of the potlatch, respectively—for our understanding of the character of religion; and the ways in which the very term "religion," including its definition, application, and extension, does not, in fact, belong solely to the academy but is constantly at stake in the interchanges of cultural discourses and practices.

THE CHURCH OF BASEBALL

To return to the testimony of Buck O'Neil, baseball is a religion because it is an enduring institution governed by established rules. "If you go by the rules," he explains, "it is right." Baseball is a religion according to Buck O'Neil, then, because "it taught me and it teaches everyone else to live by the rules, to abide by the rules."[2]

This definition of religion as rule-governed behavior, however, is not sufficiently comprehensive or detailed to capture what Ken Burns presents as the religious character of baseball. The "church of baseball" is much more than merely the rule book. It is a religious institution that maintains the continuity, uniformity, sacred space, and sacred time of American life. As the "faith of fifty million people," baseball does everything that we conventionally understand the institution of the church to do.

First, baseball ensures a sense of continuity in the midst of a constantly changing America, through the forces of tradition, heritage, and collective memory. As Donald Hall suggests, "Baseball, because of its continuity over the space of America and the time of America, is a place where memory gathers."[3] Certainly, this emphasis on collective memory dominates Burns's documentary on baseball. But it also characterizes the religious character of the sport in American culture as a whole. Like a church, Major League Baseball institutionalizes a sacred memory of the past that informs the present.

Second, baseball supports a sense of uniformity, a sense of belonging to a vast, extended American family that attends the same church. As journalist Thomas Boswell reports in his detailed discussion in "The Church of Baseball," his mother was devoted to baseball because "it made her feel like she was in church." Like her church, Boswell explains, baseball provided his mother with "a place where she could—by sharing a fabric of beliefs, symbols, and mutual agreements with those around her—feel calm and whole."[4] Boswell draws out a series of analogies between baseball and his mother's church: both feature organs; both encourage hand-clapping to their hymns; both have distinctive robes and vestments; and in both everyone is equal before God. Although his analogy between the basepaths of a diamond and the Christian Cross seems a bit strained, Boswell provides sufficient justification for asserting that his mother regarded her attendance of baseball games as roughly equivalent to belonging to a church.

Third, the religion of baseball represents the sacred space of home. In this respect, baseball is a religion of the domestic, of the familiar, and even of the obvious. As Boswell explains:

> Baseball is a religion that worships the obvious and gives thanks that things are exactly as they seem. Instead of celebrating mysteries, baseball rejoices in the absence of mysteries and trusts that, if we watch what is laid before our

eyes, down to the last detail, we will cultivate the gift of seeing things as they really are.

The vision of reality that baseball affords, therefore, is a kind of normality, the ordinary viewed through a prism that only enhances its familiarity. While many religions point to a perfect world beyond this world, Boswell observes, baseball creates a "perfect universe in microcosm within the real world." [5] By producing such a ritualized space within the world, baseball domesticates the sacred and gives it a home.

Fourth, the religion of baseball represents the sacred time of ritual. "Everything is high-polish ritual and full-dress procession," Boswell notes. The entire action of the game is coordinated through a ritualization of time. But baseball also affords those extraordinary moments of ecstasy and enthusiasm, revelation and inspiration, that seem to stand outside of the ordinary temporal flow. His mother experienced those moments of "ritual epiphany" in church, according to Boswell, and "[b]asically, that's how she felt about baseball, too." [6] Through ritual and revelation, baseball provides an experience of sacred time that liberates its devotees from time's constraints.

In these terms, therefore, baseball is a church, a "community of believers." Certainly, the church of baseball is confronted by the presence of unbelievers within the larger society. As Thomas Boswell reports, his father failed to find his rightful place among the faithful in the church of baseball: "The appeal of baseball mystified him, just as all religions confound the innocent bewildered atheist." [7] Like any church, however, baseball has its committed faithful, its true believers. The opening speech of Annie Savoy in the film *Bull Durham* can be invoked as a passionate statement of religious devotion to baseball. "I believe in the church of baseball," she declares. The religion of baseball, however, promises a freedom beyond guilt. Although she observes the analogy between baseball and the Christian church, which is supported by the curious equivalence between 108 beads on the rosary and 108 stitches on a baseball, Annie Savoy proclaims baseball as a church in its own right. "I've tried them all, I really have," she concludes, "and the only church that truly feeds the soul, day in, day out, is the church of baseball." [8]

"What nonsense!" an unbeliever might understandably conclude in response to all this testimony about the church of baseball. Baseball is not a religion. It is recreation; it is entertainment; supported by the monopoly granted to Major League Baseball, it is very big business. All this religious language merely mystifies the genuine character of the sport in American society.

For all the apparent mystification, strained analogies, and improbable statements of faith, however, the depiction of baseball as a church represents a highly significant development in attempts to locate religion in American popular culture. In earlier anthropological accounts, especially those produced by the anthropologist-from-Mars school of cultural anthropology that gave us the "Nacirema" tribe ("American" spelled backwards), baseball registers as "magic" rather than "religion."[9] For example, a frequently anthologized article titled "Baseball Magic" records the magical techniques employed by baseball players to manipulate unseen forces and control events.[10] Using various kinds of amulets for good luck, players engage in specific practices—never stepping on the foul line, always spitting before entering the batter's box—that appear, in Freudian terms, just like "what are called obsessive acts in neurotics." In their magical practices, baseball players display an obsession with "little preoccupations, performances, restrictions and arrangements in certain activities of everyday life which have to be carried out always in the same or in a methodically varied way."[11] Although Freud held that such "obsessive acts" characterized the practice of both ritual and magic, the author of "Baseball Magic" implicitly upholds the familiar analytical distinction between the two. Instead of interpreting baseball as religion, however, he highlights its superstitious practices of magic.

This account of baseball magic raises two theoretical problems. First, by characterizing baseball as magic, the author pushes us back to the basic opposition between "religion" and "superstition" that has been crucial to the very definition of religion in Western culture. The ancient Latin term *religio,* indicating an authentic, careful, and faithful way of acting, was defined by its opposite, *superstitio,* a kind of conduct that was allegedly based on ignorance, fear, or fraud. In these terms, "we" have religion; "they" have superstition. But only rarely has the inherently oppositional character of the notion of "religion" been recognized: Thomas Hobbes, for example, observed that the "fear of things invisible is the natural seed of that, which everyone in himself calleth religion; and in them that worship or fear that power otherwise than they do, superstition," and the linguist Emile Benveniste observed that "the notion of 'religion' requires, so to speak, by opposition, that of 'superstition.'"[12] Baseball magic, therefore, is not religion. It is a repertoire of superstitious beliefs and practices that stands as the defining opposite of authentic religion. From the perspective of the anthropologist who stands outside and observes, baseball magic is clearly something very strange that "they" do; it is not "our" religion.

The second problem raised by the argument of "Baseball Magic" is that its author recalls the tension between the individual and society that has long characterized academic reflections on the difference between magic and religion. Following Emile Durkheim's classic formulation, magic is essentially individualistic and potentially antisocial. Unlike religious ritual, which affirms and reinforces the social solidarity of a community, magic manipulates unseen forces in the service of self-interest. As Durkheim insisted, there can be no "church of magic." Accordingly, if baseball is magic, there can be no "church of baseball."

Ken Burns intervenes in these theoretical debates by reversing their terms. Simply by presenting baseball as religion rather than magic, he represents the game as an authentic religious affirmation of the traditional continuity, uniformity, and solidarity of American society. Adopting a functional definition of religion, Burns documents the ways in which baseball operates like a church by meeting personal needs and reinforcing social integration. In fact, his implicit theoretical model of religion seems to be informed by the kind of functional assumptions found in J. Milton Yinger's definition of a universal church as "a religious structure that is relatively successful in supporting the integration of society, while at the same time satisfying, by its pattern of beliefs and observances, many of the personality needs of individuals on all levels of society." [13] Like a church, with its orthodoxy and heresies, its canonical myths and professions of faith, its rites of communion and excommunication, baseball appears in these terms as the functional religion of America.

Of course, this account of the church of baseball is positioned in a historical moment of great public disillusionment with the professional game. Feeling betrayed by both greedy players and arrogant owners, many devotees have become apostates of the religion of baseball. In this context, the phrase "church of baseball" shifts from metaphor to irony; it becomes a figure of ironic displacement as collective memory is transformed from commemoration of an enduring tradition into nostalgia for a lost world. From this vantage point, the continuity and uniformity of baseball tradition, the sacred time and sacred space of the baseball religion, can only be re-created in memory.

THE FETISH OF COCA-COLA

A very different theoretical model of religion is developed in Mark Pendergrast's For God, Country, and Coca-Cola. Drawing upon the famil-

iar definition of religion provided by Clifford Geertz, Pendergrast proposes that Coca-Cola is a religion because it is

> a system of symbols which acts to establish powerful, pervasive, and long-
> lasting moods and motivations in men by formulating conceptions of a gen-
> eral order of existence and clothing these conceptions in such an aura of fac-
> tuality that the moods and motivations seem uniquely realistic.[14]

To his credit, Pendergrast does not force his history of Coca-Cola into
the mold of Geertz's definition. Rather, he allows the major actors in the
drama to evoke their religious moods and motivations in their own
voices. Here, I will mention only some of the more striking examples.

From the beginning, the beverage was enveloped in a sacred aura: its
inventor, John Pemberton, referred to one of Coca-Cola's original in-
gredients, cocaine (which remained in the mix from 1886 until 1902), as
"the greatest blessing to the human family, Nature's (God's) best gift in
medicine" (27). During the 1890s, Coca-Cola emerged as a popular tonic
in the soda fountains that a contemporary commentator described as
"temples resplendent in crystal marble and silver" (16). Eventually, however, the blessings of Coca-Cola moved out of the temple and into the
world.

Company executives, advertisers, bottlers, and distributors displayed
distinctively religious moods and motivations in relation to the sacred
beverage. Asa Candler, the Atlanta entrepreneur who started the Coca-
Cola empire, was described by his son as regarding the drink with "an
almost mystical faith" (68). Candler eventually "initiated" his son "into
the mysteries of the secret flavoring formula" as if he were inducting him
into the "Holy of Holies" (61). Robert Woodruff, who became president
of the company in 1923, "demonstrated a devotion to Coca-Cola which
approached idolatry" (160). Harrison Jones, the leading bottler of the
1920s, often referred to the beverage as "holy water" (146). Even the
bottle itself was a sacred object that could not be changed. At a 1936 bottlers convention, Harrison Jones declared, "The Four Horsemen of the
Apocalypse may charge over the earth and back again—and Coca-Cola
will remain!" (178). Archie Lee, who assumed direction of Coca-Cola advertising in the 1920s, complained that the "doctrines of our churches
are meaningless words," but he speculated that "some great thinker may
arise with a new religion" (147). Apparently, Archie Lee, along with
many other "Coca-Cola men," found that new religion in Coca-Cola.

Throughout the second half of the twentieth century, the Coca-Cola
religion inspired a missionary fervor. At the first international conven-

tion, at Atlantic City in 1948, an executive prayed "May Providence give us the faith . . . to serve those two billion customers who are only waiting for us to bring our product to them" (238). Delony Sledge, an advertising director in the early 1950s, proclaimed, "Our work is a religion rather than a business" (261). Obviously, the Coca-Cola Company has imagined its enterprise as a religious mission.

Coca-Cola has also assumed religious significance for the consumer, having "entered the lives of more people," as one executive put it, "than any other product or ideology, including the Christian religion" (406). In the jive vocabulary of the 1930s, Coca-Cola was known as "heavenly dew." But the religious significance of Coca-Cola extends far beyond such playful invocations. Coca-Cola gave America its orthodox image of Santa Claus in 1931, by presenting a fat, bearded, jolly old character dressed up in Coca-Cola red; it became the most important icon of the American way of life for U.S. soldiers during World War II; it represented an extraordinary sacred time—the "pause that refreshes"—redeemed from ordinary postwar routines of work and consumption; and from the 1960s on, it promised to build a better world "in perfect harmony." One indication of the popular religious devotion to the drink was the public outcry at the changed formula of "New Coke" in 1985, which caused one executive to exclaim, "They talk as if Coca-Cola had just killed God" (364). In these profoundly religious terms, as editor William Allen White observed in 1938, Coca-Cola became a potent symbol of the "sublimated essence of America" (198).

Although the popular religion of Coca-Cola has pervaded American society, it has also been global. Represented in over 185 countries—more countries, Pendergrast notes, than are in the United Nations—the Coca-Cola Company has extended its religion all over the world. As company president Roberto Goizueta put it: "Our success will largely depend on the degree to which we make it impossible for the consumer around the globe to escape Coca-Cola" (397). The 1980s film *The Gods Must Be Crazy* suggests precisely this impossibility of escaping the religion of Coca-Cola, with its absurd parable of Coca-Cola's effect among a remote community of Bushmen in southern Africa. As Pendergrast notes, the film opens with "the totemic bottle fall[ing] out of the sky onto the sands of the Kalahari Desert, where it completely transforms the lives of the innocent Bushmen as surely as Eve's apple in Eden" (406). Here we find Coca-Cola as a sacred sign: a sign subject to local misreading, perhaps, but nevertheless the fetish of a global religion, an icon of the West, a symbol that can mark an initiatory entry into modernity. Through massive global exchanges and specific local effects, the religion of Coca-Cola has placed its sacred fetish "within arm's reach of desire" (376) all over the world.

"What utter nonsense!" a skeptic might justifiably conclude after reviewing this alleged evidence for the existence of a Coca-Cola religion. Coca-Cola is not a religion. It is a consumer product that has been successfully advertised, marketed, and distributed. In the best tradition of American advertising, the Coca-Cola Company has created the desire for a product that no one needs. Even if it has led to the "Coca-colonization" of the world, this manipulation of desire through effective advertising has nothing to do with religion.

In the study of popular culture, however, the religious character of advertising, consumerism, and commodity fetishism has often been noted. "That advertising may have become 'the new religion of modern capitalist society,'" Marshall W. Fishwick has recently observed, "has become one of the clichés of our time." [15] Advertising-as-religion has transformed "commodity fetishism" into a redundant phrase. In the symbolic system of modern capitalist society that is animated by advertising, the commodity is a fetish object.

As a model for defining and locating religion, the fetish raises its own theoretical problems. As William Pietz has shown in a series of articles, the term "fetish" has been a focal point for ongoing controversies in Western culture over what counts as authentic making. From the Latin *facere*, "to make or to do," the term has carried the semantic burden of indicating artificial, illicit, or evil making, especially in the production of objects of uncertain meaning or unstable value. In this respect, the fetish is not an object; it is a subject for arguments about meaning and value in human relations.

As a modern dilemma, the problem of the fetish arises in complex relations of encounter and exchange between "us" and "them." On the one hand, the fetish is something "they" make. Recalling the evil making— the *maleficium*—of black magic, Portuguese traders on the west coast of Africa in the seventeenth century found that Africans made *fetissos*, objects beyond rational comprehension or economic evaluation. Likewise, for generations of anthropologists, the fetish was an object that "they" make, a sign of their "primitive" uncertainty over meaning and inability to evaluate objects. On the other hand, Marx, Freud, and their intellectual descendants have found that the fetish is something "we" make—the desired object, the objectification of desire—something integral to modern subjectivities and social relations.[16]

Drawing upon this ambivalent genealogy of the fetish in Western culture, Michael Taussig has recently emphasized the importance of "state fetishism" in both making and masking the rationality and terror of the modern political order.[17] This recognition of the role of fetishized making in the production and reinforcement of the state resonates with recent research on the making of those collective subjectivities—the imagined communities, the invented traditions, the political mythologies—that animate the modern world.[18] All of these things are made, not found, but they are made in the ways in which only the sacred or society can be produced.

Unlike the historical continuity and social solidarity represented by the church, therefore, the fetish provides a model for religion in which religion is inherently unstable. As an object of indeterminate meaning and variable value, the fetish represents an unstable center for a shifting constellation of religious symbols. Although the fetishized object might inspire religious moods and motivations, it is constantly at risk of being unmasked as something made and therefore as an artificial focus for religious desire. The study of religion in popular culture is faced with the challenge of exploring and explicating the ways in which such "artificial" religious constructions can generate genuine enthusiasms and produce real effects in the world.

THE POTLATCH OF ROCK 'N' ROLL

As if it were not enough to bestow religious status on baseball and Coca-Cola, we now have to confront the possibility that rock 'n' roll should also count as religion. Certainly the ambivalent relations between rock and religion have often been noticed. As Jay R. Howard has observed, "Religion and rock music have long had a love/hate relationship."[19] On the one hand, rock 'n' roll has occasionally converged with religion. Rock music has sometimes embraced explicitly religious themes, serving as a vehicle for a range of religious interests, from heavy metal Satanism to contemporary Christian evangelism.[20] On the other hand, rock 'n' roll has often been the target of Christian crusades against the evils that allegedly threaten religion in American society. From this perspective, rock music appears as the antithesis of religion: not merely an offensive art form but a blasphemous, sacrilegious, and antireligious force in society.[21]

Rock's ambivalent relationship with religion is obvious. Less apparent, perhaps, is the inherently religious character of rock 'n' roll, and yet attempts have been made to theorize rock 'n' roll as religion. For example, rock 'n' roll has given rise to "a religion without beliefs"; it has given scope for the emergence of a new kind of "divinely inspired shaman"; it has revived nineteenth-century Romantic pantheism; rock music, concerts, and videos have provided occasions for what Durkheim called "ecstasy ritual"; and a new academic discipline—"theomusicology"—has included rock 'n' roll in its mission "to examine secular music for its religiosity."[22] From various perspectives, therefore, rock 'n' roll has approximated some of the elementary forms of the religious life.

In one of the most sustained and insightful analyses of the religious character of rock 'n' roll, Dave Marsh's book-length cultural analysis of the archetypal rock song, "Louie, Louie," explores the secret of its meaning, power, and rhythm, the "sacred duh duh duh. duh duh."[23] He issues a daunting assessment of all previous attempts to address his topic: the "academic study of the magic and majesty of duh duh duh. duh duh," as Marsh puts it bluntly, "sucks" (77). To avoid this condemnation, we must proceed not with caution, but with the recklessness that the song requires. We must say, with the song's African-American composer Richard Berry, who first recorded "Louie, Louie" as a calypso tune in 1956, "Me gotta go now," and see where that going takes us.

As Dave Marsh follows the sacred rhythm of "Louie, Louie," especially as it was incarnated by the Kingsmen in 1963, he dismisses previous attempts to explain the secret of the song's appeal as the result of effective marketing or the intentional mystification produced by its unintelligible lyrics. In rejecting economic and rhetorical explanations, Marsh advances an analysis of the secret of "Louie, Louie" in explicitly religious terms. His analysis uncovers layers of religious significance that are all associated with a "gift." Although his discussion is inspired by the dramatic prelude to the instrumental break—"Let's Give It to 'Em, Right Now!"—it is also directly related to the power of giving and receiving in the history of religions.

The song might be regarded as if it were a divine gift. As Marsh's colleague Greil Marcus puts it, by the 1980s "the tune was all pervasive, like a law of nature or an act of God." Marsh plays upon this theme: If the song was a gift from God or the gods, "he, she, or they chose a vehicle cut from strange cloth, indeed—deus ex cartoona" (78). However, the sacred gift of "Louie, Louie," the hierophany of incoherence, three chords, and a cloud of dust, cannot be accounted for in the conventional terms of any orthodox theology. Accordingly, Marsh turns to a passage in the gnostic Gospel of Thomas that seems to capture the "holy heartbeat" of "Louie, Louie."

> Jesus said, "If you bring forth what is within you, what you bring forth will save you. If you do not bring forth what is within you, what you do not bring forth will destroy you."

Bringing forth all that is within them, the gnostic celebrants of "Louie, Louie" are saved—if not "eternally," as Marsh clarifies, then at least temporarily, during the liberating moment when they participate in the rhythm of the "sacred duh duh duh. duh duh" and the "magical incantation" of "Let's Give It to 'Em, Right Now!" (73–4).

Ultimately, however, the religious significance of the gift must be located in relations of exchange. Here a Native American ritual—the potlatch—provides a model for giving and receiving in which the gift assumes a sacred aura. From a Chinook term meaning simply "to give," the potlatch practiced by indigenous communities of the Pacific Northwest signifies the ritualized display, distribution, and sometimes destruction of valued objects at ceremonial occasions.[24]

Although potlatch has variously been interpreted in the ethnographic literature as religious ritual, status competition, a kind of banking system, or even a periodic outburst of "unabashed megalomania," Marsh focuses on three aspects. First, the gift is total. The potlatch demands giving "everything you had: your food, your clothing, your house, your name, your rank and title." As a ritual occasion for giving everything away, the potlatch demonstrates an "insane exuberance of generosity." Second, the gift is competitive. In ritual relations of exchange, tribes compete with each other to move to the "next higher plane of value." Third, the sacred secret of the gift is ultimately revealed in destruction. As the ritualized exchanges of ceremonial gift giving escalate in value, the supreme value of the gift is realized by destroying valued objects, so that, as Marsh concludes, "eventually a whole village might be burned to the ground in order that the rules of the ceremony could be properly honored" (79–80).

By an odd coincidence, the Pacific Northwest was home to both the Native American societies that performed the potlatch, and the rock 'n' roll bands of the early 1960s that played the song "Louie, Louie." In Marsh's account, both demonstrate the religious "secret" of the gift, especially as it was revealed in acts of conspicuous destruction, in ritual acts that "violated every moral and legal tenet of non–Native American civilization, encumbered as it was with the even stranger socioreligious assumption that God most honored men by allowing them to accumulate possessions beyond all utility in this life, let alone the next" (80). In these "socioreligious" terms, the "modern day electronic potlatch" of rock 'n' roll violates Euro-American religious commitments to capitalist production and accumulation, to property rights and propriety, by reviving the sacred secret of the gift.

In defense of the capitalist order, J. Edgar Hoover's FBI pursued a four-year investigation of "Louie, Louie" during the 1960s, in search of evidence of subversion and obscenity in the song and its performers. As Marsh recalls, Hoover's mission "consisted precisely of visiting the plague of federal surveillance upon any revival of the potlatch mentality" (80). But "Louie, Louie" survived this state-sponsored inquisition. Defying all attempts to suppress it, the song remains the archetype of the sacred gift at the religious heart of the potlatch of rock 'n' roll.

"What utter, absolute, and perverse nonsense!" anyone might conclude after being subjected to this tortuous exposition of the religion of rock music. Rock 'n' roll is not religion. Besides the obvious fact that it is a major part of the entertainment industry, rock 'n' roll is a cultural medium in which all the "anarchistic, nihilistic impulses of perverse modernism have been grafted onto popular music." As a result, it is not a religion; it is a "cult of obscenity, brutality, and sonic abuse."[25]

The model of the potlatch, however, refocuses the definition of religion. As exemplified most clearly by rituals of giving and receiving, religion is a repertoire of cultural practices and performances, of human relations and exchanges, in which people conduct symbolic negotiations over material objects and material negotiations over sacred symbols. If this theoretical model—religion as symbolic, material practice—seems to blur the boundaries separating religious, social, and economic activity, then that is a function of the gift itself, which, as Marcel Mauss insists in his classic treatment, is a "total" social phenomenon in which "all kinds of institutions find simultaneous expression: religious, legal, moral, and economic."[26] According to Mauss, the potlatch, as ritual event, social contest, and economic exchange, displays the complex symbolic and material interests that are inevitably interwoven in religion. Similar interests, Dave Marsh and Greil Marcus argue, can be located in rock 'n' roll.

In the performance of the potlatch, Mauss observes, the contested nature of symbolic and material negotiations becomes particularly apparent; the "agonistic character of the prestation is pronounced."[27] If contests over the ownership of sacred symbols characterize the potlatch, what is the contest that is conducted in the potlatch of rock 'n' roll? It is not merely the competition among musical groups, a competition waged in the "battle of the bands" that Marsh identifies as an important element of the history of "Louie, Louie." It is a contest with a distinctively religious character. In broad agreement with rock critics Marsh and Marcus, anthropologist Victor Turner proposes that rock 'n' roll is engaged in a contest over something as basic as what it means to be a human being in a human society. "Rock is clearly a cultural expression and instrumentality of that style of communitas," Turner suggests, "which has arisen as the antithesis of the 'square,' 'organization man' type of bureaucratic social structure of mid-twentieth-century America." [28] By this account, rock 'n' roll, as antistructure to the dominant American social structure, achieves the human solidarity, mutuality, and spontaneity that Turner captures in the term "communitas." It happens in religious ritual; it happens in rock 'n' roll.

This "agonistic character" of the potlatch of rock 'n' roll, however, is not only evident in America. As Greil Marcus has proposed, the potlatch might unlock the "secret history of the twentieth century." [29] Tracking a disconnected narrative that links Dada, surrealism, litterists, situationists, and performance art, Marcus rewrites the cultural history of the twentieth century from the vantage point of the punk rock that was epitomized in 1976 by the Sex Pistols. Surprisingly, perhaps, that revised history depends heavily upon a sociology of religion that is implicitly rooted in the foundational work of Emile Durkheim and extended by Marcel Mauss's seminal essay on the gift, but it is a left-hand sociology of religion that takes an unexpected turn through the world of the French social critic, surrealist, and student of religion Georges Bataille.

In his 1933 essay "The Notion of Expenditure," Bataille takes up the topic of the potlatch to draw a distinction between two kinds of economic activity: production and expenditure. While production represents "the minimum necessary for the continuation of life," expenditure is premised on excess and extravagance, on loss and destruction, or, in a word, on the gift. This alternative range of economic activity "is represented by so-called unproductive expenditures: luxury, mourning, war, cults, the construction of sumptuary monuments, spectacles, arts, perverse sexual activity (i.e., deflected from genital finality)—all these represent activities which, at least in primitive circumstances, have no end beyond themselves." While productive economic activity is directed towards goals of subsistence, gain, and accumulation, expenditure is de-

voted to achieving dramatic, spectacular loss. In expenditure, according
to Bataille, "the accent is placed on a loss that must be as great as possible in order for the activity to take on its true meaning." [30] In the performance of the potlatch, especially when gift giving escalates to the destruction of property, Bataille finds a model of expenditure that informs
his entire theory of religion.

As exemplified by the potlatch, religion intersects with rock 'n' roll
because both are cultural practices of expenditure. The gift—as in "Let's
Give It to 'Em, Right Now!"—reopens the complex ritual negotiations
over meaning and power, over place and position, over contested issues
of value in modern American society. In that context, religion in American popular culture is neither a church, nor a symbolic system revolv-
ing around a fetish. Beyond the constraints of any institution or the play
of any desire, religion is defined as religion by the practices, performances, relations, and exchanges that rise and fall and rise again through
the ritualized giving and receiving of the gift.

RELIGION IN AMERICAN POPULAR CULTURE

So now where are we? After this long journey through the religious contours and contents of baseball, Coca-Cola, and rock 'n' roll, we are still
left with the question: where is religion in American popular culture?
How do we answer that question? Where do we look? If we only relied
upon the standard academic definitions of religion, those definitions that
have tried to identify the essence of religion, we would certainly be informed by the wisdom of classic scholarship, but we would also still
be lost.

In the history of the academic study of religion, religion has been defined, following the minimal definition of religion proposed in the 1870s
by E. B. Tylor, as beliefs and practices relating to spiritual, supernatural,
or superhuman beings.[31] This approach to defining religion continues to
find its advocates, both among scholars and in the discourse of popular
culture. The extraordinary athlete, for example, can easily become the
focus of religion to the extent that he or she is regarded as a superhuman
being. When Michael Jordan returned to basketball in 1995, his "sec
ond coming" was portrayed in precisely these superhuman terms. While
Sports Illustrated recorded Michael Jordan's embarrassment at being regarded as the superhuman focus of religious regard—"When it is perceived as religion," Jordan complained, "that's when I'm embarrassed

by it"—it also added that this reservation was expressed by "the holy Bull himself" about "the attention his second coming has attracted." Adding to the embarrassment, the same article quoted Brad Riggert, head of merchandising at Chicago's United Center, who celebrated the return of Michael Jordan by declaring that this "god of merchandising broke all our records for sales." [32] In this case, therefore, Michael Jordan—the "holy Bull," the "god of merchandising"—registers as a superhuman being that should satisfy Tylor's minimal definition of religion.

In a second classic attempt to define religion, Emile Durkheim stipulated in 1912 that religion was constituted by beliefs and practices that revolve around a sacred focus, a sacred focus that serves to unify a community.[33] In this approach to defining religion, which also continues to have its proponents, religion depends upon beliefs and practices that identify and maintain a distinction between the sacred and its opposite, the profane. That distinction between the sacred and the profane has also appeared in the discourse of American popular culture. For example, during the long and difficult development of a crucial new software product, Microsoft hired a project manager who undertook the task with religious conviction. According to the unofficial historian of this project, that manager "divided the world into Us and Them. This opposition echoed the profound distinction between sacred and profane: We are clean; they are dirty. We are the chosen people; they are the scorned. We will succeed; they will fail." [34] According to this account, therefore, the cutting edge of religion—the radical rift between the sacred and the profane—appears at the cutting edge of American technology.

Like church, fetish, and potlatch, these classic definitions of religion—belief in supernatural beings, the distinction between sacred and profane—are at play in American culture. As a result, religion is revealed, once again, not only as a cluster concept or a fuzzy set but also as a figure of speech that is subject to journalistic license, rhetorical excess, and intellectual sleight of hand.[35] For the study of religion, however, this realization bears an important lesson: the entire history of academic effort in defining religion has been subject to precisely such vagaries of metaphorical play.

As I have argued in detail elsewhere, the study of religion and religious diversity can be seen as originating in the surprising discovery by Europeans of people who have no religion. During the eras of exploration and colonization, Europeans found indigenous populations all over the world who supposedly lacked any trace of religion. Gradually, however, European observers found ways to recognize—by comparison, by anal-

ogy, and by metaphoric transference from the familiar to the strange—
the religious character of beliefs and practices among people all over the
world. This discovery did not depend upon intellectual innovations in
defining the essence of religion; it depended upon localized European
initiatives that extended the familiar metaphors already associated with
religion, such as the belief in God, rites of worship, or the maintenance
of moral order, to the strange beliefs and practices of other human populations.[36] In the study of religion in American popular culture, I would
suggest, we are confronted with the same theoretical dilemma of mediating between the familiar and the strange.

The theoretical models of religion that we have considered allow some
of the strangely religious forms of popular culture—baseball, Coca-
Cola, and rock 'n' roll—to become refamiliarized as if they were religion. These models allow them to appear as the church, the fetish, and
the sacred gift of the ritual potlatch in American popular culture. Why
not? Why should these cultural forms not be regarded as religion?

The determination of what counts as religion is not the sole preserve
of academics. The very term "religion" is contested and at stake in the
discourses and practices of popular culture. Recall, for instance, the disdain expressed by the critic who dismissed rock 'n' roll as a "cult of obscenity, brutality, and sonic abuse." In this formulation, the term "cult"
signifies the absence of religion, the opposite of "religion." The usage of
the term "cult," however it might be intended, inevitably resonates with
the discourse of an extensive and pervasive anticult campaign that has
endeavored to deny the status of "religion" to a variety of new religious
movements by labeling them as entrepreneurial businesses, politically
subversive movements, or coercive, mind-controlling, and brainwashing
"cults." In that context, if we should ever speak about the "cult" of baseball, Coca-Cola, or rock 'n' roll, we could be certain about one thing:
we would not be speaking about religion.

The very definition of religion, therefore, continues to be contested in
American popular culture. However, if we look again at the privileged
examples considered above—baseball, Coca-Cola, and rock 'n' roll—
they seem to encompass a wildly diverse but somehow representative
range of possibilities for what might count as religion. They evoke familiar metaphors—the religious institution of the church, the religious
desires attached to the fetish, and the religious exchanges surrounding
the sacred gift—that resonate with other discourses, practices, experiences, and social formations that we are prepared to include within the
orbit of religion. Why do they not count as religion?

In the end, we will need to answer that question. In this case, however, "we" refers to all of us who are in one way or another engaged in the professionalized and institutionalized academic study of religion. Participants in American popular culture have advanced their own answers. As a baseball player, Buck O'Neil certainly had an answer: "It's a religion." As a Coca-Cola executive, Delony Sledge definitely had an answer: "Our work is a religion." As a rock 'n' roller, John Lennon had his own distinctive and controversial answer: "Christianity will go. It will vanish and shrink. I needn't argue about that. I'm right and I will be proved right. We're more popular than Jesus now." [37] These claims from outside the discipline raise problems of definition and analysis which need to be addressed within the study of religion. In different ways, as I have tried to suggest, the terms "church," "fetish," and "potlatch" signify both the problem of defining religion and the complex presence of religion in American popular culture.

NOTES

1. Mark Pendergrast, *For God, Country, and Coca-Cola: The Unauthorized History of the World's Most Popular Soft Drink* (New York: Charles Scribner's Sons, 1993), 400.

2. Buck O'Neil, "Why Would You Feel Sorry for Me? An Interview with Buck O'Neil," in *Baseball: An Illustrated History,* ed. Geoffrey C. Ward and Ken Burns (New York: Alfred A. Knopf, 1994), 226–31, quotation from 231.

3. Quoted in Ken Burns and Lynn Novick, "Preface: Where Memory Gathers," in Ward and Burns, *Baseball,* xvii–xviii, quotation from xviii.

4. Thomas Boswell, "The Church of Baseball," in Ward and Burns, *Baseball,* 189–93, quotation from 189.

5. Ibid., 193.

6. Ibid., 189–90.

7. Ibid., 189.

8. See Joseph L. Price's essay in this volume for another account of this speech from *Bull Durham.*

9. See, for example, Horace Miner, "Body Ritual Among the Nacirema," *American Anthropologist* 58, no. 3 (1956): 503–7.

10. George Gmelch, "Baseball Magic," in *Conformity and Conflict: Readings in Cultural Anthropology,* ed. James P. Spradley and David W. McCurdy (Glenview, Ill.: Scot, Foresman, 1978), 373–83.

11. Sigmund Freud, "Obsessive Acts and Religious Practices," in *The Standard Edition of the Complete Psychological Works of Sigmund Freud,* ed. James Strachey (London: Hogarth Press, 1953), 9:117–27.

12. Thomas Hobbes, *Leviathan,* ed. Michael Oakeshot (New York: Collier Books, 1962), 69; Emile Benveniste, *Indo-European Language and Society,* trans. Elizabeth Palmer (London: Faber and Faber, 1973), 522.

13. J. Milton Yinger, *Religion, Society, and the Individual* (New York: Macmillan, 1957), 147.

14. Pendergrast, *God, Country, and Coca-Cola,* 400; further citations will be made in parentheses in the text. For Clifford Geertz's definition of religion as "a system of symbols," see "Religion as a Cultural System," in *Anthropological Approaches to the Study of Religion,* ed. Michael Banton (London: Tavistock, 1966), 1–46, especially 4.

15. Marshall Fishwick, review of Sut Jhally, *The Codes of Advertising, Journal of Popular Culture* 26, no. 2 (1992): 155–6, quotation from 155.

16. William Pietz, "The Problem of the Fetish, I," *Res: Anthropology and Aesthetics* 9 (Spring 1985): 5–17; "The Problem of the Fetish, II," *Res: Anthropology and Aesthetics* 13 (Spring 1987): 23–45; "The Problem of the Fetish, IIIa," *Res: Anthropology and Aesthetics* 16 (Autumn 1988): 105–23. For further development of the problem of the fetish in contemporary cultural analysis, see Emily Apter and William Pietz, eds., *Fetishism as Cultural Discourse* (Ithaca: Cornell University Press, 1993), and Patricia Spyer, ed., *Border Fetishisms: Material Objects in Unstable Places* (New York: Routledge, 1998).

17. Michael Taussig, "Maleficium: State Fetishism," *The Nervous System* (London: Routledge, 1992), 111–40.

18. See, for example, Benedict Anderson, *Imagined Communities: Reflections on the Origin and Spread of Nationalism* (London: Verso, 1991); Eric Hobsbawm and Terrence Ranger, eds., *The Invention of Tradition* (Cambridge: Cambridge University Press, 1985); Leonard Thompson, *The Political Mythology of Apartheid* (New Haven: Yale University Press, 1985).

19. Jay R. Howard, "Contemporary Christian Music: Where Rock Meets Religion," *Journal of Popular Culture* 26, no. 1 (1992): 123–30, quotation from 123.

20. See Robert L. Gross, "Heavy Metal Music: A New Subculture in American Society," *Journal of Popular Culture* 24, no. 1 (1990): 119–30; Davin Seay and Mary Neely, *Stairway to Heaven: The Spiritual Roots of Rock 'n' Roll* (New York: Ballantine, 1986); and William D. Romanowski's discussion of Contemporary Christian Music in chapter 5 of the present volume.

21. Bob Larson, *Rock and Roll: The Devil's Diversion* (McCook, Nebr.: Larson, 1967); Linda Martin and Kerry Segrave, *Anti-Rock: The Opposition to Rock 'n' Roll* (Hamden, Conn.: Archon Books, 1988); Dan Peters, Steve Peters, and Cher Merrill, *What About Christian Rock?* (Minneapolis: Bethany, 1986).

22. David Shenk and Steve Silberman, *Skeleton Key: A Dictionary for Deadheads* (New York: Doubleday, 1994), ix; Tony Magistrale, "Wild Child: Jim Morrision's Poetic Journeys," *Journal of Popular Culture* 26, no. 3 (1992): 133–44; Robert Pattison, *The Triumph of Vulgarity: Rock Music in the Mirror of Romanticism* (Oxford: Oxford University Press, 1987); Lisa St. Clair Harvey, "Temporary Insanity: Fun, Games, and Transformational Ritual in American Music Video," *Journal of Popular Culture* 24, no. 1 (1990): 39–64; Jon Michael Spen-

cer, "Overview of American Popular Music in a Theological Perspective," in *Theomusicology,* ed. Jon Michael Spencer (Durham, N.C.: Duke University Press, 1994), 205–17, quotation from 205.

23. Dave Marsh, *Louie, Louie* (New York: Hyperion, 1993), 74; further citations will be made in parentheses in the text.

24. For a useful review of literature on the potlatch, see Steven Vertovec, "Potlatching and the Mythic Past: A Re-evaluation of the Traditional Northwest Coast American Indian Complex," *Religion* 13 (1983): 323–44. See also Sergei Kan, *Symbolic Immortality: The Tlingit Potlatch of the Nineteenth Century* (Washington: Smithsonian Institution Press, 1989).

25. Martha Bayles, *Hole in Our Soul: The Loss of Beauty and Meaning in American Popular Music* (New York: Free Press, 1994), 12.

26. Marcel Mauss, *The Gift: Forms and Functions of Exchange in Archaic Societies,* trans. Ian Cunnison (London: Cohen & West, 1969), 1.

27. Ibid., 4.

28. Victor Turner, *Dramas, Fields, and Metaphors: Symbolic Action in Human Society* (Ithaca: Cornell University Press, 1974), 262.

29. Greil Marcus, *Lipstick Traces: A Secret History of the Twentieth Century* (Cambridge: Harvard University Press, 1989).

30. Georges Bataille, "The Notion of Expenditure," in *Visions of Excess: Selected Writings, 1927–1939,* ed. Allan Stoekly, trans. Allan Stoekly, Carl R. Lovitt, and Donald M. Lesie, Jr. (Minneapolis: University of Minnesota Press, 1985), 116–29, quotations from 118.

31. E. B. Tylor, *Primitive Culture.* 2 vols. (London: John Murray, 1870), 1:424.

32. *Sports Illustrated,* 10 April 1995, 92.

33. Emile Durkheim, *The Elementary Forms of the Religious Life,* trans. Joseph Ward Swain (New York: Free Press, 1965), 62.

34. G. Pascal Zachary, *Showstopper: The Breakneck Race to Create Windows NT and the Next Generation at Microsoft* (New York: Free Press, 1994), 281.

35. On the significance for the study of religion of the polythetic categories "cluster concept" and "fuzzy set," see Fitz John Porter Poole, "Metaphors and Maps: Towards Comparison in the Anthropology of Religion," *Journal of the American Academy of Religion* 54 (1986): 411–57, especially 428, and Jonathan Z. Smith, *Drudgery Divine: On the Comparison of Early Christianities and the Religions of Late Antiquity* (Chicago: University of Chicago Press, 1990), especially 50.

36. See David Chidester, *Savage Systems: Colonialism and Comparative Religion in Southern Africa* (Charlottesville: University Press of Virginia, 1996).

37. Quoted in Fred Bronson, *The Billboard Book of Number One Hits* (New York: Billboard Publications, 1985), 201.

PART FOUR

RELIGION AND
POPULAR CULTURE
IN DIALOGUE

When a Roman Catholic activist, a Muslim imam, or a Lakota holy man criticizes certain features of popular culture, or when Sinead O'Connor tears up a picture of the pope on national television, their activity does not quite fit into the previous relationships between religion and popular culture: Religion in Popular Culture, Popular Culture in Religion, and Popular Culture as Religion. Critiques of popular culture by representatives of religious communities, and challenges to religious understandings by figures from popular culture, open the door to conversation between the two; thus our fourth type of interaction is Religion and Popular Culture *in Dialogue*. Reference to dialogue between religion and popular culture is not meant to imply that the two are totally discrete, separate realities. They interpenetrate one another, and many of the participants in this dialogue are themselves involved both in a religious community and in popular culture. For many, however, religion provides an interpretive lens through which culture may be read and critiqued, and popular culture raises realities and themes that cast religion in a different light. The three essays in this section all participate in this conversation.

Robert Jewett's reflection on Clint Eastwood's *Pale Rider* represents a Christian biblical scholar's dialogue with themes that emerge from popular culture. By comparing the appeal to vengeance in the Eastwood film to Paul's discussion of vengeance in Christian scripture (Romans 12), Jewett finds that cultural realities lead him to new insights about the biblical passage, while he also uses his understanding of Paul to provide a theological critique of American culture.

Anthony Pinn draws on insights derived from blues and rap music to critique African American religious explanations of suffering and evil. In a reversal of the more common pattern, in which critics utilize their religious principles to critique popular culture, Pinn's critique moves in the other direction. For him, African American popular music raises questions about the adequacy of the theological formulations offered by the black church.

Meredith Underwood establishes a dialogue with and about cyberculture, specifically the worldwide web and its disembodied presentation of women. Working from a self-consciously Christian feminist perspective, she doubts the utopian claims of gender equality in a computer-based world. She raises religiously based questions about how women are presented and served by the web, while drawing pragmatic conclusions about the way "wired women" will make use of cyberspace.

These three essays illustrate that dialogue between religion and popular culture can take several forms. Often, religion critiques the values and assumptions of popular culture, offering appreciation, criticism, or both. Yet commentators also can use themes and insights from popular culture to critique religion, raising questions about its relevance or adequacy. In either case, the discussions provoke clarification of implicit values and assumptions in both religion and popular culture.

THE DISGUISE OF VENGEANCE
IN PALE RIDER

> Beloved, do not avenge yourselves,
> but give way to the wrath [of God],
> for it is written,
> "Vengeance is for me, I will repay,"
>   says the Lord.
> But if "your enemy is hungry, feed him;
> if he is thirsty, give him drink;
> for by doing this you will pile up
>   burning coals upon his head."
> Do not be conquered by the evil
> but conquer the evil with the good.
>
> (Romans 12:19–21)[1]

Paul's warning against vengeance runs counter to the widely shared sentiment several years ago regarding the capture of a mass murderer in the city where I live. After a killing spree through the Midwest, Alton Coleman was captured without resistance by police in Evanston, Illinois. I heard one professional woman state the view that many others held: "I wish he had been killed in a shootout with the police!" The yearning for vengeance—quick and final—assumes a most peculiar form in American society, where popular myths frequently picture the police or private detectives acting as avenging judges and executioners.

A popular preference for shootouts resulting in the death of criminals is expressed in classical form in *Pale Rider*,[2] with Clint Eastwood playing the role of the nameless stranger who rids a small town of murderous predators in the employ of a ruthless mining corporation. Since the stranger had earlier been shot by these same predators, there is an element of personal vengeance disguised in this traditional tale of the selfless redemption of a helpless community. The movie has some fascinating links with Romans 12–13 that may shed light on how to counter the siege of violence that threatens to engulf the country.

VENGEANCE AND VIGILANTISM

"Beloved, never avenge yourselves," writes Paul to the Roman Christians. It is an admonition that flatly counters the sentiments expressed about an American serial killer. But rather than condemning those who feel the need for direct and effective vengeance in the case of particularly heinous criminals, I would like to explore the cultural origin of this sentiment. It can be traced back to early American traditions of using violent stories from the Bible to justify taking the law into one's own hands. Derived from Biblical stories such as that of Phinehas the lyncher in Numbers 25, there has long been an ideal of holy vengeance in our society. Acting on the premise that God inspires and justifies the righteous to take vengeance in his behalf, we have celebrated a succession of heroes who took the law into their own hands—from the disguised citizens of the Boston Tea Party through John Brown in his Harper's Ferry raid, from the Phantom and Dick Tracy through the Avengers of contemporary comics.

The vigilante ethos justifies direct violence so long as the evil is clearcut, the vigilantes disinterested, and their identity kept secret. The appeal of this vigilante tradition has been that quick justice could be achieved for crimes which might otherwise go unpunished, and achieved through private channels, without encouraging feuds or reprisals.

To understand how citizens could prefer that the defenders of the law would sometimes take the law into their own hands and execute vengeance on criminals requires a grasp of the widely popular myth system that developed in the wake of the vigilante tradition. The large number of popular superheroes and heroines in modern entertainment derive from earlier forms of the cowboy western and detective stories that have embodied this vigilante plot.

A crucial example of this kind of story is *The Virginian,* Owen Wister's 1902 novel that contains the first duel on Main Street in American literature.[3] The story is set in the context of struggles between farmers and ranchers in Wyoming, specifically the 1892 range war in Johnson

County, in which lynching and systematic thievery was practiced by both sides. The ranchers imported a trainload of Texas gunmen equipped with dynamite to put down the resistance of the farmers who were home-steading land in the public domain that the ranchers had used without rent for years. Widespread violence came to a climax near Buffalo, Wyoming, where federal troops finally intervened.

Wister romanticized the ranchers' side of this struggle in the creation of the Virginian, a tall, nameless cowboy who becomes the foreman of Sunk Creek Ranch. He is forced to track down a rustling gang, capturing two of its members, one of whom was formerly his best friend. True to the vigilante code, the Virginian renounces friendship and has the thieves hung. But the chief rustler, Trampas, escapes with a guileless side-kick, and when the trackers approach, Trampas shoots him in the back so he can escape on their only horse.

Several years later, Trampas is seen by the Virginian and his fiancée, Molly the schoolteacher. She comments that it seems "wicked that this murderer" should go free when others were hanged for rustling. "He was never even arrested," says the girl. "No, he helped elect the sheriff in that county," replies the Virginian (385–6).

In the dramatic climax of this novel, which became required reading for high school classes all over the U.S., the rustler issues a formal chal-lenge for a Main Street duel. The Virginian seeks the counsel of the clergy-man who was to perform the wedding ceremony. The bishop was con-vinced that the rustlers had to be dealt with by vigilante tactics, that "they elected their men to office, and controlled juries; that they were a star-ing menace to Wyoming. His heart was with the Virginian. But there was his Gospel that he preached, and believed, and tried to live." He reminds the Virginian of the Biblical injunction not to kill. The heroic cowboy re-sponds, "Mighty plain to me, seh. Make it plain to Trampas, and there'll be no killin.'" As they parry about the contradictory demands of reli-gion and law, the Virginian poses the key question: "How about instru-ments of Providence, seh?" In other words, what about the Biblical idea of providence taking the form of heroic vigilantes who rid the world of evil-doers? As the hero reluctantly departs for the duel that threatens to prevent his hoped-for marriage and end even his life, the bishop finds he cannot repress the words, "God bless him! God bless him!" (404–6)

We all know the end of the story, even without having read *The Vir-ginian* or seen the film in which Gary Cooper played the title role. In the archetypal duel with Trampas, the bad guy draws and shoots first, but is killed by the Virginian's bullets. The hero's friends marvel, "You were that cool! That quick!" (416), which expresses the cool ethos of the vigilante tradition. The state of Wyoming is redeemed from the reign of crime, which results in a paradisal condition in which all problems are solved. Even Molly's New England conscience, which had resisted the vigilante tactic so strongly, finally relents, and she marries the Virginian. The novel ends with the hero and his family ensconced in prosperity and long life. The Virginian becomes a wealthy rancher and mine owner, passing the redemptive task onto the next generation.

This novel produced hundreds of imitations, including *Pale Rider*. The cinematic triumph of *The Virginian* in 1929 was soon followed by the emergence of serialized stories featuring the supercowboy ("The Lone Ranger"), the supercop ("Dick Tracy") and superheroes ("Superman," "Wonderwoman," and "Captain America")—tales that embody the same kind of plot. It is one of the most pervasive tales in American culture,[4] giving shape to the yearning for quick and effective public redemption, but not with the legally sanctioned public means. Here is violent redemption without due process of law, accomplished with dignity and heroic self-restraint. The public does not take the law into its own hands in this kind of story; "instruments of providence" take up the task of the "wrath of God" which Paul believed should never be shouldered by people in their own behalf.

The ingenious result of this widely popular myth is that it allows Americans to imagine gaining retribution without incurring personal risk. They gain in fantasy a perfect form of public justice, but never feel the need to call it vengeance. It is disguised as a story of courageous redemption of helpless communities by selfless heroes. This kind of story has the immense advantage of occurring without the slow and cumbersome machinery of public means in a constitutional society. The United States has police forces without judicial powers, a court system bound by constitutional restraints, and forms of punishment that often seem awkward and ineffective. Compared with this, who would not prefer the "miracle" of a Pale Rider?

CINEMATIC MIRACLES AS DISGUISED VENGEANCE

Megan Wheeler is burying her puppy after the marauders hired by the mining corporation have made yet another raid on the defenseless miners at Carbon Canyon. She breaks off the recitation of the Twenty-third

Psalm to look skyward: "But they killed my dog! Why did you let them kill my dog?" When there is no reply from the silent heavens, she returns to the psalm: "For thou art with me. Thy rod and thy staff comfort me— but we need more than comfort. We need a miracle . . . Mother says miracles happen, sometimes. The book says they happen" (13–4). On her way back from the hillside grave, young Megan sees a horseman with a broad-brimmed hat riding slowly into town. It is, of course, Clint Eastwood, playing the role of the Preacher who ultimately takes his .44 caliber pistol out of storage to redeem the community from its corporate outlaws.

On one level, the redemption promised by the Pale Rider seems to fit the parameters of the divine "wrath" that Paul hopes will be provided in the place of human vengeance. When the stranger rescues one of the beleaguered miners from three of the hired gunmen, he is invited to Megan's home for supper. After cleaning up from his redemptive exertions, the stranger appears with a clerical collar. Everyone else is stunned that so skilled a fighter could be a preacher, but not Megan: "She knew a miracle when she met one" (53). Later, she describes the uncanny stranger with a line from the Book of Revelation that provides the title of the movie: "And I looked, and beheld a pale horse: and his name that sat on him was death, and hell followed with him" (Rev. 6:8). The tall stranger demonstrates a miraculous ability to prevail against the bullies hired by the mining corporation, smashing them with effortless ease in encounter after encounter. His presence in Carbon Canyon causes an incredible revival of morale, and the miners set about restoring their homes and mining sluices. He reappears with uncanny timing to rescue Megan from a gang rape at the hands of the corporate thugs, and acts as a divinely appointed judge to dynamite the mining operation that destroys entire hillsides and valleys with its gigantic water cannon. This "god of some sort" [5] prevails against incredible odds in the final duel against a gang of hired gunmen, killing them all with the relentless accuracy of an apocalyptic avenger.

The profile of the gunmen hired to contend with the tall preacher matches the Biblical archetype of agents of the antichrist. In Stephen Chapman's words, "The enemy is the devil himself. . . . Even the villainous lawman's name, Stockburn, conjures up flames." [6] The six gunmen along with Stockburn are made to appear like the antipode of the seven horsemen of the apocalypse. Alan Dean Foster's novelization of the film provides this chilling description of the scene in front of Stockburn's headquarters, when the corporation's telegram arrives to summon these dark angels of destruction into battle:

> There were seven horses tied to the hitching rail that fronted the lawman's office. Each had a black saddle on its back. A black leather rifle holster slashed at an angle on the right-hand side of each seat. Their oiled walnut stocks gleaming, seven Winchesters filled the holsters. Expensive guns, worth a lot of money in a bustling frontier community like Yuba City. They sat there in plain sight, apparently unguarded. There was nothing to prevent a resourceful thief from making off with the lot of them.
>   Nothing except knowing better. (129)

When they arrive in the mining community, the gunmen begin by shooting down an unarmed miner with uncanny coordination and accuracy. After making him dance in the streets for a while by firing at his feet, Stockburn gives a slight nod and all seven guns fire simultaneously into his defenseless body. It is the kind of law that the Preacher had explained to the miners after they decided to refuse the offer to be bought out by the corporation. "I don't know how he ever managed to get himself appointed Marshal, but that doesn't matter. . . . Stockburn's got six deputies been with him a long time. Six—and they'll uphold whatever law pays them the most. Killing's their way of life" (113).

The model for this kind of figure within the Pauline tradition is the "lawless one" who usurps the place of a properly lawful agent, deluding people "with all power and with pretended signs and wonders, and with all wicked deception" (2 Thess. 2:9). So it is appropriate that these evil gunmen are slain in the end by divine agency, fulfilling the Biblical paradigm (2 Thess. 2:8). In the most incredible duel scene in cowboy western history, the Preacher alone prevails in a Main Street face-off with all seven killers, who come within twenty-three yards before anyone fires. This is the final miracle, doubtless achieved by more than human powers, which is probably the reason why the "Inspirational Films" lobby group touted the "positive Christian values" in *Pale Rider*.[7]

Yet there is a major discrepancy in this picture of impartial, superheroic redemption. After all of his partners are killed by the tall stranger, Stockburn is cut down by a hail of bullets, fired more quickly than even the most experienced gunman could get off from a single gun: "The shells ripped an eight-inch circle into the Marshal's chest" (215). This odd detail matches the strange sight caught by the camera earlier in the movie while the Preacher was washing up for dinner in the Wheelers' home. The scars on his back would have caught the eye of the most indifferent observer. There were five of them. Each was a half inch in diameter and evenly spaced from its neighbor. They formed a neat circle. Though long since healed over, their origin was unmistakeable.

They were bullet holes. (45)

This explains why Stockburn suddenly recognizes the tall stranger in the duel scene, having earlier dismissed reports of similarities to someone he used to know. "Couldn't be him," Stockburn had told his corporate employer earlier in the story, because the "man I'm thinking about is dead" (170). Stockburn had evidently fired that circle of bullets in the back of the tall stranger and left him for dead.[8] The duel on main street is therefore an act of personal vengeance: as the tall stranger explains before the battle, "It's an old score. There's more to it than the problems of the folks in Carbon Canyon. Time's come to settle things" (190).

So this particular superhero tale disguises what really amounts to private vengeance, carried out in the precise fashion of tit for tat, an eye for an eye, and a tooth for a tooth. The symmetry is almost Biblical, a kind of holy battle against a demonic enemy who receives a precisely measured rebribution. Yet the greatness of this particular Clint Eastwood film is that the disguise is fleetingly lifted. Behind the facade of a story of superheroic redemption, with all its apocalyptic references to the pale horse of the Book of Revelation, there lies a tale of personal vengeance.[9]

MOVING PAST VENGEANCE

The relevance of Paul's view in Romans to this popular American view of vengeance gains cogency when we realize that Paul was facing similar myths in the first century. In particular, large segments of the Jewish community in the period prior to the Jewish-Roman war of A.D. 66–70 favored a vigilante strategy. Modeling their behavior on the same heroic tales in the Old Testament that inspired early vigilantes in our society, zealous Jews believed that their violence against evildoers would achieve divine ends.[10] In particular, these advocates of Jewish vigilantism felt that the Roman governing authorities should be opposed on principle, and with force.[11] And it was natural in this kind of environment that many persons who had suffered injustices at the hands of the authorities felt themselves called by the heroic myths to take the law into their own hands, to avenge themselves and thus avenge Israel.

It is in this context that Paul's admonition—"Beloved, never avenge yourselves, but leave it to the wrath of God"—assumes significance. He was tapping the ancient tradition of never being a judge in one's own cause, a principle embodied in Jewish as well as Greco-Roman law. It is a crucial principle as well for modern jurisprudence. The trouble with the police or private citizens taking the law in their own hands is that the omniscience and impartiality of myths such as *The Virginian* and *Pale Rider* rarely work out in reality. Zealotism is presumptuous, Paul implies here, for it refuses to "give way" to the prerogatives of divine justice ("give way to the wrath of God; for it is written, 'Vengeance is mine, I will repay, says the Lord'").[12]

It is significant in this connection that Paul does not deny the principle of vengeance.[13] He realizes that in this imperfect and violent world, human beings yearn for some kind of justice. When people have suffered at the hands of thieves and murderers, they usually hope that such evil will someday be overcome. The belief that the universe is as unfair as everyday experience is would be too demoralizing to tolerate. This may be one reason why the Judeo-Christian and Islamic religions have developed such elaborate systems of belief in the final judgment, when all accounts will be paid in full, for both good and ill. What Paul counsels in Romans is patient reliance on the instruments of divine justice.

The most significant question with regard to vengeance is what to do in the meanwhile. If people simply harbor their hatred and fail to express it, they sicken; if they give way to the desire for vengeance and take the law into their own hands, they usually suffer disastrous consequences. As Thomas Wilson once said, "It costs more to avenge injuries than to bear them."[14] In place of zealous vigilantism, Paul advises two things— an active concern for the life and well-being of one's adversary, and submission to lawful governmental authority—but at first glance these appear to be flatly contradictory.

Paul treats the concern for the good of one's enemies first. "Instead, if your enemy is hungry, feed him; if he is thirsty, give to drink. For in so doing you heap coals of fire on his head" (Rom. 12:20). This verse specifies what was meant earlier in this chapter by the admonition "Repay no one evil for evil" (Rom. 12:17). Whereas the natural tendency is to respond to violence with violence, to meanness with reprisals, the actions of mercy aim to break the deadly cycle. The abiding guideline of the church is the commitment to "overcome evil with good," as the following verse sets forth (Rom. 12:21).

William Klassen has made a convincing case that the metaphor of burning charcoal on the adversaries' heads is meant to represent their repentance and remorse rather than painful vengeance inflicted on them.[15] The strategy Paul recommends seeks not only the well-being but also the transformation of persecutors and criminals: "Do not be overcome by evil, but overcome evil with good" (Rom. 12:21). This is not to say that what one aims to achieve will actually be accomplished in every instance.[16] Those commentators who accuse Paul of being an incurable optimist in these verses confuse, in my opinion, intentions with results. As Paul knew from personal experience, there are some adversaries who redouble their hatred when shamed by such unanticipated gestures of love.

But one aims to achieve, in the final analysis, not vengeance but transformation. We are seeing a remarkable embodiment of this idea in the "Truth and Reconciliation Commission" in the Republic of South Africa. Archbishop Desmond Tutu explained the rationale of this commission to reporter Colin Greer:

> To pursue the path of healing for our nation, we need to remember what we have endured. But we must not simply pass on the violence of that experience through the pursuit of punishment. We seek to do justice to the suffering without perpetuating the hatred aroused. We think of this as *restorative justice* . . . focused on restoring the personhood that is damaged or lost. . . . Restorative justice is different from *retributive* justice. Retributive justice will adjudicate guilt, then the case is closed. But restorative justice is about the profound inability of retributive justice to effect *permanent* closure on great human atrocities. . . . Vengeance leads only to revenge.[17]

This transformist viewpoint is consistent with the Apostle Paul, whose final goal was to "conquer the evil with the good."

The other half of the counsel Paul offers, besides concern for one's enemy's well-being, is submission to lawful authority. This is laid out in Rom. 13:1–7, one of the most controversial passages in the Pauline epistles.[18] Here Paul flatly states that those who resist governing authorities resist God, for the government serves as "the servant of God to execute God's wrath on the wrongdoer." The idea is that a primary component of what the Virginian called "instruments of providence" is governmental law enforcement.[19]

There are mitigating circumstances that help us understand why Paul was so positive in his appraisal of the Roman government. At the time of writing Rom. 13, an exemplary period of Roman justice and law enforcement was nearing its end. The court system was being administered with unusual fairness; the conspiracy laws had been abolished; the emperor himself was obeying the law—a fact worth mentioning, given that he was Nero, who would violate every law in the book within a few years. Paul did not foresee what was to come when he made the sweeping claims in this passage, and thus we are justified in taking his views with a grain or two of salt. When the law is perverted by a Marshal Stockburn, some form of resistance seems justified. Yet the most serious question this passage raises is the question of whether or not it contradicts the business of heaping coals on the head of one's enemy, feeding him, and giving him drink.

How could Paul have it both ways? How could he call upon the Christian community to pray for its enemies and bless those who persecute it, and at the same time urge obedience to the government, which "bears the sword" to execute divine wrath on criminals?

PAUL'S HOLY INCONSISTENCY

The common sense answer is surely that Paul is inconsistent, that one or the other side of his position should be abandoned. This is, in fact, what Christian communities have usually done. Advocates of law and order have taken Rom. 13:1–7 and have dropped the idea of loving the enemy: from the tradition of the divine right of kings to the proponents of submission to Adolf Hitler in Lutheran and Catholic Germany, the word has been to obey the emperor or the Führer as a kind of God, and as for the enemies, let them be rooted out, harrassed, and destroyed. Others in the Christian tradition have taken Rom. 12 and abandoned 13, urging the love of enemies no matter what their scale of provocation, no matter how many atrocities they may have committed. The pacifists holding this preference have tended to oppose the use of law enforcement powers to punish criminals, and resist the use of warmaking powers to curb the actions of tyrants.

I would grant that either position has a kind of consistency that Paul seems to lack. But as I mull over this passage, I find myself wondering whether there is not a deeper consistency of human experience that Paul is tapping into in Rom. 12–13. Look at the record of our American cultural tradition: having resisted strong law enforcement ever since our struggle against the British crown, we have tolerated remarkably high levels of violence and disorder. On the American frontier in the decades before *The Virginian* was written, for example, there was very lax law enforcement, little protection for the rights of the weak, and a series of economic disorders that proved destructive to stable relationships. Hundreds of vigilante actions occurred in response to those evils, some of them inspired by the religious heritage I sketched earlier. But vigilantism also frequently disguised what amounted to personal vengeance. The net result of such actions was the further erosion of security and a popularization of violence. Lacking a widely shared belief in the government as the agency of divine wrath against criminals, we found it necessary to invent "instruments of providence" in the form of frontiersmen, tall cowboys, and, later, superheroic figures.

The problem is that such superhero stories serve to popularize the very antisocial behavior that causes much of the problem in the first place. I believe that the impact of such superheroic "disguises for vengeance" is visible not only in the unusually high crime statistics in the United States, but also in the increasing frequency of mass murderers. The society influenced by these stories is facing a virtual epidemic of cool and relentless killers.[20] Several years ago, a colleague and I presented a paper on this topic, suggesting that recent assassins and mass murderers have tended to model their behavior after the avengers of the superheroic dramas.[21] They differ from "normal" citizens in that they take the mythic paradigm of the Virginian seriously, tracking down persons they imagine are offenders and giving them vigilante justice, swift and direct.

These considerations lead me to wonder whether the seeming contradiction of Paul's perspective may not be superior to the tradition our culture has favored. If you abandon the idea of the government as the agent of divine wrath, then you will have to invent such agents—which is precisely what our culture has done. People who are suffering from abuse and injustice simply will not tolerate a world in which there is no hope for tidying up the score. But to glorify the heroes of vigilante justice is to sow the seeds of our own destruction. It is to allow us to think that we might become vigilante heroes or heroines ourselves, or at least elect one to the Marshal's office or the White House. When that happens, respect for the law disintegrates, and the yearning for violent resolution of the quick and easy sort gains highly dangerous, public forms.

Is there not perhaps a more healthy balance in Paul's view? A kind of holy inconsistency? Paul holds fast to the idea of divine vengeance, both in the world to come and in the form of vigorous law enforcement by a duly constituted government. At the same time, he strongly resists any involvement in vengeance on one's own behalf—"Beloved, never avenge yourselves"— because no one should ever attempt to become a judge in one's own cause. And to counter the poison of vengeance that afflicts anyone who is abused and persecuted, as the early Christians were, Paul counsels that "if your enemy is hungry, feed him; if he is thirsty, give him drink; for by doing this you will pile up burning coals upon his head." As Desmond Tutu has suggested in advocating a policy of divine inconsistency, "restorative justice" rests on the premise that "we live in a moral universe after all. What's right matters." So, he explains, "we aim to remember, to forgive and to go on, with full recognition of how fragile the threads of community are."[22]

Is there perhaps a deeper, more divine logic at work here? Are humans really capable of such actions if they are not entirely certain of the final judgment of God, the final triumph of righteousness? How can persecuted people counter despair without such a hope? How can they gain the power to respond creatively with burning coals except by trusting, finally, in the power of God either to transform or to punish the wicked? Is there not perhaps a deeper understanding of the human psyche in Paul's apparent inconsistency than in our current cultural simplicities?

TWO CONCLUDING SUGGESTIONS

I leave these questions for you to ponder, because they are larger than I can comprehend on my own. Yet to take Paul's position seriously is to question certain aspects of our cultural tradition, to challenge our attitudes toward popular entertainment, and to alter our perspective on the proper role of government. It provokes us to think about what Roger Bacon wrote in his *Essays:* "Revenge is a kind of wild justice; which the more man's nature runs to, the more ought law to weed it out."[23] Private vengeance disguised as selfless redemption has now reached such proportions in our society that we must begin to develop a new respect for the law, and for equal but firm justice under law. This pondering leads to two practical suggestions.

The first relates to Paul's concern for an impartial system of law enforcement. Obviously, if we seek the perfection of the myths, we shall find any legal system fatally flawed; there were numerous loopholes in Paul's time as well. But when our system works fairly well, we should not stifle expressions of support and appreciation. When the five Evanston police arrested mass murderer Alton Coleman quickly, efficiently, and without undue use of force, we had every reason to be proud. We should find ways to express our gratitude when a system patterned on Paul's ideal of due process of law functions properly. And we should constantly be ready to support and pay for international institutions of this sort, comparable to the kind of international law enforcement that the Roman Empire offered when this letter was written.

Secondly, there is a need to develop contemporary forms of "heaping up burning coals" on the heads of adversaries. While relying on the final vengeance of God, whether in this life or the next, there is the practical task of feeding enemies and seeking the welfare of abusers. Rather than retaliating against neighbors, the challenge is to find ways to help them within the context of truthfulness about crimes committed. Rather than simply seeking the defeat of national adversaries, the challenge is to discover ways to assist them. This is not to condone their crimes or to diminish the injuries they have caused; if Paul is right, the crimes of our enemies and ourselves will be avenged in God's good time, both in this world and the next. In the meanwhile, it makes sense to set about the business of seeking to overcome evil with good. Only in this way shall it be possible truly to become instruments of God's peace. For "vengeance is mine, I will repay, says the Lord."

NOTES

This essay is adapted from Robert Jewett, *Saint Paul at the Movies: The Apostle's Dialogue with American Culture* (Louisville, Ky.: Westminster/John Knox, 1993), chapter 10.

1. See the rhetorical analysis of this material in Walter T. Wilson, *Love without Pretense: Romans 12.9–21 and Hellenistic-Jewish Wisdom Literature* (Tübingen: Mohr-Siebeck, 1991), 132–6.

2. *Pale Rider* was directed and produced by Clint Eastwood and released by Warner Brothers in 1985. Citations will be drawn from Alan Dean Foster, *Pale Rider: A Novelization* (New York: Warner, 1985), and made parenthetically in the text.

3. This material about Wister's *The Virginian* is adapted from Robert Jewett and John Shelton Lawrence, *The American Monomyth* (Garden City, N.Y.: Anchor Press/Doubleday, 1977), 180–5. Citation from Wister will be taken from *The Virginian: Horseman of the Plains* (Lincoln: University of Nebraska Press, 1992), and will be made parenthetically in the text.

4. See the description of the *American Monomyth* in Bruce David Forbes's introduction to this volume; see also Tom Shales, "Reign of TV Terror Floods Viewers in Vigilantism," *Chicago Tribune,* 17 January 1986, section 5, 5.

5. Vincent Canby, "Vengeance Is His," *New York Times,* 28 June 1985, C8.

6. Stephen Chapman, "Who is the Pale Rider?" *Chicago Tribune,* 7 July 1985, section 5, 3.

7. John M. Kraps reports this detail in "The Gospel According to Eastwood," *Christian Century,* 14 August 1985, 740.

8. I am not inclined to follow Vincent Canby's suggestion in "Vengeance Is

His" that "resurrection also is the key to 'Pale Rider.'" I am more inclined to agree that "just who this fellow was in his previous incarnation is left so vague you have a right to suspect that he might have been Him," i.e., God (C8).

9. See Will Wright's discussion of the "vengeance variation" in *Six-Guns and Society: A Structural Study of the Western* (Berkeley: University of California Press, 1975), 59–74.

10. See Torrey Seland, *Establishment Violence in Philo and Luke: A Study of Nonconformity to the Torah and the Jewish Vigilante Reactions* (Leiden: Brill, 1995).

11. See particularly Martin Hengel, *The Zealots: Investigations into the Jewish Freedom Movement in the Period from Herod I Until 70 A.D.*, trans. D. Smith (Edinburgh: Clark, 1989), 206–32, 283–6.

12. See William Klassen, *Love of Enemies: The Way to Peace* (Philadelphia: Fortress, 1984), 119: "To God alone belongs vengeance. We must believe that God will repay. To preempt God's act is to put ourselves in the place of God. It is the ultimate act of unbelief."

13. See Simon Légasse, "Vengeance humaine et vengeance divine en Romains 12,14–21," in *La Vie de la parole de l'Ancien au Nouveau Testament. Études d'exégèse et d'herméneutique bibliques offertes à Pierre Grelot* (Paris: Desclée, 1987), 281–91.

14. Quoted in Jacob M. Braude, *Lifetime Speaker's Encyclopedia* (Englewood Cliffs, N.J.: Prentice-Hall, 1962), 2:700.

15. William Klassen, "Coals of Fire: Sign of Repentance or Revenge," *New Testament Studies* 9 (1962–63): 337–50; his view is reiterated in *Love of Enemies*, 120; see also S. Bartina, "Carbones encendidos, ¿sobre la cabeza o sobre en veneno? (Prov 25,21–22; Rom 12:20)," *Estudios bíblicos* 31 (1972): 201–3.

16. See Krister Stendahl, "Hate, Non-Retaliation, and Love. 1 QS x, 17–20 and Rom. 12:19–21," *Harvard Theological Review* 55 (1962): 343–55, reprinted in *Meanings: The Bible as Document and as Guide* (Philadelphia: Fortress, 1984), 137–49.

17. Colin Greer, "'Without Memory, There is No Healing. Without Forgiveness, There is No Future,'" *Parade*, 11 January 1998, 4–6, quotation from 6.

18. A survey of the immense literature on this discussion is provided by the Finnish scholar Vilho Riekkinen, *Römer 13. Aufzeichnung und Weiterführung der exegetischen Diskussion, Annales academiae scientiarum fennicae: Dissertationes humanarum litterarum* 23 (Helsinki: Suomalainen Tiedeakatemia, 1980); more recent debate is covered by Jan Botha, *Subject to Whose Authority? Multiple Readings of Romans 13, Emory Studies in Early Christianity* 4 (Atlanta: Scholars, 1994). The most discerning recent study is Stanley E. Porter, "Romans 13:1–7 as Pauline Political Rhetoric," *Filología neotestamentaria* 3 (1990): 115–39.

19. See particularly Robert H. Stein, "The Argument of Romans 13:1–7," *Novum Testamentum* 31 (1989): 332–6.

20. See Dave Grossman, *On Killing: The Psychological Cost of Learning to Kill in War and Society* (Boston: Little, Brown, 1995), 299–322.

21. Robert Jewett and John Shelton Lawrence, "The Fantasy Factor in Civil Religion: Assassinations and Mass Murders in the Media Age," *explor: A Jour-*

nal of Theology 7 (1984): 71–80; reprinted in *Sunstone* 7 (1982): 28–33 and *Mission Journal* 17, no. 2 (1983): 3–7, 17.

22. Greer, "Without Memory," 6.

23. Burton F. Stevenson, *The Home Book of Quotations: Classical and Modern* (New York: Dodd, Mead, 1967), 1711.

13

Anthony Pinn

RAP MUSIC AND ITS MESSAGE

On Interpreting the Contact between Religion and Popular Culture

INTRODUCTION

George Clinton and Parliament would be in town doing some of their classic cuts—"Flashlight," etc. My friends were going and part of me wanted to attend, but, as a good "church boy," I was torn. Should a Christian attend such a "worldly" event, listening to songs that did not address themes of spiritual uplift? Granted, I did on occasion listen to these songs, but I always believed this was somehow wrong. Could there be a relationship between these two worlds? Initially I thought not. My friends went to the concert and I stayed home. It would be years before I would see George Clinton live, only after I was able to recognize and appreciate the natural conversation or convergence between popular culture and religiosity.

Media sources tend to highlight the negative and reactionary interaction between religious ideologies and popular culture; one need only think about the friction between Rev. Calvin Butts and several "gangsta" rap artists. The former argues that this form of musical production erodes moral values and religious sensibilities; the artists respond that they are speaking of reality and are misunderstood and disrespected. This, however, is only one form of interaction between religion and popular culture. On another level, Paul Tillich is correct; they work in harmony—revising and rethinking each other, interpreting each other for the benefit of larger communities. As Bruce David Forbes writes in the introduction: "Because popular culture surrounds us, it seems reasonable to assume that its messages and subtle themes influence us as well as reflecting us. If popular culture reflects values we already hold, that reflection also serves to reinforce our values and deepen our commitment to them" (p. 5).

This essay is my attempt to discuss this form of interaction between religion and popular culture. The question is, how do those who are interested in understanding and exploring the connections between these two worldviews interpret the dialogue? My goal is not to outline or rehearse the conversation, but rather to provide a methodology for exploring this conversation, a method growing out of the source material. I have labeled this approach "nitty gritty hermeneutics."

"NITTY GRITTY HERMENEUTICS" DEFINED

The term "nitty gritty" denotes a hard and concrete orientation in which the "raw natural facts" are of tremendous importance, irrespective of their ramifications. While serving to confine vision and orientation to certain parameters of roughness, it also uncompromisingly expands the meaning and possibility of life to its full limits. Thus nitty gritty hermeneutics seeks a clear and unromanticized understanding of a hostile world, and entails "telling it like it is" and taking risks.

Aspects of this hermeneutic include a sense of heuristic rebelliousness as well as raw and uncompromised insight. This hermeneutical approach takes the material of life that goes unspoken and hidden, and expresses it. In Foucault's terms, this hermeneutic ruptures American dialogue by both surfacing "subjugated knowledge," which dismantles false perceptions and harmful practices, and by altering popular perceptions and life values.[1]

Defined by its nitty gritty character, nitty gritty hermeneutics exhibits a sense of nonconformity. It ridicules interpretations and interpreters who seek to inhibit or restrict liberative movement and hard inquiries into the problems of life. The nitty gritty "thang," so to speak, forces a confrontation with the "funky stuff" of life, and, oddly enough, finds strength in the challenge posed. These two principles—rootedness in rebelliousness and raw, uncompromising insight—not only give shape to this hermeneutic, but are also found in cultural expressions such as the blues. That is to say, the blues illustrates the nature and function of nitty gritty hermeneutics.[2] I do not mean to suggest an endorsement of oppressive opinions held within the blues or other forms of musical expression such as rap. However, I am not willing to reject these forms of expression simply because they contain some of the misguided tendencies of the larger society. Rather, I am suggesting that the positive expressions of this music (i.e., the examples of this music which have a constructive intention) suggest a hermeneutic which is worthy of investigation and implementation by those interested in the connections between religion and popular culture, because it already entails this very conversation between religious realities and cultural production.

NITTY GRITTY HERMENEUTICS IN ACTION: THE BLUES

The historical origin of the blues as a musical form is virtually impossible to pinpoint. It is, however, safe to say that blues songs took form long before their actual recording, and likely developed alongside spirituals and secular work songs. Consequently, existential and musical contexts informing work songs and spirituals determined the content, shape, and sound of the blues. Yet whereas the spirituals—"religious songs"—tell the story of Black life in terms of a collective reality, blues songs connote a shift to an individualized and personal accounting of existence within a hostile society.[3]

Within these songs, the promises of the spirituals were weighed and tested in light of life's controlling hardships, and utopian ideals were found wanting. Hence the blues as a musical form is concerned with truth as it arises out of experience. That is, for blues artists "truth is experience and experience is the truth."[4] The blues's commitment to the unpolished expression of Black life made some segments of the Black community uncomfortable. For example, the blues met with the disapproval of Black churches because the lyrical content and "seductive" nature of the music fell outside of the norms, values, and morality advocated by Black church tradition. Raw or "gutbucket" experiences were poetically presented, critiqued, and synthesized, yet unapologetically understood as real and unavoidable. No subject was taboo, although most were shrouded in metaphorical language. The rejection of the blues stems from the "hard living" and hard questioning noted in the lyrics. In this manner, blues performers openly discussed aspects of life that church folk would just as soon keep hidden, and challenged espoused yet unpracticed principles of religion.[5]

Blues artists often found traditionally religious interpretations of life fundamentally flawed and unproductive. The blues critiqued the hypocrisy and inactivity of Black churches and used this as fuel for significations and sarcasm. J. T. "Funny Paper" Smith hits upon this point when singing the following lines:

> Some of the good Lawd's children, some of them aint no good,
> Some of the good Lawd's children, some of them aint no good.
> Some of them are the devil, ooh, well, well,
>   and won't help you if they could.

> Some of the good Lawd's children kneel upon their knees and pray,
> Some of the good Lawd's children kneel upon their knees and pray.
> You serve the devil in the night, ooh, well
>   and serve the Lawd in the day.[6]

Smith's questioning of banal theological formulations and sarcasm towards hyper-optimistic religiosity, when he sings about the traditional notion of a good God held by Black Christian religion, is also typical of the blues. He sings:

> I used to ask God questions, then answer that question my self,
> I used to ask God questions, then answer that question my self,
> 'Bout when I was born, wonder was there any mercy left?

> You know it must be the devil I'm servin', I know it can't be Jesus Christ,
> You know it must be the devil I'm servin', I know it can't be Jesus Christ,
> 'Cause I ask him to save me and look like he tryin' to take my life.[7]

Looking over the course of his life, Smith is unable to accept traditional conceptions of God (as compassionate and historically involved), nor is he willing to explain his continual hardship through divine mystery. Taking a hard look at his condition and Christian faith, Smith raises subtle questions concerning the evidence of God's involvement in the world and one's ability to decipher this involvement.

The blues forces a rethinking of what religion is and what it means to be religious. In this way, blues players expanded the narrow perceptions of religiosity beyond the confines of mainstream Black traditional approaches. Hence, with respect to the blues, it is unacceptable to limit religion and religiosity to traditional Black Christian (or theistic) models. Consider the following lines:

> Yes I went out on the mountain, looked over in Jerusalem,
> Yes I went out on the mountain, looked over in Jerusalem,
> Well, I see them hoodoo women, ooh Lord, makin' up in their
>   low-down tents.

> Well I'm going to Newport to see Aunt Caroline Dye,
> Well I'm going to Newport to see Aunt Caroline Dye,
> She's a fortune-teller, oh Lord, she sure don't tell no lie.[8]

Productive religiosity comes to mean a religiosity whose principles have felt consequences for daily life. Doctrinal and theological "purity" pale in comparison to existential need. Usable religion must not place abstraction and neat theological categories above human experience: only that which is proven by experience holds value. Religious expression is here defined by its commitment to human accountability, and responsibility for human occurrences. To a large extent, productive religiosity is fluid, in that its dynamics alter with the existential situation; thus it avoids dilemmas of applicability resulting from the rigid demands and dictates of tradition.

The nitty gritty hermeneutics surfacing in the blues interprets religion based upon complex Black life as a tool, by which humans are encouraged to remove psychologically comforting theological "crutches" and develop themselves as liberators. Ralph Ellison captures this meaning in "Richard Wright's Blues":

> The blues is an impulse to keep the painful details and episodes of a brutal experience alive in one's aching consciousness, to finger its jagged edge and to transcend it, not by the consolation of philosophy [or religious constructs] but by squeezing from it a near-tragic, near-cosmic lyricism. As a form, the blues is an autobiographical chronicle of personal catastrophe expressed lyrically. . . .
>
> [Blues songs'] attraction lies in this, that they at once express both the agony of life and the possibility of conquering it through sheer toughness of spirit. They fall short of tragedy only in that they provide no solution, offer no scapegoat but the self.[9]

There is a sense in which blues tones, such as those mentioned above, carve out a space of creativity and ingenuity in the middle of oppressive circumstances, and this space belongs to both those who sing and those who listen. I believe there is much for academics to learn from the contours of this made space.

NITTY GRITTY HERMENEUTICS IN ACTION: RAP

Blues songs make use of the same creative and existential materials as the spirituals, thereby creating a continuum of musical expression. But perpetual hardship, and the need to respond creatively to it, continues into the present, resulting in a new musical exploration that is both continuous with the earlier one, and appropriate to current conditions and contexts. This new form is rap music. Consequently, the substance of this nascent method of interpretation—nitty gritty hermeneutics—also appears in rap.[10]

An accurate history of rap music must understand it in connection to the larger development of hip hop culture. Hip hop first emerges as a cultural and creative response to the matrix of industrial decline, social isolation, and political decay endemic to the Bronx in New York City.[11] Faced with declining opportunities for socioeconomic mobility, and the accompanying marginality, young artists made use of their creative resources to establish an alternative "way of being" in the world, complete with a vocabulary, style of dress, visual artistic expression (graffiti art emerges as early as 1971), and dance (break dancing is present as early as 1973) uniquely their own.[12]

In essence, hip hop culture and its musical voice—rap—signal both cultural resistance and, in keeping with this essay's theme, a continued dialogue with religious ideals and institutions. The music behind rap lyrics, with its sampling and strong beats, rethinks traditional understandings of proper musical formation, and finds pleasure in the sounds the music industry labeled undesirable. As Tricia Rose insightfully points out,

> Although famous rock musicians have used recognizable samples from other prominent musicians as part of their album material, for the most part, samples were used to "flesh out" or accent. . . . Rap producers have inverted this logic, using samples as a point of reference, as a means by which the process of repetition and recontextualization can be highlighted and privileged.[13]

On another level, rap lyrics—the verbal expression of hip hop's more general affirmation of identity and critique of the larger society—present a "postmodern" articulation of themes, lifestyles, and behaviors found in Black oral traditions. Rap music has roots in African musical techniques and African influenced oral practices, and uses folk heroes such as "Bad Niggers," Brer Rabbit, Signifying Monkey, Stagolee, and Dolemite as models in order to develop ways of outsmarting and temporarily gaining the upper hand over the dominant society while still rehearsing the realities of Black urban life. More recent influences include storytellers such as the Last Poets and Gil Scott-Heron, as well as midcentury radio personalities such as Douglas "Jocko" Henderson.[14]

Most rap music afficionados mark the emergence of what became contemporary rap with the arrival of DJ Kool Herc in New York City, from Jamaica, in 1972. DJ Kool Herc used the Jamaican tradition of toasting or speaking over extended beats and, like Afrika Bambaataa and Grandmaster Flash, began holding open-air parties in the Bronx. In 1979, "Rapper's Delight" was recorded by the Sugar Hill Gang (on Sugar Hill Records), and sold millions of copies.[15] The Sugar Hill Gang, from New Jersey, brought rap to a larger audience by making it available to groups outside select New York circles. Prior to this, MCs and DJs distributed their goods using dubbing devices and cassette players known as "boom boxes," but with the success of "Rapper's Delight," the commercialization of rap music was underway.

In the early 1980s, East Coast hip hop made its way to the West Coast, where Soul Sonic Force and Afrika Bambaataa toured in 1980. Captured by the rap music craze, Los Angeles residents used two skating rinks, "World on Wheels" and "Skateland," as rapper training camps, where contests sponsored by radio station KDAY were held. This style gave way to the creativity of Eazy E, Dr. Dre (formerly of the World Class Wreckin' Crew), Ice Cube, and the other members of NWA (Niggaz With Attitude). NWA firmly established a style of rap based upon the hard facts of L.A. gang and hustler life. Granted, Schooly D and KRS-One (with Scott La Rock) on the East Coast and Ice-T ("Six in the Morning" and "Colors") on the West Coast had already pioneered this hard-life form of rap music, and I do not mean to downplay the national attention they gained. Yet it was not until NWA recorded "Straight Outta Compton" (as a Macola Company/Ruthless record production for sale out of car trunks) and successfully adopted "gangsta" personae that this style gained a large audience. As Brian Cross says: "NWA placed themselves on the hiphop map with authenticity, capturing the aggression and anger of the streets of South Central in their intonation and timbre. This places the listener in an intimate position relative to their rhymes. Ice-T sounds like a narrator by comparison." [16]

The raw aggression and reckless lifestyle portrayed by this form of rap caught the attention of rap fans and defined the West Coast as the center of "realism" rap or gangsta rap.[17] New York's rap was "flavored" by the dynamics of hip hop culture, and so West Coast rap highlighted, in response, its culture's own defining features, most prominently gang culture. Compton was in direct competition with the Bronx.[18] The reputation of West Coast rap has been enhanced, in recent years, by the work of Cypress Hill, Snoop Doggy Dogg, Dr. Dre, Warren G., Ice Cube, and Yo-Yo.

The above history, although brief, presents the social and cultural context, creative dynamics, and scope—East Coast and West Coast— of rap music's development. What is needed at this point is a typology to clarify the thematic structure of rap's lyrical content. I argue that there are three major (at times overlapping) categories of rap music: "status" rap, "gangsta" rap, and "progressive" rap.

The "status" strand of rap first appears in the Sugar Hill Gang's "Rapper's Delight." This cut consists of braggadocio's rhythms and mild signification, which denote a strong concern with "status" and social prowess. At one point in this rap, "Big Bank Hank" outlines his superior skills and sexual attractiveness. He boasts that a

> Reporter stopped me for an interview
> She said, She's heard stories and She's heard fables
> That I'm vicious on the mike and the turntables.
> This young reporter I did adore,
> So I rocked the mike like I never did before,
> She said damn fly-guy I'm in love with you,
> the casanova legend must have been true.
> I said by the way baby what's your name,
> She said I go by the name of Lois Lane.
> She said you can be my boyfriend, you surely can,
> Just let me quit my boyfriend called Superman.[19]

This style of rap music, emerging early, is concerned with distinguishing artists from their competitors. "Status" rap, combined with break-dance movements, served as the major tool within this struggle for artistic dominance. Both cultural expressions highlighted competitor's flaws and shortcomings while emphasizing the rapper's or dancer's own prowess.

The social critique offered in this brand of rap is usually limited to the assertion of self in opposition to a society that is seeking Black nonexistence. This rupture is often expressed sexually and overtly, such as in the lyrics of New York's "Heavy D" (born Dwight Myers). The following lines are from "Mr. Big Stuff" (1990):

> I'm a fly girl lover and a woman pleaser
> Girls say, "Heavy, let me squeeze you"
> An incredible
> Overweight, huggable
> Prince of poetry
> That's why I'm so lovable.[20]

Groups such as Salt-n-Pepa effectively brought Black women into the rap world beyond roles as sexual objects and targets for male aggression and distrust, highlighting the personal value and strength of Black women. Salt-n-Pepa (the trio of "Salt" [Cheryl James], "Pepa" [Sandy Denton], and "Spinderella" [Dee Dee Roper, the DJ]) argue for self-appreciation—the creation of strong and assertive individuals—and, in so doing, promote the value of human personality. "It's About Expression" (1991):

> You know life is all about expression
> You only live once, you're not coming back
> So express yourself . . .
>
> Express yourself
> You gotta be you and only you, baby
> Express yourself
> Let me be me
> Express yourself
> Don't tell me what I cannot do, baby
> Express yourself.[21]

More recent artists such as Li'l Kim and Foxy Brown also signify and challenge sexual stereotypes.

Although "status" rap contains an implicit political agenda, it explicitly discusses the social "living of life." As Michael Dyson recounts, rap of this nature allows rappers, and by extension their listeners, to momentarily move beyond physical demise and enjoy the material benefits of the American Dream.[22] Unfortunately, this struggle for individual, ontological, and material "space" often results in counterproductive and oppressive tendencies, which can be seen in the sexism, patriarchal ideals, and problematic consumerism that much "status" rap expresses. On one level, this brand of rap strikes at the dehumanizing tendencies of American society; on another level, it buys into the structures and attitudes fostering such dehumanizing practices.

"Gangsta" rap presents this dual message in even stronger terms, responding to the same dehumanizing effects of life in the United States with much more overt intracommunal and extracommunal aggression. The first major gangsta group, NWA, consciously plays out America's nightmare—depicting itself as ruthlessly dominating its environment. However, one notices an implied critique of American racism. Take, for example, NWA's controversial rap "Fuck Tha Police" (1989):

> Fuck the police, comin' straight from the underground
> A young nigger got it bad because I'm brown
> And not the other color. Some police think
> They have the authority to kill a minority
> Fuck that shit 'cause I ain't the one
> For a punk motherfucker with a badge and a gun.[23]

The members of this group point out the manner in which "law and order" operates on principles that encourage the victimizing of young people based upon style of dress and skin color. Whereas some acquiesce to this treatment, NWA promotes resistance to such practices, in order to maintain a sense of self-worth and importance.

If NWA is correct in its analysis, the anger and violence expressed in gangsta rap is reflective of American society in general. In other words, violence and crime do not originate with rap music, but are part of the American fabric and merely magnified by musical expression.

> We ain't the problems, we ain't the villains
> Its the suckers deprivin' the truth from our children
> You can't hide the fact, Jack
> There's violence in the streets everyday
> Any fool can recognize that
> But you try to lie and lie
> And say America's some motherfuckin' apple pie.[24]

Dr. Dre uses the "Americanness" of gangsta rap's lyrics to justify the violence of his album, *The Chronic* (1993). In an interview with *Rolling Stone,* Dr. Dre says:

> People are always telling me my records are violent[,] . . . that they say bad things about women, but those are the topics they bring up themselves. . . . They don't want to talk about the good shit because that doesn't interest them, and it's not going to interest their readers. . . . If I'm promoting violence, they're doing it just as much as I am by focusing on it in the article. That really bugs me out—you know, if it weren't going on, I couldn't talk about it.[25]

In addition to pointing out the oppressive nature of American society, gangsta rap outlines the practices within the "hood" that allow survival. As with "status" rap, gangsta style often entails using counterproductive tools in order to achieve identity and material comfort. A consequence of this is the sexist and misogynistic attitude glorified in the music. Women are often viewed as the enemy, the ones who destroy Black manhood and thereby bring into question the gangsta's survival.[26] As a result of this assumed threat, women are dealt with harshly; they are stopped at all cost from ending the G's quest for success. Rappers, without question, must be held responsible for the oppression supported in their music. At the same time, however, critics and fans must recognize that gangsta rap echoes oppressive precepts acknowledged and encouraged by the larger society.[27]

Even with these flaws, gangsta rap (and to a lesser extent status rap) provides a brief glimpse of the interpretative honesty, roughness, and concern for personal identity inherent in nitty gritty hermeneutics. The appeal to reality at all cost, and despite the possibility of more comfortable agendas, is clear in these two forms of rap. Still, this critical insight is most forcefully presented in the "progressive" strain of rap. Aware of the same existential hardships and contradictions as gangsta rap, progressive rap seeks to address these concerns without intracommunal aggression and in terms of political and cultural education, providing an interpretation of American society and a constructive agenda (e.g., self-respect, knowledge, pride, and unity) for the uplift of Black America. It is also within progressive rap that one encounters a more overt dialogue with and interpretation of Black religiosity.[28]

Nascent progressive rap gained popular attention with "The Message" (1982), by New York rappers Grand Master Flash and the Furious Five. Using a portrait of life amid industrial decline, social alienation, and political corruption, this rap interprets the cycle of poverty and dehumanization producing limited life options and despair. It speaks to the destructiveness of systemically imposed "ghetto" existence.

> You'll grow in the ghetto living second-rate
> And your eyes will sing a song of deep hate
> The places you play and where you stay
> Looks like one great big alleyway.[29]

Grand Master Flash and the Furious Five's appeal stemmed, in part, from the group's uncompromising attention to the "underbelly" of U.S. economic and sociopolitical structures. Yet implicit within this depiction of daily hardships in urban centers was an understanding that knowledge might produce the struggle necessary for transformation.

Progressive rap seeks, first, to change the system, using Black history and cultural developments as well as a critique of social structures to point out the intrinsic value of Black life, and increase positive Black self-expression. A classic representative of this agenda is the group Public Enemy. Its lead rapper, Chuck D, understands rap music as an arena for the exchange of vital information. Rap deciphers the muddled ideologies of political, economic, and social institutions and makes listeners aware of necessary steps leading to self-determination.[30]

As the self-proclaimed "prophet of rage," Chuck D sees the meaning of American society as centering around the control and destruction of Black minds and bodies. Through raps such as "Fight the Power," "Bring the Noise," "Shut 'Em Down," "Party for Your Right to Fight," and "White Heaven / Black Hell," Public Enemy outlines this control and the methods for breaking its grip. Public Enemy's interpretive eye is not focused solely upon the larger society and its flaws, but also chastises African Americans for the role they play in their own destruction.

Of more direct interest here is Chuck D's insight into Black religion. He argues that Black religion should contribute to the liberation of Black people. The meaning of Black religion is found in its support of Black identity and consciousness, and its rejection of status quo politics, economics, and social relations. Chuck D's support of the Nation of Islam suggests that Black churches, as representative of majority Black religious expression, are not in line with religion's ultimate purpose and that the "Nation's" praxis better fulfills the meaning of religion. Public Enemy understands the Nation of Islam as redemptive because it provides the quest for African American progress with a vivifying spiritual base. The 1990 album *Fear of a Black Planet* presents a musical interpretation of the Nation of Islam, inspiring critics to make comments such as this:

> [Public Enemy] has become the spokesperson for a new wave of African-American consciousness shaped in the tradition of Elijah Muhammad, Malcolm X, and Louis Farrakhan. [It] is not the only rap group influenced by the symbols and rhetoric of the Nation of Islam, they are [sic] by far its most significant and most consistent proponents.[31]

Through its Islam-influenced lyrics and rebellious beats, Public Enemy provided a "jeremiad" calling attention to the hypocrisy of white America. Chuck D also reprimanded African Americans for involvement in their own oppression, while pointing out their potential for liberative action. Such a thick and layered message is the hallmark of progressive rap.

Although Public Enemy is generally the primary example used to define the nature and content of progressive rap, it is my opinion that some of the best progressive rap in this decade has been produced by Arrested Development (from Atlanta), notwithstanding the lack of attention given the group within academic treatments. AD, as the group is commonly called, exhibits a hybridization of Afrocentrism and the 1960s Black aesthetic. In keeping with the interpretation of American society provided by Public Enemy, AD sees the fundamental meaning of U.S. institutions and ideologies as demarcated by the ontological and epistemological demise of Black individuals and communities. Through raps such as "People Everday" and "Ache'n for Acres," Arrested Development illustrates the self-destructive and community-eroding effects of consumer-

ism and sociopolitical alienation. Seeing through the ideological plat-
forms aimed at the extirpation of Black life, Arrested Development offers a regenerative program based upon pan-African cultural nationalism, social cohesion, economic cooperation, and proactive politics.

In stronger terms than the other groups mentioned, AD provides a
critique of religiosity which demonstrates the tenacity of nitty gritty hermeneutics. A clear example of this is the rap "Fishin' 4 Religion," from
their album *3 Years, 5 Months and 2 Days in the Life of . . .* (Chrysalis
Records, 1992). In this rap, AD critiques Black ministers' promotion of
passivity as a sign of righteousness, as well as the lack of sustained and
direct community involvement by Black churches. In part, this involves
an attack upon the symbolic and imagistic grounding of Black religion,
by critiquing the inconsistencies between the demands for liberation and
the conception of God peddled by Black Christian churches. Using liberation as a theological norm, AD determines that many Black churches
do not embody the true nature and meaning of Black religion's objective.
Black religion must promote ontological and epistemological "black-
ness" and thereby encourage the holistic survival of the Black community. Unfortunately, however, Black churches are "praising a God that
watches you weep, and doesn't want you to do a damn thing about it."
Thus the activism suggested by Black religion is actually counterproductive, because it does not extend beyond emotional outburst and spiritual platitudes. Resolutions of this nature have no relationship to temporal and proactive plans for social transformation; they are far too
spiritualized to be of any worldly good.

> When they want change the preacher says shout it,
> Does shoutin' bring about the change, I doubt it.
> All shoutin' does is make you lose your voice.

In the words of MC Speech (the group's leader), Black churches fail to
"nurture" African Americans, and instead enslave them within a web of
opiatic eschatology and debilitating consternation. In this way, the essence or genuine meaning of religion is transmuted into a plea for religiously coded banality and "turn-the-other-cheek" benignancy. AD expresses this while relaying a particular church scene:

> . . . sitting in church hearing legitimate woes.
> Pastor tells the lady it'll be alright,
> Just pray so you can see the pearly gates so white.
> The Lady prays and prays, prays, prays, it's everlasting.
> There's nothing wrong with prayin', it's what she's askin'.

According to this critique, many Black churches are unwilling to address the hard issues of life. Therefore, in Marx's phrase, they are the opiate of the people. Individualistic and indolent religiosity promoted by churches is a major factor in the underdevelopment of Black America.

Arrested Development musically outlines a religiosity committed to the hands-on deliverance of Black people from a profusion of existential dilemmas, without respect to traditional theology and doctrine. In this—AD's constructive project—one sees another aspect of nitty gritty hermeneutics: the uncovering and revitalizing of religion outside the confines of long-standing but ineffectual theological tradition. It is a project steeped in realism, in the primacy of experience over doctrine.

For example, in keeping with traditional African religions,[32] Arrested Development extols the earth and calls union with the earth a "divine" source of power and a chief objective of any vibrant religious system. Such a religious system is constructed from the rudimentary and rather Manichean treatment of certain life principles, for example in the rap "Washed Away." Here, the delusion of righteousness and goodness is metaphorically depicted as the destruction of a seashore by demonic tides. AD urges humans to fight the trickster serpent's efforts to destroy the seashore:

> Why do we let them wash it away
> Why are we allowing them to take what's good
> Why won't we teach our children what is real
> Why don't we collect & save what is real
> Look very hard & swim the ocean
> We must find what needs to be found.
> Look all around & find a wise man
> To feed us the truth & keep us sound.

From this sense of connectedness, to a scene much larger than oneself, comes the inspiration for transformation. That is, the proper working of a religion must involve both collective efforts to identify the sources of oppression, and the storing up (and sharing) of vital, self-affirming cultural information. Only a religiosity that participates in and affirms the cultural life of the community, and speaks plainly to pressing issues without paying tribute to unproved theological assertions—no new wine in old skins—is in keeping with the meaning of religion.

The interaction between religious ideals and popular culture is extremely important because it says something about who we are and what is of fundamental importance to us. But how are we to unpack this interaction, this dialogue? The answer rests within the interaction itself, within the contact; it is present in the depictions of life, the raw facts of existence exposed by the coming together of worldviews represented by religion and popular culture. I have labeled the interpretative process involved in the religion / popular culture dialogue nitty gritty hermeneutics. Hopefully this will help scholars of religious studies recognize, among other things, that there are more than riddles in the rap rhymes.

NOTES

This essay is an altered version of Anthony Pinn, *Why, Lord? Suffering and Evil in Black Theology* (New York: Continuum, 1995), chapter 5.

1. See Michel Foucault, *Power/Knowledge: Selected Interviews and Other Writings, 1972–1977* (New York: Pantheon Books, 1980).

2. I thank one of my students, Abraham Wheeler, for valuable information on certain blues figures.

3. See LeRoi Jones, *Blues People: The Negro Experience in White America and the Music That Developed from It* (New York: Morrow Quill, 1963), 63–8. For a more detailed history of the blues, see William Barlow, *"Looking Up at Down": The Emergence of Blues Culture* (Philadelphia: Temple University Press, 1989); Charles Keil, *Urban Blues,* 2d ed. (Chicago: University of Chicago Press, 1969); Paul Oliver, *Blues Fell This Morning: The Meaning of the Blues,* 2d ed., foreword by Richard Wright (New York: Cambridge University Press, 1990); and Jon Michael Spencer, *Blues in Evil* (Knoxville: University of Tennessee Press, 1993).

4. James Cone, *The Spirituals and the Blues: An Interpretation* (New York: Seabury Press, 1972), 78.

5. Part of this critique involves the sarcastic lampooning of repressive Christian sex codes. The blues responds to this aspect of Black religion by openly celebrating expressed sexuality as a vital component of freedom. Using easily deciphered metaphors such as "jelly rolling," blues artists promoted sexuality as a vital and invaluable aspect of humanity. In this way, blues figures such as Ma Rainey, Robert Johnson, Muddy Waters, Koko Taylor, and others moved away from provincial (church inspired) ethical codes and restraining sensibilities, and embraced the full depiction of their being in the world. This implies a hermeneutic or norm of interpretation that examines tradition and rejects religion's allegiance to the nineteenth-century codes of conduct that problematized Black sexuality, thereby denying African Americans a full range of human expression. Nitty gritty hermeneutics, as expressed in the blues, interprets religious conduct codes as properly encouraging the full expression of one's humanity as a symbol of freedom. Religious systems and practices that hamper full human expression are thus inherently hypocritical.

6. James Cone, "The Blues: A Secular Spiritual," in *Sacred Music of the Secular City: From Blues to Rap,* ed. Jon Michael Spencer (Durham: Duke Univer-

sity Press, 1992), 68–97, song quoted on 93. This volume is a special issue of *Black Sacred Music: A Journal of Theomusicology* 6, no. 1 (Spring 1992).

7. Quoted in Oliver, *Blues Fell This Morning*, 118.

8. Quoted in ibid., 128.

9. Quoted in Jerry G. Watts, *Heroism and the Black Intellectual: Ralph Ellison, Politics, and Afro-American Intellectual Life* (Chapel Hill: University of North Carolina Press, 1994), 54–5.

10. This blues-rap continuum extends the spiritual-blues impulse discussed by Cornel West in the article "On Afro-American Popular Music: From Bebop to Rap," in his *Prophetic Fragments* (Grand Rapids: William B. Eerdmans Publishing Co., 1988), 177–88, especially 182–3.

11. See Tricia Rose, *Black Noise: Rap Music and Black Culture in Contemporary America* (Hanover: Wesleyan University Press/University Press of New England, 1994), 21–5. For a more detailed and complete history and analysis of rap music than presented in this essay, see, in addition to Rose, Mark Costello and David Foster, *Signifying Rappers: Rap and Race in the Urban Present* (New York: Ecco, 1990); Brian Cross, *It's Not about a Salary: Rap, Race and Resistance in Los Angeles* (New York: Verso, 1993); William Eric Perkins, ed., *Droppin' Science: Critical Essays on Rap Music and Hip Hop Culture* (Philadelphia: Temple University Press, 1996). Also of interest are magazines such as *The Source, Vibe,* and *RapPages.*

12. Break dancing and graffiti art did not remain exclusively within the Black community. Movies such as *Breakdance* and *Wild Style* commercialized these art forms and brought them to a larger audience. Rapper Fab 5 Freddy's graffiti art, for example, was eventually displayed in New York City galleries.

13. Rose, *Black Noise,* 73. An analysis of the musical element of rap is beyond the scope of this essay; for further information, see Thomas Schumacher, "'This Is a Sampling Sport': Digital Sampling, Rap Music and the Law in Cultural Production," *Media, Culture and Society* 17, no. 2 (April 1995): 253–63; "Rap: Taking It from the Streets," *Keyboard* 14, no. 11 (November 1988): 32–45. See also Tricia Rose, "Soul Sonic Forces: Technology, Orality, and Black Cultural Practices in Rap Music," in *Sounding Off: Music as Subversion/Resistance/Revolution,* ed. Ron Sakolsky and Fred Wei-Han Ho (Brooklyn: Autonomedia, 1995), 97–108, a version of *Black Noise,* chapter 3.

Jon Michael Spencer is aware of the manner in which analysis of the music is often missing from discussions of rap music and other forms of musical expression. In much of his early work, Spencer developed a method for exploring both music and lyrics, as a way of better understanding the religious and theological importance of musical developments. He named this approach theomusicology. Information on his approach might prove helpful for readers: see Jon Michael Spencer, ed., *Theomusicology,* a special issue of *Black Sacred Music: A Journal of Theomusicology* 8, no. 1 (Spring 1994).

14. Douglas "Jocko" Henderson was a disk jockey known for his rhythmic sign on. For an example of this, see Mel Watkins, *On the Real Side: Laughing, Lying, and Signifying; The Underground Tradition of African-American Humor That Transformed American Culture, from Slavery to Richard Pryor* (New York:

Simon & Schuster – Touchstone, 1994), 297. Stagolee (or Staggerlee) is a major figure in African American folklore. He is a "badman" whose activities carve out a space of independence while also causing destruction within the African American communities he touches. For additional information, see ibid., chapter 11, especially 461–9.

15. It should be noted that other rap songs were recorded during this early period, including "King Tim III" by Fatback. However, this and others like it were small releases that did not make the same impact as "Rapper's Delight."

16. Cross, *It's Not about a Salary,* 37. See chapter 1 for a history of rap music on the West Coast.

17. Ibid., 24. Houston's Geto Boys also present a strong example of gangsta rap. ScarFace, formerly of the Geto Boys, continues this image as a solo artist in, e.g., *Mr. ScarFace Is Bak* (1991), *The Diary* (1994), and most recently *The Untouchables* (1997).

18. The distinction between the two schools of rap must not be too strongly stated, since the line between East Coast and West Coast is blurred as a result of rapid growth and blending of styles.

19. Quoted in B. Adler and Janette Beckman, ed., *Rap: Portraits and Lyrics of a Generation of Black Rockers* (New York: St. Martin's Press, 1991), 41.

20. Quoted in ibid., 59.

21. Quoted in ibid., 55.

22. Michael Eric Dyson, "Rap Culture, the Church, and American Society," in Spencer, *Sacred Music of the Secular City,* 268–73, especially 270.

23. NWA, "Fuck Tha Police," *Straight Outta Compton* (Priority Records, 1989).

24. Quoted in ibid., 75, from "Freedom of Speech" (1990) by L.A.'s Ice-T.

25. Jonathan Gold, "Dr. Dre and Snoop Doggy Dogg: One Nation Under a G Thang," *Rolling Stone,* 30 September 1993, 38–43, quotation from 124. There are certainly more recent examples of this "gangsta" attitude, including the recently deceased Tupac and The Notorious B. I. G. However, Dr. Dre and *The Chronic* mark a major turning point in the marketing of gangsta rap and, as a result, continue to serve as a useful example.

26. I continue this line of argument in "'Gettin' Grown': Notes on Gangsta Rap Music and Notions of Manhood," *Journal of African American Men* 2, no. 1 (Summer 1996): 61–73.

27. bell hooks makes this argument in "Gangsta Culture—Sexism and Misogyny: Who Will Take the Rap," in *Outlaw Culture* (New York: Routledge, 1994), 115–23, especially 117.

28. For examples of this sort of explicit critique in gangsta rap, see pieces such as Ice Cube's "When I Get to Heaven" and ScarFace's "Mind Playin' Tricks on Me, 1994."

29. Quoted in Adler and Beckman, *Rap,* 19.

30. See Robert Christagau and Gret Tate, "Chuck D All Over the Map," *Village Voice, Rock & Roll Quarterly* (Fall 1991): 12–8. For more in-depth information, see Chuck D with Yusuf Jah, *Fight the Power: Rap, Race, and Reality* (New York: Delacorte Press, 1997).

31. William Eric Perkins, "Nation of Islam Ideology in the Rap of Public En-

emy," in *The Emergency of Black and the Emergence of Rap,* ed. Jon Michael Spencer (Durham: Duke University Press, 1992), 41–50, quotation from 41–2. This volume is a special issue of *Black Sacred Music: A Journal of Theomusicology* 5, no. 1 (Spring 1991). Other rap groups such as Poor Righteous Teachers embrace the philosophy of the 5% Nation, a Nation of Islam splinter group formed by Clarence 13X. This group argues that 85 percent of the people are ignorant, 10 percent are capable of initiating liberation but fail to do so, and 5 percent have the truth and are poor righteous teachers.

32. The African basis of AD's religiosity is hinted at in the group's make-up, which includes the Baba (Ojay) figures. This name—Baba—is given to African spiritual advisors.

14

Meredith Underwood

LOST IN CYBERSPACE?

*Gender, Difference, and the
Internet "Utopia"*

> There are no races
> There are no genders
> There is no age
> There are no infirmities
> There are only minds
>> Television commercial for
>> MCI Internet Services

Our society has a tough time dealing with difference. We celebrate the virtues of multiculturalism and pluralism, then claim that underneath we're all alike. Black people, Asians, and Hispanics are "just like us," white Americans say (but never, as Elizabeth Spelman points out, the other way around).[1] So what we give with one hand, we take back with the other. If the Bible can be considered one of the founding documents of Western civilization, we can trace the origins of our ambivalence back at least that far. "God created them male and female," declares the creation narrative in Genesis. "In Christ, there is neither male nor female," proclaims the New Testament in turn. So which is it? Are men and women fundamentally different, or deep down the same? Is gender difference a good thing, to be glorified and preserved? Or is it something to be transcended, whether through the establishment of an androgynous society in this world or the attainment of an asexual spiritual body in the next?

Today, modern technology is putting a new spin on this age-old question. For instance, a television commercial advertising internet services promotes a web culture free from distinctions of gender, race, and other physical characteristics.

> People here communicate mind to mind. Not black to white. Not man to woman. Not young to old. Not short to tall. Or handsome to homely. Just thought to thought. Idea to Idea. What is this place? Utopia? No. The Internet.[2]

In a society torn by racial strife and the war between the sexes, obsessed with appearance and style, what could be better? Here is equal participation, the free exchange of ideas judged solely on merit rather than the superficialities of whose ideas they are and what kinds of bodies they come from. What could be more democratic, more objective, and, thus, more fair?

Of course, the internet, as almost anyone who has surfed it well knows, isn't all it's cracked up to be. That probably doesn't surprise us very much; we're generally cynical about advertising claims. But I wonder whether or not the so-called internet utopia, even if it did exist, would really be a liberating vision for the future.

I bring two approaches to this question, which overlap in feminist theology. My feminist perspective makes me suspicious when I hear lines like "There are no genders . . . There are only minds." In the history of Western thought, only the male has been able to transcend gender and become a neutral, universal human subject. He has likewise staked his claim on the domain of reason. Hence, a genderless world of only minds might as well come with a sign over the entrance: no women allowed. My Christian theological perspective makes me pause when I consider a world where embodied human beings no longer exist (or no longer matter). What has happened to God's good creation? To the Word made flesh?

Before proceeding, though, I offer this word of caution. If embodiment is a fact of human existence, then no cultural analysis—feminist, religious, or otherwise—can be conclusive solely on theoretical grounds. All theory must strive to become a "theory in the flesh."[3] It must take into account the concrete particularities of historical context, social location, and our embeddedness in the world of material realities and human relations. Does touting the internet as egalitarian utopia constitute a transcendence or an erasure of gender? Is it good news or bad news for women (and others who have been culturally marked as "different")? This question can only be decided by examining the practices and effects of internet culture. If I'm inclined to resist the idealization of the internet, I'm equally reluctant to contribute to its demonization. The internet, like all elements of popular culture (and of religious systems), is neither inherently liberating nor inherently oppressive. It becomes one or the other—or some combination of both—only in the context of its on-going actualization and use.

IS THIS A GREAT TIME OR WHAT? :-)

So ran the tag line for the 1997 advertising campaign that launched MCI into the arena of public internet services. The internet has been pitched to us, in this campaign and others like it, as a kinder, gentler world than its formidable technology would lead us to expect, and certainly than the real ("non-virtual") world we live in everyday. This approach was no accident, but an intentional marketing strategy with a particular history.

By 1995, it became abundantly clear to companies specializing in communications technology that the internet could be phenomenally big business. What was once the limited resource of the scientific community might have other, more popular applications. Corporate and entrepreneurial use certainly provided one lucrative market. But given the large numbers of people buying personal computers, the home market was wide open. Prodigy and CompuServe, then America OnLine, were among the first Internet Service Providers (ISPs) to exploit this market. Not long after, telecommunications companies like Sprint and MCI threw their hats into the competitive ring. With a vengeance.

Industry predictions had it that these "telcos," as they were dubbed, would quickly own the lion's share of internet access accounts, easily surpassing the traditional ISPs.[4] More than just internet access, the telcos were able to provide convenience and breadth of service through a practice called "bundling." In a single package, heralds an online press kit,

> MCI One provides consumers with Internet software and access as well as other communications services such as a cellular phone, a pager, a calling card, long distance and five free hours of e-mail. Consumers receive one single monthly invoice and a one-stop customer service number.[5]

Through various partnerships and agreements with software producers, international communications companies, and news networks, telcos like MCI have also offered customers free access to their preferred internet browsers, proprietary network content, website design, and a host of other products and services, only increasing their market share. The amounts of money at stake have been staggering: while exact figures varied, depending on the source of the prediction and factors considered, industry pundits forecast that the internet would explode within a few short years into a multibillion-dollar business.

This exponential growth in internet profits was matched only by the rise in advertising dollars to promote it. In one year, the traditional ISPs tripled what they spent on television advertising.[6] In early 1997, Sprint and MCI both launched their long-awaited campaigns, while AT&T continued promoting its full range of services—all showing the "Many Ways Our Friend Mr. Telecommunications Touches Our Lives."[7] The trend has been toward humanization, giving high tech a personal touch rather than emphasizing all the gizmos and wizardry.

Many of these campaigns have been pitched explicitly or implicitly to women. This, too, is no accident. Traditionally "underusers" of the new internet technology, women, as a female executive at one of MCI's on-line services put it, "have always been an underserved 'net population."[8] Yet a 1995 survey reported that one-third of all internet users were women, and predicted a steady increase in that figure, prompting companies and marketers to scurry about looking for ways to reach that untapped audience. The age-old question "What do women really want?" quickly became "What do women want online?"[9] Growing interest in the women's market seems to have been instrumental in making "humanization" the typical advertising ploy. Indeed, one marketing executive at CompuServe described a holiday campaign in terms of "a much more emotional pitch . . . that may strike core values particularly present in women."[10]

Given the potential for nearly unimaginable profit, we might well suspect that the utopian impulse present in these internet marketing campaigns is less munificent than it appears on the surface. These ads are not primarily about justice, but about expansion of the market. They are an attempt to make those who previously felt excluded feel welcome, by featuring images of women, children, people of color, non–Euro-Americans, older and physically challenged adults. They seldom if ever picture white, privileged males; that audience has already been reached and won. Just as significantly, they never show images of people from lower classes, nor make reference to overcoming class difference. Not only would those folks not have the necessary income to access the internet, they would not have the purchasing power to make providing it to them worthwhile. Internet access itself is merely the tip of the iceberg; the money is to be made through the products and services that go along with it. Though we are encouraged to think otherwise, the internet isn't a global village in cyberspace. Rather, it's an audience delivery system:

the "next mass medium." [11] While providers have been busy pitching the internet to us, they have also been pitching us—its users—to corporations, as ready-made consumers.

All this being true, so what? So ISPs and telecommunications giants have their own best interests at heart in presenting their vision of the internet as utopia. Whatever the impetus for this vision, and despite the fact that it remains far from reality, isn't the vision itself still worthwhile? Something to aspire to? Well, maybe yes, maybe no.

THE DIFFERENCE DIFFERENCE MAKES

Feminist thought is organized around the issue of gender. It investigates what difference it makes that women and men are considered "different"—whether that difference is taken as biologically based or socially constructed.[12] When a television commercial opens with the line "There are no genders," this raises a number of feminist concerns. Does it mean "gender doesn't exist"? Or "gender doesn't matter"? The ad plays on the slippage between these two meanings. To say that gender, race, age, and physical infirmity do not exist is patently false, if not ridiculous. But to say that they do not matter is to make a very comfortable and familiar claim. It comes straight out of the classic liberal humanism of the post-Enlightenment period—the very social vision that guided our founding "fathers" in the creation of American democracy and continues to hold a great deal of influence over our thinking. "Oh, I get it," we say to ourselves by the end of the ad. "Physical differences are superficial. Underneath lies what truly counts—mind, thought, consciousness, soul—the character of our common humanity."

As compelling as this vision may be, it is not as benign as it seems. Feminist scholars from a variety of disciplines have pointed out several problems with it, particularly for women and others who have been marked as "different" by society. The fundamental ambiguity this ad plays upon—between saying "difference doesn't matter" and "difference doesn't exist"—is nothing new. Historically, it has functioned to deny the social, material fact that bodies are different and that this difference indeed counts, as well as to obscure the fact that not every body gets to be included in this supposedly neutral, universal utopia of disembodied minds.

The trouble stems from the underlying assumptions that define and support this utopian vision—that make it tick. This vision presupposes a certain notion of what it means to be human (anthropology), and an understanding of how we human beings know things (epistemology), all based on a certain concept of the nature of reality, of what exists (ontology). All these presuppositions, feminists say, have their origin in a masculine view of the world, a view grounded in male experience—not surprisingly, since until recently it was men who determined the way we think, because they were the ones writing the philosophical treatises, science manuals, and history books. In this way, what has been passed off as the generic human being with a universal social vision is in fact a very particular sort of human, located in his body, embedded within his own experience and history, and therefore limited by the circumference of his perspective and interests. But the fact of his particularity—and the corresponding limitations on his thought—are precisely what a long tradition of Western philosophy has tried to cover up.

To discover how this happened, we must go back to the period before the Enlightenment. Tired of religious wars and political conflicts, equally fearful of doubt and dogma, philosophers of the early seventeenth century were engaged in a desperate search for clarity and certainty. They found it, so they believed, in the supposedly one characteristic that human beings shared with God, the thing that elevated them above brute nature and dumb animals: reason. But this was reason understood in a very specific way, as a result of the historical, social, and intellectual developments of this early modern period.

In medieval times, the natural or material world was imbued with the presence and purpose of God. Human embeddedness in this world was, in Susan R. Bordo's words, a "source of intellectual and spiritual satisfaction." In the modern period this changed. Nature and history became secularized, no longer a physical incarnation of the divine. The natural world and the human body came to be thought of in mechanistic terms, like an intricate but lifeless machine. Thus human embeddedness in the material and social world now seemed to be a distortion rather than a revelation. Only reason linked "man" to God. What was necessary, then, was to release the "clear and distinct ideas" from "their obscuring material prison." [13]

Though a mind/body dualism had always been present in Western thought, all the way back to Plato, these modern thinkers, especially Descartes, drew the line between mind and body much more starkly. "The body is pure *res extensa*—unconscious, extended stuff, brute materiality. . . . The soul, on the other hand, is pure *res cogitans*—mental, incorporeal, without location, *bodyless*." Mind and body were not merely distinct, but opposed. The body was seen to betray us in a number of ways: it hinders our progress when we must stop to feed it or give it rest; it resists our attempts at control; it muddies our thoughts with feelings of aversion and desire; most of all, it is an unavoidable sign of our fini-tude, a "pressing and ubiquitous reminder of how located and perspec-tival our experience and thought is, how bounded in time and space." The "purity of the intellect" could be guaranteed only "through its abil-ity to transcend the body." Thus the Enlightenment subject—what this way of thinking considers the ideal human being—sought to develop a "view from nowhere," untainted by bodily sensations and passions, un-fettered by historical particularity and social location.[14]

What is it, though, that made this understanding of human being, knowledge, and the world specifically masculine? For one thing, and most simply, it was described as such by those who developed it. "The founders of modern science," Bordo writes, "consciously and explicitly proclaimed the 'masculinity' of science as inaugurating a new era." In so doing, they contrasted this "more objective and more disciplined epis-temological relation to the world" with "feminine" ways of knowing, variously described in terms of sympathy, intuition, and a merging of subject and object, all taken as the more "erotic [and thus less pure] ori-entation toward knowledge."[15] This sexualization of women's relation to and knowledge of the world sealed her embeddedness in the material realm. Long associated throughout Christian tradition with nature and corporeality, women in Enlightenment thought as well were their bod-ies, in ways that men were not.[16]

For another thing, Western philosophers and theologians have made no secret of their suspicion that women might not, in fact, be human—at least not in the same sense men are. They have debated all along whether women possess the faculty of reason, or even whether they have souls.[17] Such conversations belie the claim that "man" is a generic term for "human being," including females as well as males. Metaphysically and materially, philosophically and practically, gender difference has al-ways made a difference.

In all this, we see a kind of symmetry between "embodiment" and "difference." Those who are not marked as different can appear as if their bodies don't matter. They are considered "normal," and so don't stand out. But since the male has provided our image of the human, women cannot help but be "other" than the norm, readily apparent as such and in need of explaining. In this context, then, to say that "There are no genders . . . There are only minds" is redundant. The realm of ungendered minds is by definition a male-only club. Only they can pass, because only their bodies remain unnoticed, unremarkable. Discounting or denying gender does not open up that world, however; it simply reinforces what women already know. To enter, you must leave your body—with its disturbing gender difference—at the door. In other words, become male. But of course that's something women cannot do.

Nor, feminists argue, would they want to. Even if a world of "only minds" were possible, it would be highly undesirable. For without our embodiment—including the plethora of physical differences and limitations accompanying it—we lose one of our greatest resources. The body is a deep well of both strength and wisdom. We know in, with, and through our bodies. To assert otherwise is to vastly misconstrue, even distort, the nature of human experience, in ways that are highly damaging not only to women, but to every person on this planet—indeed, to the planet itself.

THE SACREDNESS OF DIFFERENT BODIES

Feminist theology shares feminist theory's general critique of Western philosophy around issues of embodiment and difference. In fact, early feminist theologians were at the forefront of this critique, exposing the roots of this philosophical tradition in the doctrines of Western Christianity by showing how the apotheosis of masculine reason was related to the worship of a masculine deity, conceived as separate and aloof from the world, purely spirit, and absolutely other than corrupt human flesh.[18] Feminist theologians likewise explored the deeply conflicted relationship between Christian faith and the body, discovering that women often bore the brunt of the tensions this relationship produced. "In Christianity," writes Margaret Miles, "the body scorned, the naked body, is a female body."[19]

But despite this often violent struggle between spirit and flesh in Scripture and practice, nothing can erase a central fact of Christian existence: the Incarnation. Other doctrines attest to the importance, even the fundamental goodness of the body: the creation story in Genesis; the constant affirmation of God's presence in nature and activity in history; the doctrine of *imago dei,* that we are all made in the image of God. But, for Christians, all these culminate in the doctrine of the Incarnation—that in Jesus Christ, God became human and dwelt among us. And not only do we assert that God was incarnate in a human body, we further claim that Jesus was both fully divine and fully human, and that the two "aspects" of his nature can be neither distinguished nor divided.

Feminist theologians seeking a "usable past" in Christian tradition have found a friend in this doctrine. In itself, it affirms human embodiment in all its concrete particularity as blessed and embraced by God. Moreover, it allows us to interpret the message and ministry of Jesus, as well as the entire corpus of Christian tradition, in terms that acknowledge and value the body and all that embodiment implies. At the very least, it counteracts the claim that reason, and reason alone, is the *imago dei,* the only faculty enabling us to know God. Rather, bodies as well as minds (indeed, how can they be separate?) link us to the divine. We have what might be called body-knowledge of God, just as we have body-knowledge of ourselves and the world around us.

Theologian Sallie McFague has developed perhaps the most extensive statement of this feminist theology of embodiment. "The body is not a discardable garment cloaking the real self or essence of a person," she maintains, "rather, it is the shape or form of who we are." But we in our culture suffer a "deep sickness" of ambivalence, even aversion toward the body. This sickness takes two forms: somatophobia ("disdain for the body") and pletherophobia ("fear of different kinds of bodies"). To overcome this sickness, we must learn to love and value bodies—in the plural. She further recommends we take the fundamental fact of our embodiment as our starting point for theological reflection. To that end, she suggests considering the universe "as God's body." According to this image or model, God's body would encompass all life-forms and all matter on our planet, in fact in the whole universe. We would see ourselves "not as a spirit among bodies, but as a spirited body among other spirited bodies," and so think of God as the "embodied spirit of all that is." [20]

For my purposes here, McFague's model of the universe as God's body has a number of important advantages. First of all, it overcomes the mind/body dualism discussed above. In her model, she argues, "there is no mind directing the body, but rather a body suffused with the breath and power of life." Furthermore, because mind and body, spirit and matter, are fully integrated, this model brings together immanence and transcendence: "God would not be transcendent over the universe in the sense of external to or apart from, but would be the source, power, and goal—the spirit—that enlivens (and loves) the entire process and its material forms." [21] Thirdly, the universe as God's body allows for both unity and diversity, without preferring or slighting either. McFague bases her model on the common creation story, what we popularly refer to as the big bang theory. All matter, all life, has a common origin. Yet from this single point has evolved a vast, almost overwhelming, array of different kinds of matter and different forms of life, which are nonetheless, for all their infinite variety, mutually interrelated and interdependent. This model, then, recommends and supports

> a view of meaning and truth that takes seriously the diversity of embodied sites from which human beings make such claims: the sites that take into account race, class, gender, sexual orientation, handicapping situations, and so forth. Since there is no one universal, ideal embodiment but many, diverse forms of it, truth and meaning for human beings must begin from these embodied locations.[22]

Like McFague's model, Margaret Miles's work suggests that the cyberbody which leaves behind its cultural markers of difference also leaves behind its religious meaning, good or bad. In her study of Christian representations of the female body, she draws upon the distinction between nakedness and nudity: "the nude body is a representation of a naked body from which subjectivity, along with moles and lumps, has been elided." But it is in the concrete imperfections of embodiment, not in abstract or exemplary form, that religious meaning is located—a view that accords well with McFague's location of the sacred in the multiple diverse bodies of the universe. The "sexism of Christian societies" throughout Western history, argues Miles, has subverted the "central project" of Christianity, a project she describes as "carnal knowing," doctrinally expressed as "the incarnation of God in human flesh." One of the tasks of feminist theology is to complete this project by recovering and representing the female body "not as the object of fascination and scorn, but as revelation and subjectivity."[23] Likewise, McFague urges that we practice "embodied knowing and doing," which rests

> not upon the one ideal body (the white, fit and able, male, human body) that would absorb all its parts and all differences into itself for its own well-being. Rather, embodied knowing and doing should rest, for all intents and purposes, upon the infinite number of bodies in all their differences that constitute the universe.[24]

We are by now a far cry from the so-called utopia of a genderless, raceless, ageless world in which only disembodied minds exist or matter. Such a utopian vision constitutes, given McFague's model of the universe as God's body, not only a refusal of the fundamental fact and inestimable value of our (many different) bodies, but, even more importantly, a subversion of what makes the world sacred. Indeed, it constitutes a denial of the very body of God itself.

:-)-8 USER IS A BIG GIRL

The negative image of one ideal body that absorbs everything into itself, which McFague rejects, seems perilously close to an internet "utopia" envisioned as one worldwide web in which the many lose their markers of difference, and thereby both their subjectivity and the revelatory power that comes with it. In other words, the critique of disembodied reason by feminist theory, and the affirmation by feminist theology that embodiment in all its forms is sacred, together suggest that the utopian vision pitched to us by television ad campaigns is in fact a dystopia, disturbing in its implications. If the Cartesian masculinization of reason was a modern attempt to achieve the neutral and pristine view from nowhere, then perhaps the disembodied mind of cyberspace is a postmodern attempt at the view from everywhere—the elusive and illusory dream that connecting with nodes and nets from around the world, while bound to no one location, will enable us to transcend our all-too-human bodies and societies along with their frustrating limitations.

But we should ask in whose best interest is it to promote such an alleged "utopia"? The revelatory power of gendered subjectivity—in the embodied knowing of all its lived contradictions (is woman Eve or Mary? temptress or madonna?)—can challenge the gender stereotypes prevalent in our culture. To preserve the status quo and the market stability that goes with it, it is better she leave her body at the door and merge with the man's world of only mind. But there is another sort of contradiction complicating this picture. The image of the singular ideal is no longer an effective sales tool; it takes multiple and diverse consumers, convinced that they too may join this new utopia, to increase the market base. Internet service providers, consciously or not, know this well. Which is why, despite the fact that they often pitch the internet as a genderless utopia, these ad campaigns as a whole are thoroughly gendered in their appeal.

When not busy showing how the internet can be directly useful to women, these ads show how it can indirectly help women fulfill their desires in the traditional domain of home and family. Though the ad's vignette may be a father doing homework with his children at night via internet resources, or a busy executive ordering flowers online for his wife's anniversary, these ads nonetheless portray men who are better able to fulfill their familial and relational roles—undoubtedly seen as a pre-eminent desire of the women in their lives—through internet technology. The sales pitch, in other words, is directed to the woman as much as, or more than, it is to the man whose image appears in the commercial.

Still another dimension of this trend in internet advertising has been its heavy emphasis on domestic space—the so-called private realm of women as opposed to the public, "male" realm of work, government, law, and finance. These ad campaigns have pitched the internet as a technology that can bridge this gap, arguably a recent concern of women who must juggle the demands of boss and client on the one hand, husband and children on the other. MCI's second offering in its 1997 campaign provides a beautiful example. Entitled "Confessions of a Telecommuter," it features a young woman comfortably ensconced at home—wearing flannel pajamas and bunny slippers, in fact—making an online business presentation to a roomful of corporate execs who never know the difference. You can have it both ways, these ads seem to say. You can be a successful career person without ever leaving the confines of your traditional domestic space. But, as usual, the message is mixed: by entering the genderless world of the internet you can better fulfill your gender roles.

Let's face it: there are genders in cyberspace. And, just as in "non-virtual" reality, sometimes this is a good thing for women, sometimes not. In many ways, the information superhighway is not that much different from a suburban sidewalk or a city block. As Ann Snitow says, "one can be recalled to 'woman' anytime—by things as terrible as rape, as trivial as a rude shout on the street."[25] Women online suffer harassment, abuse, and sexual objectification. One of the primary concerns of those creating new networks specifically for women has been the issue of online safety, of protection from "unsavory characters" who inhabit cyberspace just as they do homes, neighborhoods, and the workplace.[26] The answer to "what women want online" is as varied as the answers typically are in daily life. Women's websites run the gamut from offering beauty, fashion, and child-raising tips, to providing professional networking and career advice, to connecting radical feminists involved in all sorts of political activism. As such, internet culture is a replication of the cultures we inhabit everyday. Most likely, women negotiate cyberspace much the same way they learn to negotiate "non-virtual" space:

Even when a woman chooses which shoes she'll wear today—is it to be the running shoes, the flats, the spikes?—she's deciding where to place herself for

> the moment on the current possible spectrum of images of 'woman.' What-
> ever our habitual position on the divide, in daily life we travel back and forth,
> or, to change metaphors, we scramble for whatever toehold we can.[27]

The divide Ann Snitow refers to here is the "common divide" in feminist thinking between the "minimizers" and "maximizers" of gender—between those who emphasize difference (the distinctive qualities of women should be acknowledged, celebrated, and nourished), and those who urge equality (women should be treated just like men). Try as we might, and many feminists have, there's no resolving this contradiction, no third position which transcends or harmonizes its poles. As Teresa de Lauretis points out, the divide is "a result of the divisions . . . in the social itself," a product of our history of ambivalence about gender, difference and embodiment.[28] Thus, Snitow concludes, "The urgent contradiction women constantly experience between the pressure to be a woman and the pressure not to be one will change only through a historical process; it cannot be dissolved through thought alone."[29] So, just as the internet reproduces many of the cultural realities of "non-virtual" space, so it reproduces the contradictions we have inherited regarding the gendered body. Whichever position on the divide we take up in cyberspace, the question still remains. Is it liberating or oppressive? Does it break the bonds of gender stereotyping or once again render women invisible, no body at all?

To this, we must finally add the testimony of "wired women"—those who already inhabit cyberspace and whose experiences belie either a simple endorsement or condemnation of the internet "utopia." On the one hand, as Deborah Lupton points out, computer culture generally takes embodiment to be a distraction and a barrier.

> In cyberwriting, the body is often referred to as the "meat," the dead flesh
> that surrounds the active mind which constitutes the "authentic" self. . . . The
> dream of cyberculture is to leave the "meat" behind and to become distilled
> in a clean, pure, uncontaminated relationship with computer technology.[30]

Lupton connects this attitude with the mind/body dualism of Western tradition, now writ into cyberspace. On the other hand, we may be witnessing the creation of another form of embodiment, its significance yet to be determined. Women in cyberspace often write in these terms. Lupton remarks how our interactions with computers "'inscribe' our bodies, so that, for example, pens start to feel awkward as writing instruments."[31] Elizabeth Reba Weise says, "My computer felt to me, feels to me still, the way wings must feel to a bird, making flight possible."[32]

Though this is an image of transcendence, it is certainly not a disembodied one, but rather a metaphor for taking on a different sort of body.

As a feminist theologian concerned about the practices and effects of popular culture, I'm called both to critique popular culture when it's bad for women, and to applaud and nurture it when it's good for them. But I'm also called to attend to the variety of forms oppression and liberation may take in any given social context. There is no one ideal body, nor one set of implications for any given form of embodiment. Thus, what the gendered body of cyberspace is, or will become, remains in a constant process of creation. Women and others—including the corporations and technologies that interface with women's bodies through the internet products and services they provide—will determine this as cyberhistory unfolds. Moreover, if we believe that nothing, no reality—virtual or otherwise—is separate from God's embrace, then cyberbodies, too, for good or ill, will become part of the universe as God's body. And if, as Margaret Miles suggests, bodies are revelatory of religious meaning, what kind of theological significance might cyberbodies bear? Constructing the answer to that question will be one of the more fascinating tasks for feminist theology in the future.

NOTES

1. Elizabeth V. Spelman, *Inessential Woman: Problems of Exclusion in Feminist Thought* (Boston: Beacon Press, 1988), 12.

2. Television commercial for MCI Internet Services, quoted in Bob Garfield, "Is Internet Utopia? Good Heavens No," *Advertising Age,* 20 January 1997, 49.

3. Cherríe Moraga and Gloria Anzaldúa, eds., *This Bridge Called My Back: Writings by Radical Women of Color* (New York: Women of Color Press - Kitchen Table, 1983), 24.

4. "Telcos Take on the ISPs," *Advertising Age,* 23 December 1996, 21.

5. "MCI and the Internet," http://www.mci.com/aboutmci/press/content/internet.shtml, 10 April 1997.

6. Kim Cleland and Jane Hodges, "Experts Predict Spending Will Triple as Telcos, Onliners Target Mass Market," http://www.adage.com/interactive/articles/19960318/article2.html, 9 April 1997.

7. Bob Garfield, "AT&T Presses Right High-tech Buttons," *Advertising Age,* 10 March 1997, 47.

8. Kim Cleland, "Look Out MSN, Here Comes MCI," http://adage.com/interactive/articles/19950814/article2.html, 10 April 1997.

9. Jane Hodges, "What Women Want Online," http://adage.com/interactive/articles/19951106/article2.html, 9 April 1997.

10. Ibid.

11. Marian Salzman, "What Lies Ahead in the Brave New World of Technology," *Advertising Age*, 11 November 1996, A34.

12. Gender, of course, is only one axis of difference among many others that have been marked as significant in our society. Through a series of fruitful, if often painful, developments, feminist theory has come to realize that gender never exists or operates separately from other axes of difference, such as race, class, age, sexual orientation, and physical ability. The assertion or denial of one kind of difference is often related in complex ways to other kinds of difference. So to envision a world where there are no races, for instance, should give a feminist as much cause for concern as envisioning a world where there are no genders. For the purposes of this discussion, I am focusing on gender with only minimal reference to the other axes of difference equally at stake. Such an approach is admittedly inadequate. Nor should we assume that what is said of gender will be similarly true of race, class, age, etc., without substantial revision. For instance, in the critique of Enlightenment humanism that follows, my discussion of how the male became the norm for generic, universal human being refers to the able-bodied, heterosexual, propertied, and above all white male. A black man would never have been considered generically human, any more than, say, a gay man or poor man.

13. Susan R. Bordo, *The Flight to Objectivity: Essays on Cartesianism and Culture* (Albany: State University of New York Press), 98.

14. Ibid., 93–4, 95, 99; Susan R. Bordo, "Feminism, Postmodernism, and Gender-Skepticism," in *Feminism/Postmodernism*, ed. Linda J. Nicholson (New York: Routledge, 1990), 133–56, especially 136.

15. Bordo, *Flight to Objectivity*, 105.

16. The peculiar thing is that these thinkers could assert the neutrality and universality of their perspective while at the very same time indulging in sexual metaphors to describe both women's *and* men's ways of knowing. The sexual metaphors were decidedly different, however, depending on gender. While women's knowing was a kind of convergence or union, men's (or "man's") knowledge, particularly scientific investigation, was described in terms of penetration, seduction, and even rape, to which nature inevitably responded by yielding up her secrets (see Carolyn Merchant, *The Death of Nature: Women, Ecology and the Scientific Revolution* [San Francisco: Harper and Row, 1980]). Thus the denial of embodiment presupposed by Enlightenment reason was itself, in contradictory fashion, not only based on a series of gendered assumptions and values, but also stated via gendered assertions.

17. Feminist analysis and critique on this point is extensive, but for a general introduction regarding women and rationality, see Genevieve Lloyd, *The Man of Reason: "Male" and "Female" in Western Philosophy* (Minneapolis: University of Minnesota Press, 1984), and regarding women's spiritual nature and status, see Rosemary Radford Ruether, *New Woman/New Earth: Sexist Ideologies and Human Liberation* (New York: Seabury Press, 1975).

18. Two representative texts are Mary Daly, *Beyond God the Father: Toward a Philosophy of Women's Liberation* (Boston: Beacon Press, 1973), and Rosemary Radford Ruether, *Sexism and God-Talk: Toward a Feminist Theology*

(Boston: Beacon Press, 1983).

19. Margaret R. Miles, *Carnal Knowing: Female Nakedness and Religious Meaning in the Christian West* (Boston: Beacon Press, 1989), 185.

20. Sallie McFague, *The Body of God: An Ecological Theology* (Minneapolis: Fortress Press, 1993), 16, 53, 17, 19, 20.

21. Ibid., 156, 20.

22. Ibid., 48.

23. Miles, *Carnal Knowing*, 14, 185.

24. McFague, *Body of God*, 54.

25. Ann Snitow, "A Gender Diary," in *Conflicts in Feminism*, ed. MariAnn Hirsch and Evelyn Fox Keller (New York and London: Routledge, 1990), 9–43, quotation from 36.

26. Hodges, "What Women Want Online."

27. Snitow, "Gender Diary," 34.

28. Teresa de Lauretis, "Upping the Anti (sic) in Feminist Theory," in *Conflicts in Feminism*, ed. MariAnn Hirsch and Evelyn Fox Keller (New York: Routledge, 1990), 255–70, quotation from 264.

29. Snitow, "Gender Diary," 19.

30. Deborah Lupton, "The Embodied Computer/User," in *Cyberspace/Cyberbodies/Cyberpunk: Cultures of Technological Embodiment*, ed. Mike Featherstone and Roger Burrows (London: Sage Publications, 1995), 97–112, quotation from 100.

31. Ibid., 99.

32. Elizabeth Reba Weise, "A Thousand Aunts with Modems," in *Wired Women: Gender and New Realities in Cyberspace*, ed. Lynn Cherny and Elizabeth Reba Weise (Seattle: Seal Press, 1996), vii–xv, quotation from viii.

Jeffrey H. Mahan

CONCLUSION

*Establishing a Dialogue about
Religion and Popular Culture*

In looking back on *Religion and Popular Culture in America,* it is clear that two sets of questions interest the contributors to this project. First, we are drawn to questions about how religion interacts with popular culture. We ask whether American popular culture has a religious face, and if so what it looks like, or wonder how religion has developed and adapted in the midst of a consumer culture. Second, we are interested in the form the conversation about these questions has taken. Who is thinking and writing about the relationship between religion and popular culture? What concerns, theories, and methodologies unite and divide the conversations about these relationships? What new things might we learn by paying attention to the questions others are raising about religion and popular culture and to the assumptions inherent in their approaches?

UNDERSTANDING POPULAR CULTURE

Traditionally, religious studies has tended to focus on the doctrine or practice of established religious groups and cultural elites. Yet in recent years, scholars of religion, like their counterparts in other fields of cultural study, have begun to focus more on the lives of everyday people. When scholars have turned their attention from the activities of religious leaders and institutions to the way ordinary people experience their religious lives, they discover a variety of relationships between religion and popular culture. In the opening essay of this volume, Bruce David Forbes lays out four distinct interactions between religion and popular culture which have interested scholars. As we have seen in the intervening essays, each of the four interactions reflects a distinctive concern about what studying religion and popular culture should tell us.

For some, popular culture is primarily a subset of art. It includes the forms of music, film, television, and literature that have found the widest audiences. Robert J. Thompson's examination of network television's Christmas specials, like Mark D. Hulsether's discussion of Madonna's music videos and Robert Jewett's analysis of the popular western movie *Pale Rider,* are examples of this approach. Here, "the popular" is identified with material that reaches a broad and *general* audience. Such readings help us to think about patterns that we might describe as normatively American. The danger of such approaches, cut off from other kinds of readings, is that they can suggest too homogenized a culture. Jane Naomi Iwamura's reflection on the image of the Oriental monk in American film and television suggests the importance of hearing minority readings of dominant culture materials, while William D. Romanowski's discussion of contemporary Christian music and Anthony Pinn's of rap and the blues remind us that minority cultures have their own distinctive forms of popular art.

Michael Jindra's analysis of *Star Trek* fandom, and much of Joseph L. Price's and David Chidester's discussions of sports rituals, shift our attention from the "official" performance of the work of art to the performance activity of the audience. For such critics, the focus is not so much on the structures and themes of the art work, or on the game on the field, but on the use that audience members make of these things. Drawing on a term from religious studies, the Super Bowl game, the songs of a pop star, or the episodes of *Star Trek* might be said to provide a popular culture *canon* of legitimated "texts," in which case the fans, as participant/consumers, are the "readers" of these "texts." But, at least in the examples discussed in these essays, the fans are quite active readers and the popular culture event, properly understood, includes both the text and the activity of the readers. In other words, these essays counter the criticism that popular culture reduces its audience to passive viewers, by directing our attention away from the event itself towards other people's engagement with that event.[1] In fact, as is most explicit in Jindra's discussion of *Star Trek,* the participant/consumers may even create non-canonical texts of their own. They write themselves into the popular culture event through their activity, which includes wearing costumes, belonging to fan clubs, attending conventions, memorizing lore, and even creating and enacting their own tales.

An adequate discussion of popular culture, and of its relationship to the religious, must therefore not be limited to a consideration of aesthetic texts as traditionally understood. Stewart M. Hoover's and Gregor Goethals's discussions of the practice of Protestant worship, along with David Chidester's reflections on Coca-Cola and baseball and Meredith Underwood's and Michelle M. Lelwica's feminist critiques of cyberspace and dieting, suggest that the concept of popular culture embraces much more than the art world. Ritual activities of everyday people and mass-produced cultural objects are a significant part of popular culture.

Setting limits remains difficult. "Popular culture" refers to a range of cultural material and activity which is understood, as Forbes discusses in the opening essay, at least in part by its distinction from high or elite culture on one hand and folk culture on the other. Those who find the concept of popular culture useful do so for the way that it combines an interest in aesthetics and cultural form with an interest in social meaning and influence and a concern for non-elite publics.

UNDERSTANDING RELIGION

Intuitively, most Americans are confident that they know what is meant by "religion." Most of us think of organized devotional practice focused on a concept of God or gods. Several of our authors reflect on these traditional expressions of religion: Hoover's discussion of the famous megachurch at Willow Creek, Goethals's discussion of evangelical worship on television, and Pinn's critique of the black church are the most obvious reflections on the cultural expressions of traditional religious groups. Meanwhile, a feminist Christian community provides the basis for Underwood's critique of cyberspace, and Romanowski is concerned with helping the evangelical community make sense of the way its faith and secular popular culture come together in the world of contemporary Christian music.

Some essays in this collection push us to expand our definition of religion still further, beyond the bounds of denomination or theological orientation. The examination of religious or theological images and concepts in literature, film, and television (Iwamura, Jewett, Muck, and Thompson) remind us that religion may be thought of as a particular consciousness which we bring with us to, or find expressed in, art. The essays in the section on popular culture as religion (Chidester, Jindra, Lelwica, and Price) see religion primarily as ritualized activity expressive of ultimate values. In contrast, Goethals's discussion of architecture and icon, and Chidester's discussion of Coca-Cola as fetish, see religion as embodied in symbolic objects. A full understanding of religion must include religion as belief, as activity, as symbol or object, and as organization.

FOUR DIVERSE AUDIENCES

Within each of the four interactions between religion and popular culture we find writers not only addressing a range of different issues, but also writing for diverse *audiences*. Four audiences are implied in the essays, two of them primarily academic and two broader, each interested in a somewhat different set of questions. The first academic audience is interested primarily in the *description and analysis of specific cultural phenomena* which reveal particular relationships between religion and popular culture. A second academic audience is more concerned with *reflection on the methodologies* which help us see the broader relationships between religion and popular culture. A third audience is made up of religious women and men who want to *clarify the practice of the religious life*. A fourth audience is made up of thinking members of the culture at large, religious and secular, who are engaged in a conversation about *social or cultural reform*.[2]

Audience One: Seeks Description and Analysis

All of the authors in this volume are academics who write for students and scholars interested in thinking analytically about American culture and religion. This is perhaps most evident in the descriptions of the phenomena of fandom among sports and *Star Trek* enthusiasts, or in the discussions of television Christmas specials. The authors are seeking not to reform these cultural practices, nor to instruct the participants or audiences in the ways of this practice, but to help us make sense of these phenomena. Simply put, their goal is to understand "what is going on." The distinction between this and other approaches can be seen by contrasting the two essays which deal with the western genre: Terry C. Muck writes for an audience primarily interested in understanding literary patterns and conventions, whereas Jewett writes for an audience interested in clarifying and reforming religious and social practice.

Audience Two: Seeks Methodological Reflection

A second group, also addressing an academic audience, is primarily interested in helping develop the theoretical underpinnings of this emerging field of study. For Chidester, Goethals, Hoover, and Hulsether, the specific expressions of religion or popular culture—the fetishistic function of Coca-Cola, the practices of a particular television preacher, the specifics of worship at Willow Creek Church, or the form and content of a specific music video—are not so important in and of themselves. Rather, they provide the critic with illustration of a broader argument which is really about the nature of religion and popular culture and the methodology of those who study them. These theoreticians and their readers are ultimately interested in clarifying our definitions and sharpening our analytical tools. For them, the compelling questions are about the theories of religion, culture, narrative, and art on which such analysis rests. This work teaches us how to think critically, and its intended audience is colleagues and students who want to deepen their own analytical work.

Audience Three: Seeks to Clarify the Religious Life

Still other writers are particularly concerned with helping religious people and communities think about their practice of religion in a mass-media culture. Implicit in Romanowski's essay is his desire to help evangelicals interact more freely with popular culture while remaining clear about their distinctive religious identity. Hulsether gives particular attention to our second audience, academics interested in theory, but his scholarly interest in reading Madonna grew out of efforts to interpret popular music with and to church youth groups. While Jewett is broadly concerned with American cultural values, he is particularly concerned with helping mainstream Christians access the Bible in ways which are culturally rich and formative. And, though Pinn's essay is critical of traditional black church theology, it implicitly suggests a reformist concern for the church much like Jewett's and Romanowski's. The implied audience for these essays are thinking practitioners of religion who desire to more clearly understand the interactions between faith and culture, in order to enable lives of religious integrity.

Audience Four: Seeks Social or Cultural Reform

Most explicitly in the Dialogue category, several essays address society at large and hope to encourage social change, or at least social awareness. Jewett's essay, with its attention to social practice around vengeance and justice, clearly bridges this and the previous category, and Pinn's use of rap and the blues to critique the black church, like Underwood's look at women and the internet, invites action as well as awareness. However, this commitment to moral suasion is evident in some of the essays in other sections as well. When Lelwica looks at eating disorders among women, or Iwamura at the portrayal of Oriental religion in the popular arts, they are doing more than describing interesting social patterns. They hope to establish a transformational conversation that will lead readers to make different choices. These writers share with the third group a desire to impact the behavior of their readers, but whereas scholars in the third group are primarily interested in addressing religious subcultures within the broader society, these scholars hope to enter into a broader cultural conversation. They bring a religious perspective into dialogue with the entire community about American cultural life.

TWO CAMPS OF SCHOLARS

In part, this diversity of audience, and the diversity of intention it points to, grows out of a fundamental division among students of popular culture in general. What is the purpose of studying popular culture and what methodologies best help us understand it?

On one side is the Popular Culture Association and its companion organization the American Culture Association (PCA/ACA), where humanities-based approaches to the study of culture predominate. The PCA/ACA, like the popular culture program at Bowling Green State University which has been important in the development of these associations, were formed at a time when the very idea of studying popular art and literature was suspect within academia. Those who saw the university's task as initiating students into elite culture attacked both the material of popular culture and the interest of scholars who studied it. Popular culture was dismissed as simple, boringly repetitive, and at odds with the best values of society. Needing to defend both the seriousness of their work and the material they studied, PCA/ACA scholars tended to focus on aesthetic patterns within the work and social practices in the audience. They gave little attention to the market forces which shaped and limited what was available to the audience, and to the question of how the values of those who controlled the means of cultural production shaped popular materials. They argued that studying popular culture brings to the surface the aesthetics, cultural values, and social and personal concerns of everyday people in society. As such, popular culture is worthy of respectful attention by scholars. These concerns and interests have lead the PCA/ACA scholars to focus on the relationship between popular material and their audience, and to draw conclusions about the audience's values and concerns.

On the other side are cultural studies scholars, whose interests were shaped by theoretical developments in England that brought together social theory, Marxist analysis of race, gender, and class, and a focus on material and cultural practice. They gave particular attention to the means of production of popular culture. Whereas PCA/ACA scholars usually focus on the values of the popular audience, cultural studies critiques are likely to focus on the way that attitudes, values, and prejudices of the dominant society are expressed in popular culture, and on the ways in which it functions as a form of social control and release.

Those primarily rooted in cultural studies are inclined to see their PCA/ACA colleagues as too focused on narrative and as not sufficiently rooted in postmodern and deconstructionist perspectives. At the same time, cultural studies critics, with their roots in social theory and Marxist analysis, are often criticized by PCA/ACA-oriented colleagues as too ideological, too rooted in obscure theories and jargon, and unable to adequately understand the aesthetic and critical traditions which shaped the popular arts.

To understand how Americans experience the religious, we must continue to think about the religious content of mass media tales and rituals, *and* about the powerful institutions which produce and distribute popular culture. We must also reflect on the complex social process through which religious institutions both critique the media and remake themselves to respond to a media culture. It should be clear that no single approach to the study of religion and popular culture provides a complete analysis of their complex relationships. A diversity of approaches is likely to give us the fullest understanding of those relationships between religion and popular culture, and, as a result, our understanding of how religion and popular culture interact has not been well served by the fundamental distrust between PCA/ACA and cultural studies scholars. To expand our understanding of the varied and complex ways religion and popular culture interact, we must overcome scholarly distrust and learn from each other in order to see more fully how Americans and American culture give expression to the religious impulse.

NOTES

1. For a discussion of the postmodern concept of "readerly" as opposed to "writerly" texts, see Roland Barthes *S/Z* (New York: Hill and Wang, 1974), especially 4–6.

2. Note that these audiences do not align with the four relationships between religion and popular culture. We find authors speaking to different audiences in each of the categories.

Contributors

David Chidester is Professor of Comparative Religion, Head of the Department of Religious Studies, and Director of the Institute for Comparative Religion in Southern Africa at the University of Cape Town, South Africa. His recent books include *Word and Light: Seeing, Hearing, and Religious Discourse* (University of Illinois Press, 1992); *American Sacred Space* (Indiana University Press, 1995), edited with Edward T. Linenthal; and *Savage Systems: Colonialism and Comparative Religion in Southern Africa* (University Press of Virginia, 1996).

Bruce David Forbes is Professor of Religious Studies at Morningside College in Sioux City, Iowa. With a formal educational background and publications in American religious history, he also has published several articles on popular culture and religion. He has served on the national board of the American Academy of Religion, and is cochair of the AAR Religion and Popular Culture Group.

Gregor Goethals is Emerita Professor of Art History at the Rhode Island School of Design. Her publications include *The TV Ritual: Worship at the Video Altar* (Beacon Press, 1981) and *The Electronic Golden Calf: Images, Religion, and the Making of Meaning* (Cowley, 1990).

Stewart M. Hoover, Professor of Media Studies at the University of Colorado at Boulder, is a scholar of media and culture who has focused his work on questions of religion in the media age. His recent publications include *Religion in the Media Age* (forthcoming), *Religion in the News: Faith and Journalism in American Public Discourse* (Sage, 1998), and *Rethinking Media, Religion and Culture* (Sage, 1997), which he coedited with Knut Lundby.

Mark D. Hulsether is Assistant Professor of Religious Studies and American Studies at the University of Tennessee. He has published numerous articles on culture, politics, and religion in the twentieth-century U.S., as well as *Building a Protestant Left:* Christianity and Crisis Magazine, *1941–1993* (University of Tennessee Press, 1999). He is currently working on *Religion, Culture, and Politics in Modern America* (Edinburgh University Press).

Jane Naomi Iwamura is a Ph.D. candidate in the Department of Rhetoric at the University of California at Berkeley. She is currently working on her dissertation, an extended study of the Oriental Monk in American popular culture. She has written on Asian American religions and religious experience, and her works include "Homage to Ancestors: Exploring the Horizons of Asian American Religious Identity" (*Amerasia Journal* 22, no. 1).

Robert Jewett is Harry R. Kendall Senior Professor of New Testament Interpretation at Garrett-Evangelical Theological Seminary in Evanston, Illinois. His publications on religion and popular culture include *Saint Paul Returns to the Movies: Triumph over Shame* (Eerdmans, 1998); *Paul the Apostle to America: Cultural Trends and Pauline Scholarship* (Westminster/John Knox, 1994); *Saint Paul at the Movies: The Apostle's Dialogue with American Culture* (Westminster/John Knox, 1993); *The American Monomyth* (Anchor Press/Doubleday, 1977), cowritten with John Shelton Lawrence; and *The Captain America Complex* (Westminster, 1973).

Michael Jindra is Assistant Professor of Social Sciences at Bethany Lutheran College in Mankato, Minnesota. He received a Ph.D. in Cultural Anthropology in 1997 from the University of Wisconsin at Madison; his dissertation was a study of "death celebrations" in Cameroon.

Michelle M. Lelwica is Assistant Professor of Religious Studies at Saint Mary's College of California. She holds a doctorate from Harvard Divinity School in the area of Religion and Gender in Culture, and is the author of *Starving for Salvation: The Spiritual Dimensions of Eating Problems among American Girls and Women* (Oxford University Press, 1999).

Jeffrey H. Mahan is Associate Professor of Ministry, Media and Culture at the Iliff School of Theology in Denver, Colorado. His publications include *A Long Way from Solving That One: Psycho/Social and Ethical Implications of Ross Macdonald's Lew Archer Tales* (University Press of America, 1990), and *American Television Genres* (Nelson Hall, 1985), cowritten with Stuart Kaminsky. He has served on ecumenical juries at the Montreal, Cannes, and Berlin International Film Festivals, and he cochairs the AAR Religion and Popular Culture Group.

Terry C. Muck is Professor of Comparative Religion at Austin Presbyterian Theological Seminary in Austin, Texas. He received a Ph.D. from Northwestern University in the history of religions, and is author of nine books, including *A Guide to American Religion* (Doubleday, forthcoming), and many articles, including "Warner Sallman's Head of Christ" (*Insights* 112, no. 2 [1997]).

Anthony Pinn is Associate Professor of Religious Studies and Director of African American Studies at Macalester College. His work on African American culture and religion includes *Why, Lord? Suffering and Evil in Black Theology* (Continuum, 1995), *Varieties of African American Religious Experience* (Fortress, 1998) and the edited volume *Making the Gospel Plain: Writings by and about Bishop Reverdy C. Ransom* (Trinity Press International, 1999).

Joseph L. Price is Professor of Religious Studies at Whittier College in Whittier, California. His long-standing interest in sports and religion is reflected in two forthcoming edited volumes: *From Season to Season: Sports as American Religion* and *Fusing the Spirits: Religion and the Sporting Spirit in Recent American Literature and Film.*

William D. Romanowski is Professor of Communication Arts and Sciences at Calvin College in Grand Rapids, Michigan. His most recent book is *Pop Culture Wars: Religion and the Role of Entertainment in American Life* (InterVarsity, 1996). He is a contributing author of *Dancing in the Dark: Youth, Popular Culture and the Electronic Media* (Ecrdmans, 1991), and coauthor of *Risky Business: Rock in Film* (Transaction, 1991).

Robert J. Thompson, Professor at the S. I. Newhouse School of Public Communication at Syracuse University in New York, is director of the Center for the Study of Popular Television. Recent publications include *Television's Second Golden Age: From Hill Street Blues to ER* (Continuum, 1996). He is past vice-president of the Popular Culture Association.

Meredith Underwood is a degree candidate in the joint doctoral program at the Iliff School of Theology/University of Denver studying theology, philosophy of religion, and cultural theory. She has previously served as a staff producer, writer, and director for United Methodist Communications, and has television production experience on such shows as *Star Trek: The Next Generation, War of the Worlds,* and *Doogie Howser, M.D.*

The following books have been selected from a much larger potential list of works. They are suggested as a helpful beginning to introduce interested persons to the field of religion and popular culture. This bibliography includes general works on the topic, as well as examples of literature pertaining to specific features of popular culture: film, television, popular literature, holidays, and so on. This list does not include basic works in related fields, such as cultural studies, popular culture, film studies, and others, unless they pertain directly to religion as well.

Dyson, Michael Eric. *Between God and Gangsta Rap: Bearing Witness to Black Culture.* New York: Oxford University Press, 1996.
Essays by a Baptist minister, professor, and cultural critic about religious meanings and African American culture.

Ferré, John P., ed. *Channels of Belief: Religion and American Commercial Television.* Ames: Iowa State University Press, 1990.
Six essays about religious representations in, and the religious significance of, commercial television, including prime-time entertainment programs, advertising, and news.

Fore, William F. *Television and Religion: The Shaping of Faith, Values, and Culture.* Minneapolis: Augsburg, 1987.
A mainstream Protestant theological examination of a wide range of issues pertaining to television, including implicit values in secular television programs, controversies about media violence, concentrations of power in the media, and television evangelism.

Gardella, Peter. *Domestic Religion: Work, Food, Sex and Other Commitments.* Cleveland, Ohio: Pilgrim Press, 1998.
An examination of the daily choices that human beings make, related to topics such as success, work, food, sports, entertainment, drink and sobriety, sex, and exercise, arguing that they constitute a domestic religion which also influences the shape of traditional religions.

Goethals, Gregor. *The TV Ritual: Worship at the Video Altar.* Boston: Beacon Press, 1981.
A classic book by an art historian, which discusses television's role as a "substitute for sacraments," offering icons and rituals to its viewers.

————. *The Electronic Golden Calf: Images, Religion, and the Making of Meaning.* Cambridge, Mass.: Cowley Publications, 1990.
A later addition to the discussion started by *The TV Ritual,* this book places television in the context of art history and the role images have played in "making meaning."

Greeley, Andrew M. *God in Popular Culture.* Chicago: Thomas More Press, 1988.
A collection of essays about a great range of popular culture, from comic strips to Clint Eastwood to Madonna, discussed in light of what he calls the "Catholic theological imagination."

Higgs, Robert J. *God in the Stadium: Sports and Religion in America.* Lexington: University Press of Kentucky, 1995.
Using mostly a literary approach, this volume examines the intersections between sports and religion and claims that both have been "warped" by the relationship.

Hoover, Stewart M. *Mass Media Religion: The Social Sources of the Electronic Church.* Newbury Park, Calif.: Sage, 1988.
This treatment of contemporary religious broadcasting includes interviews with representative television viewers as well as historical research and case studies.

Ingebretsen, Edward J., S.J. *Maps of Heaven, Maps of Hell: Religious Terror as Memory from the Puritans to Stephen King.* Armonk, N.Y.: M. E. Sharpe, 1996.
An argument that the American genre of horror fiction is historically related to the Puritan use of terror for conversion.

Jewett, Robert. *St. Paul at the Movies: The Apostle's Dialogue with American Culture.* Louisville, Ky.: Westminster/John Knox Press, 1993.
With Bernard Brandon Scott's *Hollywood Dreams and Biblical Stories* (below), an example of a Christian Biblical scholar reflecting upon the themes of American popular films.

Jewett, Robert, and John Shelton Lawrence. *The American Monomyth*. Garden City, N.Y.: Anchor Press/Doubleday, 1977. 2d ed. Lanham, Md.: University Press of America, 1988.

For a summary of this book's argument that most American popular culture follows a singular mythic pattern (basically a redemption drama), see our introduction (p. 11).

Journal of the American Academy of Religion 64, no. 4 (Winter 1996).

This special issue has the theme of "Religion and American Popular Culture." While all other entries in this bibliography are books, this special issue deserves inclusion, since the American Academy of Religion is the largest academic association of religion scholars in the United States.

Kreuziger, Frederick A. *The Religion of Science Fiction*. Bowling Green, Ohio: Bowling Green State University Popular Press, 1986.

A discussion of the appeal of science fiction and the popular mythology it provides, focusing upon apocalyptic themes.

Lippy, Charles H. *Being Religious, American Style: A History of Popular Religiosity in the United States*. Westport, Conn.: Greenwood Press, 1994.

Although the study of "religion and popular culture" is not identical to the study of "popular religion," they overlap. This book, along with the volume by Peter W. Williams below, provides a helpful introduction to the study of popular religion.

Martin, Joel W., and Conrad E. Oswalt, Jr., eds. *Screening the Sacred: Religion, Myth, and Ideology in Popular American Film*. Boulder, Colo.: Westview Press, 1995.

A collection of essays representing "theological, mythological, and ideological criticism" of popular movies, as a means to learn about American religion.

McDannell, Colleen. *Material Christianity: Religion and Popular Culture in America*. New Haven: Yale University Press, 1995.

A discussion of religious material objects (such as the Bible in the Victorian home, or Lourdes water, or Mormon garments) aimed at helping readers understand the religious experiences and perspectives of average American Christians in the last 150 years.

Medved, Michael. *Hollywood vs. America: Popular Culture and the War on Traditional Values*. New York: HarperCollins, 1992.

A film critic's attack on Hollywood as a "poison factory," arguing that it is antireligious, antifamily, anti-American, violent, and offensive. Medved's criticisms have served as a catalyst for responses of all kinds.

Miles, Margaret. *Seeing and Believing: Religion and Values in the Movies*. Boston: Beacon Press, 1996.

A cultural studies approach to issues such as religion, gender, race, class, and sexuality, noting movies that challenge existing norms and others that do not.

Moore, R. Laurence. *Selling God: American Religion in the Marketplace of Culture*. New York: Oxford University Press, 1994.

An historical survey of religion in American commercial culture, showing how religious leaders have used commercial practices to promote religion, and how business leaders have used religion for commercial purposes.

Morgan, David. *Visual Piety: A History and Theory of Popular Religious Images*. Berkeley: University of California Press, 1997.

A discussion of the intersection between popular religious art and popular piety, focusing especially on Warner Sallman's popular artistic renderings of Jesus. Morgan is also the editor of an earlier collection of essays on Sallman: *Icons of American Protestantism: The Art of Warner Sallman* (New Haven: Yale University Press, 1996).

Myers, Kenneth A. *All God's Children and Blue Suede Shoes: Christians and Popular Culture*. Wheaton, Ill.: Crossway Books, 1989.

An evangelical Christian assessment and critique of the importance of popular culture.

Nelson, John Wiley. *Your God is Alive and Well and Appearing in Popular Culture*. Philadelphia: Westminster Press, 1976.

A classic early work on religion and popular culture that argues for the existence of an "American cultural religion," and claims that popular culture serves as the "worship service" confirming the beliefs of that religion. Nelson includes chapters on film, country music, popular magazines, television, and detective fiction.

Postman, Neil. *Amusing Ourselves to Death: Public Discourse in the Age of Show Business*. New York: Penguin Books, 1985.

A critique of the impact of television, claiming that the nature of the medium itself is oriented toward entertainment and undermines coherent, serious, rational discourse (chapter 8 applies this thesis to religion on television).

Prebish, Charles S., [et al.]. *Religion and Sport: The Meeting of Sacred and Profane*. Westwood, Conn: Greenwood Press, 1993.

Three essays by Prebish arguing that sport has become an American religion, plus five previously published essays by other scholars that expand upon his thesis.

Real, Michael R. *Mass-Mediated Culture*. Englewood Cliffs, N.J.: Prentice-Hall, 1977.

A theoretical discussion of popular culture and mass communications, arguing that "mass-mediated culture primarily serves the interests of the relatively small political-economic power elite." Connections are made with religion in a chapter on Billy Graham, and in discussions of the Disney universe as morality play and the Super Bowl as mythic spectacle. A more recent text by the same author on many of the same themes, but with less attention to religion, is *Exploring Media Culture: A Guide* (Thousand Oaks, Calif.: Sage, 1996).

Romanowski, William D. *Pop Culture Wars: Religion and the Role of Entertainment in American Life.* Downers Grove, Ill.: InterVarsity Press, 1996.
An attempt to reframe the "culture wars" in American life by encouraging readers to see religion as creatively and critically engaged with popular entertainment.

Sample, Tex. *White Soul: Country Music, the Church, and Working Americans.* Nashville: Abingdon Press, 1996.
An argument that country music "speaks" the life of working people, whereas mainline Christianity has lost touch with that social class.

Schmidt, Leigh Eric. *Consumer Rites: The Buying and Selling of American Holidays.* Princeton: Princeton University Press, 1995.
A cultural history of the commercialization of American holidays (Valentine's Day, Christmas, Easter, and Mother's Day), not condemning the results of commercialization as spiritually empty but instead describing a blend of religious and secular forms.

Schultze, Quentin J. *Televangelism and American Culture: The Business of Popular Culture.* Grand Rapids, Mich.: Baker Book House, 1991.
Argues that television evangelists represent wider cultural tendencies of commodification and the focus on material success, and that these are issues for the culture at large, not televangelism alone.

———. *Redeeming Television: How TV Changes Christians—How Christians Can Change TV.* Downers Grove, Ill.: InterVarsity Press, 1992.
An evangelical Christian critique of television by a communications professor who also critiques the "typical" Christian responses.

Schultze, Quentin J., Roy M. Anker, et al. *Dancing in the Dark: Youth, Popular Culture and the Electronic Media.* Grand Rapids, Mich.: Eerdmans, 1991.
A collaborative effort by Calvin College faculty, examining music, videos, and other elements of youth culture from a variety of perspectives, without predictable adult critiques.

Scott, Bernard Brandon. *Hollywood Dreams and Biblical Stories.* Minneapolis: Fortress Press, 1994.
A Christian Biblical scholar's discussion of more than fifty recent American movies, considering mythic dimensions of both the films and Christian scriptures to encourage conversation and mutual criticism.

Spencer, William David. *Mysterium and Mystery: The Clerical Crime Novel.* Ann Arbor, Mich: UMI Research Press, 1989.
A survey of the mysteries available in English that feature clerics (rabbis, priests, nuns, ministers, and missionaries) as crime solvers.

Stausbaugh, John. *Reflections on the Birth of the Elvis Faith.* New York: Blast Books, 1995.
The associate editor of New York Press argues that "Elvisism" is a religion, with pilgrimages, icons, miracles, canon, and priesthood.

Stout, Daniel A., and Judith M. Buddenbaum, eds. *Religion and Mass Media: Audiences and Adaptations*. Thousand Oaks, Calif.: Sage, 1996.
Audience-centered essays, using social science research methods, unlike most studies of popular culture, which focus more on examples of popular culture and their content than on the audiences that receive them.

Warren, Michael. *Seeing Through the Media: A Religious View of Communications and Cultural Analysis*. Harrisburg, Penn.: Trinity Press International, 1997.
A book significantly influenced by the sociological theories of Raymond Williams, and intended to help religious people and communities acquire the basic skills and tools for analyzing and critiquing popular culture.

Williams, Peter W. *Popular Religion in America: Symbolic Change and the Modernization Process in Historical Perspective*. Englewood Cliffs, N.J.: Prentice-Hall, Inc., 1980.
Like the Lippy volume above, a study of popular religion, which relates closely to the study of religion and popular culture.

Index

Text:	Sabon
Display:	Franklin Gothic Book and Demi
Composition:	G & S Typesetters, Inc.
Printing and Binding:	Edwards Brothers, Inc.